T0214436

Lecture Notes of the Institute for Computer Sciences, Social Informatics and Telecommunications Engineering 258

More information about this series at http://www.springer.com/series/8197

Jun Zheng · Wei Xiang
Pascal Lorenz · Shiwen Mao
Feng Yan (Eds.)

Ad Hoc Networks

10th EAI International Conference, ADHOCNETS 2018
Cairns, Australia, September 20–23, 2018
Proceedings

 Springer

Editors
Jun Zheng
National Mobile Communications Research
Laboratory
Southeast University
Nanjing, China

Shiwen Mao
Department of Electrical and Computer
Engineering
Auburn University
Auburn, AL, USA

Wei Xiang
College of Science and Engineering
James Cook University
Cairns, QLD, Australia

Feng Yan
National Mobile Communications Research
Laboratory
Southeast University
Nanjing, China

Pascal Lorenz
IUT
University of Haute Alsace
Colmar, France

ISSN 1867-8211 ISSN 1867-822X (electronic)
Lecture Notes of the Institute for Computer Sciences, Social Informatics
and Telecommunications Engineering
ISBN 978-3-030-05887-6 ISBN 978-3-030-05888-3 (eBook)
https://doi.org/10.1007/978-3-030-05888-3

Library of Congress Control Number: 2018964126

This Springer imprint is published by the registered company Springer Nature Switzerland AG
The registered company address is: Gewerbestrasse 11, 6330 Cham, Switzerland

Preface

An ad hoc network is a wireless system for a specific purpose, in which mobile or static nodes are connected using wireless links and dynamically auto-configure themselves into a network without the requirement for any infrastructures such as access points or base stations. Ad hoc networking covers a variety of network paradigms, including mobile ad hoc networks, sensor networks, vehicular networks, unmanned aerial vehicle (UAV) networks, underwater networks, airborne networks, underground networks, personal area networks, device-to-device (D2D) communications in 5G cellular networks, and home networks etc. It promises a wide range of applications in civilian, commercial, and military areas. In contrast to the traditional wireless networking paradigm, this new networking paradigm is characterized by sporadic connections, distributed autonomous operations, and fragile multi-hop relay paths, which have introduced many formidable challenges, such as scalability, quality of service, reliability and security, and energy-constrained operations. Thus, while it is essential to advance theoretical research on fundamental and practical research on efficient architectures and protocols for ad hoc networks, it is also critical to develop useful applications, experimental prototypes, and real-world deployments to achieve immediate impacts on the society for the success of this wireless networking paradigm.

The annual International Conference on Ad Hoc Networks (AdHocNets) aims at providing a forum to bring together researchers from academia as well as practitioners from industry to meet and exchange ideas and recent research work on all aspects of ad hoc networks. As the tenth edition of this event, AdHocNets 2018 was successfully held in Cairns, Australia, during September 20–23, 2018. The conference featured one keynote speech, by Dr. Guoqiang Mao from the University of Technology Sydney (UTS), Australia. The technical program of the conference included 27 regular papers that were selected out of 50 submissions through a rigorous review process.

This volume of proceedings includes all the technical papers that were presented at AdHocNets 2018. We hope that it will become a useful reference for researchers and practitioners working in the area of ad hoc networks.

November 2018

Jun Zheng
Wei Xiang
Pascal Lorenz
Shiwen Mao
Feng Yan

Organization

Steering Committee

Imrich Chlamtac	University of Trento, Italy
Shiwen Mao	Auburn University, USA
Jun Zheng	Southeast University, China

Organizing Committee

General Chair

Jun Zheng	Southeast University, China

TPC Chair and Co-chairs

Wei Xiang	James Cook University, Australia
Pascal Lorenz	University of Haute-Alsace, France
Shiwen Mao	Auburn University, USA

Local Chair

Ickjai Lee	James Cook University, Australia

Workshops Co-chairs

Nirwan Ansari	New Jersey Institute of Technology, USA
Weixiao Meng	Harbin Institute of Technology, China

Publicity and Social Media Co-chairs

Yonghui Li	University of Sydney, Australia
Nathalie Mitton	Inria, Lille-Nord Europe, France
Baoxian Zhang	University of Chinese Academy of Sciences, China

Publications Chair

Feng Yan	Southeast University, China

Web Co-chairs

Bingying Wang	Southeast University, China
Yuying Wu	Southeast University, China

Conference Manager

Andrea Piekova	European Alliance for Innovation

Technical Program Committee

Hamada Alshaer	University of Edinburgh, UK
Jalel Ben-Othman	Université de Paris 13, France
David Brown	Defence Research and Development, Canada
Claude Chaudet	Telecom ParisTech, France
Yin Chen	Keio University, Japan
Omer Farooq	University College Cork, Ireland
Antoine Gallais	Université de Strasbourg, France
Shuai Han	Harbin Institute of Technology, China
Changle Li	Xidian University, China
Pascal Lorenz	University of Haute Alsace, France
Shiwen Mao	Auburn University, USA
Nathalie Mitton	Inria Lille – Nord Europe, France
Amiya Nayak	University of Ottawa, Canada
Symeon Papavassiliou	National Technical University of Athens, Greece
Joel Rodrigues	University of Beira Interior, Portugal
Alex Sprintson	Texas A&M University, USA
Marc St-Hilaire	Carleton University, Canada
Zhi Sun	State University of New York at Buffalo, USA
Kun Wang	Nanjing University of Posts and Telecommunications, China
Kui Wu	University of Victoria, Canada
Wei Xiang	James Cook University, Australia
Feng Yan	Southeast University, China
Jie Zeng	Tsinghua University, China
Baoxian Zhang	University of China Academy of Sciences, China
Sihai Zhang	University of Science and Technology of China, China
Yuan Zhang	Southeast University, China
Jun Zheng	Southeast University, China
Sheng Zhou	Tsinghua University, China

Contents

Security

Miscellaneous Topics in Wireless Networks

Ad Hoc Networks

Task Assignment for Semi-opportunistic Mobile Crowdsensing

Wei Gong[1], Baoxian Zhang[1]([✉]), and Cheng Li[2,3]

[1] Research Center of Ubiquitous Sensor Networks,
University of Chinese Academy of Sciences, Beijing 100049, China
gongwei11@mails.ucas.ac.cn, bxzhang@ucas.ac.cn
[2] School of Computer and Information Engineering, Tianjin Chengjian University,
Tianjin 300384, China
[3] Faculty of Engineering and Applied Science, Memorial University,
St. John's, NL A1B 3X5, Canada
licheng@mun.ca

Abstract. In this paper, we propose a novel crowdsensing paradigm called semi-opportunistic sensing, which is aimed to achieve high task quality with low human involvement. In this paradigm, each mobile user can provide multiple path choices to reach her destination, which largely broadens the task assignment space. We formulate the task assignment problem in this paradigm of maximizing total task quality under incentive budget constraint and user travel time constraints. We prove this problem is NP-hard and then propose two efficient heuristic algorithms. First, we propose a Best Path/Task first algorithm (BPT) which always chooses current best path and current best task into the assignment list. Second, we propose an LP-relaxation based algorithm (LPR), which greedily assigns paths and tasks with the largest values in LP relaxation solution. We deduce the computational complexities of the proposed algorithms. We evaluate the performance of our algorithms using real-world traces. Simulation results show that our proposed crowdsensing paradigm can largely increase overall task quality compared with the opportunistic sensing paradigm where each user has only one fixed path. Simulation results also show that our proposed algorithms are efficient and their performance is close to the optimal solution.

Keywords: Mobile crowdsensing · Task assignment
Semi-opportunistic sensing

1 Introduction

Recently, mobile crowdsensing [2] has become a cost-effective way to collect massive sensing data and thus enabled tremendous real-world applications such

This work was supported in part by the NSF of China under Grant Nos. 61531006, 61471339, 61872331, the Natural Sciences and Engineering Research Council (NSERC) of Canada (Discovery Grant RGPIN-2018-03792), and the InnovateNL SensorTECH Grant 5404-2061-101.

J. Zheng et al. (Eds.): ADHOCNETS 2018, LNICST 258, pp. 3–14, 2019.
https://doi.org/10.1007/978-3-030-05888-3_1

as environment monitoring, traffic condition monitoring, and smart city [3, 7, 8, 12]. In a mobile crowdsensing system, the service platform recruits mobile users to perform tasks by exploiting the sensing and computing ability of smart devices at the users.

Based on whether tasks are performed consciously by users, existing work for mobile crowdsensing can be categorized into two types: opportunistic sensing and participatory sensing. In opportunistic sensing, users move following their daily routines and complete sensing tasks with minimum disturbance. Sensing data along their moving paths can be collected automatically without human involvement and thus leads to low employment expenses of opportunistic sensing users. However, since the paths taken by opportunistic sensing users are predetermined based on users' moving patterns, tasks not on any mobile user's path will not be performed. This often results in limited task coverage. In contrast, the moving paths of participatory sensing users are scheduled by the service platform. Service platform can ask such users to move to any task location within their travel capability to perform tasks at the cost of high employment expenses.

Task assignment [4] is one of the most important problems for mobile crowdsensing. In participatory sensing, [9] aims to minimize the task expiration penalty by user selection and path planning, while [5] studied the problem of user selection and path planning in an online manner to maximize total task quality under given travel budget. In opportunistic crowdsensing, [10] studied the multi-objective optimization problem of maximizing total task quality under energy consumption constraints of users' smart devices. [11] studied the problem of maximizing total task quality under incentive budget constraint and proposed an approximation algorithm exploiting the submodular property of the used utility function. High task quality and low employment expenses are two crucial goals in the design of effective task assignment mechanisms for mobile crowdsensing. However, the above two crowdsensing paradigms cannot meet these two goals simultaneously. In this paper, we propose a new mobile crowdsensing paradigm called semi-opportunistic mobile crowdsensing. The motivation behind our work in this paper is as follows. For traditional opportunistic mobile crowdsensing, each user moves to predetermined destination along a fixed path. However, in reality, a user may take one path from multiple choices (e.g., most frequently taken paths or most economical paths) to reach the same destination without much disturbance of her daily routine. For a mobile user, each such path is a reasonably good choice for her to make the trip. For the platform, the task assignment performance can be significantly improved since tasks are typically randomly distributed at different locations and in this case the platform has much more choices for task assignment due to the increased path set from the user side. In this way, task coverage probability can be greatly improved with slightly increased human involvement.

In this paper, we first propose the semi-opportunistic mobile crowdsensing paradigm. In this paradigm, each user provides multiple candidate paths for the service platform to choose from. We describe in details how this new paradigm works. We then formulate the optimal task assignment problem, which jointly chooses mobile users and their taken paths and also tasks for them to perform with an objective to maximize the total task quality subject to given incentive budget constraint and user travel time constraints. We prove this problem is NP-hard and then propose two efficient heuristic algorithms to address this problem. First, we propose a Best Path/Task first algorithm (BPT) which always chooses current best path and current best task into the assignment list. Second, we propose an LP-relaxation based algorithm (LPR), which greedily assigns paths and tasks with the largest values in LP relaxation solution. We deduce the computational complexities of the proposed algorithms. We evaluate the performance of our algorithms on real-world traces. Simulation results show our proposed algorithms are very close to the optimal solution and significantly outperform the case when pre-determined single path is used for each user.

The rest of this paper is organized as follows. We describe the system model and formulate the problem under study in Sect. 2. We propose our algorithms in Sect. 3. We present the simulation results in Sect. 4. We conclude the paper in Sect. 5.

2   Problem Statement

In this section, we describe the semi-opportunistic sensing system, formulate the problem under study, and prove its NP hardness.

2.1   Crowdsensing Paradigm

In this subsection, we introduce the semi-opportunistic sensing system, which consists of a crowdsensing service platform and a set of mobile users.

Mobile User. A mobile user is going to some place in a future time interval (e.g., 7:00–9:00 tomorrow morning). She has a travel time budget (e.g., two hours of commuting time), and fortunately, the actual travel time is less than that. She can use the remaining time to perform some sensing tasks on her travel path to make some money. To reach her destination, she may have multiple candidate paths for the trip. Due to different traffic conditions, each path has distinct travel time and thus distinct remaining time for task performing. She can ask the service platform for compensation of her task performing behavior. She then submits her application form containing her suggested paths to the service platform along with corresponding estimated available task performing time and also demanded compensation for each path. Without causing confusion, hereafter, we shall use the terms "user" and "worker" interchangeably unless otherwise stated.

Service Platform. The crowdsensing service platform receives a set of task performing requests which need to be done in a specific future time interval with a total incentive budget to support the task performing. Each task is submitted with detailed task attributes including task location, task performing time, and task quality requirement. We will discuss the task model in Subsect. 2.2. The platform also receives a list of task performing applications with detailed path information from mobile users who are willing to perform tasks in this time interval. The platform jointly chooses mobile users and their taken paths and also tasks for them to perform. The objective is to maximize the sum of task quality subject to total incentive budget and user's path travel time budget.

Semi-opportunistic Crowdsensing Paradigm. Our crowdsensing paradigm is composed of the following steps:

- First, the crowdsensing service platform announces a specific future time interval and recruits mobile user to perform tasks in this time interval.
- Second, each mobile user who is willing to undertake tasks in that future time interval submits to the service platform her suggested moving paths in that time interval, with corresponding task performing time and demanded compensation for each path.
- Third, the platform selects mobile users to perform tasks and informs each selected user which path to take and also which task(s) to perform.
- Fourth, each mobile user travels along the designated path, performs assigned task(s), and finally receives demanded compensation.

2.2   System Model

The three layer task assignment process is illustrated in Fig. 1. The platform selects a set of mobile users to perform tasks on their paths. For each user, one path in her given path set is selected by the platform, if the user is chosen for performing task(s). Some task(s) on this path are then assigned to the user as long as her travel time budget is not violated.

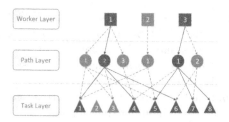

Fig. 1. Three layer task assignment process. The red ones are selected. (Color figure online)

Worker Model. We denote the users by user set $\mathcal{I} = \{1, 2, \cdots, I\}$. Each user has a starting point and a destination point. Each user has several path choices for her to reach her destination. We define decision variable $x_i = 1$ if the user $i \in \mathcal{I}$ is selected to perform task, or otherwise $x_i = 0$.

Path Model. Each user has multiple path choices to reach her destination. We denote the path set of user $i \in \mathcal{I}$ as path set $\mathcal{K}_i = \{1, 2, \cdots, K_i\}$. Each path is a simple path from a departure place to a destination passing through a few streets or blocks. Each path $k_i \in \mathcal{K}_i$ has a fixed incentive reward r_{ik_i} and a time budget T_{ik_i} for performing tasks on this path. Different workers demand different incentive rewards for different paths which depend on time budgets of the paths and labor costs per unit time for recruiting the users. We define decision variable $y_{ik_i} = 1$ if user i is selected to travel along path k_i, or otherwise $y_{ik_i} = 0$. Each user can only take one of her provided path choices, and thus we have:

$$x_i = \sum_{k_i} y_{ik_i}, \quad \forall i \in \mathcal{I} \tag{1}$$

The total incentive cannot exceed the platform given incentive budget B, thus we have:

$$\sum_i \sum_{k_i} r_{ik_i} \cdot y_{ik_i} \leq B \tag{2}$$

Task Model. We denote the task set as $\mathcal{J} = \{1, 2, \cdots, J\}$. Each task $j \in \mathcal{J}$ is associated with a specific location, task performing time t_j, and task quality q_j. Due to different task types and performing difficulties, tasks have different performing times. Task quality can be indicated by the information value of the task location [11] or the probability of giving a correct answer for an event by majority voting [5]. We define $w_{ik_ij} = 1$ if task $j \in \mathcal{J}$ is along the path k_i of user i, or otherwise $w_{ik_ij} = 0$. We define decision variable $z_{ik_ij} = 1$ if task $j \in \mathcal{J}$ is assigned to user i on her path $k_i \in \mathcal{K}_i$, or otherwise 0. We have

$$z_{ik_ij} \leq w_{ik_ij}, \quad \forall j \in \mathcal{J}, i \in \mathcal{I}, k_i \in \mathcal{K}_i \tag{3}$$

Each path is associated with zero, one, or several tasks to perform and the total task performing time cannot exceed the path-related task performing time budget. Therefore, we have:

$$\sum_j t_j \cdot z_{ik_ij} \leq T_{ik_i} \cdot y_{ik_i}, \quad \forall i \in \mathcal{I}, k_i \in \mathcal{K}_i \tag{4}$$

Task j can only be performed by user i taking path k_i if path k_i of user i is selected by the platform, thus we have:

$$z_{ik_ij} \leq y_{ik_i}, \quad \forall j \in \mathcal{J}, i \in \mathcal{I}, k_i \in \mathcal{K}_i \tag{5}$$

We assume each task needs to be done no more than once. Thus, we have

$$\sum_i \sum_{k_i} z_{ik_ij} \leq 1, \quad \forall j \in \mathcal{J} \tag{6}$$

2.3 Problem Formulation

The task assignment problem of maximizing the sum of quality of all the tasks subject to the incentive budget constraint and travel time constraints is formulated as follows:

$$max \sum_{i,k_i,j} q_j \cdot z_{ik_ij} \tag{7}$$

$$s.t. \quad (1) - (6)$$
$$var. \quad x_i \in \{0,1\}, \qquad \forall i \in \mathcal{I}$$
$$y_{ik_i} \in \{0,1\}, \qquad \forall k_i \in \mathcal{K}_i, \forall i \in \mathcal{I}$$
$$z_{ik_ij} \in \{0,1\}, \quad \forall k_i \in \mathcal{K}_i, \forall i \in \mathcal{I}, \forall j \in \mathcal{J}$$

The hardness of the above problem is given as follows. We consider a simplified case where there is only one user who has exactly one path to take and the platform can afford her incentive reward. Then the problem is to maximize the total task quality under the user's task performing time budget. This is a 0-1 knapsack problem. Here, the item weight is task performing time and the sum of item weights cannot exceed the weight capacity (i.e., the user's task performing time budget). Moreover, here, the value of an item is the quality of a task and the objective is to maximize the sum of values of chosen items. The 0-1 knapsack problem is known to be NP-hard. Therefore, the problem under study in this paper is also an NP-hard problem.

3 Proposed Task Assignment Algorithms

There are two resource constraints (i.e., incentive reward and per-path-related task performing time) in the task assignment problem under study. Incentive reward constraint is a high-layer constraint from the service platform and path-related task performing time constraint is a low-layer constraint from the user side. In this section, we propose two efficient heuristic algorithms to address the NP-hard task assignment problem formulated in Subsect. 2.3. First, we propose Best Path/Task First Algorithm (BPT) which always chooses current best path and current best task into the assignment list. Second, we propose an LP-relaxation based algorithm, which greedily assigns paths and tasks with largest values into the LP relaxation solution.

3.1 Best Path/Task First Algorithm (BPT)

In this subsection, we propose BPT algorithm. The algorithm is composed of two major components: TASK SELECTION and PATH SELECTION.

TASK SELECTION. For each of the candidate paths provided by users, the TASK SELECTION process selects a set of still available tasks leading to the maximum task quality while meeting the path-related task performing time constraint. This is a 0-1 knapsack problem and is known to be NP-hard. Here, an approximate algorithm is presented for the TASK SELECTION, which works as follows.

1. Sort all still available tasks on this path in the descending order according to the ratio of task quality and performing time.
2. If the sum of task performing time of all still available tasks is no larger than task performing time budget, then all tasks are selected.

3. Otherwise, find the maximum number m such that the first m tasks in the task list meet the following condition: These m tasks' total task performing time is smaller than or equal to the task performing time budget while the first $(m + 1)$ tasks' total task performing time is larger than the task performing time budget. If the sum of task quality of the first m tasks are smaller than the task quality of the $(m + 1)^{th}$ task and the task performing time of the $(m + 1)^{th}$ task is not larger than the task performing time budget, then the $(m + 1)^{th}$ task is selected, otherwise the first m tasks are selected.

The above steps for TASK SELECTION work in spirit similar to the 2-approximate algorithm in [1] and thus also has an approximate ratio of two.

PATH SELECTION. This process aims to select a set of users and designate a specific path to each of them with an objective of maximizing the total task quality under incentive budget. For this purpose, we propose a greedy algorithm which works as follows.

1. Compute the sum of task quality of tasks available to be performed on each candidate path using the above TASK SELECTION algorithm.
2. Compute the quality/incentive ratio (i.e., the ratio of sum of quality of all tasks (temporarily) assigned to a path to the path-related incentive reward) of each path.
3. Select the path with the largest ratio and go to step 1 if the incentive budget constraint is not violated after the selection.
4. If the incentive budget constraint is violated after adding the path in the above step, and if the total task quality of this path is larger than the sum of total task quality of all previously selected paths, then abandon all the previously-selected paths and take this path.

The detailed procedure for BPT is given in Algorithm 1. Lines 1–2 are for initialization. Lines 3–40 iteratively choose the path leading to the largest quality/incentive ratio while Lines 10–26 give detailed procedure for selecting tasks for each candidate path. More specifically, line 3 ensures that the incentive budget constraint is not violated. In line 4, i^*, k^*, and Q^* record the user, path, and path-specific total task quality for the so far best path, respectively. P records the ratio of total task quality and incentive for the so far best path, whose initial value is zero. Lines 6–8 ensure that at most one path is selected for each user. Line 10 ensures to choose tasks which are on the current path and further have not been selected by any other path. Lines 12–13 consider the case when the task performing time budget is large enough to cover all the tasks on the path. Lines 14–22 determine whether to take the first m tasks or the $(m + 1)^{th}$ task. Lines 24–26 select the path with the largest ratio of overall task quality to the incentive for taking the path. Lines 30–32 add paths into the assignment list if the incentive budget constraint is not violated. Lines 34–38 take the last path and abandon all previously-selected paths if the task quality of the last path is larger than the sum of all the previously-selected paths.

The computational complexity for the TASK SELECTION in lines 10–26 is $O(Jlog(J))$ due to the task sorting operation. Thus, the computational complexity of BPT is $O(I^2 K J log(J))$, where I, K, J denote the number of users, number of path choices of a user, and number of tasks, respectively.

Algorithm 1 Procedure for BPT.

Input: $\mathcal{I}$, $\mathcal{K}_i$, $\mathcal{J}$, B, r_{ik_i}, T_{ik_i}, t_j, q_j, w_{ik_ij}

Output: x_i, y_{ik_i}, z_{ik_ij}

1: set any x_i, y_{ik_i}, z_{ik_ij} to 0.
2: $sumB \leftarrow 0, Q^+ \leftarrow 0$
3: **while** $sumB < B$ **do**
4:   $i^* \leftarrow null, k^* \leftarrow null, Q^* \leftarrow 0, P \leftarrow 0$
5:   **for** $i \in \mathcal{I}$ **do**
6:     **if** $x_i = 1$ **then**
7:       continue;
8:     **end if**
9:     **for** $k_i \in \mathcal{K}_i$ **do**
10:       $\mathcal{J}_{ik_i} \leftarrow \left\{ j | \forall j, w_{ik_ij} = 1, \sum_i \sum_{k_i} z_{ik_ij} = 0 \right\}$
11:       Sort $j \in \mathcal{J}_{ik_i}$ in the descending order of q_j / t_j
12:       **if** $\sum_{j \in \mathcal{J}_{ik_i}} t_j \leq T_{ik_i}$ **then**
13:         $Q_{ik_i} \leftarrow \sum_{j \in \mathcal{J}_{ik_i}} q_j$
14:       **else**
15:         $m^* \leftarrow \arg\max_m \sum_{j \in \text{the first } m \text{ tasks in } \mathcal{J}_{ik_i}} t_j \leq T_{ik_i} < \sum_{j \in \text{the first } m+1 \text{ tasks in } \mathcal{J}_{ik_i}} t_j$
16:         $j^* \leftarrow$ the $(m^*+1)^{th}$ task in $\mathcal{J}_{ik_i}$
17:         **if** $\sum_{j \in \text{the first } m^* \text{ tasks in } \mathcal{J}_{ik_i}} q_j < q_{j^*}$ and $t_{j^*} \leq T_{ik_i}$ **then**
18:           $Q_{ik_i} \leftarrow q_{j^*}, \mathcal{J}^* \leftarrow \{j^*\}$
19:         **else**
20:           $Q_{ik_i} \leftarrow \sum_{j \in \text{the first } m^* \text{ tasks in } \mathcal{J}_{ik_i}} q_j$
21:           $\mathcal{J}^* \leftarrow \{\text{the first } m^* \text{ tasks in } \mathcal{J}_{ik_i}\}$
22:         **end if**
23:       **end if**
24:       **if** $Q_{ik_i} / r_{k_i} > P$ **then**
25:         $P \leftarrow Q_{ik_i} / r_{k_i}, Q^* \leftarrow Q_{ik_i}, i^* \leftarrow i, k^* \leftarrow k_i$
26:       **end if**
27:     **end for**
28:   **end for**
29:   $sumB \leftarrow sumB + r_{i^*k^*}$
30:   **if** $sumB \leq B$ **then**
31:     $x_{i^*} \leftarrow 1, y_{i^*k^*} \leftarrow 1, Q^+ \leftarrow Q^+ + Q^*$
32:     $z_{i^*k^*j} \leftarrow 1, \forall j \in \mathcal{J}^*$
33:   **else**
34:     **if** $Q^* > Q^+$ and $r_{i^*k^*} \leq B$ **then**
35:       set any x_i, y_{ik_i}, z_{ik_ij} to 0.
36:       $x_{i^*} \leftarrow 1, y_{i^*k^*} \leftarrow 1$
37:       $z_{i^*k^*j} \leftarrow 1, \forall j \in \mathcal{J}^*$
38:     **end if**
39:   **end if**
40: **end while**

3.2   LP-Relaxation Based Algorithm(LPR)

We propose an LP-relaxation based algorithm, which greedily assigns paths and tasks with largest values in Linear Programming(LP) relaxation solution. The algorithm is composed of LP-relaxation based initialization and greedy task assignment.

LP-Relaxation Based Initialization. The 0–1 integer constraints of x_i, y_{ik_i}, and z_{ik_ij} are relaxed as follows:

$$0 \le x_i \le 1, 0 \le y_{ik_i} \le 1, 0 \le z_{ik_ij} \le 1, \quad \forall j \in \mathcal{J}, i \in \mathcal{I}, k_i \in \mathcal{K}_i \qquad (8)$$

Algorithm 2 Procedure for LPR.

Input: $\mathcal{I}$, $\mathcal{K}_i$, $\mathcal{J}$, B, r_{ik_i}, T_{ik_i}, t_j, q_j, w_{ik_ij}
Output: x_i, y_{ik_i}, z_{ik_ij}
1: set any x_i, y_{ik_i}, z_{ik_ij} to 0.
2: x_i^*, $y_{ik_i}^*$, $z_{ik_ij}^* \leftarrow$ Run LP algorithm
3: $sumB \leftarrow 0, Q^+ \leftarrow 0$
4: **while** $sumB < B$ **do**
5:     $y^* \leftarrow$ largest $y_{ik_i}^*$(if user i has not been selected yet)
6:     $i^* \leftarrow arg_i$ largest $y_{ik_i}^*$, $k^* \leftarrow arg_{k_i}$ largest $y_{ik_i}^*$
7:     $sumB \leftarrow sumB + r_{i^*k^*}$
8:     **if** $sumB \le B$ **then**
9:         $x_{i^*} \leftarrow 1, y_{i^*k^*} \leftarrow 1$
10:        $sumT \leftarrow 0$
11:        **while** $sumT < T_{i^*k^*}$ **do**
12:            $z^* \leftarrow$ largest $z_{i^*k^*j}^*$(if task j has not been selected yet)
13:            $j^* \leftarrow arg_j$ largest $z_{i^*k^*j}^*$
14:            $sumT = sumT + t_{j^*}$
15:            **if** $sumT \le T_{i^*k^*}$ **then**
16:                $z_{i^*k^*j^*} \leftarrow 1$
17:            **end if**
18:        **end while**
19:    **end if**
20: **end while**

After the relaxation, the new problem can be solved by a linear programming solver in polynomial time. And we use x_i^*, $y_{ik_i}^*$, $z_{ik_ij}^*$ to denote the optimal solution of this linear programming problem.

Greedy Task Assignment. The greedy task assignment is composed of path selection and task selection. The algorithm iteratively selects the path with the highest value of $y_{ik_i}^*$ if the user of this path has not yet been selected and the total incentive budget is not violated after selecting this path. For each selected path, the algorithm iteratively selects the task with the highest value of $z_{ik_ij}^*$ if the task j has not yet been selected and the total task performing time budget of this path is not violated after selecting this task. This algorithm is feasible since the incentive budget constraint and task performing time constraint are not violated.

LPR is described in Algorithm 2. Line 2 runs the linear programming algorithm to obtain the relaxed solution. Lines 5–9 select the path with the maximum value of $y^*_{ik_i}$ into the assignment list. Lines 11–18 iteratively select the task with the maximum value of $z^*_{i^*k^*j}$ into the assignment list.

The computational complexity of solving linear programming problem is polynomial. The computational complexity of Greedy Task Assignment is $O(IKJ)$. Therefore the computational complexity of LPR is polynomial.

4 Performance Evaluation

In this section, we conduct extensive simulations to evaluate the performance of our proposed algorithms. We shall describe detailed simulation settings, the traces that we use, and finally present the simulation results.

We compare our algorithms with optimal solution on real-world traces. The optimal solution is obtained by using branch and cut algorithm which is a time-consuming algorithm. We denote the optimal solution as *Semi_opt*. We also compare our algorithms with the traditional opportunistic sensing paradigm where each mobile user only takes one pre-determined path which is her most frequently taken path. The optimal solution for this traditional opportunistic sensing paradigm is referred to as *Oppt_opt*. In addition, in our simulations, average task quality equals to total task quality divided by total task number. The default parameter settings are shown in Table 1.

Table 1. Default parameter settings.

Parameters	Values
Path number for a user	$N(3,1)^1$
Worker number	20
Task number	200
Task performing time of a task	$N(20,10)$
Task performing time budget for a path	$N(100,30)$
Path incentive	$N(100,30)$
Task quality	$N(100,30)$

[1] $N(x,y)$ means normal distribution whose mean value is x and standard deviation is y

We use two real-world traces Geolife dataset [13] and NCCU dataset [6] to evaluate the performance of our proposed algorithms. Geolife dataset [13] was collected by 182 users and contains 17,621 trajectories. The majority of the data was created in Beijing, China. We use trajectories in main urban zone of Beijing city which is of $17\,\text{km} \times 18\,\text{km}$. The transportation mode of these users includes driving, taking a bus, riding a bike, and walking. NCCU dataset [6] was collected by 115 college students for 15 days in a campus environment of $3764\,\text{m} \times 3420\,\text{m}$. Similar to [10], we divide the areas into square subareas. Mobile users move among different subareas and user paths are sequences of subarea indexes. We divide the area of Geolife dataset into 20×20 subareas and divide the area of NCCU dataset into 10×10 subareas. In these two datasets, paths were chosen based on frequencies that they were taken in the datasets.

We evaluate the average performance of different algorithms on real-world traces. In Figs. 2(a) and 2(b), as the number of paths K increases, average task quality of *Semi_opt*, LPR, and BPT increases as well. The performance of LPR and BPT is close to *Semi_opt*. The performance of *Semi_opt* and that of *Oppt_opt* are the same when $K = 1$ since they both choose the most frequently taken path for each user and use optimal algorithm for task assignment. When $K > 1$, *Semi_opt*, LPR, and BPT have better performance than *Oppt_opt* which again validates the effectiveness of our proposed crowdsensing paradigm.

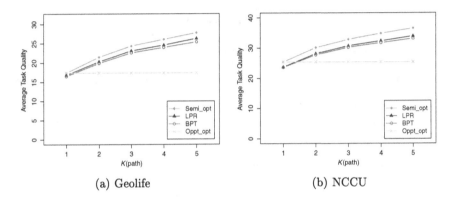

| | (a) Geolife | (b) NCCU |

Fig. 2. Performance comparison of different algorithms on real-world traces.

5   Conclusion

In this paper, we proposed a new mobile crowdsensing paradigm called semi-opportunistic sensing where each mobile user has multiple path choices to take to reach her destination. We formulated the optimal task assignment problem, which aims to select proper mobile users taking proper paths and assign tasks to maximize the total task quality while meeting given incentive budget constraint and travel time constraints. We proved the problem is NP-hard and proposed two efficient algorithms. We presented detailed algorithm design and deduced their computational complexities. We conducted extensive simulations on real-world traces. Simulation results validate the effectiveness of our proposed crowdsensing paradigm and further the results show that the performance of our proposed algorithms is close to the optimal solution.

References

1. Du, D.Z., Ko, K.I., Hu, X.: Design and Analysis of Approximation Algorithms. Springer, New York (2012). https://doi.org/10.1007/978-1-4614-1701-9
2. Ganti, R.K., Ye, F., Lei, H.: Mobile crowdsensing: current state and future challenges. IEEE Commun. Mag. **49**(11), 32–39 (2011)
3. Gao, R., et al.: Jigsaw: indoor floor plan reconstruction via mobile crowdsensing. In: Proceedings of ACM MobiCom 2014, pp. 249–260 (2014)
4. Gong, W., Zhang, B., Li, C.: Task assignment in mobile crowdsensing: present and future directions. IEEE Netw. https://doi.org/10.1109/MNET.2018.1700331
5. Gong, W., Zhang, B., Li, C.: Location-based online task scheduling in mobile crowdsensing. In: Proceedings of IEEE GLOBECOM 2017, Singapore, pp. 1–6, December 2017
6. Tsai, T.C., Chan, H.H.: NCCU trace: social-network-aware mobility trace. IEEE Commun. Mag. **53**(10), 144–149 (2015)
7. Wang, X., Zhang, J., Tian, X., Gan, X., Guan, Y., Wang, X.: Crowdsensing-based consensus incident report for road traffic acquisition. IEEE Trans. Intell. Transport. Syst., October 2017. https://doi.org/10.1109/TITS.2017.2750169
8. Xu, C., Li, S., Zhang, Y., Miluzzo, E., Chen, Y.: Crowdsensing the speaker count in the wild: implications and applications. IEEE Commun. Mag. **52**(10), 92–99 (2014)
9. Yang, F., Lu, J.L., Zhu, Y., Peng, J., Shu, W., Wu, M.Y.: Heterogeneous task allocation in participatory sensing. In: Proceedings of IEEE GLOBECOM 2015, pp. 1–6, December 2015
10. Zhang, B., Song, Z., Liu, C.H., Ma, J., Wang, W.: An event-driven qoi-aware participatory sensing framework with energy and budget constraints. ACM Trans. Intell. Syst. Technol. **6**(3), 1–19 (2015)
11. Zhang, M., et al.: Quality-aware sensing coverage in budget-constrained mobile crowdsensing networks. IEEE Trans. Veh. Technol. **65**(9), 7698–7707 (2016)
12. Zheng, Y., Liu, F., Hsieh, H.: U-Air: when urban air quality inference meets big data. In: Proceedings of ACM KDD 2013, pp. 1436–1444, August 2013
13. Zheng, Y., Xie, X., Ma, W.Y.: GeoLife: a collaborative social networking service among user, location and trajectory. IEEE Data Eng. Bull. **33**(2), 32–40 (2010)

Caching on Vehicles: A Lyapunov Based Online Algorithm

Yao Zhang, Changle Li[✉], Tom H. Luan, Yuchuan Fu, and Lina Zhu

State Key Laboratory of Integrated Services Networks, Xidian University,
Xi'an 710071, China
{yzhang_01,ycfu}@stu.xidian.edu.cn, clli@mail.xidian.edu.cn,
{tom.luan,lnzhu}@xidian.edu.cn

Abstract. With the explosive increase of mobile data and users, data tsunami seriously challenges the mobile operators worldwide. The vehicular caching, which caches mobile data on widely distributed vehicles, is an efficient method to solve this problem. In this paper, we explore the impact of vehicular caching on cellular networks. Specifically, targeting on network performance in energy efficiency, we first formulate a fractional optimization model by considering the network throughput and energy consumption. We then apply nonlinear programming and Lyapunov technology to relax the nonlinear and nonconvex model. Based on analysis, we propose a novel online task decision algorithm. Based on this algorithm, vehicles determine to act either as servers or task schedulers for the requests of users. The burden of cellular MBS (Macro Base Station) then can be alleviated. Extensive simulations are finally conducted and results verify the effectiveness of our proposal.

Keywords: Caching · Nonlinear programming
Lyapunov optimization

1 Introduction

As indicated in [1], the monthly global mobile data traffic would be 49 exabytes by 2021 under 11.6 billion mobile connected devices, which increases about sevenfold between 2016 and 2021. Mobile users thus can enjoy a large number of new applications and fairly rich network experience. However, the data tsunami also pushes a huge challenge to the mobile operators all over the world for their network capacity in terms of network throughput, and processing delay.

To solve above problem, a variety of techniques focus on the improvement of edge process capacity by applying edge computing technology on network edge, including offloading technologies [2,3], edge caching schemes [4,5]. However, most

This work was supported by the National Natural Science Foundation of China under Grant No. 61571350 and No. 61601344, Key Research and Development Program of Shaanxi (Contract No. 2017KW-004, 2017ZDXM-GY-022, and 2018ZDXM-GY-038), and the 111 Project (B08038).

J. Zheng et al. (Eds.): ADHOCNETS 2018, LNICST 258, pp. 15–24, 2019.
https://doi.org/10.1007/978-3-030-05888-3_2

of these researches relay on the deployment of large-scale infrastructure, resulting in huge deployment and maintenance cost. To cope with this problem, we aim to make a full use of the moving vehicles to cache mobile data and then serve mobile users. Compared with traditional SBS (Small Base Station) or AP (Access Point), vehicles as data carriers are widely distributed and cost-effective. Besides, the V2X (Vehicle-to-Everything) technology has been specified in the 5G communication standard, which makes vehicle-to-user communications be efficient and reliable.

In this paper, we aim to explore the impact of caching vehicles on the energy efficiency of cellular network. To this end, we assume that the communications with caching vehicles are default setting in mobile users, and caching vehicles act as task schedulers to determine the requests of users are served by themselves or MBS. Specifically, to obtain the optimal task decision from global perspective, we first formulate a fraction optimization model towards to the minimization of network energy efficiency. Based on the solution for the optimization model, we then develop a new online algorithm, which is used to obtain the real-time task decision for vehicles. Assisted by caching vehicles, the burden of MBS can be alleviated. We proceed in three steps. (1) *ProblemFormulation* : Based on the analysis on network throughput and energy consumption, we formulate the task decision problem as a fraction optimization model. The task decision of all caching vehicles can be obtained by solving this model. (2) *AlgorithmDesign* : We then transform the nonlinear and nonconvex model as a linear and convex model based on the nonlinear programming. To solve the transformed model, a novel online task decision algorithm is developed based on Lyapunov optimization theory. (3) *Simulations* : To evaluate the performance of the proposed algorithm, we conduct extensive simulations. Results show that our algorithm achieve obvious improvement in energy efficiency compared with traditional network paradigm.

The remainder of this paper is structured as follows: Sect. 2 illustrates the system models and formulate the optimization model. Section 3 presents the algorithm design, which is based on the solution of the optimization model. Section 4 evaluate the performance of the algorithm based on simulation results while Sect. 5 concludes our study.

2   System Description and Problem Formulation

In this section, we mainly make a description about the system scenario in our study, and finally formulate a fractional optimization problem.

2.1   System Description

We consider a scenario that includes three types of nodes, MBS, caching vehicles, and mobile users. In this scenario, a part of vehicles caching the popular mobile data act as task schedulers to alleviate the burden of MBS. Mobile users can be served either by cellular MBS or caching vehicles. Specifically, when detecting the caching vehicle within the communication range, mobile users will send requests to it and ask for services. According to the task decision, the caching vehicle determines whether to serve the requests or not. Once the request of the user are declined, it will receive a feedback from the vehicle and then switch to cellular network. It is assumed that networks operate in slotted time, *i.e.*, the time slot t is within the time interval $[t, t+1)$, $t \in \{0, 1, 2, ...\}$. As such, our goal is to determine the task decision $\mathbf{T} = \{T_1(t), T_2(t), T_3(t), ...T_n(t)\}$ on caching vehicles, where $T_n(t) \in [0, 1]$ is a fractional variable and denotes the task decision of the vehicle n. We make some basic assumptions to simplify our analysis as follows.

To represent the spatial distribution of mobile users, we refer to [6] and use the Poisson point process (PPP) to calculate the distribution probability with mean rate λ_u. The exponential distribution is commonly used to model the distribution of vehicles on roads. In our analysis, the contact time between a user and vehicles is assumed to follow the exponential distribution [7]. To simplify the analysis, we assume the data catalogue consists of N_f files with same size, *i.e.*, $\mathbf{F} = \{F_1, F_2, ...F_{N_f}\}$. This assumption is reasonable in the analysis of edge caching since files can be divided into multiple fragments with same size [8]. To model the request probability of different files, we apply the widely used Zipf-like distribution [9]. Specifically, let p_n denote the request probability of the file n, it can be calculated as $p_n = \frac{1}{\left(\sum_{n=1}^{N_f} 1/n^\phi\right)n^\phi}$, where ϕ is the Zipf exponent.

2.2 Problem Formulation

Communication Model. There are two communication modes in our network, *i.e.*, vehicle-to-user communications and cellular communications. As many existing communication protocols, such as DSRC, LTE-A, and upcoming 5G for vehicular communicaions, rate adaptation mechanism is adopted to characterize the diversity of data rates. Note that, the communication mode of V2P (Vehicle-to-Pedestrian) is similar with V2V excepted the limited power consumption on the mobile devices of pedestrian users [10]. In this paper, we make a simplified assumption that data rates between users and vehicles are determined by Euclidean distance, and the mean rate is $R_v = 5$ Mbps [11]. The mean data rate in cellular network, due to the large-power MBS, is assumed as $R_m = R_v + \xi$, where $\xi \geq 0$. It means the data rate of cellular network is larger than that from vehicle to user.

The total network throughput in our network is

$$R_{tot}(t) = \sum_{m=1}^{N_m} R_m\{\mathbf{T}(t)\} + \sum_{v=1}^{N_v} R_v\{\mathbf{T}(t)\}, \tag{1}$$

where N_m and N_b are the number of requests served by caching vehicles and MBS, respectively.

Energy Consumption. Energy consumption is considered an important metric. On the one hand, green communications in wireless cellular networks have been an important task for a long time [2]. On the other hand, with the development of battery electric vehicles, the energy consumption management in vehicular networks becomes an major challenge [12]. As such, we explore the vehicular caching algorithm targeting at the full use of energy consumption. Since we assume that $R_m \geq R_v$, MBS may result in large throughput with a more transmission power due to the large-power transmitter. By contrast, caching more data on vehicles saves total energy consumption with a cost of the decrease of throughput. For simplicity, we only consider the energy consumption that can be impacted by the caching policy, *i.e.*, transport energy from MBS, transport energy and caching energy from caching vehicles. Therefore, we aim to find a trade-off between the energy consumption and network throughout. A series of energy consumption models are given below.

By referring to [13], we use the linear energy consumption model to calculate the transport energy consumed by MBS. At each time slot, the transport energy is

$$P_m(t) = \sum_{m=1}^{N_m} R_m\{\mathbf{T}(t)\}\omega_t^m, \tag{2}$$

where ω_t^m denotes the energy consumption rate of transmission from MBS (in Watt/bit).

The energy consumption at caching vehicles consists of two parts [4], transport energy and caching energy, *i.e.*, $P_{cv}(t) = P_t^v(t) + P_{ca}(t)$. Specifically, P_t^v is a function of the transmit power of caching vehicles

$$P_t^v(t) = \zeta_v P_{tx}^v(t), \tag{3}$$

where ζ_v is a simplified impact parameter for power amplifier cooling, and power supply. The energy-proportional model is used to represent the caching energy

$$P_{ca}(t) = R_v(t)\omega_c, \tag{4}$$

where ω_c is the caching factor (in Watt/bit).

Based on the analysis above, the total energy consumed at time slot t is

$$P_{tot}(t) = P_{cv}(t) + P_m(t) \tag{5}$$

Fraction Optimization. The problem of task decision at vehicles can be formulated as a fraction optimization model. Specifically, from the perspective of long-term optimization, the network energy efficiency model is

$$\min \eta_{EE} = \lim_{K \to \infty} \frac{\frac{1}{K}\sum_{t=0}^{K-1} P_{tot}(t)}{\frac{1}{K}\sum_{t \to 0}^{K-1} R_{tot}(t)} = \frac{\overline{P_{tot}}}{\overline{R_{tot}}} \tag{6}$$

$$\text{s.t. C1: } Q_n(t) \text{ are mean rate stable, } \forall n \in \{1, ..., N_u\}$$
$$\text{C2: } 0 \leq T_n(t) \leq 1, \forall j \in \{1, ..., N_v\},$$

where C1 is the constraint that guarantees the stability of user queue. $T_n(t)$ is the task decision of vehicle n at time slot t.

3   Algorithm Design

3.1   Problem Transformation

In this part, we refer to [14] and transform the fractional and nonconvex model (6) to a linear and convex one.

To make the transformation, we have the following theorem.

Theorem 1. *The problem (6) equals to minimizing $\overline{P}tot - \eta_{EE}^{opt}\overline{R}_{tot}$ subject to the same constraints.*

Proof. To prove Theorem 1, we assume that $\mathbf{T}^*(t)$ is the optimal task decision at time slot t. The proof is divided into two parts, *i.e.*, necessity proof and sufficiency proof.

The necessity proof is to prove that $\mathbf{T}^*$ is the solution of $\min \overline{P}tot - \eta_{EE}\overline{R}_{tot}$ because it is the solution of (6).

Specifically, since $\mathbf{T}^*$ is the optimal solution of optimization problem (6), we have

$$\eta_{EE}^{opt} = \frac{\overline{P}_{tot}(\mathbf{T}^*)}{\overline{R}_{tot}(\mathbf{T}^*)} \leq \frac{\overline{P}_{tot}(\mathbf{T})}{\overline{R}_{tot}(\mathbf{T})}. \tag{7}$$

We further transform (7) to

$$\overline{P}_{tot}(\mathbf{T}^*) - \eta_{EE}^{opt}\overline{R}_{tot}(\mathbf{T}^*) = 0, \tag{8}$$

$$\overline{P}_{tot}(\mathbf{T}) - \eta_{EE}^{opt}\overline{R}_{tot}(\mathbf{T}) \geq 0, \tag{9}$$

Therefore, we can obtain the following equation.

$$\min \overline{P}_{tot}(\mathbf{T}) - \eta_{EE}^{opt}\overline{R}_{tot}(\mathbf{T}) \tag{10}$$
$$= \overline{P}_{tot}(\mathbf{T}^*) - \eta_{EE}^{opt}\overline{R}_{tot}(\mathbf{T}^*)$$
$$= 0.$$

The proof for the necessity of Theorem 1 is completed.

For sufficiency proof, we aim to prove that $\mathbf{T}^*$ is the solution of problem (7) with the assumption below that it is the solution of $\min \overline{P}tot - \eta_{EE}\overline{R}_{tot}$. Firstly, we assume the following equation hold

$$\min \overline{P}_{tot}(\mathbf{T}) - \eta_{EE}^{opt}\overline{R}_{tot}(\mathbf{T}) \tag{11}$$
$$= \overline{P}_{tot}(\mathbf{T}^*) - \eta_{EE}^{opt}\overline{R}_{tot}(\mathbf{T}^*)$$
$$= 0,$$

where $\mathbf{T}^*$ is the optimal task decision. By rearranging above equation, we obtain

$$0 = \overline{P}_{tot}(\mathbf{T}^*) - \eta_{EE}^{opt}\overline{R}_{tot}(\mathbf{T}^*) \leq \overline{P}_{tot}(\mathbf{T}) - \eta_{EE}^{opt}\overline{R}_{tot}(\mathbf{T}). \tag{12}$$

Furthermore, we obtain

$$\eta_{EE}^{opt} = \frac{\overline{P}_{tot}(\mathbf{T}^*)}{\overline{R}_{tot}(\mathbf{T}^*)} \leq \frac{\overline{P}_{tot}(\mathbf{T})}{\overline{R}_{tot}(\mathbf{T})}. \tag{13}$$

It can seen that $\mathbf{T}^*$ is also the solution of (7). The proof of Theorem 1 is completed.

Hence, the fractional optimization problem (6) is transformed to

$$\min \overline{P}_{tot} - \eta_{EE}\overline{R}_{tot} \tag{14}$$
$$\text{s.t. C1, C2.}$$

The original problem now becomes a linear and convex one [14].

3.2 Lyapunov Optimization Based Online Algorithm

In this part, we develop a Lyapunov optimization based online task decision algorithm. The Lyapunov optimization theory is an effective method to deal with the problems of resource allocation in wireless networks [15]. The application of Lyapunov optimization in our paper is due to that the traditional heuristic or iterative algorithm may incur large overhead and latency, which are not tolerant in the delay-sensitive vehicular environments. We first define the Lyapunov function as follows.

Let $\Theta(t) \stackrel{\triangle}{=} \mathbf{Q}(t)$ denote the combined queue backlog vector. The quadratic Lyapunov function is defined as

$$L(\Theta(t)) \stackrel{\triangle}{=} \frac{1}{2} \sum_{n=1}^{N_u} Q_n(t)^2 \tag{15}$$

Then, the one-slot Lyapunov drift can be obtained as

$$\Delta(\Theta(t)) = L(\Theta(t+1)) - L(\Theta(t)) \tag{16}$$

We further use the drift-plus-penalty method to guarantee the stability of queues and solve the optimizaiton problem. The drift-plus-penalty is defined as

$$\min \Delta(\Theta(t)) + VE\{P_{tot}(t) - \eta_{EE}(t)R_{tot}(t)\} \tag{17}$$

The bound of drift-plus-penalty is defined as

$$\Delta(\Theta(t)) + VE\{P_{tot}(t) - \eta_{EE}(t)R_{tot}(t)|\Theta(t)\} \leq B$$
$$+ \sum_{n=1}^{N_u} Q_n(t)E\{A_n(t) - R_n(t)|\Theta(t)\} \tag{18}$$
$$+ VE\{P_{tot}(t) - \eta_{EE}(t)R_{tot}(t)|\Theta(t)\},$$

where

$$B \geq \frac{1}{2} \sum_{n=1}^{N_u} E\{A_n(t)^2 + R_n(t)^2|\Theta(t)\} \tag{19}$$

Proof. Assuming that the queue $Q_n(t)$ is updated as

$$Q_n(t+1) = max[Q_n(t) - R_n(t), 0] + A_n(t), \tag{20}$$

where $A_n(t)$ is the data arrival at time slot t, and $R_n(t)$ is the service rate of user n.

By squaring two sides of Eq. (20) and rearranging terms, we have

$$\frac{1}{2}[Q_n(t+1)^2 - Q_n(t)^2] \leq \frac{1}{2}[R_n(t)^2 + A_n(t)^2] + Q_n(t)(A_n(t) - R_n(t)) \quad (21)$$

Summing over $n \in \{1, ... N_u\}$ for (21) and taking a conditional expectation, we have

$$\Delta(\Theta(t)) \leq \sum_{n=1}^{N_u} \frac{1}{2}[R_n(t)^2 + A_n(t)^2|\Theta(t)] + \sum_{n=1}^{N_u}[Q_n(t)E\{A_n(t) - R_n(t)\}|\Theta(t)] \quad (22)$$

By adding the term of $VE\{P_{tot}(t) - \eta_{EE}(t)R_{tot}(t)|\Theta(t)\}$ on both sides of (22), it becomes

$$\begin{aligned}\Delta(\Theta(t)) + VE\{P_{tot}(t) - \eta_{EE}(t)R_{tot}(t)|\Theta(t)\} &\leq B \\ &+ VE\{P_{tot}(t) - \eta_{EE}(t)R_{tot}(t)|\Theta(t)\} \\ &+ \sum_{n=1}^{N_u} Q_n(t)E\{A_n(t) - R_n(t)|\Theta(t)\}\end{aligned} \quad (23)$$

Therefore, the Eq. (18) is proved, where

$$B \geq \sum_{n=1}^{N_u} \frac{1}{2}[R_n(t)^2 + A_n(t)^2|\Theta(t)] \quad (24)$$

The proof of (18)–(19) is completed.

In this case, the optimization problem of (14) can be solved by minimizing the right-side of inequality (23). Specifically, we finally obtain $\mathbf{T}^*$ according to

$$\min V\{P_{tot}(t) - \eta_{EE}(t)R_{tot}(t)\} - \sum_{n=1}^{N_u} Q_n(t)R_n(t)$$

s.t. C1, C2. $\quad (25)$

3.3 Online Algorithm

By the analysis in Subsects. 3.1–3.2, we successfully transfer the original optimization model (6) into the minimization of the right side of the drifty-plus-penalty (18). We hence define a novel online task decision algorithm to schedule the requests of users, as shown in Algorithm 1. At the beginning of time slot, the user requests are predicted by carrying out the Zipf-like model. Due to the limitation of vehicular storage, only a part of requests can be served by vehicles. After selecting the requests served by caching vehicles, the optimal task decision is determined by solving (25). Finally, the queue $Q_n(t)$ and $\eta_{EE}(t)$ are updated.

Algorithm 1. Online task decision.

Input: t, $Q_n(t)$, $\eta_{EE}(t)$

Output: $\mathbf{T}^*$

 1: For time slot $[t, t+1)$

 2: **while** At the beginning of time slot t **do**

 3:     **Step 1:**Obtain the number of requests at time slot t based on Zipf-like model

 4:     **Step 2:**Determine the numbers of requests that can be served by caching vehicles

 5:     **Step 3:**Calculate the $\mathbf{T}^*$ by solve (25)

 6:     **Step 4:**Update $Q_n(t)$ according to (20) and update $\eta_{EE}(t)$ according to

$$\eta_{EE}(t) = \frac{\sum_{t=0}^{K-1} P_{tot}(\mathbf{T}^*)}{\sum_{t \to 0}^{K-1} R_{tot}(\mathbf{T}^*)}$$

 7: **end while**

---

4 Simulations

To evaluate the performance of the newly proposed algorithm, we conduct extensive simulations using Matlab.

In all simulations, we consider a hexagonal cellular region with radius 350 m. Considering a four-lane bidirectional road within the coverage of cellular network, the density of vehicles is assumed as 0.086 vehicle/m. Vehicles adapt their velocity at each time slot following Normal distribution with the mean value is within $[20, 60]$ km/h and the standard deviation is 10 km/h. It is assumed that 50% vehicles cache the mobile data. The normalized cache capacity is denoted by η, which is an important parameter in following performance evaluation. Mobile users can get real-time communication with MBS, while the communication with vehicles has a maximum distance of 300 m. The mean rate of user distribution PPP is assumed as $\lambda_u = 1/10$ user/m^2. For Zipf-like model, we assume that $\phi = 0.7$. For energy model, we assume $w_t^m = 0.5 * 10^{-8}$ J/bit, $\zeta_v = 15.13$, and $\omega_c = 6.25 * 10^{-12}$W/bit according to [13]. The energy efficiency performance is shown in Figs. 1 and 2.

In Fig. 1, we assume that the arrival of the requests of users follows Poisson distribution with mean rate is $\lambda_r = 1$ request/s. We evaluate the impact of parameter V on the energy efficiency η_{EE}. The parameter V, as shown in (25), is used to control the trade-off between network performance and queue stability. We plot three data sets, determined by $\eta = 0.001$, $\eta = 0.01$, and $\eta = 0.1$. From Fig. 1 we can see, the energy efficiency decreases with V increasing. It means that the larger the V, the better energy efficiency can be achieved by Algorithm 1. However, the high-efficiency energy consumption is achieved with the cost of the stability of user queue. Therefore, Fig. 1 gives a reference for the application of Algorithm 1. Besides, the large η means that vehicles can cache more mobile data. It can be seen that large caching capacity achieves the lower

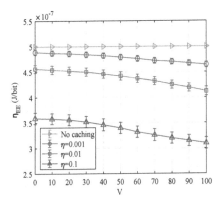

Fig. 1. Relationship between energy efficiency and V

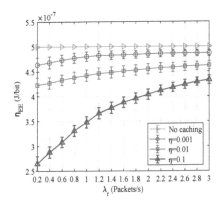

Fig. 2. Relationship between energy efficiency and packet arrival rate

energy efficiency, which however results in large cost. Therefore, there should be a trade-off between energy efficiency performance and storage cost.

In Fig. 2, we set V to be 50 to evaluate the impact of user requests on energy efficiency performance. From Fig. 2 we can see, when λ_r is small, the Algorithm 1 based vehicular task schedule achieves significant performance improvement compared with no caching, especially when $\eta = 0.1$. However, with the increase of λ_r, the advantage of energy efficiency in vehicular caching is gradually reduced and approached that of no caching. In this time, the number of requests is too large so that most of them must be served by MBS. The vehicular caching now has a little influence on the energy efficiency performance. Besides, the similar conclusion about different η with Fig. 1 can also be obtained.

5   Conclusion

This paper explores the performance of vehicular caching when alleviating the burden of MBS. We first analyze the system model in the cellular network incorporating vehicular caching. The problem of energy efficiency is then formulated as a fractional optimization model. However, this model is non-linear and non-convex, which is difficult to solve directly. We further transform this model into a linear and convex model based on the nonlinear programming. To relax the time-related variable in the transformed model, we then explore the application of the Lyapunov optimization theory on our optimization model. After detailed derivation, the original problem is solved in a simple method. Based on this solution, an online task decision algorithm is developed to schedule the requests of users for vehicles. Extensive simulations are conducted to evaluate the performance of the proposed algorithm. Results show that our algorithm achieves good performance in energy efficiency and gives a reference of application of vehicular caching.

References

1. Index: Global mobile data traffic forecast update. 2016–2021 white paper, Cisco Visual Networking. Accessed 2 May 2017
2. Yu, H., Cheung, M.-H., Iosifidis, G., Gao, L., Tassiulas, L., Huang, J.: Mobile data offloading for green wireless networks. IEEE Wirel. Commun. 24(4), 31–37 (2017)
3. Xu, J., Chen, L., Ren, S.: Online learning for offloading and autoscaling in energy harvesting mobile edge computing. IEEE Trans. Cogn. Commun. Netw. 3(3), 361–373 (2017)
4. Liu, D., Yang, C.: Energy efficiency of downlink networks with caching at base stations. IEEE J. Sel. Areas. Commun. 34(4), 907–922 (2016)
5. Chen, M., Qian, Y., Hao, Y., Li, Y., Song, J.: Data-driven computing and caching in 5G networks: architecture and delay analysis. IEEE Wirel. Commun. 25(1), 2–8 (2018)
6. Li, C., Zhang, J., Letaief, K.-B.: Throughput and energy efficiency analysis of small cell networks with multi-antenna base stations. IEEE Trans. Wirel. Commun. 13(5), 2505–2517 (2014)
7. Karagiannis, T., Le Boudec, J.-Y., Vojnovic, M.: Power law and exponential decay of intercontact times between mobile devices. IEEE Trans. Mob. Comput. 9(10), 1377–1390 (2010)
8. Vigneri, L., Pecoraro, S., Spyropoulos, T., Barakat, C.: Per chunk caching for video streaming from a vehicular cloud. In: ACM MobiCom Workshop on Challenged Networks (CHANTS) (2017)
9. Breslau, L., Cao, P., Fan, L., Phillips, G., Shenker, S.: Web caching and zipf-like distributions: evidence and implications. In: Proceedings IEEE Eighteenth Annual Joint Conference of the IEEE Computer and Communications Societies, vol. 1, pp. 126–134. IEEE (1999)
10. Yang, H., Zheng, K., Zhao, L., Zhang, K., Chatzimisios, P., Teng, Y.: High reliability and low latency for vehicular networks: Challenges and solutions. arXiv preprint arXiv:1712.00537 (2017)
11. Vigneri, L., Spyropoulos, T., Barakat, C.: Quality of experience-aware mobile edge caching through a vehicular cloud. In: 20th ACM International Conference on Modelling, Analysis and Simulation of Wireless and Mobile Systems, pp. 91–98 (2017)
12. Zhang, S., Luo, Y., Li, K., Li, V.: Real-time energy-efficient control for fully electric vehicles based on explicit model predictive control method. IEEE Trans. Veh. Technol. 67(6), 4693–4701 (2018)
13. Gabry, F., Bioglio, V., Land, I.: On energy-efficient edge caching in heterogeneous networks. IEEE J. Sel. Areas Commun. 34(12), 3288–3298 (2016)
14. Dinkelbach, W.: On nonlinear fractional programming. Manag. Sci. 13(7), 492–498 (1967)
15. Neely, M.J.: Stochastic network optimization with application to communication and queueing systems. Synth. Lect. Commun. Netw. 3(1), 1–211 (2010)

Simplicial Complex Reduction Algorithm for Simplifying WSN's Topology

Wenyu Ma[1], Feng Yan[1,2(✉)], Xuzhou Zuo[3], Jin Hu[4], Weiwei Xia[1], and Lianfeng Shen[1]

[1] National Mobile Communications Research Laboratory, Southeast University, Nanjing 210096, China
{mwy,feng.yan,wwxia,lfshen}@seu.edu.cn
[2] State key Laboratory of Networking and Switching Technology, Beijing University of Posts and Telecommunications, Beijing, China
[3] School of Information and Software Engineering, University of Electronic Science and Technology of China, Chengdu 610054, China
zuoxuzhou@uestc.edu.cn
[4] 724 Research Institute of CSIC, Nanjing 211153, China
hj662@163.com

Abstract. In this paper, a reduction algorithm aiming at simplifying the topology of wireless sensor networks (WSNs) is proposed. First, we use simplicial complex as the tool to represent the topology of the WSNs. Then, we present a reduction algorithm which recurrently deletes redundant vertices and edges while keeping the homology of the network invariant. By reducing the number of simplexes, we make the simplicial complex graph nearly planar and easy for computation. Finally, the performance of the proposed scheme is investigated. Simulations under different node intensities are presented and the results indicate that the proposed algorithm performs well in reducing the number of simplexes under various situations.

Keywords: Simplicial complex · Reduction algorithm
Wireless sensor networks

1 Introduction

There is a growing interest in the research of wireless sensor networks due to the extent of their applications and the progress made in decreasing the costs and sizes of the sensor nodes. Wireless sensor networks can be applied in battlefield surveillances, environmental monitoring, target tracing and so on. In most of these applications, coverage is one crucial factor to ensure the quality

This work is supported in part by the National Natural Science Foundation of China (No. 61601122, 61471164 and 61741102), and Open Foundation of State key Laboratory of Networking and Switching Technology (Beijing University of Posts and Telecommunications) (SKLNST-2016-2-16).

J. Zheng et al. (Eds.): ADHOCNETS 2018, LNICST 258, pp. 25–35, 2019.
https://doi.org/10.1007/978-3-030-05888-3_3

of service provided by the network. However, in practical situation, sensors are randomly deployed in the target field and the topology of the network can be time-variant due to many reasons, such as node destruction or lack of energy. Thus, the knowledge of the network's topology and coverage is necessary for practical applications. Extensive research has been dedicated to coverage problem in wireless sensor networks and they can be classified into three categories: location-based, range-based and connectivity-based. Location-based and range-based approaches need either the precise coordinate information of all sensors or the distance information between each two neighboring nodes, which are difficult to obtain and the performance of the algorithms rely heavily on the accuracy of coordinate and distance measurements. In recent years, connectivity-based approach attracts particular attention due to its powerful tools for discovering coverage holes which only using connectivity information.

The connectivity-based approach uses algebraic tools to study the topological properties of the network. In this category, Čech complex and Rips complex are two most useful abstract simplicial complex to study the coverage problem. The authors in [1] first introduced homology to discover coverage holes by constructing Čech complex to represent wireless sensor networks. This approach can discover the existence and location of the coverage holes accurately. However, the complexity to compute Čech complex is rather high and may explode with the size of the simplicial complex. Another simplicial complex named Rips complex is more easily computable, while it may miss some holes. The relationship between Čech and Rips complexes in terms of coverage holes detection in planar target field was analyzed in [2], and the author shown that the proportion of the holes' area missed by Rips complex is related to the ratio between communication and sensing radius of sensor nodes. In [3], the author presented a scheme based on combinational Laplacians for coverage verification and localized the coverage holes by formulating the problem as an optimization problem for computing a sparse generator of the first homology. The authors in [4] introduced a method for detection and localization of coverage holes by processing information embedded in the hole-equivalent planer graph of the network. In [5], the author classified coverage holes into triangular and non-triangular holes, and proposed a connectivity-based algorithm to discover non-triangular holes.

However, the computation complexity of the above algorithms still remain high for the size of simplicial complex increases sharply with the number of sensor nodes. In addition, for wireless sensor network with nodes randomly deployed, there may exist redundant nodes which can be turn off to save energy. Therefore, we can remove a subset of simplicial complex while keep the homology of the network unchanged. In [6], the author proposed a distributed scheme based on game theoretic approach for power management. This method need precise coordinate information which is either impractical or expensive in practical applications. In [7], a distributed algorithm involved reduction and co-reduction of simplicial complexes for coverage verification was proposed. The work in [8] removed vertices and edges according to a homology-preserving transformation rule without changing the homology while making Rips complex sparser and nearly planar.

In [9] and [10], two reduction algorithms which reduced the number of vertices while keeping connectivity and coverage unchanged were proposed. However, both of the schemes need to calculate the k-th Betti number of the network which is of high computation complexity.

In this paper, we present a reduction algorithm for abstract simplicial complex. The algorithm aims at simplifying the network's topology while keeping the connectivity and coverage intact. We simplify the topology of the wireless sensor network by recurrently deleting vertices according to a strong collapse approach and remove redundant edges to make the simplicial complex graph as planar as possible. Simulations under different node intensities are presented and the results indicate that the proposed algorithm performs well in reducing the number of simplexes under various situations.

The remainder of the paper is organized as follows. First, we give some definitions and properties of simplicial complex and homology in Sect. 2. Then in Sect. 3, we describe the reduction algorithm in details. The performance of the proposed scheme is investigated in Sect. 4. Finally, Sect. 5 concludes the paper.

2   Simplicial Complex and Network Models

The wireless sensor network can be denoted as a graph $G = (V, E)$, which models 2-dimensional information of the network through vertices and edges [11]. Furthermore, graph can be generalized to more generic combinatorial objects known as simplicial complexes. Given a set of vertices V, a k-simplex σ is an unordered set $\{v_0, v_1, ..., v_k\} \subseteq V$, where $v_i \neq v_j$ for all $i \neq j$ and k is the dimension of the simplex. As illustrated in Fig. 1, a 0-simplex is a point, a 1-simplex is an edge, a 2-simplex is a triangle including its interior and a 3-simplex is a tetrahedron with its interior included. Any subset of $\{v_0, v_1, ..., v_k\}$ is called a face of σ. Note that when $k > 2$, the k-simplexes are no longer planar.

A simplicial complex χ is a collection of simplexes that satisfies the following conditions.

1. Any face of a simplex from χ is also in χ;
2. The intersection of any two simplexes σ_1 and σ_2 is a face of both σ_1 and σ_2.

An abstract simplicial complex is a purely combinatorial description of the geometric notion of a simplicial complex, and it does not need the second property. For simplexes in χ, a maximal simplex is a simplex that is not a face of any other simplex, which is also called a facet of the complex.

Definition 1 (Rips complex). *For a set of vertexes V and a parameter ε, the Rips complex is the abstract simplicial complex whose k-simplex satisfies that the (k+1) vertexes are all within the distance ε of each other [12].*

Consider a wireless sensor network comprised of a collection of stationary sensors (also called nodes), nodes are deployed randomly on a planar target field according to a Poisson point process with intensity λ. All nodes are isomorphic

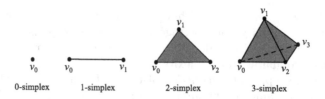

Fig. 1. 0-, 1-, 2- and 3-simplex.

and each sensor is capable of monitoring a region within a circle of sensing radius R_s and communicating with adjacent nodes within its communication radius R_c, as shown in Fig. 2(a). For any two nodes that locate within the sensing radius of each other, they are said to be neighbors. Each node u is capable of acquiring the complete knowledge of its neighbor set N_u. The Rips complex of the wireless sensor network can be constructed as follows. Each node in the target field can be denoted as a 0-simplex. For any two neighboring nodes, they can be denoted as a 1-simplex. For a set of nodes $V_k = \{v_0, v_1, ..., v_k\}$, they compose a k-simplex if $v_i \in N_j$ for any $v_i, v_j \in V_k$.

Then, the wireless sensor network can be modeled by constructing the corresponding Rips complex, as shown in Fig. 2(b). Note that the induced simplicial complex graph can be very complicated and non-planar. When analyzing the coverage, it is not necessary to keep all the information of the simplexes, we can remove a certain subset of simplicial complex and make the complex as planar as possible to reduce the computation complexity. It is important to mention that these deletions of simplexes do not change the homology of the network, which means the properties of the network such as connectivity, number and size of coverage holes remain the same.

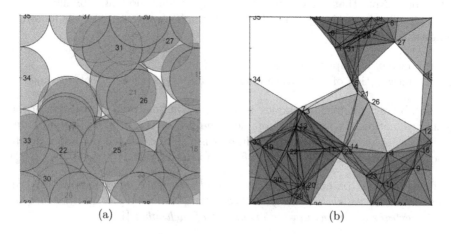

Fig. 2. The network and the corresponding Rips complex.

3   Simplical Complex Reduction Algorithm

In this section, we present a reduction algorithm for wireless sensor network, aiming at simplifying the topology of the network while keeping the homology invariant. The algorithm consists of two component, node collapse and edge collapse. Both of these two components only use connectivity information. In the first component, we delete nodes according to a strong collapse approach. By deleting several nodes, we reduce the number of simplexes while maintain the number and size of coverage holes unchanged. In the second component, we firstly present and prove a corollary that indicates the relations between the maximal simplexes and the common neighbor set incident to an edge. Then we propose a scheme to decide whether an edge is dominates by another. The simplicial complex is further simplified by removing these dominated edges. After that, there may exist new nodes that can be deleted, and the above two steps iterates until the simplicial complex stabilizes. The whole process of the reduction algorithm is illustrated in Fig. 3.

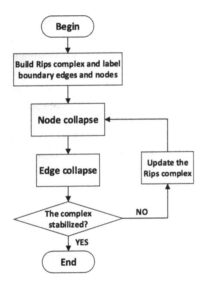

Fig. 3. The algorithm flowchart

3.1   Node Collapse

The strong collapse approach is firstly presented by Barmak and Minian in [13]. The authors introduce the theory of strong homotopy type of simplicial complex, and the strong homotopy type can be described by elementary moves like strong collapse. For a vertex $u \in V$, if there exists another node v that every maximal simplex that containing node u also contains node v, it is considered that node u is dominated by node v and can be removed. Two theorems introduced in [14] shows that strong collapse does not change the connectivity and coverage of the network, as well as the number and location of the coverage holes. We define the size of a coverage holes in Definition 2. As illustrated in Fig. 2(b), the size of the coverage hole on the left is 6 and the one on the right is 5 according to length of the shortest path around each hole. We can know from Theorem 2 that strong collapse also keep the size of the coverage holes invariant.

Theorem 1. *The strong collapse leaves the homology of the complex unchanged* [14].

Theorem 2. *The strong collapse preserves at least one of the shortest paths around each coverage hole in the network* [14].

Definition 2 (Size of the coverage hole). *For a coverage hole in the network, the size of the hole is the length of the shortest path that bordering the hole.*

In [15], the authors prove that for two neighboring nodes u and v, every maximal simplex incident to u is also incident to v if and only if N_u belongs to N_v. Thus, we can decide whether a node u is dominated by one of its adjacent nodes through comparing their neighbor nodes set.

Firstly, we construct the corresponding Rips complex of the network, which only using the connectivity information. We can see from Fig. 2(b) that for any edge uv that has at most one neighbor, the edge locates beside a boundary hole. We call these edges as boundary edges and the nodes that compose them as boundary nodes. For these special nodes and edges, we mark them with a label and the labeled edges and nodes cannot be deleted. Then, for each unlabeled node $u \in V$, check whether there exists a node v that is adjacent to all neighbors of node u. If node v dominates node u, remove node u and all the simplexes that containing node u. Note that a node can be dominated by several different nodes at the same time, we choose the node with the most neighbors as the domination node and it cannot be deleted in the current round of strong collapse. The corresponding Rips complex of the network after the first strong collapse is shown in Fig. 4.

Algorithm 1. Node Collapse

```
 1: for each active interior node u do
 2:     v_dom = 0
 3:     N_{v_dom} = ∅
 4:     if u is not labeled and u is not a domination node then
 5:         N_u = {v_j} is the immediate neighbors of node u
 6:         for j = 1 → m do
 7:             if N_u ⊆ N_{v_j} and |N_{v_j}| > |N_{v_dom}| then
 8:                 v_j → v_dom
 9:             end if
10:         end for
11:         if v_dom ≠ 0 then
12:             node v_dom dominates node u
13:             mark node u for removal and node v_dom for domination node
14:             update the neighbor set of node u's neighbors
15:         end if
16:     end if
17: end for
```

Algorithm 2. Edge Collapse

```
 1: for each unlabeled edge uv do
 2:     N_uv is the common neighbor of node u and v
 3:     if edge uv is only incident to one maximal simplex then
 4:         continue
 5:     else
 6:         for each two node v_i, v_j ∈ {N_uv/{u, v}} do
 7:             if v_i ∈ N_{v_j} and edge v_i v_j is not a domination edge then
 8:                 if N_uv ⊆ N_{v_i v_j} then
 9:                     edge uv is dominated by edge v_i v_j
10:                     mark edge uv for removal and v_i v_j for domination edge
11:                     update neighbor set of node u and v
12:                 end if
13:             end if
14:         end for
15:     end if
16: end for
```

3.2 Edge Collapse

After the strong collapse for nodes, the Rips complex of the network are simplified to a certain extent. However, as shown in Fig. 4, there still remains many overlapped simplexes. In the second component, we proposed a scheme for deleting edges, i.e. the 1-simplexes in the complex.

We extend the strong collapse approach for 1-simplex. For an edge uv, we say a different edge wx dominates uv if every maximal simplexes that contains uv also contains wx. Note that edge uv and wx do not share common nodes. Similar to the theorem given in [15], we can reach to the following corollary, where N_{uv} denotes for the union set of $\{u, v\}$ and common neighbors of node u and v.

Corollary 1. *For two edges uv and wx without common nodes, N_{uv} belongs to N_{wx} if and only if every maximal simplex that contains edge uv also contains edge wx.*

Proof: ($\Rightarrow$) Let Δ be a maximal simplex that incident to edge uv, without loss of generality, $\Delta = \{v_1, v_2, ..., v_n, u, v\}$. We have $v_i \in N_{uv}$ for every $i = 1, 2, ..., n$. According to the assumption, v_i also belongs to N_{wx} for every $i = 1, 2, ..., n$, so $\{w, x\} \cup \Delta$ is a simplex incident to edge uv. While Δ is a maximal simplex of edge uv, we have $\{w, x\} \cup \Delta \subseteq \Delta$, which means there exist different $j, k \in \{1, 2, 3, ..., n\}$ for which $v_j = w$ and $v_k = x$. Therefore Δ also contains edge wx.

($\Leftarrow$) Let Δ be a maximal simplex that incident to edge uv, any two nodes in the simplex are neighbors of each other. According to the assumption, edge wx is also in the simplex, thus node w and x are common neighbors of edge uv. For any node v_i belongs to N_{uv}, there is at least one maximal simplex Δ_i of edge uv that contains node v_i, i.e. $\{u, v, v_i\} = \sigma_j \subseteq \Delta_i$, since edge wx is also in Δ_i, we have $\{w, x, v_i\} = \sigma_j \subseteq \Delta_i$, and so N_{uv} belongs to N_{wx}. ∎

If an edge wx dominates uv, edge uv and the simplexes incident to it can all be removed without creating new coverage holes. However, it is important to mention that unlike strong collapse for nodes, removing edges that locate adjacent to a coverage hole may enlarge the size of the hole. The proposed scheme aims at reducing the number of simplexes to make the simplicial complex planar, while keeping the size of the coverage holes invariant as far as possible. Therefore, a few more restrictions need to be draw when we decide whether an edge is dominated by others and can be removed, and avoid mistaken deletion of edges that neighboring coverage holes as far as possible.

For all of the unlabeled edges, we calculate the number and dimension of maximal simplex incident to the edge. If the edge only has one maximal simplex, we do not delete the edge. The remaining edges are checked whether there exists a dominating edge. All edges that are dominated by another edge are deleted and the corresponding dominating edge cannot be deleted in the current round of edge collapse.

After the edge collapse, there may exists more nodes that can be collapse, the node and edge collapse processes iterate until the complex stabilizes. After several rounds of collapse, the stable simplicial complex of the network is shown in Fig. 5. It can be observed from the figure that the complex are simplified to nearly planar.

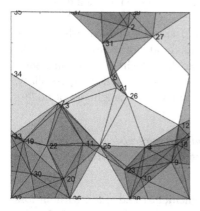

Fig. 4. The Rips complex after the first node collapse.

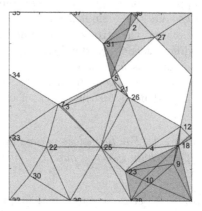

Fig. 5. The stabilized simplicial complex after collapse.

4 Simulation and Performance Evaluation

In this section, complexity of the proposed algorithm will be analyzed and performance of the algorithm will be presented.

4.1 Complexity Analysis

In the node collapse component, each node need to determine whether there exists a dominating node by checking all of its neighbors. Complexity of this step is $\mathcal{O}(n)$, where n is the number of neighbors of each node. In the edge collapse component, each edge firstly need to check whether it is incident to only one maximal simplex. This can be achieved by checking whether there exists two nodes in the neighbor set of the edge that are not neighbors of each other. In the worst case, computation complexity of this step is $\mathcal{O}(n^2)$. Then, for all edges that are incident to more than one maximal simplexes, each of them needs to determine whether there exists an edge that dominates it, and complexity of this step is $\mathcal{O}(n^2)$. Therefore, the overall complexity of edge collapse component is $\mathcal{O}(n^2)$. The total worst-case computation complexity in each round of the proposed algorithm is $\mathcal{O}(n^2)$, where n is the average number of neighboring nodes.

4.2 Performance Evaluation

The algorithm is simulated with MATLAB and we choose a square area of $60 \times 60 \, \mathrm{m}^2$ to be the target field. The sensing radius of each node is set to be $10 \, \mathrm{m}$ and the communication radius is $20 \, \mathrm{m}$. Sensors are deployed randomly in the target field according to a Poisson point process with intensity λ, and the algorithm also works for other random distributions.

Figure 6 illustrates the average number of different dimensional simplexes before and after the reduction algorithm (RA), in which 100 different simulations are performed under average number of nodes 35. It shows that the proposed algorithm can reduce a significant number of different dimensional simplexes in the network, especially simplexes with higher dimension.

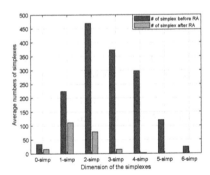
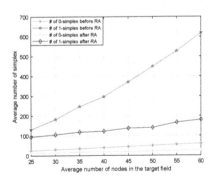

Fig. 6. Numbers of different dimensional simplexes before and after reduction algorithm under average number of nodes 35.

Fig. 7. Number of 0- and 1-simplex before and after reduction algorithm under various node intensities.

Figure 7 shows the average number of 0-simplex and 1-simplex before and after conducting the algorithm, simulations are implemented under various node densities for evaluating the different performance of the proposed algorithm. For each node density, 100 different simulations are performed. It is shown in Fig. 7

that the reduction algorithm can reduce more than 60% of nodes (0-simplex) in the original network under different situations. The number of edges (1-simplex) in the original network raises sharply with the increase of nodes, while there is only a slight increase in the number of remaining edges after the reduction algorithm.

5   Conclusion

In this paper, we propose an efficient reduction algorithm for wireless sensor network, which only uses connectivity information. The proposed algorithm simplifies the corresponding Rips complex of the network by recurrently deleting vertices and edges, while keep the coverage and hole locations invariant. The algorithm is simulated under different node intensities, and the results show that the algorithm can reduce a significant number of different dimensional simplexes under various node intensities. The complexity of our algorithm is $\mathcal{O}(n^2)$, where n is the number of neighboring nodes.

References

1. Ghrist, R., Muhammad, A.: Coverage and hole-detection in sensor networks via homology. In: Proceedings of the 4th International Conference on Information Processing in Sensor Networks, pp. 254–260. IEEE Press, Boise (2005)
2. Yan, F., Martins, P., Decreusefond, L.: Accuracy of homology based coverage hole detection for wireless sensor networks on sphere. IEEE Trans. Wireless Commun. **13**(7), 3583–3595 (2014)
3. Tahbaz-Salehi, A., Jadbabaie, A.: Distributed coverage verification in sensor networks without location information. IEEE Trans. Autom. Control **55**(8), 1837–1849 (2008)
4. Kanno, J., Buchart, J.G., Selmic, R.R., Phoha, V.: Detecting coverage holes in wireless sensor networks. In: IEEE Mediterranean Conference on Control and Automation, pp. 452–457. IEEE Press, Thessaloniki (2009)
5. Yan, F., Martins, P., Decreusefond, L.: Connectivity-based distributed coverage hole detection in wireless sensor networks. In: IEEE Global Telecommunications Conference, pp. 1–6. IEEE Press, Kathmandu (2011)
6. Campos-Nanez, E., Garcia, A., Li, C.: A game-theoretic approach to efficient power management in sensor networks. Oper. Res. **56**(3), 552–561 (2008)
7. Dlotko, P., Ghrist, R., Juda, M., Mrozek, M.: Distributed computation of coverage in sensor networks by homological methods. Appl. Algebra Eng. Commun. Comput. **23**(1–2), 29–58 (2012)
8. Yan, F., Vergne, A., Martins, P., Decreusefond, L.: Homology-based distributed coverage hole detection in wireless sensor networks. IEEE/ACM Trans. Networking **23**(6), 1705–1718 (2015)
9. Vergne, A., Decreusefond, L., Martins, P.: Reduction algorithm for simplicial complexes. In: 2013 Proceedings of IEEE INFOCOM, pp. 475–479. IEEE Press, Turin (2013)

10. Cao, Z., Yan, F., Deng, S., Xia, W., Shen, L., Li, Z.: A topology control algorithm based on homology theory in software-defined sensor networks. In: IEEE/CIC International Conference on Communications, pp. 1–6. IEEE Press, Qingdao (2017)
11. An, W., Qu, N., Shao, F., Shao, F., Ci, S.: Coverage hole problem under sensing topology in flat wireless sensor networks. Wirel. Commun. Mob. Comput. **16**(5), 578–589 (2016)
12. Silva, V.D., Ghrist, R.: Coverage in sensor networks via persistent homology. Algebr. Geom. Topol. **7**(1), 339–358 (2007)
13. Barmak, J.A., Minian, E.G.: Strong homotopy types, nerves and collapses. Discret. Comput. Geom. **47**(2), 301–328 (2012)
14. Wilkerson, A.C., Moore, T.J., Swami, A., Krim, H.: Simplifying the homology of networks via strong collapses. In: IEEE International Conference on Acoustics, Speech and Signal Processing, pp. 5258–5262. IEEE Press, Vancouver (2013)
15. Wilkerson, A.C., Chintakunta, H., Krim, H., Moore, T.J., Swami, A.: A distributed collapse of a network's dimensionality. In: Global Conference on Signal and Information Processing, pp. 595–598. IEEE Press, Atlanta (2014)

Resource Allocation

Resource Allocation Scheme for D2D Communication Based on ILA

Zhifang Gu[(⊠)], Pingping Xu, Guilu Wu, and Hao Liu

National Mobile Communications Research Laboratory, Southeast University,
Nanjing, China
{zhifang_gu,xpp,wgl,liuhao_seu}@seu.edu.cn

Abstract. Resource allocation is one of the most crucial issues in Device-to-Device (D2D) communication, which can achieve high spectrum efficiency and enhance system capacity. However, the interference generated by multiplexing users makes resource allocation more complicated. In this paper, a resource allocation algorithm based on interference limited area (ILA-based) is proposed to manage the interference. First, the system capacity of D2D communication is analyzed. Next, the ILA is divided and the resource pool is selected. Finally, it is verified that the proposed algorithm can effectively improve the overall capacity of the communication system with a relatively low complexity.

Keywords: D2D communication · Resource allocation algorithm · ILA

1 Introduction

With the rapid development of mobile communication technologies, every industry has undergone tremendous changes. The 5G standardization process has been completed recently. D2D technology, as one of the key technologies of 5G, increasingly attracts the attention of researchers. It is a kind of communication method that directly communicates between user terminals without passing through a base station or the core network, but uses the operator-authorized spectrum for point-to-point communication under the system control.

D2D communication underlaying cellular network can bring significant improvement to system capacity and spectrum efficiency [4]. While D2D technology brings numerous advantages, it also increases the complexity of the existing communication system. More importantly, it is inevitable to guarantee that the D2D communication does not generate excessive interference to the original cellular system. Therefore, an effective resource allocation is necessary to manage the interference and improve the overall performance of the system.

Many efforts have been taken in order to deal with the problem of interference. The research in [1] proposed an interference management algorithm to maximize the performance of the D2D communication while satisfying the

Supported by the National Natural Science Foundation of China (No. 61771126).

J. Zheng et al. (Eds.): ADHOCNETS 2018, LNICST 258, pp. 39–48, 2019.
https://doi.org/10.1007/978-3-030-05888-3_4

quality-of-service requirements of the cellular communications in both uplink and downlink phases. Specifically, the admission control and power allocation were conducted to ensure that the interference from D2D communication does not affect to the cellular communications. In [6], an iterative resource allocation algorithm combined with power control was proposed to achieve higher performance of the system. A pricing framework for interference management was proposed in [3], where the base station protects itself (or its serving cellular users) by pricing the cross-tier interference caused from the D2D users. A social-community-aware D2D resource allocation framework in [5] was adopted to D2D communications, which exploited social ties in human-formed social networks.

The above algorithms generally adopt the method of traversing all the available resources and have a high system complexity. A resource allocation algorithm based on ILA is proposed to manage the interference generated by multiplexing users. For the scenario of D2D users multiplexing with cellular network uplink, the proposed algorithm filters the reusable resource pool instead of traversing all the resources, which can greatly reduce the complexity of the system and approximate the optimal ergodic algorithm.

The rest of this paper is organized as follows. Section 2 introduces the system model and analyses the performance of D2D communication multiplexing with cellular uplink network. In Sect. 3, the interference limited area and the proposed resource allocation algorithm are discussed in detail. The simulation results are presented and analyzed in Sect. 4. Finally, the conclusions are given in Sect. 5.

2   System Model

2.1   Scenario Description

The uplink of the D2D multiplexing cellular system model is shown in Fig. 1. The figure includes cellular users to base station uplink communication links, D2D multiplexing uplinks, cellular users to D2D users and D2D users to base station interference links. Assume that there are M cellular users in the cellular system, which are denoted as Cellular User Equipment (CUE) and are uniformly distributed in the cell. In addition, there is a pair of D2D users randomly distributed in the cell, and they are all managed by the base station. The base station transmits signals to M $CUEs$, at the same time, D2D Transmitting User Equipment (TUE) transmits signals to D2D Receiving User Equipment (RUE). In order to facilitate the analysis of the interference of the D2D multiplexing mode, it is assumed that the frequency band resources of CUE_1 are multiplexed by D2D users, and then the D2D receiver is subject to uplink multiplexing interference from CUE_1. On the other hand, the base station receives interference from the D2D sender while receiving the CUE_1 useful signal. Because the main user in the cellular system is the CUE, it is necessary to manage the interference caused by the D2D multiplexing mode through a reasonable resource allocation algorithm.

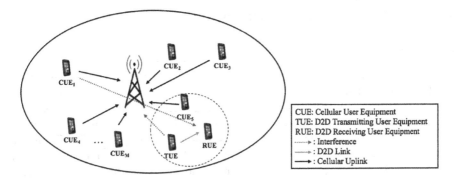

Fig. 1. D2D communication system model with multiplexing interference

2.2 System Capacity

According to the system model shown in Fig. 1, the Signal to Interference plus Noise Ratio ($SINR$) of a cellular user without multiplex interference, a cellular user with multiplex interference, and a D2D user can be obtained as

$$SINR_{CUE_i} = \frac{P_{CUE_i} G_{BS,CUE_i}}{N_0 + I_{d,CUE_i}}, \tag{1}$$

$$SINR_{CUE_j} = \frac{P_{CUE_j} G_{BS,CUE_j}}{N_0}, \tag{2}$$

$$SINR_d = \frac{P_d G_d}{N_0 + I_c}, \tag{3}$$

where P_{CUE_i} is the transmit power of CUE_i, I_{d,CUE_i} is the multiplexing interference to CUE_i, I_c is the multiplexing interference to D2D user. N_0 is the power spectral density of the Additive White Gaussian Noise (AWGN). G_{BS,CUE_i}, G_{BS,CUE_j} are the channel coefficients between the base station and cellular users with interference, between the base station and the cellular users without interference, respectively. G_d is the channel coefficient between D2D users. Therefore, the total capacity of the cellular users and the D2D users can be expressed as

$$R_c = \sum_{i=1}^{K} log_2(1 + SINR_{CUE_i}) + \sum_{j=1}^{M-K} log_2(1 + SINR_{CUE_j}), \tag{4}$$

$$R_d = K log_2(1 + SINR_d), \tag{5}$$

where K is the number of resources needed to be multiplexed. The total capacity, R_{total}, of the system can be shown

$$R_{total} = R_c + R_d. \tag{6}$$

3 ILA-Based Resource Allocation Scheme

3.1 ILA Construction

In a cellular communication system, geographic location information of each cellular user is easily acquired by the base station and can be used to better allocate resources for D2D users [2]. The allocation of resources based on ILA is a scheme for utilizing geographic information. First, the number of physical resource blocks required by a D2D user is estimated when satisfying the preset transmission rate requirement. Secondly, the interference limited area is divided by using the ILA-based scheme. At the same time, to satisfy the quality of service of the base station, the power control of the cellular user is required. Then to meet the D2D receiver's quality of service, D2D transmitter power needs to be controlled. Finally, the resources are allocated after analyzing the interference generated by D2D multiplexing with the ILA-based scheme.

When the D2D user uses the multiplexing uplink mode, the RUE may receive uplink interference from the cellular user, and the D2D transmitter may interfere with the base station which should receive the cellular user uplink signal. In the proposed resources allocation method, first, with the ILA-based algorithm, cellular users that can be multiplexed with D2D are divided to ensure that D2D communication will not cause excessive interference to normal cellular communication. At the same time, it is analyzed whether the distance between D2D users is appropriate and whether the communication quality meets the requirements, so as to ensure that D2D links can be establish normally. When the D2D user uses the multiplexing uplink mode, the base station receives the signal from the cellular user, which can be expressed as

$$y_{CUE_i} = \sqrt{P_{CUE_i} d_{CUE_i,BS}^{-\alpha}} h_{CUE_i,BS} x_i + \sqrt{P_{TUE_i} d_{TUE_i,BS}^{-\alpha}} h_{TUE_i,BS} x_{TUE,i} + n_i. \quad (7)$$

where P_{CUE_i} is the transmit power of CUE_i on the i-th Resource Block (RBi), with the bandwidth of W. P_{TUE_i} is the transmit power of the D2D sender on RB_i. $d_{CUE_i,BS}^{-\alpha}$ is the large-scale fading from CUE_i to the base station, $d_{CUE_i,BS}$ is the distance from CUE_i to the base station, and α is the path loss index. Similarly, $d_{TUE_i,BS}^{-\alpha}$ is the large-scale fading from TUE_i to the base station on RB_i, and $d_{TUE_i,BS}$ is the distance from the D2D sender to the base station. $h_{CUE_i,BS}$ is the channel coefficient between the cellular user and the base station, while $h_{TUE_i,BS}$ is the channel coefficient between the D2D sender and the base station on RB_i. x_i and $x_{TUE,i}$ represent the signal that the CUE sends to the base station and the signal that the D2D sender sends to the D2D receiver on RB_i, respectively. It is assumed that $E\{|x_i|^2\} = 1$ and $E\{|x_{TUE_i}|^2\} = 1$. n_i is AWGN signal.

Since the signal from the CUE received by the base station is subject to interference from the TUE, the $SINR$ on RB_i is:

$$SINR_{CUE_i} = \frac{P_{CUE_i} d_{CUE_i,BS}^{-\alpha} |h_{CUE_i,BS}|^2}{N_0 + P_{TUE_i} d_{TUE_i,BS}^{-\alpha} |h_{TUE_i,BS}|^2}. \quad (8)$$

In order to make the interference to the CUE under the control of the base station, it is assumed that the $SINR$ of the CUE should be greater than a certain threshold value which is set to δ_{CUE_i}, that is

$$SINR_{CUE_i} > \delta_{CUE_i}. \tag{9}$$

Therefore, to meet the QoS requirements of cellular users, $d_{TUE_i,BS}$ needs to meet:

$$d_{TUE_i,BS} > (\frac{P_{CUE_i}d_{CUE_i,BS}^{-\alpha}|h_{CUE_i,BS}|^2 - N\delta_{CUE_i}}{\delta_{CUE_i}P_{TUE_i}|h_{TUE_i,BS}|^2})^{1/\alpha} = D_{TUE,BS,min}, \tag{10}$$

TUE should be far away from the base station, and the minimum distance for normal D2D communication is $D_{TUE,BS,min}$. Similarly, the minimum distance between RUE and the CUE whose resources are multiplexed can be expressed by

$$d_{CUE_i,RUE} > (\frac{P_{TUE_i}d_{TUE,RUE}^{-\alpha}|h_{TUE_i,RUE}|^2 - N\delta_{RUE_i}}{\delta_{RUE_i}P_{CUE_i}|h_{CUE_i,RUE}|^2})^{1/\alpha} = D_{CUE,RUE,min}. \tag{11}$$

where all parameters are the counterparts of the CUE and RUE, which are defined in the same way. The cell radius is r. $D_{TUE,BS,min}$ and $D_{CUE,RUE,min}$ can be used to indicate the Interference Limited Area as Fig. 2 shows.

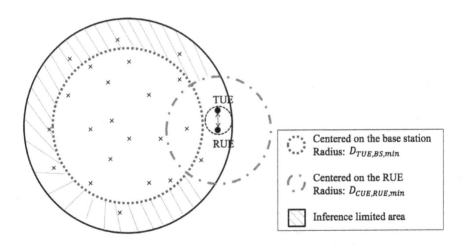

Fig. 2. Interference limited area in D2D communication system

3.2   ILA-Based Resource Allocation Algorithm

According to the interference limited area shown in Fig. 2, a complete ILA-based resource pool can be established as

$$pool = [RB_1', RB_2', RB_3', \ldots, RB_{M'}'], \tag{12}$$

where RB'_i represents the resource blocks occupied by the cellular users that satisfy the ILA requirement, and M' is the total number of resource blocks that satisfy the ILA requirement. Obviously, assuming that there are many cellular users in the application scenario of the D2D user, when solving the above optimization problem, the base station needs to control all cellular users in the resource pool to measure the channel status of each link. In an actual situation, this traversal scheme is obviously not practical.

Secondary modification is conducted to the original resource pool, which greatly reduces the size of the resource pool, thereby reducing system complexity and adapting to future large-scale D2D scenarios. In the proposed method, L times the number of cellular users for the demand of D2D users are randomly selected, and the total selected number is far less than the original resource pool size. Next, the optimization problem is calculated in the modified resource pool to allocate the resource block for the D2D user. At the same time an optimized resource list is established:

$$List_L = \begin{bmatrix} SINR_{CUE_RB'_1} \dots SINR_{CUE_RB'_L} \\ SINR_{RUE_RB'_1} \dots SINR_{RUE_RB'_L} \end{bmatrix}. \tag{13}$$

$List_L$ records $SINR$ of CUE and RUE, which can be used to more easily calculate the optimization problem. The proposed resource allocation algorithm uses a slight drop in performance in exchange for time-consuming reduction and the reduced complexity.

4   Simulation Results

The design of the D2D simulation platform is mainly modified on the basis of the traditional cellular system by adding D2D users and their related links. Through simulation results, the performance of the proposed ILA-based D2D resource allocation method is evaluated. The simulation is based on orthogonal frequency division multiple access in a cellular system. Resources are divided into resource blocks, and each resource block does not interfere with each other. Considering the limited capacity of the base station in the future, the pool of D2D reusable resources is reduced to simulate the occurrence of congestion. The simulation parameters are shown in Table 1. In Fig. 3, the comparison of the total capacity of the cellular system in the proposed algorithm, random algorithm and traversal optimal algorithm is conducted. As can be seen from Fig. 3, the total system capacity increases first and then decreases with the base station interference threshold increasing. The performance of the proposed algorithm is obviously better than the random allocation method because the proposed solution makes full use of the ILA information, which excludes cellular users with heavy interference from the resource pool. In contrast, random allocation method may allocate these resource blocks to D2D users. The reason why the performance of the proposed scheme is slightly lower than the optimization scheme is that the system reduces the computational complexity and the signaling overhead to adapt to the actual scenario. By setting the $SINR$ threshold, some reusable resources are eliminated. Therefore, the size of the resource pool and the system load pressure is reduced by the slight sacrifice in performance. When the $SINR$ threshold rises in the initial stage, resource blocks with relatively low transmitting power or poor link condition are excluded from the resource pool. Because this algorithm ensures that the interference received by the base station is within a certain range, the curve increases at the beginning. However, when the $SINR$ continues to increase, the decrease of the average TUE transmit power in the resource pool reduces the multiplexing gain of D2D. In this case, the overall capacity of the system finally showed a downward trend. The simulation results show that the threshold should be set reasonably according to the actual situation of the system.

Figure 4 shows the relationship between the total system capacity and the simulated distance between D2D users. The power threshold of the base station

Table 1. Simulation parameters in D2D communication system

System parameter	Value
Cell radius, r	$500\,\mathrm{m}$
Resource block bandwidth, W	$180\,\mathrm{KHz}$
Maximum transmit power of the terminal, P_{TUE}	$23\,\mathrm{dBm}$
Power spectral density of AWGN, N_0	$-174\,\mathrm{dBm/Hz}$
System outage probability threshold, p	0.8

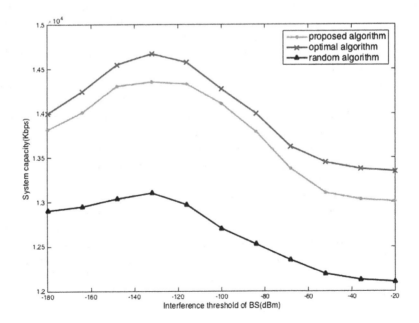

Fig. 3. The capacity of the system with various interference threshold of BS

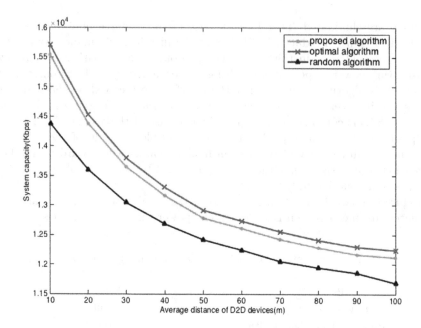

Fig. 4. The capacity of the system with various distances of D2D devices

receiving RUE is set to $-110\,$dBm, and other parameters of the system remain unchanged. From this figure, it can be seen that the system capacity decreases with the increase of the simulation distance between D2D users. The performance of the proposed scheme is significantly better than the randomization scheme, while it is slightly lower than that of the optimization scheme. As the distance of the D2D devices increase, the average power of the received signal transmitted from TUE to RUE decreases, so that the gain of the multiplexed signal between the D2Ds and the overall capacity of the system decrease. This is the reason that the total system capacity decreases as the distance between D2Ds increases. Because of the proposed ILA-based algorithm, the initial resource pool has removed some resource blocks that may generate excessive reuse interference. Therefore, the overall system performance can still approach the optimal solution but with a relatively low complexity.

It can be seen from Fig. 5 that the overall system capacity increases as the number of cellular users in the system increases. The performance of the proposed algorithm is lower than but close to the optimal solution, and is superior to the randomized resource allocation method. Simulation results show that for a single pair of D2D users, the greater the number of cellular users in the system, the better the overall capacity of the system. Because the larger the D2D resource pool, the more likely the system allocates resources that have less interference to D2D users.

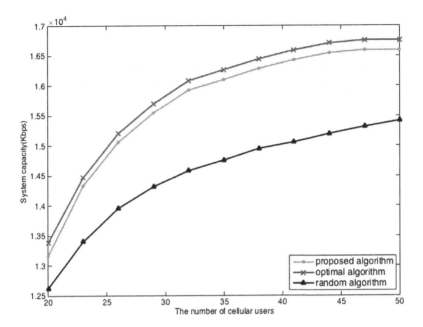

Fig. 5. The capacity of the system with various numbers of cellular users

5   Conclusion

An ILA-based resource allocation algorithm is proposed to effectively manage resources and reduce interference in D2D multiplexing communication. With the proposed algorithm, the system resource pool is modified to reduce the complexity of the system and can be more competitive in future dense communications networks. Through the simulation experiments, the performance of the proposed algorithm can be very close to the optimal traversing method, and with a significantly lower system complexity.

References

1. Huynh, T., Onuma, T., Kuroda, K., Hasegawa, M., Hwang, W.J.: Joint downlink and uplink interference management for device to device communication underlaying cellular networks. IEEE Access **4**, 4420–4430 (2016)
2. Li, X., Wang, Z., Sun, Y., Gu, Y., Hu, J.: Mathematical characteristics of uplink and downlink interference regions in D2D communications underlaying cellular networks. Wirel. Pers. Commun. **93**(4), 917–932 (2017)
3. Liu, Y., Wang, R., Han, Z.: Interference-constrained pricing for D2D networks. IEEE Trans. Wirel. Commun. **16**(1), 475–486 (2017)
4. Shah, S.T., Hasan, S.F., Seet, B.C., Chong, P.H.J., Chung, M.Y.: Device-to-device communications: a contemporary survey. Wirel. Pers. Commun. **98**(1), 1247–1284 (2018)

5. Wang, F., Li, Y., Wang, Z., Yang, Z.: Social-community-aware resource allocation for D2D communications underlaying cellular networks. IEEE Trans. Veh. Technol. **65**(5), 3628–3640 (2016)
6. Yang, Z., Huang, N., Xu, H., Pan, Y., Li, Y., Chen, M.: Downlink resource allocation and power control for device-to-device communication underlaying cellular networks. IEEE Commun. Lett. **20**(7), 1449–1452 (2016)

Content Aware Resource Allocation for Video Service Provisioning in Wireless Networks

Yongxiang Zhao, Yunpeng Song, and Chunxi Li[(⊠)]

Beijing JiaoTong University, Beijing 100044, China
{yxzhao,17120113,chxli1}@bjtu.edu.cn

Abstract. Video service has been a killer application over wireless networks. Many cross-layer optimization techniques have been proposed to improve the quality of video services in wireless networks. However, most of them did not consider video content type information in resource allocation, which greatly affects the quality of users' watching experience. In this paper, we take video type information into consideration for resource allocation at base stations. Accordingly, for given transmission power at base station, we build an optimal model to achieve maximal achievable total Mean Opinion Score (MOS) by allocating appropriate powers and video rates for different users watching different types of videos. Numerical results show that our model can achieve much higher MOS compared with existing scheme that does not consider such video type information.

Keywords: MOS · Video content · Resource allocation · Wireless networks

1 Introduction

Video services have been a killer application over mobile networks and smart devices. According to a cisco report [1], mobile video traffic has accounted for 55% of the total mobile data in 2015 and is expected to grow approximately to 75% in 2020.

Many cross-layer techniques have been proposed to improve video quality in wireless environment. In [2], Gross et al. proposed to schedule packet transmissions over orthogonal frequency-division multiplexing (OFDM) channels in a way such that higher priority is given to more important packets (e.g., Iframes in video traffic). In [3], Li et al. built an optimal model to minimize the distortion of reconstructed videos at user side in multi-user wireless video transmission environment. They assume that all users use the same rate-distortion function. In [4], Chuah et al. considered scalable video in multicast communications and used signal-to-noise ratio and packet delivery rate as video quality measures. However, they did not consider perceptual quality at users. In [5], Danish et al. proposed a resource allocation algorithm, which assigns video bitrate and subcarriers to users with an expectation to maximize users' perceptual quality of video services. However, they did not consider how to allocate network resources among users watching different types of videos. In summary, all the above existing work did not take video content type information (e.g., whether a video is an action movie or a romance video) into consideration when making decision on resource allocation among different users so as to improve the overall perceptual quality of video services at users.

J. Zheng et al. (Eds.): ADHOCNETS 2018, LNICST 258, pp. 49–58, 2019.
https://doi.org/10.1007/978-3-030-05888-3_5

Video type has big impact on the MOS (Mean Opinion Score) of video service at user side. In this aspect, Ref. [6] found that the MOS (Mean Opinion Score) of a video watching experience is not only related to video bitrate, frame rate, and packet loss probability, but also related to video type. In addition, the impact of bitrate, frame rate, and packet loss probability on the MOS for different video types are also different. For example, the MOS of an action movie with violently changing pictures will be smaller than that of a landscape film with smoothly changing pictures under the same setting of bitrate, frame rate, and packet loss probability. Thus, we have the following two inferences: Base station needs to allocate more transmit power to users watching action videos than to users watching landscape videos in order for them to enjoy same level of MOS in video watching; Given transmit power allocated to a user, we also need to consider the balance between video bitrate and packet loss probability in order to maximize the user's MOS.

Based on the above observations, in this paper, we build a content aware resource allocation model by considering video content type information in wireless resource allocation. We assume video type information is known for resource allocation at base stations. Accordingly, for given total transmission power at base station, we build an optimal model to achieve maximal total achievable MOS by allocating appropriate transmit powers and video rates for different users watching different types of videos. Numerical results show that our model can achieve much higher total MOS compared with existing scheme that does not use such video type information.

The rest of this paper is organized as follows. In Sect. 2, we introduce some related work. In Sect. 3, we first introduce application scenario under study and feasibility of MOS maximization by considering video type information. In Sect. 4, we build the optimal content aware resource allocation model. In Sect. 5, we provide numerical results for performance evaluation. Finally, in Sect. 6, we conclude the paper.

2   Related Work

Existing work for supporting video streaming services in wireless networks can roughly be classified into following two types: top-down approaches and bottom-up approaches. The former type of approaches adapts video's features to network layer/data link layer/physical layer's parameter tuning. In contrast, the latter type of approaches adapts network layer/data link layer/physical layer's parameters to the tuning of video streaming parameters [7]. Next, we shall introduce typical work belonging to either type.

Typical top-down approaches are as follows. In [2], Gross et al. suggested to transmit important video packets (Iframes) with high priority over OFDM channels. In [8], Lee et al. suggested that a mobile terminal should control its video bitrate according to its video content characteristics in order to achieve improved energy efficiency. This idea was extended to three-dimensional (3D) videos where QoE (Quality of Experience) is used as base measure to determine SNR (Signal Noise Ratio) threshold for adaptive modulation and coding over IEEE802.16e wireless channels [9].

Typical bottom-up approaches are as follows. Refs. [3, 4] formulated the optimal resource allocation problem by maximizing the video quality of users subject to transmission energy and channel access constraints. Ref. [10] built an optimal model to allocate bandwidth to users according to their video contents. However, [10] only considers bandwidth constraint without considering the relationship among power, bandwidth, and packet loss probability. Ref. [5] is the closest to our work in this paper. Given a target minimal power requirement, Ref. [5] proposed a scheme to assign video bitrate and subcarriers to users in order to maximize the users' perceptual quality of videos. However, Ref. [5] assumes that packet loss probability is given (fixed) and users' perceptual quality of videos is only relevant to video bitrates. They did not consider the relationship between video bitrate and packet loss probability. Moreover, it did not consider power allocation among users watching different types of videos. In our work in this paper, perceptual quality of a video is relevant to transmit power, packet loss probability, and video bitrate. Furthermore, packet loss probability is a function of both transmit power and video bitrate.

3 Application Scenario and Key Idea

Figure 1 shows the application scenario under study in this paper. In this figure, a number of wireless video-watching users are scattered in a cell covered by a base station. These users can be classified into the following three types based on the types of video they are watching [6]: videos with Slight Movement (SM), videos with Gentle Walking (GW), and videos with Rapid Movement (RM).

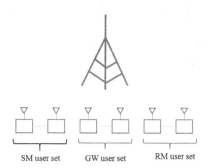

Fig. 1. Application scenario.

According to [6], the MOSs of SM, GW, and RM videos can be calculated as follows, respectively:

$$\text{MOS}_{\text{SM}} = 0.0075r - 0.014f - 3.79l + 3.4 \tag{1.a}$$

$$\text{MOS}_{\text{GW}} = 0.0065r - 0.0092f - 5.76l + 2.98 \tag{1.b}$$

$$\text{MOS}_{\text{RM}} = 0.002r - 0.0012f - 9.53l + 3.04 \tag{1.c}$$

In (1.a), (1.b) and (1.c), r, f, l represent video bitrate, frame rate, and packet loss probability, respectively. Moreover, in this paper, we set the MOS of a video to zero when packet loss probability l is larger than nine percent since the video quality in this case usually very poor. In (1.a), (1.b) and (1.c), it is seen that the coefficients of r, f, l for different types of videos are quite different. For example, when the packet loss rate increases one percent, the MOS of a RM video will be decreased by 0.0953 while that of an SM video is only decreased by 0.0379.

The MOS of a video can be expressed as a function of transmit power (denoted by p) and video bitrate r. The reason is as follows. Firstly, packet loss probability l is a function of transmit power p, distance between transmitter and receiver (denoted by d), video bitrate r, and noise spectral density N_0 and packet size [11]. Secondly, MOS is a function of l, f, and r according to (1.a), (1.b) and (1.c). Thus, given d, N_0, packet size, and f, MOS is a function of p and r. Details are shown in Sects. 4.1 and 4.2.

Figure 2 shows the MOS for SM videos, MOS for RM videos, and also corresponding packet loss probability, respectively, due to varying video bitrate and transmit power. In this figure, the video bitrate range for both SM and RM videos is [100, 320] kbps. (Default) frame rate is fixed to be 30 frames per second. As shown in Fig. 2(a)

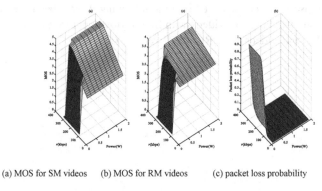

(a) MOS for SM videos   (b) MOS for RM videos   (c) packet loss probability

Fig. 2. MOS and packet loss probability of SM.

Table 1. Symbols used.

Symbols	Definition
N	Total number of users
u_j	j^{th} user
d_j	Distance between user u_j and base station
r_j	Video bitrate of u_j
p_j	Power that base station uses to transmit video to user u_j
l_j	Packet loss probability of jth user
c_j	video content type of jth user
$H(p_j, d_j, r_j)$	A function returns packet loss probability l_j for given p_j, d_j, r_j
$F(c_j, r_j, l_j)$	returns j^{th} user's MOS for given c_j, r_j, l_j

and (b), the MOSs of these two types of videos are quite different under the same combination of video bitrate and transmit power. In addition, different video types have different MOS gradients with respect to video bitrate and transmit power. Thus, these two observations suggest that we need to adjust transmit power and video bitrate simultaneously in order to maximize the total MOSs of all users.

4 Optimal Model for Content Aware Resource Allocation

In this section, we shall build an optimal content aware resource allocation model, which introduces video type information into wireless resource allocation while achieving maximal total MOS for all users.

In our model, base station is assumed to know the video type information of each video-watching user in its cell. Symbols used hereafter are listed in Table 1.

4.1 Packet Loss Probability Calculation

We use free space propagation model and DPSK modulation [11] to support the video transmissions from base station to wireless terminals. Specifically, we firstly use free space propagation model to calculate received power (denoted as P_r) at receiving terminal, which is as follows.

$$P_r = P_t G_t G_r \left(\frac{\lambda}{4\pi d}\right)^2 \tag{2}$$

Where, $P_t, G_t, G_r, \lambda,$ and d are transmission power at base station, transmitter antenna gain, receiver antenna gain, wavelength, and distance between transmitter and receiver, respectively. $\lambda = c/f$ where $c = 3 \times 10^8$ m/s is speed of radio signal and f is frequency. We set G_t, G_r, f to be 2, 1.6, and 900 MHz, respectively, as used in [11].

We assume the modulation technique is DPSK, thus bit error probability e can be calculated as follows [11].

$$e = \frac{1}{2}\exp\left(-\frac{P_r}{RN_0}\right), \tag{3}$$

where R is video bitrate and N_0 is noise power density which equals 3.2×10^{-20} J. In our analysis here, video bitrate is assumed equal to channel rate owing to the following reason. In our model, base station chooses video bitrate for each user and it can adopt transmission techniques such as OFDM or software defined radio like opening a special channel for per-user transmission based on the assigned video bitrate. Since such techniques can provide user-specific channel rate at small granularity, it is reasonable for us to assume that channel rate at the physical layer equals the video bitrate at the application layer. Although such assumption is kind of simplified, it can still largely capture major characteristics of wireless channels and in particular it enables us to focus on the video-service-provisioning-related cross layer optimization.

Accordingly, packet loss probability l can be obtained by the following equation.

$$l = 1 - (1 - e)^S \tag{4}$$

where S is packet size and its default value is 8000 bit in this paper.

In brief, for a user u_j, given p_j, d_j and r_j, we can obtain the packet loss probability l_j by using (2), (3), and (4). To ease the presentation, we shall use function $H(p_j, d_j, r_j)$ to represent the calculation of packet loss probability l_j.

4.2 MOS Calculation

We use the following method to calculate each user's MOS. As mentioned in Sect. 3, users are classified into three sets: SM, GW, and RM. We use function $F(c_i, r_i, l_i)$ to calculate a user u_i's MOS suppose his/her video content type is known. Details are as follows: select (1.a), (1.b) or (1.c) according to the value of video type c_i and replace r_i and l_i into corresponding equations to calculate the user's MOS. Note that packet loss probability is calculated using the method in the preceding subsection.

4.3 Optimal Content Aware Resource Allocation Model

Combine the results in the above two subsections, we have an optimal content aware resource allocation model as follows. Given each user's video type, his/her distance away from the base station, and the total transmit power P that the base station can use to deliver the video services, this model tries to maximize the sum of MOSs by all users. That is,

$$\max{}_{\{p_j, r_j\}} \sum_{j=1}^{N} \text{MOS}_j \tag{5}$$

Subject to:

$$l_j = H(p_j, d_j, r_j), \qquad j \in [1, \dots, N] \tag{6}$$

$$\text{MOS}_j = F(c_j, r_j, l_j), \qquad j \in [1, \dots, N] \tag{7}$$

$$\sum_{j=1}^{N} p_j \leq P, \qquad j \in [1, \dots, N] \tag{8}$$

$$l_j \leq \gamma, \qquad j \in [1, \dots, N] \tag{9}$$

$$p_L \leq p_j \leq p_B, \qquad j \in [1, \dots, N] \tag{10}$$

In this model, p_j and r_j are variables. The objective function (5) is to maximize the sum of all users' MOSs. Equation (6) finds the packet loss probability of each user. Equation (7) returns u_j's MOS. (8) requires sum of the powers allocated to all users is less than or equal to P, which represents the maximal possible (total) power that the base station can use for the transmissions and it is an input parameter. (9) requires packet loss probability l_j is less than or equal to γ which is also an input and the default of its value is set to be 0.1 in this paper or otherwise the quality of video for user u_j will be totally unacceptable. (10) requires p_j is in the range $[p_L, p_B]$, which are low bound and upper bound of the power allocated to a user and, in this paper, their default values are set to 0 and P, respectively.

5 Numerical Results

In this section, we evaluate the performance of our content aware resource allocation model via numerical results. We focus on the one-cell case such that there is only one base station with one or more users. The rate upper bound of SM, and RM is set to 320, and 1450 kbps, respectively.

For comparison purpose, here, we also realized a baseline model, which does not consider video content type in resource allocation. The baseline model works as follows: it first slices the total transmission power P equally into N share and each user is assigned with an amount of P/N power; then it finds a user's maximal MOS which can be obtained by using content aware allocation model in which P is replaced by P/N and the user set only contains this user; Finally, the outcome of the baseline model is sum of all users' maximal MOSs. The philosophy behind such a baseline model is as follows. According to [11], in a cellular network, base station is typically scheduled to transmit data to each terminal for a fixed time slice in roughly round-robin fashion. Thus, all users share the transmission power roughly equally.

5.1 One-User Case

In this experiment, we assume there is only one user whose distance away from the base station is 340 m. Then we varied the transmit power of base station from 0.1w to 2w with step size 0.1w and obtained the MOSs by different models. Figure 3 shows the numerical results when the user watches SM, GW, and RM video, respectively.

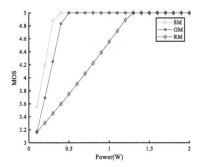

Fig. 3. MOSs by different video content types for one user case.

From Fig. 3, it is seen that the slopes of curves for different video types are different, which mean that we need to balance the power assignment among different video types when multiple users share the transmit power. Specifically, we can see that the SM curve has the steepest slope which means SM is the easiest to be saturated among the three types. That is, in case three types of video watchers with the same distance away from the base station, the priority for power allocation to different types of video watchers (from the highest to the lowest) is as follows: SM video watchers, GM video watchers, and finally RM video watchers.

5.2 Two-User Case

In this experiment, we assume there are two users watching two different types of videos: one SM user and one RM user. We chose these two types of videos because they have quite different slopes in MOS increase (see Fig. 3). In three different tests, these two users' distances away from the base station was set to (340 m, 640 m), (640 m, 340 m), and (400 m, 400 m), respectively (the former setting is for the SM user while the latter is for the RM user). In each test, we varied the transmit power of base station from 0.1w to 2w with step 0.1w and obtained the MOSs by different models. The results for the three tests are shown in Fig. 4(a), (b), and (c). Figure 5(a), (b), and (c) show the corresponding power allocated to the SM and RM users by our model. Figure 6(a), (b), and (c) show the corresponding video bitrates allocated to the SM and RM users by our model for each relevant case shown in Fig. 5.

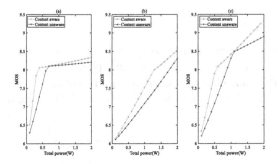

Fig. 4. MOSs under two types of videos (SM and RM videos) by different models.

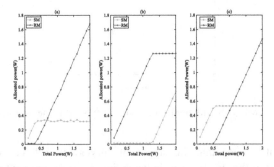

Fig. 5. Allocated powers for different video watchers by our content aware model.

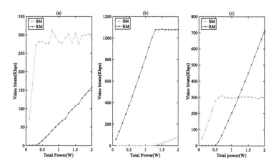

Fig. 6. Allocated video bitrates for different types of video watchers by our model.

In Fig. 4, it is seen that the curves for our content aware model are above the curves for the baseline model most of time.

Our model works to jointly optimize the power and video bitrate for each user while maximizing the sum of all users' MOSs. From Figs. 4, 5 and 6, we can see that our model tends to give high priority for allocating power to video types with faster increase rates in MOS for the same amount of power. In Fig. 5(a) (i.e., first test, leftmost subfigure in Fig. 5), our model first allocates all available power to the SM user since it is easier to increase MOS of a SM user. Because the MOS of SM is nearly saturated when transmit power = 0.4 W as can be seen in Fig. 3, the model begins to allocate remaining power to RM user when the total power exceeds 0.4 W which causes a knee point of curve of content aware model in Fig. 4(a). In Fig. 6(a), it can be seen that our model increases video bitrate of RM user until the total power exceeds 0.4 W. In the second test (i.e., the middle subfigure), the RM user is easier to increase the MOS since it is much closer to the base station than the SM user. Thus, our model first allocates all available power to RM user when the total power is below 1.2 W. After that, it begins to allocate to the SM user. The video bitrate curve of RM in Fig. 6 (b) shows similar behavior. In the third test (i.e., the rightmost subfigure), the SM user is easier to increase the MOS since the distances of the two users away from base station are the same. In this case, our model allocates available power to SM user first, then to RM user. In addition, we would like to point out that the small-scale fluctuation in transmit power allocated to SM user (see Fig. 5(a) and the approximate 20-kbps fluctuation in bitrate allocated to the SM user (see Fig. 6(a)) jointly contribute to the steady increase in MOS as shown in Fig. 4(a).

6   Conclusion

In this paper, we built an optimal resource allocation model to exploit the video content type information for provisioning of better video services in wireless environments. Numerical results show our model can improve the MOS performance as compared with baseline model.

Acknowledgement. This work was supported in part by National Natural Science Foundation of China under Grants 61572071, u1534201, 61531006, and 61471339.

References

1. Cisco Visual Networking Index. Global Mobile Data Traffic Forecast Update 2015–2020, White Paper. http://www.cisco.com/c/en/us/solutions/collateral/service-provider/visual-networking-index-vni/mobile-white-paper-c11-520862.html. Accessed 1 Feb 2016
2. Gross, J., Klau, J., Karl, H., Wolisz, A.: Cross-layer optimization of OFDM transmission systems for MPEG-4 video streaming. Comput. Commun. **27**, 1044–1055 (2004)
3. Li, P., Chang, Y., Feng, N., Yang, F.: A cross-layer algorithm of packet scheduling and resource allocation for multi-user wireless video transmission. IEEE Trans. Consum. Electron. **57**(3), 1128–1134 (2011)
4. Chuah, S.P., Chen, Z., Tan, Y.P.: Energy-efficient resource allocation and scheduling for multicast of scalable video over wireless networks. IEEE Trans. Multimedia **14**(4), 1324–1336 (2012)
5. Danish, E., Silva, V., Fernando, A., Alwis, C., Kondoz, A.: Content-aware resource allocation in OFDM systems for energy-efficient video transmission. In: Proceedings of IEEE International Conference on Consumer Electronics (ICCE), Las Vegas, NV, pp. 456–457 (2014)
6. Khan, A., Sun, L., Ifeachor, E.: Content-based video quality prediction for MPEG4 video streaming over wireless networks. J. Multimedia **4**(4), 1–5 (2009)
7. Khan, S., Peng, Y., Steinbach, E.: Application-driven cross-layer optimization for video streaming over wireless networks. IEEE Commun. Mag. **44**(1), 122–130 (2006)
8. Lee, S., Koo, J., Chung, K.: Content-aware rate control scheme to improve the energy efficiency for mobile IPTV. In: Proceedings of IEEE International Conference on Consumer Electronics (ICCE), Las Vegas, NV, pp. 445–446 (2010)
9. Danish, E., Fernando, A., Abdul-Hameed, O., Alshamrani, M., Kondoz, A.: Perceptual QoE based resource allocation for mobile 3D video communications. In: Proceedings of IEEE International Conference on Consumer Electronics (ICCE), Las Vegas, NV, pp. 454–455 (2014)
10. Wang, L., Zhao, Y., Li, C., Guo, Y.: Enabling content aware QoE network bandwidth allocation. In: Proceedings of International Conference on Wireless Communications and Signal Processing (WCSP), Nanjing, China, pp. 1–5 (2017)
11. Wireless Communication Systems. Lecture Notes. http://www.ece.utah.edu/~npatwari/pubs/lectureAll_ece5325_6325_f11.pdf. Accessed 18 Apr 2018
12. Winstein, K., Sivaraman, A., Balakrishnan, H.: Stochastic forecasts achieve high throughput and low delay over cellular networks. In: Proceedings of 10th USENIX NSDI 2013, Lombard, IL, pp. 459–471 (2013)

A Power Allocation Algorithm for D2D-Direct Communication in Relay Cellular Networks

Chenguang He[1,2(✉)], Wenbin Zhang[1], Weixiao Meng[1,2], and Yuwei Cui[1]

[1] Communication Research Center, Harbin Institute of Technology, Harbin, China
{hechenguang, zwbgxy1973, wxmeng}@hit.edu.cn,
15866632753@163.com
[2] Key Laboratory of Police Wireless Digital Communication, Ministry of Public Security, People's Republic of China, Harbin, China

Abstract. The relay and Device to device (D2D) technologies can be used to improve the Quality of Service (QoS) of a mobile user in the edge region of the cellular networks, To coordinate these two technologies, this paper considers a heterogeneous network containing the D2D-direct, D2D-non-direct and cellular communication mode. Furtherly, a system model taking throughput as optimization object is built to descript this network precisely. It is proved that the objective function and the constraints satisfy the requirements of convex function, and then a power allocation algorithm based on Lagrange Multiplier is proposed to find the optimal solver. Finally, we evaluate the performance of algorithm in terms of throughput and fairness by simulation.

Keywords: Relay · D2D-direct · Convex optimization · Throughput

1 Introduction

In recent years, the rapid development of mobile communication technologies has resulted in the diversified and complicated communication Quality of Service (QoS) required. To improve the communication quality of users in the LTE-A cell edge and other hot spots, the relay technology was introduced into the existing wireless network.

D2D, as another technology appearing recently, can share the traffic of the base station, improve the spectrum efficiency and the throughput of a communication system. D2D communication has become a hot research field. In [1], Janis proposed three D2D communication modes, which are reuse mode, dedicated mode and cellular mode. In reuse mode, the D2D communication is direct and reuses the whole resources together with the cellular communication. In dedicated mode, the D2D communication is direct and uses the specially assigned channels. In cellular mode, the D2D communication is relayed by the BS. In [2], the D2D communication underlying cellular networks was considered to improve local services and optimize the throughput over

© ICST Institute for Computer Sciences, Social Informatics and Telecommunications Engineering 2019
Published by Springer Nature Switzerland AG 2019. All Rights Reserved
J. Zheng et al. (Eds.): ADHOCNETS 2018, LNICST 258, pp. 59–70, 2019.
https://doi.org/10.1007/978-3-030-05888-3_6

the shared resources while fulfilling prioritized cellular service constraints. In [3], an resource allocation algorithm based on interference-aware was proposed for the local cellular and D2D users. In [4], Kaufman et al. presented a distributed dynamic spectrum protocol in which D2D users in an ad-hoc network randomly access and use spectrum. A new interference management mechanism was proposed to improve the reliability of D2D communication in [5]. The authors of this paper derived the probability of outages in the intensive mode and designed a mode selection algorithm to minimize the outage probability. [6] proposed the two-stage semi-distributed resource management scheme for D2D Communication in Cellular networks. In the first stage, the base station allocates resource blocks between the cellular links and D2D links in a centralized method. In the second stage, the master user in the D2D link performs an algorithm which adaptively adjust resource blocks in a distributed method. In addition, lots of different resource allocation algorithms were proposed for D2D communication in cellular networks [7–10].

To explore the effecting of D2D and relay on the LTE-A cellular networks, this paper combines these two technologies to form a heterogeneous network. In each cell of this network, there exist different communication modes, which are D2D-direct, D2D-non-direct and cellular mode. Subsequently, a system model for this heterogeneous network is built, and it is proved that the objective function and the constraints in this model satisfy the convex optimization condition. To solve this optimization problem, we propose a power allocation algorithm based on Lagrange Multiplier. Finally, we evaluate the throughput and fairness of the algorithm by theoretical analysis and simulation results.

2 System Model

We consider the uplink of the LTE-A cellular networks. As shown in the Fig. 1, each cell of the cellular system consists of one base station (BS), several relays and plenty of cellular users. Each user in coverage area of a relay can select one from two communication modes, which are D2D direct and cellular mode. The latter includes two transmission stages, one is from user to relay and the other is from relay to BS. The D2D pair and CUE in Fig. 1 stand for the D2D direct mode and cellular mode, respectively. The cellular network adopts time division duplex (TDD) mode, and the entire transmission process is divided into two time slots. The first and the second slot are occupied by the transmission from user to relay and from relay to BS, respectively. All relays transmit signals synchronously in these two time slots. The transmission process of each time slot is only interfered by other transmission processes in the same time slot. Each D2D pair shares the time and frequency resources of with CUE users.

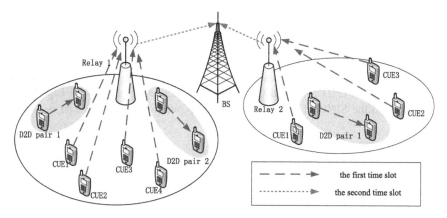

Fig. 1. System model for coexistence of D2D direct communication users and cellular users

All CUE users are represented by sets M, and the user of D2D pairs are represented by sets D^p. The whole system bandwidth is divided into N resource blocks (RBs), which can be used in each relay. B_{RB} is used to represent the bandwidth of each resource block. The relay set is represented by $L = \{1, 2, \cdots |L|\}$, and $U_l, \forall l \in L$ denote the user set in which each user is in the coverage area of relay l. The set of CUE users covered by relay l is denoted as $M_l = M \cap U_l$. The set of D2D direction users covered by relay l is denoted as $D_l^p = D^p \cap U_l$. According to the above definitions, the following relations are established: $U_l \subseteq \{D_l^p \cup M_l\}, \forall l \in L$, $\cup_l U_l = \{D^p \cup M\}$, $\cap_l U_l = \varphi, \forall l \in L$. Next, we describe the transmission procedures in each time slot in detail.

(a) Transmission in D2D pairs. The two users of each D2D pair covered by the relay l can directly communicate with each other. The SINR of the unit power signal in this process is shown in the Eq. (1). There doesn't exist interference among D2D pairs, among CUE users, and between D2D pairs and CUE users in the coverage area of a relay, because the resource blocks allocated to each transmitter in a relay are orthogonal. So, the interference only results from the D2D pairs and the CUE users of other relays. That is, for $u_l \in D_l^p$, we can obtain

$$\gamma_{u_l, u_l, 1}^{(n)} = \frac{h_{u_l, u_l}^{(n)}}{\sum\limits_{\substack{u_j \in D_j^p \\ j \neq l, j \in L}} Q_{u_j, u_j}^{(n)} \cdot g_{u_j, u_l}^{(n)} + \sum\limits_{\substack{u_j \in M_j \\ j \neq l, j \in L}} Q_{u_j, j}^{(n)} \cdot g_{u_j, u_l}^{(n)} + \sigma^2} \tag{1}$$

Where, $Q_{a,b}^{(n)}$, $h_{a,b}^{(n)}$, and $g_{a,b}^{(n)}$ respectively represent the transmitted power, the channel coefficient and interfering link channel coefficient from the transmitter a to the receiver b on the resource block n (RBn). The noise power of the receiver is $\sigma^2 = N_0 B_{RB}$, B_{RB} is the bandwidth each resource block, and N_0 is the power spectral density of noise. Therefore, the information rate of this communication process can be written as

$$R_{u_l,u_l}^{(n)} = B_{\text{RB}} \log_2\left(1 + Q_{u_l,u_l}^{(n)} \gamma_{u_l,u_l,1}^{(n)}\right) \tag{2}$$

(b) The transmission between the CUE user and the relay. This communication process is completed in the first time slot. This process is subject to interference resulting from D2D pairs and CUE users of other relays. Similar to Eq. (1), we can obtain the SINR of the unit transmitted power for each CUE user $u_l \in M_l$.

$$\gamma_{u_l,l,1}^{(n)} = \frac{h_{u_l,l}^{(n)}}{\displaystyle\sum_{\substack{u_j \in D_j^p \\ j \neq l, j \in L}} Q_{u_j,u_j}^{(n)} \cdot g_{u_j,l}^{(n)} + \sum_{\substack{u_j \in M_j \\ j \neq l, j \in L}} Q_{u_j,j}^{(n)} \cdot g_{u_j,l}^{(n)} + \sigma^2} \tag{3}$$

Where, the definition of each term in Eq. (3) is the same as that in Eq. (1). Accordingly, the information rate of this communication process can be written as:

$$R_{u_l,l}^{(n)} = B_{\text{RB}} \log_2\left(1 + Q_{u_l,l}^{(n)} \gamma_{u_l,l,1}^{(n)}\right) \tag{4}$$

(c) The transmission between relay l and base station. This communication process occupies the second time slot. During the first time slot, relay l has received the signals transmitted by the transmitter of CUE users lying in the its coverage area. During the second time slot, the relay l retransmits these signals to the base station on the resource block n. After the second time slot, base station forwards information coming from a relay to other relays of this cell or to other base stations. Assuming that during any time interval of the second time slot in a cell, only one relay transmits signals to base station. So, this communication link between relay and base station will not be interfered by other relays in this cell. Therefore, for $u_l \in M_l$, we can write the SINR per unit power as

$$\gamma_{l,eNB,2}^{(n)} = \frac{h_{l,eNB}^{(n)}}{\sigma^2} \tag{5}$$

Where, $h_{l,eNB}^{(n)}$ stands for the channel coefficient between relay l and base station on resource block n . σ^2 stands for the noise power of receiver of base station. For simplicity, we assume the noise power of relay, receiver of D2D pair and base station on any resource block are the same. Therefore, for $u_l \in M_l$, the information rate of this trasmission process can be written as:

$$R_{l,eNB}^{(n)} = B_{\text{RB}} \log_2\left(1 + Q_{l,eNB}^{(n)} \gamma_{l,eNB,2}^{(n)}\right) \tag{6}$$

In summary, for the user u_l covered by the relay l, the total information rate can be one of the following two rates, which depends on whether the transmitter and receiver of u_l are covered by the same relay.

D2D direct communication mode. In this mode, the transmitter and receiver of u_l lie in the coverage area of the same relay. The transmitter of u_l transmits signals to its receiver by D2D direct mode, and the information rate is:

$$R_D^{(n)} = R_{u_l,u_l}^{(n)} \tag{7}$$

Cellular mode. In this mode, the transmitter and receiver of u_l does not lie in the coverage area of the same relay. So CUE user u_l must spend two time slots on transmission of the uplink. The first and the second time slot are occupied by the transmission from the transmitter of u_l to relay l and the transmission from relay l to base station, respectively. So the information rate of u_l in the uplink is:

$$R_M^{(n)} = \frac{1}{2} \min\left(R_{u_l,l}^{(n)}, R_{l,eNB}^{(n)} \right) \tag{8}$$

3 Analysis of System Performance

Assuming that the transmitted power of transmitter of each D2D pair and each CUE user satisfy some constraints to guarantee their interference to the cellular network is less than some interference threshold. This section discusses how to maximize the throughput of a cell by allocating resource blocks and power on each resource blocks for D2D pairs and CUE users.

The system throughput is maximized by the allocation of resource blocks (RB) and the power. For CUE users of cellular mode, the final communication rate in the uplink is determined by the smaller of the two information rates. Denoting the maximal transmitted power of user u_l as $Q_{u_l}^{\max}$, and denoting the maximal transmitted power of the relay l as $Q_l^{\max}$. We introduce the resource block allocation factor $x_{u_l}^{(n)}$ to illustrate that each RB can only be used by one user under the coverage area of each relay. $x_{u_l}^{(n)} \in \{0,1\}$ is a binary integer variable, $x_{u_l}^{(n)} = 1$ indicates that resource block RB n is assigned to user u_l, otherwise, $x_{u_l}^{(n)} = 0$, $\bar{x}_{u_l}^{(n)} = 1 - x_{u_l}^{(n)}$. For all users u_l under the coverage area of relay l, the total information rate is $R_{u_l} = \sum_{n=1}^{N} x_{u_l}^{(n)} R_D^{(n)} + \bar{x}_{u_l}^{(n)} R_M^{(n)}$. The user's QoS requirement is represented by R_{QoS}, considering that the same RB will be occupied by the relay in two time slots. Therefore, this optimization problem can be described as:

$$\max_{x_{u_l}^{(n)}, Q_{u_l,u_l}^{(n)}, Q_{u_l,l}^{(n)}, Q_{l,eNB}^{(n)}} \sum_{l \in L} \sum_{u_l \in U_l} \sum_{n=1}^{N} x_{u_l}^{(n)} R_D^{(n)} + \bar{x}_{u_l}^{(n)} R_M^{(n)} \tag{9}$$

$$\text{subject to} \quad 0 \le \sum_{u_l \in U_l} x_{u_l}^{(n)} \le 1, \quad \forall n \in N \tag{10a}$$

$$\sum_{n=1}^{N} x_{u_l}^{(n)} Q_{u_l,u_l}^{(n)} \leq Q_{u_l}^{\max}, \forall u_l \in D_l^p, \sum_{n=1}^{N} \bar{x}_{u_l}^{(n)} Q_{u_l,l}^{(n)} \leq Q_{u_l}^{\max}, \forall u_l \in M_l \qquad (10b)$$

$$\sum_{u_l \in M_l} \sum_{n=1}^{N} \bar{x}_{u_l}^{(n)} Q_{l,eNB}^{(n)} \leq Q_l^{\max} \qquad (10c)$$

$$\sum_{u_l \in D_l^p} x_{u_l}^{(n)} Q_{u_l,u_l}^{(n)} g_{u_l,u_{l^*},1}^{(n)} \leq I_{th}^{(n)}, \quad \sum_{u_l \in M_l} \bar{x}_{u_l}^{(n)} Q_{u_l,l}^{(n)} g_{u_l,l^*,1}^{(n)} \leq I_{th}^{(n)},$$

$$\forall n \in N, \forall l \in L, l \neq l^*, \forall l^* \in L \qquad (10d)$$

$$R_{u_l} \geq R_{QoS}, \quad \forall u_l \in U_l \qquad (10e)$$

$$Q_{u_l,u_l}^{(n)} \geq 0, Q_{u_l,l}^{(n)} \geq 0, Q_{l,eNB}^{(n)} \geq 0, \forall n \in N, u_l \in U_l \qquad (10f)$$

The constraint (10a) is the condition that each allocation factor must satisfy. That is, Each RB can only be assigned to one user under each relay. (10b) and (10c) mean that transmitted power of transmitter of user and relay cannot exceed their respective maximum power limit. (10d) indicates that interference resulting from D2D users and CUE users cannot exceed the interference threshold of cellular system. (10e) means that the throughput of system must satisfy the QoS requirement. (10f) indicates that each transmitted power is non-negative.

The unit power SINR of the D2D pair in problem (9) can be written as

$$\gamma_{u_l,u_l,1}^{(n)} = \frac{h_{u_l,u_l}^{(n)}}{I_{u_l,u_l,1}^{(n)} + \sigma^2} \qquad (11)$$

Where, $I_{u_l,u_l,1}^{(n)}$ is the interference term D2D directed pair user u_l receives on resource block n.

$$I_{u_l,u_l,1}^{(n)} = \sum_{\substack{u_j \in D_j^p \\ j \neq l, j \in L}} x_{u_j}^{(n)} Q_{u_j,u_j}^{(n)} \cdot g_{u_j,u_l}^{(n)} + \sum_{\substack{u_l \in M_l \\ j \neq l, j \in L}} \bar{x}_{u_j}^{(n)} Q_{u_j,j}^{(n)} \cdot g_{u_j,u_l}^{(n)} \qquad (12)$$

For CUE users, the unit power SINR during the first time in problem (9) can be written as

$$\gamma_{u_l,l,1}^{(n)} = \frac{h_{u_l,l}^{(n)}}{I_{u_l,l,1}^{(n)} + \sigma^2} \qquad (13)$$

Where, $I_{u_l,l,1}^{(n)}$ is the interference term that the cellular user u_l receives on the resource block n in the first time slot.

$$I_{u_l,l,1}^{(n)} = \sum_{\substack{u_j \in D_j^p \\ j \neq l, j \in L}} x_{u_j}^{(n)} Q_{u_j,u_j}^{(n)} \cdot g_{u_j,l}^{(n)} + \sum_{\substack{u_l \in M_l \\ j \neq l, j \in L}} \bar{x}_{u_j}^{(n)} Q_{u_j,j}^{(n)} \cdot g_{u_j,l}^{(n)} \tag{14}$$

The total information rate $R_{\mathrm{M}}^{(n)}$ for all CUE users on resource block n:

$$
\begin{aligned}
R_{\mathrm{M}}^{(n)} &= \frac{1}{2} \min \left\{ R_{u_l,L}^{(n)}, R_{l,eNB}^{(n)} \right\} \\
&= \frac{1}{2} \min \left\{ B_{\mathrm{RB}} \log_2 \left(1 + Q_{u_l,l}^{(n)} \gamma_{u_l,l,1}^{(n)} \right), B_{\mathrm{RB}} \log_2 \left(1 + Q_{l,eNB}^{(n)} \gamma_{l,eNB,2}^{(n)} \right) \right\}
\end{aligned}
\tag{15}
$$

When $Q_{u_l,l}^{(n)} \gamma_{u_l,l,1}^{(n)} = Q_{l,eNB}^{(n)} \gamma_{l,eNB,2}^{(n)}$, $R_{\mathrm{M}}^{(n)}$ can reach its maximal value, and then $Q_{l,eNB}^{(n)}$ in the second time slot can be represented by the power in the first one, that is, $Q_{l,eNB}^{(n)} = \frac{\gamma_{u_l,l,1}^{(n)}}{\gamma_{l,eNB,2}^{(n)}} Q_{u_l,l}^{(n)}$. Therefore, the total CUE information rate $R_{\mathrm{M}}^{(n)}$ on resource block n can be rewritten as:

$$R_{\mathrm{M}}^{(n)} = \frac{1}{2} B_{\mathrm{RB}} \log_2 \left(1 + Q_{u_l,l}^{(n)} \gamma_{u_l,l,1}^{(n)} \right), \quad u_l \in M_l \tag{16}$$

In order to simplify the problem, the resource block allocation factor $x_{u_l}^{(n)}$ is first relaxed to a continuous variable, or $x_{u_l}^{(n)} \in [0, 1]$. $x_{u_l}^{(n)}$ represents the proportion of time that the resource block n is allocated to the user u_l, which still meets the constraint (10a). In addition, two new variables $S_{u_l,u_l}^{(n)} = x_{u_l}^{(n)} Q_{u_l,u_l}^{(n)}$, $T_{u_l,l}^{(n)} = \bar{x}_{u_l}^{(n)} Q_{u_l,l}^{(n)}$ are introduced as power allocation variables for the D2D user and the CUE user, respectively. These two terms represent the actual transmitted power of the user u_l on the resource block n. After condition relaxation and variable adjustment, the primitive optimization problem(9) can be reformulated into

$$\max_{x_{u_l}^{(n)}, S_{u_l,u_l}^{(n)}, T_{u_l,l}^{(n)}} \sum_{l \in L} \sum_{u_l \in U_l} \sum_{n=1}^{N} \left[x_{u_l}^{(n)} B_{\mathrm{RB}} \log_2 \left(1 + \frac{S_{u_l,u_l}^{(n)} h_{u_l,u_l}^{(n)}}{x_{u_l}^{(n)} \omega_{u_l}^{(n)}} \right) + \bar{x}_{u_l}^{(n)} \frac{1}{2} B_{\mathrm{RB}} \log_2 \left(1 + \frac{T_{u_l,l}^{(n)} h_{u_l,l}^{(n)}}{\bar{x}_{u_l}^{(n)} \mu_{u_l}^{(n)}} \right) \right] \tag{17}$$

$$\text{subject to} \quad 0 < \sum_{u_l \in U_l} x_{u_l}^{(n)} \leq 1 \quad, \forall n \in N \tag{18a}$$

$$\sum_{n=1}^{N} S_{u_l,u_l}^{(n)} \leq Q_{u_l}^{\max}, \forall u_l \in D_l^p, \sum_{n=1}^{N} T_{u_l,l}^{(n)} \leq Q_{u_l}^{\max}, \forall u_l \in M_l \tag{18b}$$

$$\sum_{u_l \in M_l} \sum_{n=1}^{N} \frac{\gamma_{u_l,l,1}^{(n)}}{\gamma_{l,eNB,2}^{(n)}} T_{u_l,l}^{(n)} \leq Q_l^{\max} \tag{18c}$$

$$\sum_{u_l \in D_l^p} S_{u_l,u_l}^{(n)} g_{u_l,u_l^*,1}^{(n)} \leq I_{th}^{(n)}, \sum_{u_l \in M_l} T_{u_l,l}^{(n)} g_{u_l,l^*,1}^{(n)} \leq I_{th}^{(n)}, \forall n \in N \tag{18d}$$

$$\sum_{n=1}^{N} \left[x_{u_l}^{(n)} B_{\text{RB}} \log_2 \left(1 + \frac{S_{u_l,u_l}^{(n)} h_{u_l,u_l}^{(n)}}{x_{u_l}^{(n)} \omega_{u_l}^{(n)}} \right) \right.$$
$$\left. + \bar{x}_{u_l}^{(n)} \frac{1}{2} B_{\text{RB}} \log_2 \left(1 + \frac{T_{u_l,u_l}^{(n)} h_{u_l,u_l}^{(n)}}{\bar{x}_{u_l}^{(n)} \mu_{u_l}^{(n)}} \right) \right] \geq R_{\text{QoS}}, \forall u_l \in U_l \tag{18e}$$

$$S_{u_l,u_l}^{(n)} \geq 0, u_l \in D_l^p, T_{u_l,l}^{(n)} \geq 0, u_l \in M_l, \forall n \in N \tag{18f}$$

$$I_{u_l,u_l,1}^{(n)} + \sigma^2 \leq \omega_{u_l}^{(n)}, u_l \in D_l^p, I_{u_l,l,1}^{(n)} + \sigma^2 \leq \mu_{u_l}^{(n)}, u_l \in M_l, \forall n \in N \tag{18g}$$

4   Power Allocation Algorithm Based on Lagrange Multiplier

By calculating, we find that the Hessian matrix of object function in (17) is negative semi-definite and the constraints in (17) are the level set of some convex functions. So (17) is a concave optimization problem. Therefore, we can use the KKT conditions in convex optimization theory to solve it. Assuming that the Lagrange multipliers of the constraints are $\delta_n, \xi_{u_l}, \varsigma_{u_l}, \upsilon_l, \psi_n, \varepsilon_n, \lambda_{u_l}, \rho_{u_l}^{(n)}, \kappa_{u_l}^{(n)}$, and the Lagrangian function can be written as

$$L = -\sum_{l \in L} \sum_{u_l \in U_l} \sum_{n=1}^{N} \left[x_{u_l}^{(n)} B_{\text{RB}} \log_2 \left(1 + \frac{S_{u_l,u_l}^{(n)} h_{u_l,u_l}^{(n)}}{x_{u_l}^{(n)} \omega_{u_l}^{(n)}} \right) + \bar{x}_{u_l}^{(n)} \frac{1}{2} B_{\text{RB}} \log_2 \left(1 + \frac{T_{u_l,l}^{(n)} h_{u_l,l}^{(n)}}{\left(1 - x_{u_l}^{(n)}\right) \mu_{u_l}^{(n)}} \right) \right]$$
$$+ \sum_{n=1}^{N} \delta_n \left(\sum_{u_l \in U_l} x_{u_l}^{(n)} - 1 \right) + \sum_{u_l \in D_l^p} \xi_{u_l} \left(\sum_{n=1}^{N} S_{u_l,u_l}^{(n)} - Q_{u_l}^{\max} \right)$$
$$+ \sum_{u_l \in M_l} \varsigma_{u_l} \left(\sum_{n=1}^{N} T_{u_l,l}^{(n)} - Q_{u_l}^{\max} \right) + \upsilon_l \left(\sum_{u_l \in M_l} \sum_{n=1}^{N} \frac{\gamma_{u_l,l,1}^{(n)}}{\gamma_{l,eNB,2}^{(n)}} T_{u_l,l}^{(n)} - Q_l^{\max} \right)$$
$$+ \sum_{n=1}^{N} \psi_n \left(\sum_{u_l \in D_l^p} S_{u_l,u_l}^{(n)} g_{u_l,u_l^*,1}^{(n)} - I_{th}^{(n)} \right) + \sum_{n=1}^{N} \varepsilon_n \left(\sum_{u_l \in M_l} T_{u_l,l}^{(n)} g_{u_l,l^*,1}^{(n)} - I_{th}^{(n)} \right)$$
$$+ \sum_{u_l \in U_l} \lambda_{u_l} \left[R_{QoS} - \sum_{n=1}^{N} \left(x_{u_l}^{(n)} B_{\text{RB}} \log_2 \left(1 + \frac{S_{u_l,u_l}^{(n)} h_{u_l,u_l}^{(n)}}{x_{u_l}^{(n)} \omega_{u_l}^{(n)}} \right) \right. \right.$$
$$\left. \left. + \bar{x}_{u_l}^{(n)} \frac{1}{2} B_{\text{RB}} \log_2 \left(1 + \frac{T_{u_l,l}^{(n)} h_{u_l,l}^{(n)}}{\bar{x}_{u_l}^{(n)} \mu_{u_l}^{(n)}} \right) \right) \right]$$
$$+ \sum_{u_l \in D_l^p} \sum_{n=1}^{N} \rho_{u_l}^{(n)} \left(I_{u,u_l,1}^{(n)} + \sigma^2 - \omega_{u_l}^{(n)} \right) + \sum_{u_l \in M_l} \sum_{n=1}^{N} \kappa_{u_l}^{(n)} \left(I_{u_l,l}^{(n)} + \sigma^2 - \mu_{u_l}^{(n)} \right)$$
$$\tag{19}$$

According to KKT conditions, let $\frac{\partial L}{\partial S_{u_l,u_l}^{(n)}} = 0$ and $\Delta_{u_l,u_l}^{(n)} = \frac{(\lambda_{u_l}+1)B_{RB}}{\ln 2\left(\xi_{u_l}+\psi_n g_{u_l,u_l^*,1}^{(n)}\right)}$, so the optimal value of transmitted power of D2D pair can be expressed as:

$$Q_{u_l,u_l}^{(n)^*} = \frac{S_{u_l,u_l}^{(n)^*}}{x_{u_l}^{(n)^*}} = \left[\Delta_{u_l,u_l}^{(n)} - \frac{\omega_{u_l}^{(n)}}{h_{u_l,u_l}^{(n)}}\right]^+ \tag{20}$$

Where, $[\xi]^+$ means that $[\xi]^+ = \max(0,\xi)$. Similarly, according to the KKT conditions in the convex optimization theory, let $\frac{\partial L}{\partial T_{u_l,l}^{(n)}} = 0$, we can obtain

$$T_{u_l,l}^{(n)} = \frac{(\lambda_{u_l}+1)\bar{x}_{u_l}^{(n)}B_{RB}}{2\ln 2\left(\varsigma_{u_l}+\upsilon_l\frac{\gamma_{u_l,l,1}^{(n)}}{\gamma_{l,eNB,2}^{(n)}}+\varepsilon_n g_{u_l,l^*,l}^{(n)}\right)} - \frac{\bar{x}_{u_l}^{(n)}\mu_{ul}^{(n)}}{h_{u_l,l}^{(n)}} \tag{21}$$

The optimal transmitted power of the CUE user can be written as

$$Q_{u_l,l}^{(n)^*} = \frac{T_{u_l,l}^{(n)^*}}{\bar{x}_{u_l}^{(n)^*}} = \left[\Delta_{u_l,l}^{(n)} - \frac{\mu_{ul}^{(n)}}{\mu_{u_l,l}^{(n)}}\right] \tag{22}$$

$$\Delta_{u_l,l}^{(n)} = \frac{(\lambda_{u_l}+1)B_{RB}}{2\ln 2\left(\varsigma_{u_l}+\upsilon_l\frac{\gamma_{u_l,l,1}^{(n)}}{\gamma_{l,eNB,2}^{(n)}}+\varepsilon_n g_{u_l,l^*,l}^{(n)}\right)} \tag{23}$$

According to the above formulas, we propose a power allocation algorithm shown in Table 1.

Table 1. A power allocation algorithm based on Lagrange multipliers

A power allocation algorithm based on Lagrange multipliers
Initializing every Lagrange multiplier in (19) and select a positive scalar ε, which is small enough.
Do: Calculating the transmitted power of D2D pairs and CUE users by formula (20) and (22), respectively;   Calculating the objective function in (17) and obtaining a value T_1; **Do:** Updating every Lagrange multiplier by sub-gradient method; **Until** every Lagrange multiplier converges to some value Calculating the transmitted power of D2D pairs and CUE users by formula (20) and (22), respectively; Calculating the objective function in (17) and obtaining a value T_2;
Until $|T_1 - T_2| \leq \varepsilon$ Output the $Q_{u_l,u_l}^{(n)^*}$ and $Q_{u_l,l}^{(n)^*}, \forall l \in L, \forall n \in N$;

5 Simulation

In order to verify the above theoretical analysis, some simulations are implemented. For simplicity, assuming that the total system bandwidth and the total number of resource blocks are fixed, and there are two relays in a cell. Furtherly, assuming that the number of users covered by each relay is the same, and the number of D2D user pairs and the number of CUE users covered by each relay are the same. The Raj Jain fairness index is used to determine the fairness of the information rate on each resource block.

Defining the fairness index as $F = \left(\sum_{n=1}^{N} R_n \right)^2 / N \sum_{n=1}^{N} R_n^2$, N is the total number of resource blocks in the system, and R_n is the information rate on resource block n. The simulation parameters are shown in Table 2.

Table 2. Simulation parameters and values

Parameter	Value
System bandwidth	2.5 MHz
Total number of resource blocks	13
Path loss of D2D link	102.9 + 18.7log[d(km)]
Path loss of CUE users to relay link	103.8 + 20.9log[d(km)]
Path loss of relay to base station link	100.7 + 23.5log[d(km)]
Shadow fade standard deviation of D2D link	3 dB
Shadow fad standard deviation of CUE users to relay link	10 dB
Shadow fade standard deviation of relay to base station link	6 dB
Transmitted power of relay	20–30 dBm
Transmitted power of user	13–23 dBm
Maximum distance between D2D links	20 m
Relay coverage radius	200 m
Distance between base station and relay	125 m
Noise power spectral density	−174 dBm/Hz
Interference threshold	−70 dBm

In the first simulation, there are two relays, and each relay covers four D2D pairs and four CUE users. Simulation results is shown in Fig. 2. Observing Fig. 2(a), we can find that with the number of iterations gradually increasing, the fairness index of resource block become better and gradually approaches 1. After 50 iterations, the information rate of each resource block is shown in Fig. 2(b). Observing Fig. 2(b), we find that the information rate on each resource block is approximately 4 Mbit/s.

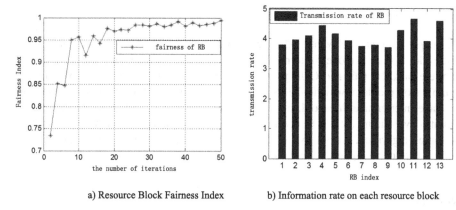

a) Resource Block Fairness Index   b) Information rate on each resource block

Fig. 2. The fairness of the system

In the second simulation, we explore the effect of the number of D2D pairs and CUE users in each relay coverage on the total throughput of the system. The number of iterations is 50 and the total number of resource blocks is 13. The simulation result is shown in Fig. 3. Observing this figure, we find that with the increasing in the number of D2D pairs and the number of CUE users under each relay, the total throughput of the system first increase linearly, and eventually reach a stable state. Especially, when the number of D2D pairs and the number of CUE users are greater than 7, the information rate is about 85 Mbit/s.

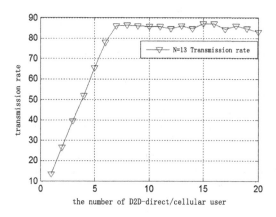

Fig. 3. The total throughput of the system

6 Conclusion

This paper integrates relay and D2D technologies into a LTE-A single cellular system, and builds a system model in terms of information rate by analyzing the influence of interfere on D2D pair and CUE users. Next, we formulate the model into a convex optimization problem, which take the total information rate of a cell as object function and take interference threshold, maximal transmitted power, and QoS of link as constraints. By utilizing the KKT conditions and Lagrange multiplier, we propose a power allocation algorithm. At last, we verify the performance of this algorithm in terms of fairness and throughput by simulation.

References

1. Jiajia, L., Kato, N., Jianfeng, M., Kadowaki, N.: Device-to-device communication in LTE-advanced networks: a survey. IEEE Commun. Surv. Tutor. **17**(4), 1923–1940 (2015)
2. Yu, C.H., Doppler, K., Ribeiro, C.B.: Resource sharing optimization for device-to-device communication underlaying cellular networks. IEEE Trans. Wirel. Commun. **10**(8), 2752–2763 (2011)
3. Janis, P., Koivunen, V., Ribeiro, C.: Interference-aware resource allocation for device-to-device radio underlaying cellular networks. In: IEEE Vehicular Technology Conference, Anchorage, USA, pp. 1–5 (2009)
4. Kaufman, B., Lilleberg, J., Aazhang, B.: Spectrum sharing scheme between cellular users and ad-hoc device-to-device users. IEEE Trans. Wirel. Commun. **12**(3), 1038–1049 (2013)
5. Min, H., Seo, W., Lee, J.: Reliability improvement using receive mode selection in the device-to-device uplink period underlaying cellular networks. IEEE Trans. Wirel. Commun. **10**(2), 413–418 (2011)
6. Dong, H.L., Choi, K.W.: Two-stage semi-distributed resource management for D2D communication in cellular networks. IEEE Trans. Wirel. Commun. **13**(4), 1908–1920 (2014)
7. Chen, B., Zheng, J., Zhang, Y.: A time division scheduling resource allocation for D2D communication in cellular networks. In: Proceedings of IEEE ICC 2015, London, UK, 8–12 (2015)
8. Xuejia, C., Jun, Z., Yuan, Z: .A graph coloring based resource allocation algorithm for D2D communication in cellular networks. In: IEEE ICC 2015, London, UK, pp. 8–12 (2015)
9. Biwei, C., Jun, Z., Yuan, Z., Hidekazu, M.: SARA: a service-aware resource allocation scheme for device-to-device communication underlaying cellular networks. In: IEEE Globecom 2014, USA, pp. 4916–4921 (2014)
10. Xuejia, C., Jun, Z., Yuan, Z., Hidekazu, M.: A capacity oriented resource allocation algorithm for device-to-device communication in mobile cellular Networks. In: IEEE ICC 2014, Sydney, Australia, pp. 10–14 (2014)

A Joint Power Control and Cooperative Transmission Scheme in Random Networks

Dan Zhang[1(✉)], Xin Su[2], Lu Ge[2], Jie Zeng[2], Bei Liu[2], and Xiangyun Zheng[2]

[1] Chongqing University of Posts and Telecommunications, Chongqing, China
zhdan@tsinghua.edu.cn
[2] Beijing National Research Center for Information Science and Technology,
Tsinghua University, Beijing, China
l_ge@tsinghua.edu.cn

Abstract. In this paper, we consider the average spectrum efficiency of edge users under the random network model. In this model, the base stations (BSs) and the users exhibit Poisson distribution. By dividing the center and cell edge users, we use the multiple BSs that are closer to the edge users to cooperative with each other to transfer the users information to improve the average spectrum efficiency of the downlink edge users. We also adopt a distance-dependent power control scheme to further reduce inter-cell interference. Using the above method comprehensively, we derive the analytical expression of the spectral efficiency of the edge user. The performance of this scheme is evaluated through simulation results. Simulation results show that the spectrum efficiency is significantly improved compared to traditional user-centric transmission and non-power control cooperative schemes.

Keywords: Random geometry · Cooperative transmission
Power control · Cell edge users · Downlink spectral efficiency

1 Introduction

In order to achieve indiscriminate coverage of 5G mobile communication systems, advanced techniques for wireless access network architecture have been extensively studied [1,2], the collaborative access network technology can better utilize various network resources to meet the user's business needs. With the increase in the number of base stations (BSs) and the number of users, inter-cell interference is an important obstacle to achieving higher spectral efficiency. Nevertheless, cooperative transmission technology applied to the cellular network is considered as a solution for effectively improving system performance, especially for cell-edge users.

Supported by the National S&T Major Project (No. 2016ZX03001017), Science and Technology Program of Beijing (No. D171100006317002) and the Ministry of Education and China Mobile Joint Scientific Research Fund (Grant No. MCM20160105).

J. Zheng et al. (Eds.): ADHOCNETS 2018, LNICST 258, pp. 71–80, 2019.
https://doi.org/10.1007/978-3-030-05888-3_7

Cooperative transmission technology plays an important role in improving system throughput and cell edge performance. However, the issue of BS cooperation in cellular networks has been extensively investigated in the past. In [3], a cell aggregation algorithm that forms a cluster adaptively based on the user's distribution and SINR is proposed, but backhaul capacity is large. [4] further proposes a noveal scheme that only shares the worst user channel state information (CSI) among BSs. It solves the problem of the backhaul link overhead and improves the throughput of the edge users. In [5], it provides a rate-adaptive modulation scheme based on cooperative transmission and power allocation based on the transmission of only the CSI, which increases the flexibility of cooperative transmission and improves the average spectrum efficiency.

With the continuous development of networks, the random deployment of BSs have introduced in cellular network, called random cellular networks [6]. Random geometry as a novel and useful technology can effectively deal with the random structures, and it can better capture the increasingly opportunistic and intensive deployment of BS. So far, methods for analyzing network performance based on stochastic geometric models have been studied from several aspects. Most work considers modeling the BS's location using the homogenous Poisson point process (PPP). Considering the cooperative transmission to improve network performance by using the random network model, [7] joint cooperation and precoding techniques eliminate inter-cell interference and further increase the coverage probability. [8] further proposed a novel downlink coordination scheme was proposed for CoMP single-user multi-input multi-output. In addition, [9] consider changes in the user's distribution density and deduces the ergodic capacity in the cooperative cluster. In [10], a method is further proposed to divide the edge users into the center users for random networks, and the effect of user density is analyzed with two resource allocation techniques on the coverage probability. In [11], the edge users are divided based on the distance ratio of the [10], and inter-cluster conflict is solved by edge coloring method to achieve similar edge throughput as the dynamic clustering method when the users are dense enough.

In this paper, we mainly study the average spectrum efficiency of downlink edge users in a PVT random cellular network. We utilize the characteristics of random networks to provide a new expression for the average spectral efficiency of edge users, which reduces the complexity of computation and simulation. In addition, we apply the cooperative transmission technology and power control scheme to further eliminate inter-cell interference and improve the average spectrum efficiency of the edge users. Finally, the average spectrum efficiency of edge users is evaluated by Matlab and compared with other existing solutions.

The rest of this paper is organized as follows. Section 2 describes the system model of the downlink cellular network and constructs the average spectral efficiency expression for the general user. The Sect. 3 analyzes the average spectral efficiency for a randomly selected edge user and gives a distinctive spectral efficiency expression. In the Sect. 4, numerical evaluation of the spectrum efficiency of the edge users is performed. Finally, the V part summarizes the paper and discusses future work.

Some notations are explained in the paper. $\Phi(.)$ indicates a set, $E(.)$ represents the expectation operator, λ denotes the distribution density, which is the number of points per square. $L(.)$ represents the Laplace transform of the function, $f(.)$ is the probability density function.

2 System Model

We consider a PVT random cellular network. The network space is divided in a Voronoi diagram. It is assumed that the BSs and the users are randomly scattered in each cell with the independent Poisson distribution. The BS set and the user set in the system are respectively represented by Φ_b and Φ_u, the corresponding distribution densities are λ_b and λ_b.

For simplify the analysis, we assume that a randomly selected user is located at the origin, and there are n cooperative BSs providing services for the user, and the cooperative BSs are sorted in order of distance. Let the distance between the user and the i-th cooperative BS be d_i, and the distance between the user and the j-th interfering BS be D_j, as shown in Fig. 1. Assuming that intra-cell users use orthogonal multiple access to eliminate inter-user interference in the cell. The channel is modeled as Rayleigh fading and follows an exponential distribution with the parameter μ^{-1}. The frequency reuse factor of the system is 1 to improve spectrum efficiency, and the transmission power of each BS is independently limited. For power control, we apply the BS's transmit power as a function of distance. e.g.$P_i = pd_i^{\rho\alpha}$, where $P_i = pd_i^{\rho\alpha}$ is a power control factor. Subsequently, we derive the average spectral efficiency expression from the general user in the network.

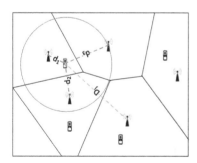

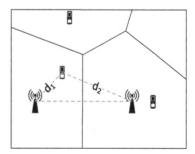

Fig. 1. Cooperative base station distribution based on Poisson point process (n = 3).

Fig. 2. An example of an edge user definition.

First of all, from the above conditions, the SINR of the general user is as follows

$$SINR = \frac{P_d}{I_d + \sigma^2} = \frac{\sum\limits_{i \in B_o} ph_i d_i^{\rho\alpha} d_i^{-\alpha}}{\sum\limits_{j \in \Phi_b \backslash B_o} ph_j d_j^{\rho\alpha} D_j^{-\alpha} + N} = \frac{\sum\limits_{i \in B_o} h_i d_i^{\alpha(\rho-1)}}{\sum\limits_{j \in \Phi_b \backslash B_o} h_j d_j^{\rho\alpha} D_j^{-\alpha} + \sigma^2/p},$$
(1)

where $h \sim E(\mu^{-1})$ follows the exponential distribution. P_d is the total received power of the expected signal. I_d is the received power of the interfering signal, and N is Gaussian white noise with mean 0 and variance σ^2. B_o denotes a circular area with the user as the origin and the distance d_n between the user and the n-th cooperative BS as a radius. Assuming that the signal transmitted is a Gaussian signal, the average spectrum efficiency of the general user is derived from the SINR expression of (1)

$$C_d = E_{\Phi_b, h}\left[In(1 + SINR)\right] = E_{\Phi_b, h}\left[In\left(1 + \frac{\sum\limits_{i=1}^{n} h_i d_i^{\alpha(\rho-1)}}{\sum\limits_{j \in \Phi_b \backslash Bo} h_j d_j^{\rho\alpha} D_j^{-\alpha} + \sigma^2/p}\right)\right].$$
(2)

Since it is a random network model, it cannot directly find the result, and it needs to be transformed by a Laplace transform to get a more exact expression. First, according to the definition of the Laplace transform, the Laplace transforms of the expected signal and interfering signals are

$$L_{P_d}(s) = E_{\Phi_b, h}\left(\prod_{i \in \Phi_b(s)} e^{-sh_i d_i^{\alpha(\rho-1)}}\right), L_{I_d}(s) = E_{\Phi_b, h}\left(\prod_{j \in \Phi_b(I)} e^{-sh_j d_j^{\rho\alpha} D_j^{-\alpha}}\right),$$
(3)

where $\Phi_b(S)$ is a set of cooperative BSs and $\Phi_b(I)$ is a set of interfering BSs. Referring to the method for solving spectral efficiency in [7], we can obtain from Eq. (2)

$$C_d = E_{\Phi_b, h}\left[In\left(1 + \frac{\sum\limits_{i=1}^{n} h_i d_i^{\alpha(\rho-1)}}{\sum\limits_{j \in \Phi_b \backslash Bo} h_j d_j^{\rho\alpha} D_j^{-\alpha} + \sigma^2/p}\right)\right]$$

$$\underset{=}{(a)} E_{\Phi_b, h}\left\{\int_0^{+\infty} \frac{e^{-z}}{z}\left[1 - \exp\left(\frac{-z \sum\limits_{i=1}^{n} h_i d_i^{\alpha(\rho-1)}}{\sum\limits_{j \in \Phi_b \backslash Bo} h_j d_j^{\rho\alpha} D_j^{-\alpha} + \sigma^2/p}\right)\right] dz\right\}$$

$$\underset{=}{(b)} E_{\Phi_b, h}\left\{\int_0^{+\infty} \frac{e^{-s\sigma^2/p}}{s} \exp\left(-s \sum\limits_{j \in \Phi_b \backslash Bo} h_j d_j^{\rho\alpha} D_j^{-\alpha}\right) \times \left[1 - \exp\left(\sum\limits_{i=1}^{n} h_i d_i^{\alpha(\rho-1)}\right)\right] ds\right\}$$

$$\underset{=}{(c)} \int_0^{+\infty} \frac{e^{-s\sigma^2/p}}{s} E_{\Phi_b, h}\left(\prod_{j \in \Phi_b(I)} e^{-sh_j d_j^{\rho\alpha} D_j^{-\alpha}}\right) \times \left[1 - E_{\Phi_b, h}\left(\prod_{i \in \Phi_b(s)} e^{-sh_i d_i^{\alpha(\rho-1)}}\right)\right] ds.$$

where (a) follows $In(1 + x) = \int_0^{+\infty} \frac{e^{-z}}{z}(1 - e^{-xz}) dz$, and (b) uses variable sub-

stitution $z = s\left(\sum\limits_{j \in \Phi_b \backslash Bo} h_j d_j^{\rho\alpha} D_j^{-\alpha} + \sigma^2/p\right)$. In (c), since the integrand is non-negative, the properties of Fubini theorem and the disjoint property of the cooperative BS set and the interfering BS set can be applied to make their integral positions interchangeable. Finally, replace the corresponding expressions with (3) to obtain the final integral expression (4) of the user's average spectral efficiency,

$$C_d\left(L_{P_d}(s), L_{I_d}(s)\right) = \int\limits_0^{+\infty} \frac{e^{-s\sigma^2/p}}{s} L_{I_d}(s)\left(1 - L_{P_d}(s)\right)ds. \tag{4}$$

From (4), we can observe that only the Laplace transform of the desired signal and the interference signal is required to obtain the spectral efficiency expression, and further consider the selection probability of edge users in the cell and the distance distribution function between the user and the BS. Thus, we can obtain the average spectral efficiency expression of the edge user. The following is divided into four parts to solve the average spectral efficiency of the edge users.

3   The Spectral Efficiency of Edge Users

3.1   Probability of Edge User Selection

Assume that only one user is scheduled in a given time slot. The edge user selection probability represents the probability that a randomly selected edge user is allocated a resource at a given time and served by a cooperating BS, as shown in Fig. 2. In order to get the probability, we first need to define the edge users.

Since the BSs are independently and randomly placed, the distance between the BSs is also random. Therefore, according to the Voronoi structure of the cell, the user's division method in [10] is cited. If $d_1/d_2 > R$, the user is called an edge user, otherwise it is called a central user, where R is the ratio of the distance between two closer points, $R \in (0, 1]$. The probability density function of the joint distribution of

$$f_{d_1,d_2}(d_1, d_2) = (2\pi\lambda_b)^2 d_1 d_2 \exp\left(-\pi\lambda_b d_2^2\right), \tag{5}$$

The selection probability of the edge user can be obtained from the above formula

$$\begin{aligned} P_u &= 1 - [d_1/d_2 \le R] \\ &= 1 - \int\limits_0^{+\infty}\int\limits_0^{d_2 R} f_{d_1,d_2}(d_1, d_2)dd_1 dd_2 \\ &= 1 - R^2 \end{aligned} \tag{6}$$

3.2   Distance Distribution Function

Assuming that a randomly selected user is served by n BSs, where the distance between the i-th cooperative BS and the selected user is d_i, no other BS can be closer to the user than d_i. Since the user needs n cooperative BSs to transmit data at the same time, at least n BSs are included in the circular area. The distribution function of the d_i can be obtained [6]

$$F_{d_i}(x_i) = 1 - p(d_i > x_i) = 1 - \sum_{t=0}^{i-1} e^{-\pi\lambda_b x_i{}^2} \frac{(\pi\lambda_b x_i{}^2)^t}{t!}$$

The the probability density function (PDF) can be derived by derivation

$$f_{d_i}(x_i) = \frac{dF_{d_i}(x_i)}{dx_i} = 2\pi\lambda_b x_i e^{-\pi\lambda_b x_i{}^2} \frac{(\pi\lambda_b x_i{}^2)^{i-1}}{(i-1)!}. \tag{7}$$

3.3 Laplace Transform of Expected Signals

Time division multiple access (TDMA) is used as a user access scheme in a multiple users in the cell and the users receive signals from each cooperating BS in a maximum ratio combining manner. we set the user receive the signal power of the i-th BS as P_i. $P_i \sim E(d_i{}^{\alpha(\rho-1)}\mu)$ can be obtained by $h_i \sim E(\mu)$. Then we can get the PDF and the Laplace transform expression of P_i

$$f_{P_i}(P_i) = d_i{}^{\alpha(\rho-1)}\mu e^{-d_i{}^{\alpha(\rho-1)1}\mu P_i}, \tag{8}$$

$$L_{P_i}(s) = E_{P_i}\left[e^{-sP_i}\right] = \int_0^{+\infty} e^{-sP_i} f_{P_i}(P_i)dP_i = \frac{d_i{}^{\alpha(\rho-1)}\mu}{s + d_i{}^{\alpha(\rho-1)}\mu}, \tag{9}$$

The total received power of the edge users is the sum of the transmission power of the cooperating BSs, and it can be transformed into the product form by the Laplace transform. Therefore, the Laplace transform of the expected signal portion can be obtained by combining Eq. (9) as follows

$$L_{P_d}(s) = L_{p_1}(s) \times L_{p_2}(s)... \times L_{p_n}(s) = \prod_{i=1}^{n} \frac{d_i{}^{\alpha(\rho-1)}\mu}{s + d_i{}^{\alpha(\rho-1)}\mu}. \tag{10}$$

3.4 Laplace Transform of Interference Part

Considering that there may not be a user in need of service in a cell in one time slot, the BS dose not cause interference to the selected user in this case, which is called an inactive BS. The probability of an inactive BS is that the BS dose not have any users in service in one slot and this probability can sparse the interference part λ_b.

In two-dimensional space, the normalized size distribution function of the approximating Voronoi cell is proposed, which is derived by the Monte Carlo method [12]

$$f_X(x) = \frac{343}{15}\sqrt{\frac{7}{2\pi}}x^{2.5}e^{-3.5x} \tag{11}$$

where X is a random variable representing the size of the Voronoi cell normalized by the $1/\lambda_b$. We assume that the number of users in the cell is M, the sparse base BS λ' can be obtained according to (12) and the probability of inactive BSs [9]

$$\lambda' = \lambda_b \left(1 - P\left(M = 0\right)\right) = \lambda_b \left[1 - \left(1 + 3.5^{-1}\frac{\lambda_u}{\lambda_b}\right)^{-3.5}\right], \tag{12}$$

It can be known from the SINR expression of the user that the interference signal power is the sum of the interference powers of the remaining BSs after removing the n cooperative BSs, e.i. the part outside the circular area. The Laplace transform of the interference part from $I_d = \sum\limits_{j \in \Phi \backslash B_0} h_j d_j^{\rho\alpha} D_j^{-\alpha}$

$$L_{I_d}(s) = E_{\Phi_b(I),h} \left[\exp\left(-s \sum_{j \in \Phi_b(I)} h_j d_j^{\rho\alpha} D_j^{-\alpha}\right)\right]$$

$$= E_{\Phi_b(I)} \left\{\prod_{j \in \Phi_b \backslash B_o} E_h \left[exp\left(-sh_j d_j^{\rho\alpha} D_j^{-\alpha}\right)\right]\right\}$$

$$\overset{(a)}{=} \exp\left(-2\pi\lambda' \int\limits_{d_n}^{+\infty} \left\{1 - \int\limits_0^{+\infty} E_h \left[exp\left(-shu^{\rho\alpha}v^{-\alpha}\right)\right]2\pi\lambda_b u e^{-\pi\lambda_b u^2} du\right\} v dv\right)$$

$$\overset{(b)}{=} \exp\left(-2\pi\lambda' \int\limits_{d_n}^{+\infty}\int\limits_0^{+\infty} \left\{1 - E_h \left[exp\left(-shu^{\rho\alpha}v^{-\alpha}\right)\right]\right\} 2\pi\lambda_b u e^{-\pi\lambda_b u^2} du v dv\right)$$

$$\overset{(c)}{=} \exp\left(-4\pi^2\lambda_b\lambda' \int\limits_{d_n}^{+\infty}\int\limits_0^{+\infty} \left(\frac{su^{\rho\alpha+1}v^{1-\alpha}}{\mu+su^{\rho\alpha}v^{-\alpha}}\right)e^{-\pi\lambda_b u^2} du dv\right),$$

$$(13)$$

where (a) is derived from the probability generation function of PPP with $\lambda(x)$,

$$E\left[\prod_{X\in\Phi} f(x)\right] = \exp\left\{\int\limits_{R^2} [f(x) - 1]\lambda(x)dx\right\}.$$ (b) is obtained by the extraction of integrands, and (c) is based on h following the exponential distribution.

After a series of calculations mentioned above, we finally bring (10) and (13) into (4) to obtain the spectrum efficiency of the general user, and add (6) and (7) to get the final downlink edge spectral efficiency expression (14)

$$C = \int\limits_0^{+\infty} \int\limits_{d_1>0} \int\limits_{d_2>d_1} \cdots \int\limits_{d_n>d_{n-1}} P_u C_d f_{d_1}(d_1) f_{d_2}(d_2)...f_{d_n}(d_n)ds dd_1 dd_2...dd_n. \tag{14}$$

4   Simulation Results and Performance Evaluation

In this section, we verify the average spectral efficiency of the edge users through extensive simulation in downlink cooperative transmission. To simplify the analysis, we consider a multi-cell coverage scenario in a specific time slot, e.t. $\lambda_b > \lambda_u$. The general setting of the simulation parameters is $\lambda_b = 2$, $\lambda_u = 0.5$, $\alpha = 4$ and

$\mu = 1$, and we ignore the influence of noise in an interference limited system $\sigma^2 = 0$; unless otherwise stated.

We define a general edge user as a user whose distance ratio is greater than $2/3$ [11]. In this paper, we set the distance ratio R to $2/3$, and the distance ratio between the closest BS and the second closest BS is $d_1/d_2 = 0.8$. Figure 3 is a simulation diagram of the spectrum efficiency according to (14) as a function of a power control factor and a number of cooperative BSs. As we can see from the figure, the two curves show that as ρ increases, the spectral efficiency of the edge user gradually increases. Focusing on the analysis of a curve, there is no power control and its performance is poor when a = 0; When a = 1, the power control completely offset the path loss and its performance is better. Comparing the two curves, as the number of cooperative BSs increases, the spectrum efficiency shows an overall upward trend.

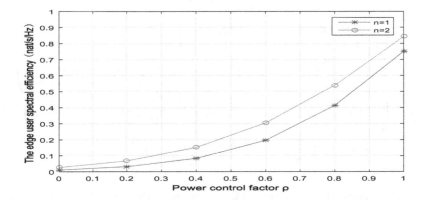

Fig. 3. Downlink edge user spectral efficiency with power control factor ρ as an variable

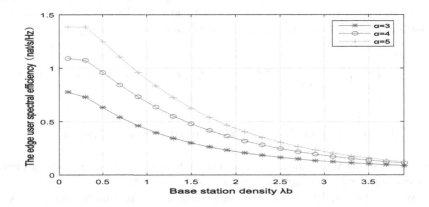

Fig. 4. The spectrum efficiency of edge users as a function of base station density λ_b

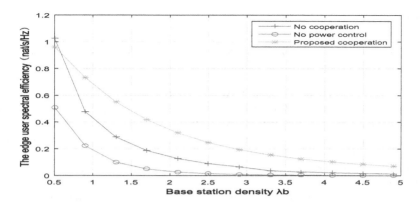

Fig. 5. The spectrum efficiency of edge users as a function of base station density λ_b

Figure 4 indicates the effect of BS density λ_b on the spectral efficiency of edge users. First analyze a curve, we can see that as the λ_b increases, the spectrum efficiency shows a smooth declining trend. This is due to the increase in the α, which increase the number of interfering BSs and decrease the distance between BSs. As a result, the intensity of interference increases sharply. Comparing the three curves, as the increase of α, the spectrum efficiency shows an upward trend. Because the greater the α, the faster the power attenuation.

Figure 5 is a comparison of three transmission schemes. The first scheme is only power control scheme without considering cooperative transmission. Second is the cooperative transmission scheme without power control. The third scheme is the optimization scheme of joint power control and cooperative transmission proposed in this paper. Considering $\lambda_b > \lambda_u$, the simulation starts from $\lambda_b = 0.5$. By comparing the three curves, it can be clearly seen that the proposed scheme is superior to the other two schemes and the spectrum efficiency of the edge users is significantly improved.

5   Conclusion

In this paper, a novel scheme is proposed for optimizing the average spectrum efficiency of edge users in a stochastic network model. It combines cooperative transmission and power control to enhance the received signal strength of the edge users and eliminate the intense inter-cell interference in the edge spectrum efficiency improvement scheme. We also deduce the average spectrum efficiency expression of the downlink edge users. Simulation results reveal that the proposed scheme is superior to the traditional cooperative transmission and the transmission scheme with the nearest base station as the serving base station. In the future, we will consider multi-user scheduling and precoding schemes for multi-user scenarios to eliminate between users interference and further increase the spectrum efficiency of edge users.

References

1. Liu, H., Su, X., You, Y., Zeng, J.: A reconfigurable software radio framework for accessing diverse resources in distributed nodes. In: Ultra Modern Telecommunications and Control Systems and Workshops, pp. 1–5. IEEE, Budapest (2011)
2. Zeng, J., Su, X., Gong, J., Rong, L, Wang, J.: 5G virtualized radio access network approach based on NO Stack framework. In: IEEE International Conference on Communications, pp. 1–5. IEEE, Paris (2017)
3. Moon, J.-M., Cho, D.-H.: Formation of cooperative cluster for coordinated transmission in multi-cell wireless networks. In: 2013 IEEE 10th Consumer Communications and Networking Conference, pp. 528–533. IEEE, Las Vegas (2013)
4. Cui, Q., Song, H., Wang, H., Valkama, M., Dowhuszko, A.A.: Capacity analysis of joint transmission CoMP with adaptive modulation. IEEE Trans. Veh. Technol. **66**(2), 1876–1881 (2017)
5. Aota, T., Higuchi, K.: A simple downlink transmission power control method for worst user throughput maximization in heterogeneous networks. In: 7th International Conference on Signal Processing and Communication Systems, pp. 1–6. IEEE, Carrara (2013)
6. ElSawy, H., Hossain, E., Haenggi, M.: Stochastic geometry for modeling, analysis, and design of multi-tier and cognitive cellular wireless networks: a survey. IEEE Commun. Surv. Tutor. **15**(3), 996–1019 (2013)
7. Baccelli, F., Giovanidis, A.: Coverage by pairwise base station cooperation under adaptive geometric policies. In: 2013 Asilomar Conference on Signals, Systems and Computers, pp. 748–753. IEEE, Pacific Grove (2013)
8. Tong, Z., Li, B., Liu, M.: Novel downlink coordination scheme for CoMP SU-MIMO. In: 2011 International Conference on Network Computing and Information Security, pp. 121–125. IEEE, Guilin (2011)
9. Yu, S.M., Kim, S.L.: Downlink capacity and base station density in cellular networks. In: 2013 11th International Symposium and Workshops on Modeling and Optimization in Mobile, Ad Hoc and Wireless Networks, pp. 119–124. IEEE, Tsukuba Science City (2013)
10. Mankar, P.D., Das, G., Pathak, S.: Load-aware performance analysis of cell center/edge users in random HetNets. IEEE Trans. Veh. Technol. **67**(3), 119–124 (2018)
11. Park, J., Lee, N., Heath, R.W.: Cooperative base station coloring for pair-wise multi-cell coordination. IEEE Trans. Commun. **64**(1), 402–415 (2016)
12. Ferenc, J.-S., Neda, Z.: On the size distribution of Poisson Voronoi cells. Stat. Mech. Appl. **385**(2), 518–526 (2007)

Routing and Network Planning

An Energy-Efficient Distributed Routing Protocol for Wireless Sensor Networks with Mobile Sinks

Hengyi Wen[1], Tao Wang[2(✉)], Daren Zha[3], and Baoxian Zhang[1]

[1] Research Center of Ubiquitous Sensor Networks,
University of Chinese Academy of Sciences, Beijing 100049, China
wenhengyi15@mails.ucas.ac.cn, bxzhang@ucas.ac.cn
[2] Network Information Center, University of Chinese Academy of Sciences,
Beijing 100049, China
wangtao2013@ucas.ac.cn
[3] Institute of Information Engineering, Chinese Academy of Sciences,
Beijing 100093, China
zhadaren@iie.ac.cn

Abstract. Mobile sink(s) can solve the hotspot issue in static wireless sensor networks (WSNs) but also cause frequent change of network topology, increase the network overhead, and thus affect the network performance. A lot of work has been done to enable efficient routing in such networks. However, little work has addressed the issue of energy efficient distributed routing in WSNs with mobile sinks (mWSNs). This paper designs an energy-efficient distributed routing protocol, which combines energy-efficient data-driven packet forwarding, trail based forwarding, and energy-efficient random walk routing, in order to achieve prolonged network lifetime performance. Detailed protocol design is presented. Simulation results show that our designed protocol can prolong the network lifetime remarkably while maintaining high packet delivery ratio performance with low protocol overhead.

Keywords: Wireless sensor networks · Mobile sinks · Energy-efficient routing

1 Introduction

Wireless sensor network with mobile sinks are often referred to as mWSN and has been a widely used sensing paradigm because mWSNs can relieve hotspot issues in static wireless sensor networks. Much work [1–3] has been carried out in the field of mWSNs, which shows that introduction of mobile sinks can significantly increase network performance. However, in mWSNs, sensor nodes typically have limited resources, and also the mobility of sink nodes brings great challenge to the design of efficient distributed routing protocols for such networks due to the unpredictable

This work was supported in part by NSF of China under grants 61531006, 61471339, and 61872331.

J. Zheng et al. (Eds.): ADHOCNETS 2018, LNICST 258, pp. 83–92, 2019.
https://doi.org/10.1007/978-3-030-05888-3_8

changes of network topology caused by sink mobility. Therefore, designing efficient routing protocols for mWSN networks has been an important issue to obtain high network performance while yielding light protocol overhead.

A lot of work has been done to enable efficient routing for mWSNs. Existing work in this aspect can be further categorized into the following four types [1–3]: Location based routing protocols, topology based routing protocols, reactive routing protocols, and energy-aware routing protocols. In location based routing protocols (such as LURP [4], TTDD [5], and ER [6]), each node needs to know node location information to make routing decisions. Specifically, such protocols require each node to have its own location, its neighbors' locations, and locations of packet destinations, which can guide hop-by-hop geographical packet forwarding. However, in many cases it difficult for nodes to get accurate location information, in particular for mobile sinks. Topology based protocols (such as AVRP [7] and MDRP [8]) can identify and maintain topological information to form efficient structure for network routing. They typically can obtain short paths at high protocol overhead. Reactive routing protocols (such as TRAIL [7], DDRP [9], and TBD [10]) can learn/update routing information in a reactive way with little overhead and thus have good performance in terms of packet delivery ratio and protocol overhead. Regarding energy-aware routing for mWSNs, Luo et al. [11] studied the issue of joint mobility scheduling and routing in an mWSN while maximizing the network lifetime while Yu et al. [12] studied how to build a quasi-polar coordinate system on an mWSN to support energy efficient ring-based forwarding in such networks.

This paper designs a distributed energy-efficient reactive routing protocol for mWSNs. The goal is to obtain improved network lifetime with low overhead and also high packet delivery performance. For this purpose, our protocol integrates energy-efficient data-driven packet forwarding, trail based forwarding, and energy-efficient random walk routing. According to the designed protocol, the following metrics are jointly utilized when making decision on next hop selections: route freshness, distance to target sink, residual energy at next hop candidates, and progress made via one-hop forwarding. Detailed protocol design is presented. Simulations are conducted and the results show that our protocol can prolong network lifetime remarkably while keeping high performance with low overhead.

The remainder of this paper is organized as below. Section 2 reviews existing work. Section 3 gives the detailed protocol. Section 4 gives simulation results.

2   Related Work

Existing work can be divided into two types: energy-unaware routing protocols and energy-aware routing protocols. Next, we will introduce typical protocols belonging to either type.

2.1   Energy-Unaware Routing in mWSNs

In this aspect, existing protocols include the following three types: Location based routing protocols, topology based routing protocols, and reactive routing protocols. Next, we will introduce typical protocols belonging to each type.

Location Based Routing Protocols

Location based routing protocols use location information of nodes for next hop selection. Major advantages of such protocols include high scalability, good routing performance, and simplicity. Typical protocols in this type contain LURP (Local Update-Based Routing Protocol) [4] and TTDD (Two-Tier Data Dissemination) [5].

In LURP, each sink node selects a small circular area around it. When it moves inside this area, it only needs to report updated location information to sensor nodes in this area, and packets outside the area need to be routed to this area first via geographical forwarding. When the sink moves outside the circular area, it will disseminate its updated location information to the entire network and further select another circular area around it for local update of its location. In this way, the overhead for location update is greatly reduced. TTDD is for multicast data delivery to multi-mobile-sinks. For such purpose, it builds a grid structure for advertisement purpose (i.e., data source node's packet availability). Packet retrieval and delivery are made along such grid structure.

Topology Based Routing Protocols

Topology based routing protocols actively build and maintain efficient routing paths from sensor nodes to sink nodes and allow data packets to be forwarded to nearby sinks with few hops. Typical protocols in this type include Anchor-based Voronoi-scoping Routing Protocol (AVRP [7]) and Multi-Stage Data Routing Protocol (MDRP [8]).

AVRP uses Voronoi-scoping for network partitioning such that each sensor nodes is likely to report its generated data packet to its nearest sink node. The problem in AVRP is the high overhead for the re-scoping caused by sink mobility. MDRP is an improved version of AVRP. Compared with AVRP, MDRP divides the scope covered by each sink into multiple layers based on hop distance, which largely reduce the frequency of wide-area topological update. Topology based routing protocols are suitable for moderate or heavily loaded mWSNs. Usually, establishing and maintaining efficient routing structure in an mWSN can cause a large amount of protocol overhead.

Reactive Routing Protocols

Reactive routing protocols can learn or update routing information adaptively. This type of protocols usually (e.g., TRAIL [7], DDRP [9] and TBD [10]) has low overhead but long route acquisition latency and is suitable for mWSNs with light traffic load.

TRAIL integrates trail-based forwarding and random walk. As a sink moves in the network, it needs to keep broadcasting beacon messages in order to leave a trail behind it. When having a data packet to report, trail based forwarding has priority to be taken, otherwise random walk routing is performed. TRAIL is suitable for dense WSNs such that trail break rarely happens. In the DDRP protocol, data packet carries an extra option in its IP packet header, in order to record the distance between the packet sender and a target sink. Sensor nodes work in promiscuous mode to learn and update local routing table via overhearing of data packet transmissions in the neighborhood. Accordingly, DDRP largely reduces the overhead for route updating and learning. TBD combines data-driven route learning/updating and trail based forwarding for improved routing performance. When a sensor node has a data packet to forward, the priorities of different routing strategies in DDRP (from the highest to the lowest) is as follows: trail-based forwarding, data-driven routing, and random walk. Simulation results show that TBD outperforms DDRP and TRAIL.

2.2   Energy-Aware Routing in WSNs

Energy-aware routing has been a critical issue in WSNs [13] and much work has been done in this area. Next, we shall briefly introduce typical work in this area.

The LEACH-C protocol [14] extends the well-known LEACH (Low-Energy Adaptive Clustering Hierarchy) protocol [15]. In these two protocols, sensor nodes are organized into a two-tier clustering regime such that a number of cluster head nodes are elected, which are responsible for communicating with base station while other regular nodes communicate with their cluster head nodes. Such elections work in a round-by-round manner. LEACH-C extends the basic LEACH protocol in the following two ways: node residual energy is considered into cluster head election and desired number of cluster heads are selected in each round. However, LEACH requires each node can directly communicate with the base station, which makes it unsuitable for large-scale WSNs. The MCBCR protocol (Efficient Minimum-Cost Bandwidth-Constrained Routing) [16] is a efficient scalable, and simple solution for mini-cost routing in wireless sensor networks and it identifies proper routes from sensors to sinks while ensuring that assigned load on each edge does not exceed the link capacity. However, operation of MCBCR needs global state information, which has the scalability issue.

There are also some energy-aware hop-by-hop routing protocols for WSNs. In [17], the authors designed an on-demand maximum residual energy routing protocol, which selects the path connecting a source-destination pair but with the maximum residual energy at intermediate nodes on the path. This protocol, however, leads to multiple search rounds for route acquisition. In [18], an energy-efficient geographical forwarding algorithm was presented, which chooses the best choice of next hop based on local network state (including local topology, state of links & nodes on the local topology). However, none of the above work considered how to enable energy-efficient routing in mWSNs, which is the focus of this paper.

There have been some work studying how to prolonging the network lifetime of mWSNs. In [11], Luo and Hubaux studied the issue of joint mobility scheduling and routing in an mWSN while maximizing the network lifetime. Paper [11] presented a generic optimization framework and proved it to be NP-hard. They first proposed an approximate algorithm for the single sink case, and then, they proposed a polynomial approximation algorithm for the general problem. In [12], Yu et al. first built multi-ring based structure in a WSN, which is actually a quasi-polar coordinate system, based on which energy-efficient ring-based forwarding is enabled for packet delivery. Different from the work in [12], in this paper, we shall introduce energy-efficient next hop selection into the joint design of trail based forwarding in TRAIL [7] and data-driven packet forwarding in DDRP [9], in order to achieve prolonged network lifetime while keeping protocol simplicity and robustness.

Our protocol in this paper is an energy-efficient enhancement of TBD, referred to as E-TBD, in order to prolong the network lifetime. Next, we shall present the design details of E-TBD.

3   E-TBD

This section presents the design details of our E-TBD protocol, which combines energy-efficient trail based forwarding, data-driven packet forwarding, and energy-efficient random walk routing for supporting energy-efficient packet forwarding. E-TBD is designed based on the following assumptions: All sensor nodes and sink nodes have omnidirectional antennas and also the same communication range, and no location information is assumed to be known.

Next, we will first give a brief review of TBD, and then give an overview about how our E-TBD protocol works, finally, we give the design details of E-TBD.

3.1   Brief Review of TBD

TBD is a reactive routing protocol such that it learns/updates routing information in a reactive way. TBD combines data-driven route learning/updating, trail based forwarding, and random walk routing. Next, we introduce how the route learning/updating and data packet forwarding in TBD work, respectively.

In TBD, each node has at most two routing entries, one for data forwarding and another for backup. The information in an entry includes the time instant when the route was generated, the distance to the target sink, the identification of the next-hop to target sink, etc. In TBD, each sink node periodically issues beacon messages to its direct neighbors as it moves, which can then learn that they are on the trail of a mobile sink. Regarding data-driven route learning, sensor nodes work in promiscuous mode to learn new routing information to reach mobile sinks via overhearing of transmissions of data packets in the neighborhood.

In TBD, for forwarding a data packet in the network, the priorities of different forwarding strategies are as follows: trail based forwarding, data-driven forwarding, and random walk. Specifically, when a sensor node receives a data packet, it will look up its own routing entries. If it is on a fresh trail, the packet will be forwarded along the trail (i.e., sending the packet to the neighbor sensor node on the trail, which has the freshest sink-related record), otherwise if it has valid routing entry in its routing cache as obtained via overhearing of neighbors' data transmission(s), the packet will be forwarded according to the corresponding entry (data-driven forwarding), otherwise it has no any routing information, random walk will be triggered.

However, design of the TBD protocol had not considered energy use efficiency at sensor nodes, which may lead to reduced energy efficiency and thus shortened network lifetime.

3.2   E-TBD Overview

To obtain high performance, E-TBD combines energy efficient trail-driven forwarding, data-driven forwarding, and energy efficient random walk routing. Energy efficient trail based forwarding makes use of the trail left by mobile sinks, at the same time, maximally prevent nodes with less residual energy from serving as forwarding nodes. Data-driven forwarding makes use of the routing information learnt via overhearing of neighbors' packet transmissions. Energy efficient random walk routing takes the residual energy of neighbor nodes into consideration when making decisions on next hop selection.

3.3 Detailed Design of E-TBD

In this subsection, we will first give how the route learning/updating in E-TBD works, and then present how the data packet forwarding in E-TBD works.

Route Learning/Updating

In the initial stage, all network nodes have no information about how to reach a sink node. When a mobile sink moves, it keeps broadcasting beacon packets to its direct neighbors, which will leave a trail behind the mobile sink. When a sensor node receives such a beacon packet, it will extract the following information from the packet:

(1) Time_stamp, which records the time when the beacon was generated,
(2) Sink_ID, which records the ID of the sink that generated this beacon.

As a sink moves in the network, the sensor nodes which receive such beacon messages can learn/update their routing tables and accordingly form a sink trail.

Meanwhile, sensors in the network can also learn or update routing table in a data-driven way. Specially, for each data packet, it contains the following extra options:

(1) Dist2mSink, which is the so far shortest distance from the sender of the packet to target sink.
(2) Time_stamp, which is the time when an entry was created. More exactly, its value equals the time when the beacon message, which triggers the construction of this route, was issued by the mobile sink.
(3) Sender_ID, which records the ID of the packet sender.

All the neighbors of the sender work in promiscuous mode and can overhear the transmission of such packet and can also extract the above information from the overheard packet. If the Time_stamp extracted from the overheard packet is fresher than the time_stamp recorded at the listening node's routing table, the routing table at the latter will be updated. Progressive route-learning among nodes in the network will let more and more network nodes learn fresh routes to mobile sinks.

Data Packet Forwarding

E-TBD combines energy-efficient data-driven packet forwarding, trail based forwarding, and energy-efficient random walk, and in descending priorities. For a sensor u, when it receives a data packet from the application layer or from a neighbor sensor node, it will look up its local routing entries, and make the following operation for packet forwarding. Specially, if it has fresh sink trail information, then perform energy efficient trail based forwarding; else if data-driven routing is applicable, then perform data-driven routing; otherwise, perform energy efficient random walk routing. Next, we will introduce how each of these processes works.

(A) *Energy-efficient trail-based forwarding*

In this case, sensor u is on a fresh trail. Accordingly, it first searches for a sink in its neighborhood. If such a sink can be found, the data packet will be forwarded to the sink directly. If not, energy efficient trail based forwarding will be taken. In this process, the holder of the packet will issue a query to check if there exists any neighbor with fresher time stamp (sink-related record) than the current node and starts a timer. A query packet includes the ID of the packet holder and a time stamp as copied from the current node's routing entry. If one reply is received, it will send the data packet to the responding node. If multiple nodes have fresher time stamps than the packet holder, energy efficient next hop selection will be triggered, which takes both trail freshness and residual energy at next hop candidates into consideration. Specifically, sensor u will assign a score to each neighbor sending it a reply in the following way:

$$\text{score} = \frac{rest\_energy}{\alpha + \beta(curr\_time - time\_stamp)}$$

where $rest\_energy$ is the residual energy of the next hop candidate node, $curr\_time$ is the current time, $time\_stamp$ is the time stamp of sink record kept at the candidate node (as indicated in the reply message), α and β are network parameters. Usually, α is a natural number to avoid the zero denominator case, β controls the proportion of importance of residual energy and freshness of time stamp. The freshness of time stamp is more important when β is larger. We can see that in the above formula, candidate nodes with more residual energy and fresher time stamp can get higher scores and thus have higher probability to serve as the next hop node. The neighbor node with the highest score will be chosen as the next hop. Then, the packet holder will send the packet to the chosen next hop.

Upon receipt of the packet, the next hop will repeat the above operation. This process keeps going until the packet arrives at a mobile sink. If no reply is received in given time, which means the trail is broken, the two-hop local broadcast mechanism in TBD is used to search for an alternate route for broken point bypassing. When two-hop local broadcast fails to find such an alternate path, node u will resort to its backup routing entry by triggering data-driven-based forwarding if it has such a routing entry in its cache. If no such entry is available, energy efficient random walk will be triggered.

(B) *Data-driven-based forwarding*

E-TBD follows the data-driven forwarding in DDRP. The use of this forwarding strategy here is exactly the same to that in TBD. In case DDRP learnt routing table is available and further data-driven-based forwarding is in triggering, the packet holder will choose the next hop in this entry for packet forwarding.

(C) *Energy-efficient random walk routing*

When sensor u does not know any route to reach a sink, energy efficient random walk routing will be triggered. For this purpose, a packet holder chooses top 20% neighbor nodes having the most residual energy and give them 80% probability to be chosen and the given the remaining 80% nodes 20% probability to be chosen. For all nodes belonging to the same type, the probabilities for each of them to be chosen are equal. In this way, we ensure certain randomness while giving more opportunity to sensor nodes with more residual energy to serve as packet forwarders and thus protect those neighbor nodes with less residual energy. Upon receipt of the data packet, a sensor node will repeat the above process until the packet reaches next hop with fresher sink record, a mobile sink, a sensor node with DDRP routing table, or timed out and then dropped.

4   Performance Evaluation

This section conducts simulations to evaluate the performance of E-TBD by comparing it with TBD. Both protocols simulated belong to reactive routing protocols and further neither of their implementations assume any location information. The simulator used here was developed using Java in Eclipse environment.

In our simulations, there are multiple mobile sinks and 200 sensor nodes deployed uniformly in a 500×500 m^2 square. The communication range of each node is 60 m. Each sink takes a random direction to move and at a given speed and it will get bounced when reaching the boundary of the sensing area. Data packets are generated at sensor nodes randomly at certain probability.

We assume that the links in the network are symmetric and the length of each packet is 1000 bit. The energy consumption of transceiver circuit is 500 nJ/bit, and the power amplifier is 100 pJ/bit/m^2. Initially, each sensor node has 2 J energy.

In the simulation, three metrics are evaluated: packet delivery ratio, normalized forwarding overhead, and network lifetime. The packet delivery ratio is the ratio of the total number of successfully delivered data packets to the number of data packets generated in the network. The normalized forwarding overhead is the ratio of the total number of packet transmissions over the number of data packets successfully delivered to sink nodes. The network lifetime is the length of time from network starts running to the time when the first sensor is dead due to running out of energy. This metric represents the energy efficiency of a protocol. In our experiments, each point in the figures is the average due to 30 different tests.

Figure 1 compares performance of different protocols in the scenario of one-sink mWSNs and the packet generation rate equals two packets/s. Specifically, Fig. 1(a) shows the delivery ratio performance with varying sink velocity, Fig. 1(b) shows the overhead with varying sink velocity and Fig. 1(c) shows the network lifetime varying sink velocity. Figure 2 shows the results for 3-sink mWSNs with the packet generation rate equals two packets/s. Figure 3 shows the results for 3-sink mWSNs but the packet generation rate equals one packet/s.

From results in Figs. 1, 2 and 3, the data delivery ratio and network overhead by E-TBD is similar to that by TBD. Meanwhile, the network lifetime by E-TBD is much longer than that by TBD. Specifically, as sink(s) move faster in the network, packet delivery ratio by both TBD and E-TBD keeps decreasing and the corresponding protocol overhead keeps increasing. In most cases, the overhead by E-TBD is a little bit higher than that TBD due to the following reasons: (1) E-TBD needs extra messages to exchange energy availability information among neighbor nodes as compared with TBD. (2) when making choice of next hop using trail based forwarding, E-TBD considers both residual energy at next hops and also progress made, while TBD

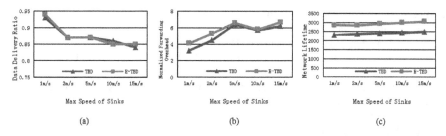

Fig. 1. Performance comparison of different algorithms with varying sink speed. In this test, there is only one sink in the network and packet generation rate is two packets/s.

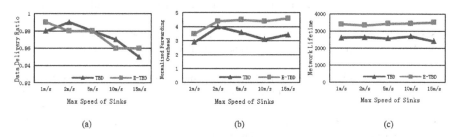

Fig. 2. Performance comparison of different algorithms with varying sink speed. In this test, there are three sinks in the network and packet generation rate is two packets/s.

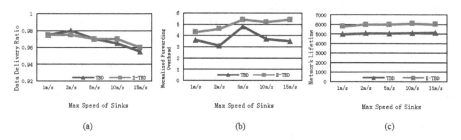

Fig. 3. Performance by of different algorithms with varying sink speed. In this test, there are three sinks and packet generation rate is one packet/s.

considers only progress made for one-hop data forwarding. Obviously, the former choice typically leads to more balancing of energy consumption among nodes but also cause more hops as compared with the latter.

References

1. Song, L.: Architecture of wireless sensor networks with mobile sinks: multiple access case. Int. J. Distrib. Sens. Netw. **3**(3), 289–310 (2007)
2. Liang, S., Hatzinakos, D.: Architecture of wireless sensor networks with mobile sinks: sparsely deployed sensors. IEEE Trans. Veh. Technol. **56**(4), 1826–1836 (2007)

3. Yu, S., et al.: Routing protocols for wireless sensor networks with mobile sinks: a survey. IEEE Commun. Mag. **52**(7), 150–157 (2014)
4. Wang, G., Wang, T., et al.: Local update-based routing protocol in wireless sensor networks with mobile sinks. In: Proceedings of IEEE ICC 2007, pp. 3094–3099. IEEE, Glasgow (2007)
5. Ye, F., Luo, H., et al.: A two-tier data dissemination model for large-scale wireless sensor networks. In: Proceedings of ACM MobiCom 2002, pp. 148–159. ACM, Atlanta (2002)
6. Yu, F., et al.: Elastic routing: a novel geographic routing for mobile sinks in wireless sensor networks. IET Commun. **4**(6), 716–727 (2010)
7. Tian, K., Zhang, B., et al.: Data gathering protocols for wireless sensor networks with mobile sinks. In: Proceedings of IEEE GLOBECOM 2010, Miami, pp. 1–6 (2010)
8. Shi, L., Yao, Z., Zhang, B., Li, C., Ma, J.: An efficient distributed routing protocol for wireless sensor networks with mobile sinks. Int. J. Commun. Syst. **28**(11), 1789–1804 (2015)
9. Shi, L., Zhang, B., Mouftah, H., Ma, J.: DDRP: an efficient data-driven routing protocol for wireless sensor networks with mobile sinks. Int. J. Commun. Syst. **26**(10), 1341–1355 (2013)
10. Wen, H., Yao, Z., Lian, H., Zhang, B.: A new distributed routing protocol for wireless sensor networks with mobile sinks. In: Li, C., Mao, S. (eds.) WiCON 2017. LNICST, vol. 230, pp. 150–159. Springer, Cham (2018). https://doi.org/10.1007/978-3-319-90802-1_13
11. Luo, J., Hubaux, J.-P.: Joint sink mobility and routing to increase the lifetime of wireless sensor networks: the case of constrained mobility. IEEE/ACM Trans. Netw. **18**(3), 871–884 (2010)
12. Yu, S., Shang, D., Yao, Z., Zhang, B., Li, C.: A lightweight ring-based routing protocol for wireless sensor networks with mobile sinks. In: Proceedings of IEEE GLOBECOM 2014, pp. 4580–4585. IEEE, Austin (2014)
13. Pantazis, N.A., Nikolidakis, S.A., Vergados, D.D.: Energy-efficient routing protocols in wireless sensor networks: a survey. IEEE Commun. Surv. Tutor. **15**(2), 551–591 (2013)
14. Vidhate, D.A., Patil, A.K., Pophale, S.S.: Performance evaluation of low energy adaptive clustering hierarchy protocol for wireless sensor networks. In: Proceedings of ICWET 2010, pp. 59–63 (2010)
15. Heinzelman, W., et al.: Energy-efficient communication protocol for wireless microsensor networks. In: Proceedings of HICSS Conference, HI, USA, p. 110 (2000)
16. Chang, J., Tassiulas, L.: Energy conserving routing in wireless ad-hoc networks. In: Proceedings of IEEE INFOCOM 2000, pp. 22–31. IEEE, Tel-Aviv (2000)
17. Zhang, B., Mouftah, H.T.: Energy-aware on-demand routing protocols for wireless ad hoc networks. Wirel. Netw. **12**(4), 481–494 (2006)
18. Yu, Q., Zhang, B., et al.: Energy-efficient geographical forwarding algorithm for wireless ad hoc and sensor networks. In: Proceedings of IEEE WCNC 2008, pp. 2468–2473. IEEE, Las Vegas (2008)

Asymptotical Performance of Ring Based Routing for Wireless Sensor Networks with a Mobile Sink: An Analysis

Sheng Yu[1], Baoxian Zhang[1(⊠)], Chunxi Li[2], Kun Hao[3], and Cheng Li[3,4]

[1] University of Chinese Academy of Sciences, Beijing 100049, China
yusheng08@mails.ucas.ac.cn, bxzhang@ucas.ac.cn
[2] Beijing Jiaotong University, Beijing 100044, China
chxlil@bjtu.edu.cn
[3] School of Computer and Information Engineering,
Tianjin Chengjian University, Tianjin, China
littlehao@126.com
[4] Memorial University of Newfoundland, St. John's, NL A1B 3X5, Canada
licheng@mun.ca

Abstract. Design of efficient routing protocols has been a critical issue in wireless sensor networks with mobile sinks (mWSN). In [1], Yu et al. proposed a distributed lightweight ring based routing protocol for mWSNs, which builds a multi-ring based network structure by creating a quasi-polar coordinate system on the network in order to support efficient ring based routing. However, in [1], only average case routing performance was reported via simulations. In this paper, we derive the asymptotical path-length performance of the ring based routing via extensive analyses. We hope the results reported in this paper can be helpful for understanding the characteristics of ring based routing.

Keywords: Wireless sensor network · Mobile sinks · Distributed routing

1 Introduction

Wireless sensor networks with mobile sinks (mWSN) have the potential to be used in many applications such as military operations, commercial, patrols, environment monitoring, and etc. Design and evaluation of mWSNs have received a lot of attention recently and much work has been carried out [1]. An mWSN typically consists of many static sensor nodes and one or more mobile sink nodes (MSs). Efficient routing for achieving high routing performance in mWSNs has been a critical issue.

This work was supported by National Natural Science Foundation of China under Grant Nos. 61471339 and 61531006, 61572071, U1534201, and the Natural Sciences and Engineering Research Council (NSERC) of Canada (Discovery Grant 293264-12), and InnovateNL SensorTECH project 5404-2061-101.

J. Zheng et al. (Eds.): ADHOCNETS 2018, LNICST 258, pp. 93–104, 2019.
https://doi.org/10.1007/978-3-030-05888-3_9

Existing routing protocols for mWSNs can be divided into location based protocols and topology based routing. In location based routing, location information of mobile sink is used to assist geographical packet forwarding. In [2], an Adaptive Location Update based Routing Protocol (ALURP) was presented to restrict the scope of location updates caused by sink mobility to a small area (called destination area) with slight sacrifice on routing distance performance. The Elastic Routing (ER) protocol [3] enables a source sensor node to keep obtaining the up-to-date location information of a mobile sink during its continuous data reporting to the sink. In [4, 5], the authors focused on how to design efficient location services for providing fresh location information of a nearby mobile sink to a sensor node with data to report while having low protocol overhead, where [4] presented a flat location service while [5] presented a hierarchical location service. Topology based routing protocols can be further divided into proactive routing protocols (e.g., AVRP [6] and MDRP [7, 8]) and reactive routing (e.g., TRAIL [6] and DDRP [9]). In proactive routing protocols, data paths from sensor nodes to mobile sink need to be established and updated from time to time, which can cause a lot of protocol overhead for route maintenance. In reactive routing protocols, overhearing on wireless channels (e.g., the passing of an MS in TRAIL [6] and transmission of a data packet in the neighborhood in DDRP [9]) is often used for path learning with minimal protocol overhead. When no such overhearing opportunity is available or previously learnt routes are outdated, random walk has to be triggered.

In [1], Yu et al. proposed an efficient lightweight reactive routing protocol called R3, which integrates ring-based routing and trail-based routing. R3 does not require location information to be kept at nodes in the network. In R3, a data packet is forwarded by using ring-based routing until it reaches a mobile sink or can be forwarded to a mobile sink along a fresh trail along which the sink moves. To support efficient ring-based routing/forwarding, R3 builds a multi-ring-based infrastructure on a multihop wireless sensor network when the network is initially deployed by creating a quasi-polar coordinate system on the network. When performing packet forwarding on a particular ring, the next hop leading to the maximum angle progress is chosen until reaching a mobile sink (or an agent node recruited by a mobile sink, or a fresh trail to reach a mobile sink). When the searching on a particular ring failed, another ring will be tried. This process continues until a mobile sink is found or no mobile sink can be found after pre-determined number of rings are tried. In [1], simulation results show that the R3 protocol outperforms existing work on average in different scenarios.

However, in [1], only average-case performance was reported. How long a shortest path along a ring, in the best and worst case, could be is not answered. In this paper, we shall tackle this issue via extensive analyses. We hope the results reported in this paper can be helpful for understanding the characteristics of ring based routing in an mWSN.

2   The R3 Protocol

The R3 protocol [1] is a lightweight distributed routing protocol targeted for mWSNs. The protocol only requires each node keep very limited routing information, which includes its node id, ring id, angle, gradient, and also its one-hop neighbor list. To support efficient data routing, R3 adopts ring-based forwarding. More specifically, each data packet is forwarded using ring-based forwarding until it reaches a mobile sink. A ring is formed by a number of nodes, all of which have the same hop distance to a base ring in the network and are expected to form an annulus for assisting packet forwarding. Packet forwarding along such an annulus is referred to as ring-based forwarding.

The network model used in R3 is as follows. A wireless multihop network can be modelled by $G(V, E)$, where $V(G)$ is constituent of one or multiple mobile sink nodes and multiple static sensor nodes and $E(G)$ represents the set of links in the network. Sensor nodes and sink nodes have the same communication range R. For each pair of nodes $u, v \in V(G)$, we have link $(u, v) \in E(G)$ if $d_{uv} \leq R$; otherwise $(u, v) \notin E(G)$. we let d_{uv} represent the geometrical distance between node u and node v. Each node is equipped with a omni-directional antenna. Nodes are uniformly deployed in a two-dimensional sensing field. Each mobile sink node moves randomly and freely in the sensing field. Nodes do not have their location information.

To support ring-based forwarding, the R3 protocol needs to first build a multi-ring-based structure on a wireless multihop sensor network when the network is initially deployed. The ring-based structure creation contains three rounds of (signaling) flooding operations. The first round of flooding prepares gradient information for sensor nodes in the WSN. To achieve this goal, a designated root node (e.g., a sensor node near the center of the WSN, see the node at the center point in Fig. 1 in our example) is chosen to start the flooding of a signaling message across the network, which enables each sensor node in the network to learn its hop distance to the designated root node as its gradient value. The second round of flooding is to build a base ring and is initiated by a sensor node with gradient of two. This round of flooding identifies a shortest cycled min-hop path, which tightly embraces a *virtual* topological hole that is artificially created in the central area of the network. This cycled shortest path is treated as the *base ring*. In the implementation of R3, all the nodes with gradients 1 and 0 (as identified in the first round of flooding operation) form the virtual hole. In Fig. 1, all the nodes in the most inner circle form the virtual hole. When multiple such cycled paths are found, the path leading to the min hop distance is chosen. In Fig. 1, the yellow nodes form the base ring. Each of the remaining (outer) rings is constituted of those sensor nodes having the same hop distance to the base ring. For example, in Fig. 1, all the green nodes have hop distance of one to the base ring. Similarly, those red, blue, and deepred nodes form each of the remaining outer rings. The creation of outer rings can be accomplished by a third round of flooding, triggered by nodes on the base ring. It should be noted that to ease the understanding and also for simplicity of illustration, in Fig. 1, each ring appears as a circular annulus. However, in reality, since the distance between different rings are measured in hops instead of geometrical distance, nodes in a ring does not necessarily form a circular annulus.

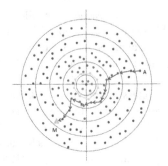

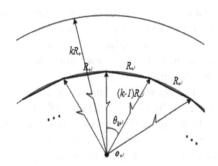

Fig. 1. Example illustrating how the R3 protocol works.

Fig. 2. Illustration of the shortest path in the best case on the k-th ring.

When carrying out ring-based packet forwarding, data packets are forwarded along nodes on a pre-selected ring along a pre-determined direction (either clockwise direction or anticlockwise direction). To enable data packets to be able to steadily move along the same direction and also minimize the path distance, virtual angle information is assigned to sensor nodes in the network in the following way: Nodes on the base ring are first assigned with virtual angles based on their positions on the cycled path (measured by their hop distances to a preselected reference node on the base ring, which can be randomly selected from nodes on the base ring, all in the same direction). In Fig. 1, suppose the lower most node in the base ring is chosen as the reference node with degree 0, then the other eight nodes in the base ring will respectively have degrees (in the closewise direction): 40°, 80°, 120°,..., 320°. The virtual angles of nodes on other outer rings are iteratively computed based on the virtual angles of their neighbor nodes (can also be seen as their farther nodes) on their immediate inner rings. In this way, a polar coordinate system can be built by assigning each node the following information: (1) a ring ID based on its distance to the base ring, and (2) a virtual angle. Such ring based structure is required to be created only once and at the network initialization phase and accordingly very limited extra protocol overhead is generated.

When performing actual packet forwarding along a selected ring, the next hop leading to max angle progress (on pre-selected direction, i.e., either clockwise direction or anti-clockwise direction) is always chosen. This hop by hop packet forwarding process continues until the packet reaches a mobile sink. A mobile sink can recruit agent nodes on the ring-based structure, one on each ring, to increase the successful probability to find mobile sink on a selected ring. When the MS searching process on a chosen ring fails, another ring will be tried. This process continues until a mobile sink is found or no mobile sink can be found when pre-determined number of rings are tried. Figure 1 shows how such ring-based forwarding can work for a sensor node A to send a packet to mobile sink M. For more details regarding how R3 works, please refer to [1].

Extensive simulation results in [1] show that R3 outperforms existing work in different scenarios. However, [1] only reported R3's average-case performance. How long a shortest path by such ring based forwarding, in the best and worst case, could be is not answered. In this paper, we shall address this issue via extensive analyses.

3 Analytical Results

This section analyzes how long a shortest route along a ring by R3 could be, in the best and worst case, respectively.

Lemma 1: For a path $P = (s = 1, 2, 3, \ldots, K - 1, K = t)$, which is a path on a particular ring returned by R3, we have: For any nodes $x, y \in P$, $y \geq x + 2$, we have $d_{xy} > R$. That is, the geometrical distance between any pair of non-neighbor nodes on P must be larger than R.

This is obvious because otherwise removal of those node(s) sitting between x and y from path P would have led to a shorter path by R3. More specifically, if $d_{xy} \leq R$ holds, the decision that node x had not chosen node y as its next hop would have violated R3's forwarding policy that each node should choose its neighbor with the maximum angle progress as its next hop. The holding of *Lemma* 1 also means that, for each node $x \in P$, we have that node $x + 2$ and its descendant nodes on P must have left x by at least R^+ distance on the anticlockwise side, where R^+ equals R plus positive infinitesimal.

Next, we present some results on the length of a shortest path constituent of nodes on a particular ring. It is easy to derive that, on a very sparse and irregular network, the length of such a path can be arbitrarily long, i.e., in the worst case, $O(|V|)$. In our analysis below, we assume that the network is densely distributed such that there exists a node at arbitrary position. For such a dense network, the width of each ring is obviously exactly R. Let o represent the common center of all the rings. To ease the analysis below, with a slight abuse of notation, for the k-th ($k \geq 2$) ring, we say it cover the space between two neighboring concentric circles, both of which are centered at o but have radius $(k - 1)R$ and kR, respectively. We call the circle with radius $(k - 1)$ R as its inner circle and the circle with radius kR its outer circle. Obviously, the so-called *base* ring identified by R3 is located in the 2nd ring. In our analysis below, we assume the exact location of each point in the network is known.

Next, we analyze the length of a shortest path to finish the travel (a closed tour) along a k-th ring ($k \geq 2$), in the best and worst case, respectively. The key factor affecting the length of such a path is the average central angle that each hop on such a path can cover. To obtain the best-case shortest path, we wish each hop to obtain the maximum angle progress. In contrast, to obtain the worst-case shortest path, we wish each hop (on average) to obtain the minimum angle progress. Note that the R3 protocol pursues short paths whenever available, by using one-hop topological information kept at each node.

Result 1: A fastest way to finish a closed tour along the k-th ring ($k \geq 2$) is that each hop advances R distance along a circle centered at o with the minimum radius on the ring, unless the last hop, which may not be that long. Let N_{min}^k denote the length of the shortest path in the best case in the k-th ring, we have

$$N_{min}^k = \left\lfloor \frac{2\pi}{\cos^{-1}\left(\frac{2(k-1)^2 - 1}{(k-1)^2}\right)} \right\rfloor + 1, \forall k \geq 2. \tag{1}$$

Figure 2 illustrates how N_{min}^k can be obtained. For the k-th ring, its inner circle is a circle centered at o with a radius $(k-1)R$. The maximum angle progress each hop can make is when two nodes are located on the inner circle and the distance between them are exactly R. Let θ_k denote that maximum angle progress that a single hop can obtain in the k-th ring. Based on the cosine theorem, we have the following equation

$$\theta_k = \cos^{-1}\left(\frac{2(k-1)^2-1}{2(k-1)^2}\right), \forall k \geq 2. \tag{2}$$

It directly follows from the above equation that in the best case, the length of the shortest path is $\left\lfloor \frac{2\pi}{\theta_k} \right\rfloor + 1$ hops in the k-th ring. Table 1 shows some values of N_{min}^k.

Table 1. Values of N_{min}^k.

k	2	3	4	5	6	7
N_{min}^k	7	13	19	26	32	38

The deduction of the worst-case length of a shortest path along a ring, however, is not easy. The key point is how slow we can achieve for traveling along such a ring along a fixed direction. *Lemma* 1 puts certain restriction on the slowness of the travel. Based on how the fastest path is created, an intuition is that at each hop, the path head node only moves forward $R/2$ (plus infinitesimal) distance instead of R (as done for creating the fastest path). This strategy works if we wish to travel along a curve or a line. We name this strategy as curve-based strategy. However, the worst case for traveling along a circular slice with certain width can be much worse than that due to the curve-based strategy because we can take a zigzag path along such a slice. To illustrate this, we provide such an example in Fig. 3(a).

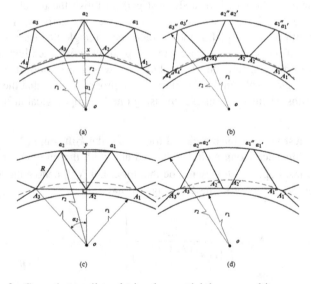

Fig. 3. Cases that equilateral triangles are tightly arranged in an annulus.

In Fig. 3(a), all the equilateral triangles are arranged on the dashed circle which makes one vertex of each of the equilateral triangles is on the outer circle of the ring and their height is exactly $\sqrt{3}R/2$. The side length of all the equilateral triangles is R. In Fig. 3(b), we further expand every vertex of the equilateral triangles to two nodes with a distance δ between them, where δ is positive infinitesimal. Note that in this expanding process, the length of each segment (A_i'', A_{i+1}'), $\forall i$, is also expanded from R to $R + \delta$, all in the same direction. This extra expansion is to keep *Lemma* 1 not violated in later path discovery. We are interested in the length of path $A_1'A_1''a_1'a_1''A_2'A_2''a_2'a_2''\ldots\ldots$ as $\delta \to 0+$ or equivalently, how many such equilateral triangles can be tightly arranged along the dashed circle. Obviously, traveling in such a zigzag manner and with such node expansions can lead to a path with a length approximately double to that due to the previously mentioned curve-based strategy[1]. We name this way of travel arrangement as triangle-based strategy. Next, we derive how many equilateral triangles can be tightly arranged on the dashed circle. Suppose the ring under study is the k-th ring, then the radius of its inner circle $r_1 = (k - 1)R$. Let x denote the middle point of line segment $\overline{A_2A_3}$ (see Fig. 3(a)). Consider the triangle A_2oA_3, we need to calculate its associated central angle $\angle A_2oA_3$. Note that $\overline{xo} = \overline{oa_2} - \overline{xa_2} = kR - \sqrt{3}R/2$. Let α_1 represent $\angle A_2oA_3$. We have $\overline{xA_3} = \overline{xA_2} = R/2$. Note $\angle oxA_3$ is a right angle and $\alpha_1 = 2\angle xoA_3$, thus

$$\alpha_1 = 2\tan^{-1}\left(\frac{xA_3}{xo}\right) = 2\tan^{-1}\left(\frac{1}{2k - \sqrt{3}}\right) \tag{3}$$

The number of equilateral triangles that can be arranged on the dashed circle in Fig. 3(a), denoted by M_1, is bounded by the following inequality,

$$\left\lfloor\frac{2\pi}{\alpha_1}\right\rfloor \leq M_1 \leq \left\lceil\frac{2\pi}{\alpha_1}\right\rceil. \tag{4}$$

Since we are interested in the worst case, we choose

$$M_1 = \left\lceil\frac{2\pi}{\alpha_1}\right\rceil \tag{5}$$

Thus, the maximum hops of a shortest path (closed tour) on such a ring due to the scenario shown in Fig. 3(a) (denoted by N_1) is as follows.

$$N_1 = 4 \times M_1 \tag{6}$$

---

[1] In the analysis, we ignore the impact of the last triangle problem, which may not be well nested there and thus lead to a few less hops on the worst-case shortest path derived based on number of equilateral triangles. Since we here focus on how worse, in the extreme case, the length of a shortest path taken by ring-based routing could be, the impact of the last triangle is ignored. Similar strategy will also be used in later analysis.

In the above expansion process, each node can only be expanded to two nodes, which are infinitely close to each other. Expanding a node to three or more such nodes will make a path containing such expanded nodes directly violate *Lemma* 1 and is thus unacceptable. Also, in Fig. 3, it is seen that the distance between original nodes (i.e., those nodes before expansions) should be exactly R (for neighbors) or larger (for non-neighbors). Let's again take a look at a triangle $\triangle A_1 a_1 A_2$ in Fig. 3(a), increasing $\overline{A_1 A_2}$ further will make the triangle unnecessarily cover larger angle or central angle (i.e., $\angle A_1 o A_2$), which would cause length reduction in the worst-case path; in contrast, decreasing $\overline{A_1 A_2}$ to be smaller than R will cause violation of *Lemma* 1 because the distance between the expanded nodes of A_1 and those of A_2 will be shorter than R. This is why equilateral triangle can well characterize the relationship among each group of three original nodes $A_i a_i A_{i+1}$. In Figs. 3(a) and (b), we have seen the power of expanding nodes in such a way for creating long paths. The purpose of such expansion is to maximally slow down the travel along a long slice at each step before proceeding further and it can easily double the worst-case path length at almost no cost.

Let us proceed to consider another extreme case as shown in Fig. 3(c) which may lead to a longer worst-case path than that shown in Fig. 3(a). We first place an equilateral triangle $a_2 A_2 a_1$ with its two vertices $a_1 a_2$ located on the outer circle, then we arrange two additional equilateral triangles, one on each side of $\triangle a_2 A_2 a_1$ with $a_2 A_2$ and $A_2 a_1$ as one edge of them, respectively. We then repeat this pattern as shown in Fig. 3 (c). Intuitively, it looks like dragging the nodes a_1 and a_2 in Fig. 3(a) closer along the outer circle until their distance is reduced to R. Also, it can be easily derived that $A_1 a_1 a_2 A_2$ is an equiangular trapezoid. In Fig. 3(d), we expand each vertex in Fig. 3(c) into two nodes with a distance δ in between like we did in Fig. 3(b). We are again interested in the length of the zigzag path $A'_1 A''_1 a'_1 a''_1 A'_2 A''_2 a'_2 a''_2 \ldots$, and how many equilateral triangles can be tightly arranged in the k-th ring as $\delta \to 0^+$ without violating *Lemma* 1. This is decided by the central angle associated with a triangle, which is the angle $\alpha_2 = \angle A_2 o A_3$ (see Fig. 3(c)). Let y denote the middle point of line segment $\overline{a_1 a_2}$. Note that $\angle o A_2 A_3$ and $\angle o y a_2$ are both right angles, $\overline{o a_2} = kR$, and $\overline{A_2 A_3} = R$. Based on the Pythagorean Theorem, we have

$$\alpha_2 = \tan^{-1} \frac{\overline{A_2 A_3}}{\overline{A_2 o}} = \tan^{-1} \frac{R}{\sqrt{k^2 R^2 - \frac{R^2}{4} - \frac{\sqrt{3}}{2} R}} = \tan^{-1} \frac{2}{\sqrt{4k^2 - 1} - \sqrt{3}}. \tag{7}$$

The number of subgraphs that can be arranged in the annulus in Fig. 3(c) in the worst case, denoted by M_2, is as follows.

$$M_2 = \left\lceil \frac{2\pi}{\alpha_2} \right\rceil \tag{8}$$

So the maximum number of hops of a shortest path (closed tour) on a ring due to the scenario shown in Fig. 3(c) (denoted by N_2) is as follows.

$$N_2 = 4 \times M_2 \tag{9}$$

By comparing (3) and (7), we have the following lemma:

Lemma 2. $\alpha_2 < \alpha_1$, for $\forall k \geq 2$.

Lemma 2 can be easily derived from (3) and (7) by using trigonometry. Following the *Lemma 2*, (6), and (9), we have

$$N_1 \leq N_2(\forall k \geq 2). \tag{10}$$

It is interesting to ask whether N_2 is the length of the shortest path in the worst case. Figure 4 shows another extreme case such that one side of each of the equilateral triangles is parallel to a radius of the ring. Intuitively, it looks like pushing nodes a_1 and a_2 in Fig. 3(a) together until they merge to one node. Figure 4(a) shows how we arrange the equilateral triangles. In Fig. 4(a), A_i, B_i, o, $\forall i$, are on the same line. We group two neighboring equilateral triangles together and called them a subgraph. We are again interested in how many such subgraphs can be embedded into a circular slice without violating *Lemma 1*. In Fig. 4(b), like what we have done in Fig. 3(b), we expand each vertex of the equilateral triangles into two nodes with a distance δ between them[2].

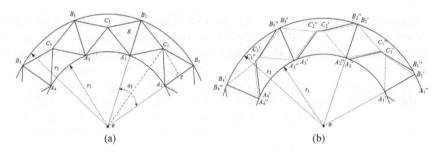

Fig. 4. Cases that equilateral triangles are perpendicular to radius of the ring.

We are interested in the length of path $A_1' A_1'' B_1' B_1'' C_1' C_1'' A_2' A_2'' B_2' B_2'' \ldots \ldots$ when $\delta \to 0+$. Note that in Fig. 4(a), lowering down C_i (even slightly) would cause a violation of *Lemma 1* since the distance between A_i and C_i would be smaller than R; In contrast, moving up a node C_i would unnecessarily increase the central angle $\angle A_{i+1} o A_i$. This is the reason why we choose to use equilateral triangles here. Next, we shall deduce the value of α_3. Note that $\overline{zo} = (k - 0.5)R$, $\overline{C_1 z} = \sqrt{3}R/2$, and $\angle C_1 z o = \pi/2$. Thus, $\angle C_1 o z = \tan^{-1}(\frac{\overline{C_1 z}}{(k-0.5)R}) = \tan^{-1}(\frac{\sqrt{3}}{2k-1})$. We have

---

[2] Actually, in the expansion, B_i' ($\forall i$) should also be put (moved) to the anticlockwise side of line $o A_i''$ with a distance ε = infinitesimal in order to keep $\overline{A_i'' B_i'} \equiv R$ because all the points on inner circle actually do not belong to the current ring under study. Because this extra procedure has no (or negligible) impact on the *asymptotical* performance, we will not discuss its impact later and simply assume o, A_i'', B_i' are on the same line and $\overline{A_i'' B_i'} \equiv R$, $\forall i$.

$$\alpha_3 = \angle C_1 o A_1 + \angle C_1 o A_2 = 2 \times \angle C_1 o z = 2 \times \tan^{-1}\left(\frac{\sqrt{3}}{2k-1}\right). \tag{11}$$

The number of subgraphs that can be arranged along a circular slice in the worst case in Fig. 4(a), denoted by M_3, is as follows.

$$M_3 = \left\lceil \frac{2\pi}{\alpha_3} \right\rceil \tag{12}$$

Thus, the maximum number of hops of a shortest path (closed tour) on a ring due to the scenario shown in Fig. 4(a) (denoted by N_3) is as follows.

$$N_3 = 6 \times M_3 \tag{13}$$

Based on (9), (10), and (13), we have a lower bound on the worst-case length of a shortest path along the k-th ring, denoted by N_{max}^k, as follows.

$$N_{max}^k = max\{N_2, N_3\}. \tag{14}$$

In reality, we may imagine to take a ring tour using quadrilateral style (e.g., squares with side R). Figure 5(a) shows such a case. However, the scenario in Fig. 5(a) will not lead to a longer worst-case path than that due to the previously used strategies because the distance between C_1 and B_2 is smaller than R such that for each square we can only visit three of its four vertices, which makes the resulting path shorter than that due to Fig. 3(a) because the dashed circle in Fig. 3(a) is longer than the inner circle used in Fig. 5(a) for arranging the squares. Or otherwise, we need to separate the squares in a way such that the distance between the closest vertices belonging to neighboring squares is exactly R (see Fig. 5(b)). In this case, a path (tour) can cover all the vertices of each square. However, it can be easily deduced that such a path is still shorter than that shown in Fig. 3(a). Note that the scenario shown in Fig. 4(a) can also be explained as a traversal of a series of identical quadrilaterals if we treat $C_i B_{i+1} C_{i+1} A_{i+1}$ (e.g., $C_1 B_2 C_2 A_2$) as a quadrilateral and in this case, we traverse two sides and a diagonal of it. Furthermore, other regular polygons (e.g., pentagon, hexagon, etc.) are not possible to be embedded into a ring without violating *Lemma* 1 due to the limited ring width if their side length is set to R.

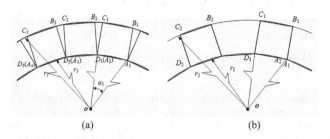

(a)   (b)

Fig. 5. Cases that quadrilaterals are arranged along the inner circle.

Now, we wish to know how close N_{max}^k obtained by using (14) is to the worst-case path length. Regarding this, we have the following. In Figs. 3 and 4, it is seen that the returned path, if excluding the impact of the last triangle (or called subgraph) problem, consists of two types of links, type I has length δ and type II has length R and these two types of links appear alternately on the path. The length of each link belonging to type II needs to be exactly R, or otherwise violation of *Lemma* 1 will be seen when node expansion is done. Accordingly, we have the following. For the two endpoints of an individual link to be expandable, the length of the link must be exactly R, otherwise, violation of *Lemma* 1 will be seen. Then, we have the following.

Observation 1: One way for creating the worst-case path is to identify a longest path consisting of original nodes (i.e., nodes before expansion) while meeting *Lemma* 1 and further keeping the distance between each pair of neighbor nodes on the path is exactly R, and then expand each original node to two nodes as we described earlier. The resulting path will be the worst-case path falling into our interest.

Observation 2: The worst-case shortest path can be obtained due to a number of identical subgraphs due to the isotropic property of a ring, if we ignore the last subgraph problem. Moreover, each subgraph itself should be symmetric with respect to a radius of the ring, in which case no extra distance (penalty) for conjunction of neighboring subgraphs will be introduced; otherwise, extra distance must be taken like the case in Fig. 5(b). For each of the identical subgraphs, we wish to traverse all its vertices (in the anticlockwise direction) along its sides and/or diagonals. Each of the traversed sides/diagonals should have length R for their endpoints to be expandable.

Obviously, all the scenarios shown in Figs. 3, 4, and 5 meet the above observations. Furthermore, using other types of quadrilateral (e.g., parallelogram, trapezoid, except those used in Figs. 3(c) and 4(a)) for guiding the tour would not lead to longer path than that using square (see Fig. 5) or parallelogram (see Fig. 4) since they will either unnecessarily occupy larger angles or not symmetric such that conjunction of neighboring such units will cause unnecessary extra costs. In this sense, we have reached a close lower bound for the longest closed tour using triangles and quadrilateral, while other polygons like pentagon, hexagon, etc., will not lead to worse paths as we discussed earlier. In this sense, we say the N_{max}^k obtained by (14) is a close lower bound on the worst-case path length for a closed shortest tour along a ring.

Result 2: Based on (14), it can be easily known that the base ring, in the best case, contains 7 hops and, in the worst case, it can contain at least 36 hops.

The base ring is a shortest cycled path on the 2nd ring. Based on the results in Table 1, we can know that the base ring, in the best case, can contain 7 hops. Based on (9), $N_2 = 36$, and based on (14), $N_3 = 36$. Thus, based on (14), the worst-case length of the base ring is lower bounded by 36 hops. However, as k exceeds a certain threshold, a worst-case path due to (9) will be longer than that due to (13). Specifically, when $k = 3$, $N_{max}^k = \max\{N_2, N_3\} = \max\{64, 60\} = 64$; when $k = 4$, $N_{max}^k = \max\{N_2, N_3\} = \max\{84, 78\} = 84$. As k increases further, the gap between N_2 and N_3 will keep increasing.

References

1. Yu, S., Zhang, B., Yao, Z., Li, C.: R3: a lightweight reactive ring based routing protocol for wireless sensor networks with mobile sinks. KSII Trans. Internet Inf. Syst. **10**(12), 5442–5463 (2016)
2. Wang, G., Wang, T., et al.: Adaptive location updates for mobile sinks in wireless sensor networks. J. Supercomput. **47**(2), 127–145 (2009)
3. Yu, F., Park, S., et al.: Elastic routing: a novel geographic routing for mobile sinks in wireless sensor networks. IET Commun. **4**(6), 716–727 (2010)
4. Zhao, Z., Zhang, B., et al.: Providing scalable location service in wireless sensor networks with mobile sinks. IET Commun. **3**(10), 1628–1637 (2009)
5. Yan, Y., Zhang, B., et al.: Hierarchical location service for wireless sensor networks with mobile sinks. Wirel. Commun. Mob. Comput. **10**(7), 899–911 (2010)
6. Tian, K. Zhang, B., et al.: Data gathering protocols for wireless sensor networks with mobile sinks. In: Proceedings of IEEE GLOBECOM 2010, pp. 1–6. IEEE Press, Miami, FL (2010)
7. Shi, L., Yao, Z., Zhang, B., Li, C., et al.: An efficient distributed routing protocol for wireless sensor networks with mobile sinks. Int. J. Commun. Syst. **28**(11), 1789–1804 (2015)
8. Shi, L., Zhang, B., et al.: An efficient multi-stage data routing protocol for wireless sensor networks with mobile sinks. In: Proceedings of IEEE Globecom 2011, pp. 1–5, Houston, TX (2011)
9. Shi, L., Zhang, B., et al.: DDRP: an efficient data-driven routing protocol for wireless sensor networks with mobile sinks. Int. J. Commun. Syst. **26**(10), 1341–1355 (2013)

Energy Efficient Based Splitting for MPTCP in Heterogeneous Networks

Huanxi Cui[1]([✉]), Xin Su[2], Jie Zeng[2], and Bei Liu[2]

[1] Broadband Wireless Access Laboratory,
Chongqing University of Posts and Telecommunications, Chongqing, China
haoxuan_c@mail.tsinghua.edu.cn
[2] Beijing National Research Center for Information Science and Technology
(Abbreviation: BNRist), Tsinghua University, Beijing, China
{suxin,zengjie,liubei}@mail.tsinghua.edu.cn

Abstract. This paper models a theoretical framework of energy efficiency concurrent multipath transfer based on MPTCP. An optimal energy efficient splitting way was proposed. By exploring the theoretical relationship between transmission rate and energy efficiency, a multinetwork concurrent multipath transmission energy efficiency optimization model is developed. For downlink and concurrent transmission scenarios in heterogeneous wireless networks, the relationship between different network channel states, energy consumption and transmission rate is studied. In order to ensure that the data leave the send queue within a limited time, the Lyapunov optimization method is used in this paper, and then obtained an optimal splitting strategy.

Keywords: Energy efficiency · Lyapunov optimization
Concurrent multi-path transfer · MPTCP

1 Introduction

With the rise of various high-speed transmission business, the demand for transmission rate is increasing, and the fifth generation mobile communication system has proposed the grand goal of increasing the network capacity by 1000 times. To solve these problems, the concurrent transmission was proposed. The multi-path transmite control protocol (MPTCP) [6] and stream control transport protocol (SCTP) [7], [8] based concurrent multi-path transfer (CMT-SCTP) [8] support communication between datacenter and users with a variety of sub-flows under a single connection session. But, MPTCP is easy to be deployed with its readily to TCP. Now, these works mainly care for the problem and some schemes such as retransmission mechanism [9], path management schemes [10], subflow assigning

Supported by the National S&T Major Project (No. 2016ZX03001017), Science and Technology Program of Beijing (No. D171100006317002) and the Ministry of Education and China Mobile Joint Scientific Research Fund (Grant No. MCM20160105).

J. Zheng et al. (Eds.): ADHOCNETS 2018, LNICST 258, pp. 105–114, 2019.
https://doi.org/10.1007/978-3-030-05888-3_10

algorithms [11], NC based deliver decision [12,13] and rate control algorithms [14] have been discussed.

Neverthless, concurrent multi-path transfer familiarly consumes more energy to remain these interfaces alive. Therefore, an optimal energy efficiency splitting scheme was proposed.

The next, this context is stated as follows. In Sect. 2, the system model was described. We present the problem formulation in Sect. 3. In Sect. 4, We derive the energy-efficiency maximum algorithm via Lyapunov optimization. Section 5, we study the performance of the algorithm. In Sect. 6, we run a simulation of the algorihm. We conclude this context and present later study directions in Sect. 7.

2   System Model Describetion and Derivation

The destination of the presentation scheme is to ensure high quality multipath deliver in a manner that maximizes energy efficient on the downlink side of the network. In the section, w'll present an overview of multipath communication systems MPTCP-based and transmitter energy models.

We consider multi-connection transmission based on MPTCP. Figure 1 shows the communication model. The request data from the internet are forwarded to many wireless networks through many paths. The user equipped with MPTCP are connected to the Internet via HetNets consisting of a lot of radio access technologies (RATs) such as IEEE802.16, 4G, 3G, WiMAX, and the like. The path can access the RAT and be out of line with other paths. The channel bandwidth, channel gain, noise power and transmit power was expressed by $B = \{B_1, B, \ldots, B_N\}$, $G = \{g_1, g_2, \ldots, g_N\}$, $\sigma^2 = \{N_0, N_0, \ldots, N_0\}$, $P = \{P_1, P_2, \ldots, P_N\}$, respectively.

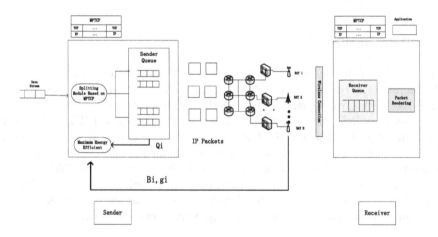

Fig. 1. System model

According to the Shannon formula, the capacity of any access network is:

$$R_i = B_i log_2(1 + \frac{g_i P_i}{B_i N_0})$$ (1)

Consequently, we can obtain the transmite power.

$$P_i = \frac{N_0 B_i}{g_i}(2^{\frac{R_i}{B_i}} - 1)$$ (2)

The energy efficiency maximization goal can be derivated as

$$max \quad \eta_e = \frac{\sum_i^N R_i}{\sum_j^N P_j(R_j)} = \frac{R_{req}}{\sum_i^N \frac{N_0 B_i}{g_i}(2^{\frac{R_i}{B_i}} - 1) + P_i^{cst}}$$ (3)

$$s.t. \quad C1 : R_i \geq 0$$ (4)

$$C2 : \sum_i^N R_i = R_{req},$$ (5)

where P_i^{cst} is the static power, and R_{req} is the request data rate. However, this is a non-convex problem (see proof in [5]). The method of convex optimization can not be used directly. The Genetic Algorithm(GA) was used to search for the optimal solution in [5], but the complexity is too high. Consequently, we will simplify this issue.

When the request rate is constant, maximizing energy efficiency can be equivalent to minimizing power consumption. We consider the concurrent transmission of the downlink, and the static power consumption is not what we care about. In this paper, we treat it as a constant, so the original optimization problem can be equivalent to be write the following problem.

$$P1: \quad min \quad \sum_i^N \frac{N_0 B_i}{g_i}(2^{\frac{R_i}{B_i}} - 1)$$ (6)

$$s.t. \quad C1 : R_i \geq 0$$ (7)

$$C2 : \sum_i^N R_i = R_{req}$$ (8)

3   Probelm Formulation

To ensure that all arriving data leave the buffer for a limited time, we introduced the idea of queue-steady. In order to maximize energy-efficient transmission, the system tends to assign more link and energy to users with better link state. However, for users with poor link states, the queue size may increase indefinitely, resulting in a large number of packet delays, which may cause severe data out-of-order. In fact, this is a trade-off between latency and power. The data queue is expressed as follows.

$$Q_i(t + 1) = max\{Q_i(t) - R_i(t) + A_i(t), 0\}$$ (9)

The $Q_i(t)$, $A_i(t)$, $R_i(t)$ are the queue size, arrival rate, and service rate, respectively. The strong stability of the queue [5] satisfies the following relationship.

$$\overline{Q_i(t)} = \lim_{t \to \infty} \frac{1}{t} \sum_{\tau=0}^{t-1} \{|Q_i(\tau)|\} < \infty \tag{10}$$

The original optimization problem can be derived from P1 as follows.

$$P2: \quad min \quad \sum_i^N \frac{N_0 B_i}{g_i} (2^{\frac{R_i}{B_i}} - 1) \tag{11}$$

$$s.t. \quad C1: R_i \geq 0 \tag{12}$$

$$C2: \sum_i^N R_i = R_{req} \tag{13}$$

$$C3: \overline{Q_i(t)} = \lim_{t \to \infty} \frac{1}{t} \sum_{\tau=0}^{t-1} \{|Q_i(\tau)|\} < \infty \tag{14}$$

4 An Energy-Efficiency Maximum Algorithm via Lyapunov Optimazation

This paper use the drift-plus-penalty (DPP) algorithm proposed in [1] to solve this optimization problem. According to [1], we can write the Lyapunov function as follows.

$$L(\boldsymbol{Q}(t)) = \sum_i Q_i^2(t) \tag{15}$$

where, the $\boldsymbol{Q}(t) = \{Q_1(t), Q_2(t), \ldots, Q_N(t)\}$. The conditional Lyapunov offset in unit time can be written as follows.

$$\Delta(\boldsymbol{Q}(t)) = L(\boldsymbol{Q}(t+1)) - L(\boldsymbol{Q}(t)) \tag{16}$$

The above problems can be described by

$$VP(t) + \Delta(\boldsymbol{Q}(t)) \tag{17}$$

where $P(t) = \sum_i^N \frac{N_0 B_i}{g_i} (2^{\frac{R_i}{B_i}} - 1)$ and V is a control parameters

Lemma 1. *Suppose that the link is independently and equally distributed (i.i.d) in each time slot. Under any splitting algorithm, $\forall V \geq 0$, and $\forall Q(t) \geq 0$, the DPP subject to the following relationships.*

$$\begin{aligned} VP(t) + \Delta(\boldsymbol{Q}(t)) \\ \leq \Im + VP(t) \\ + \sum_i^N Q_i(t)(A_i(t) - R_i(t)) \end{aligned} \tag{18}$$

where $\Im$ is more than zero, subject to for all t

$$\Im \geq \sum_i^N (A_i(t)^2 + R_i(t)^2).\tag{19}$$

Proof of Lemma 1 reference [4].

In order to minimize P2, a traffic offload scheme is presented to minimize DPP terms of P3. Therefore, we can minimize the upper bound in (18) subject to the same conditions of C1-C2 besides the C3 by the optimization theory. And then, the problem P3 can be exoressed by

$$P3: \quad min \quad V\sum_i^N P_i - \sum_i^N Q_i R_i \tag{20}$$

$$s.t. \quad C1 : R_i \geq 0 \tag{21}$$

$$C2 : \sum_i^N R_i = R_{req} \tag{22}$$

Obviously, this problem is a convex optimization problem, which is proved as follows. The second order partial derivatives of $P3(R)$ can be written as (23) and (24).

$$\frac{\partial^2 P3(R)}{\partial R_i^2} = ln^2 2 \frac{N_0}{B_i g_i} 2^{\frac{R_i}{B_i}} \tag{23}$$

$$\frac{\partial^2 P3(R)}{\partial R_i R_j} = \frac{\partial^2 P3(R)}{\partial R_j R_i} = 0 \tag{24}$$

So, the Hessian Matrix of (20) that is constructed of the second order partial derivatives of $P3(R)$ could be written as (25).

$$\boldsymbol{H} = \begin{pmatrix} ln^2 2 \frac{N_0}{B_1 \cdot g_1} 2^{\frac{R_1}{B_1}} & 0 \dots & 0 \\ 0 & ln^2 2 \frac{N_0}{B_2 \cdot g_2} 2^{\frac{R_2}{B_2}} & \dots 0 \\ \dots & & \\ 0 & 0 \dots & ln^2 2 \frac{N_0}{B_N \cdot g_N} 2^{\frac{R_N}{B_N}} \end{pmatrix} \tag{25}$$

Letting the $\boldsymbol{x}$ is the non-zero vector, we can obtain the formula as follows.

$$\boldsymbol{x}^T \boldsymbol{H} \boldsymbol{x} > 0 \tag{26}$$

Its value is always greater than zero, and the convexity can be guaranteed. Here, the convex optimization theory can be used to resolve the object issue and the optimal rate of N networks joining the concurrent transmission network can be solved. Therefore, we can use the gradient descent algorithm to find the optimal solution. The raised algorithm can be detailly presented in Algorithm 1.

Algorithm 1. Optimal splitting stratergy base on Armijio Rute algorithm

Require:
1: Initialize P_i, N_0 and R_i, B_i, Q_i.
2: Initialize capacity, denoted as $C_i = \{C_1, C_2, \ldots C_N\}$
3: Initialize rate for RAT, $\left\{R_1^{(0)}, R_2^{(0)}, \ldots R_N^{(0)}\right\}$. Initialize values of each dual variables, $\alpha_i^{(0)}, b_i^{(0)} \in \text{dom} N$.
4: **while** $\left|f_l^{(k+1)} - f_l^{(k)}\right| \leq \eta$ **do**
5:     **for** $i = 1 : N$ **do**
6:         Calculate the direction of dual variables. $\Delta\alpha_i^{(k)} = -\frac{\partial f_l}{\partial \alpha_i}$, $\Delta b_i^{(k)} = -\frac{\partial f_l}{\partial b_i}$
7:         Select the step size of dual varibles by gradient descent.
8:         The f_l is calculated from (27) updated dual variables
9:     **end for**
10: **end while**
Ensure:
11: Output the optimal rate allocation set $\{R_1^*, R_2^*, \ldots R_N^*\}$ and optimal splitting stratergy according to the (34).

For the aforementioned problem, the Lagrangian function can be presented by.

$$f_l(R, \alpha, b)$$

$$= V\sum_i^N P_i - \sum_i^N Q_i R_i + \alpha' * g(R) + b * h(R) \tag{27}$$

$$= V\sum_i^N \frac{N_0 B_i}{g_i}(2^{\frac{R_i}{B_i}} - 1) - \sum_i^N Q_i R_i + \alpha' * g(R) + b * h(R)$$

where

$$g_i = -R_i \tag{28}$$

$$h(R) = \sum_i^N R_i - R_{req} \tag{29}$$

We can write Karush-Kuhn-Tucker (KKT) conditions as follows.

$$\frac{\partial f_l(R, \alpha, b)}{\partial R_i} = \frac{N_0}{g_i}(2^{\frac{R_i}{B_i}} - 1)ln2 - Q_i - \alpha_i + b = 0 \tag{30}$$

$$h(R) = 0 \tag{31}$$

$$\sum_i^N \alpha_i g(R_i) = 0 \tag{32}$$

So

$$\frac{\partial f_l(R)}{\partial R_1}|R_1^* = \frac{\partial f_l(R)}{\partial R_2}|R_2^* = \ldots = \frac{\partial f_l(R)}{\partial R_N}|R_N^* \tag{33}$$

We can obtain the optimal rate R_i^* with the set $R^* = \{R_1^*, R_2^*, \ldots, R_N^*\}$.
For access network RAT_i, letting the splitting ratio as follows.

$$\phi_i = \frac{R_i^*}{\sum_i^N R_i^*} \tag{34}$$

The result of the object issue is the splitting vector consisting of the splitting factors of all sub-flows in R.

5   Performance Analysis

Theorem 1. *If the link state is i.i.d on each slot, then, we have the relationships about the average power and queue backlogg as follows.*

$$\overline{P} \leq \frac{\Im}{V} + \overline{P^*} \tag{35}$$

$$\overline{Q} \leq \frac{\Im + V\overline{P^*}}{\epsilon} \tag{36}$$

where ϵ is a small positive value.

Theorem 1 describes a trade-off of $[O(1/V), O(V)]$ between power consumption and data backlogg (i.e., latency). As increasing control parameter V, the power consumption can tend to the upper bound, however, the transmission latency remains increasing by (35) and (36). Proof sees the context [4].

6   Simulation

See (Table 1).

Table 1. The simulation parameters.

Network	RAT_1	RAT_2	RAT_3	RAT_4
Bandwidth (B/KHz)	220	240	280	320
Channel gain (g)	0.008	0.007	0.006	0.005
Queue length (Q, k = 1:50)	500*k	700*k	900*k	1000*k
Control parameters (V)	1–200	1–200	1–200	1–200

6.1   Impact of Request Rate (R_{req}) on Energy Efficiency ($V = 75$)

Figure 2 presents that the request rate is small, the energy efficiency of a single network operator is similar to the algorithm of this paper, and it will be higher under a certain threshold. With the increase of user request rate, the energy efficiency of single network operator declines rapidly. This is explained by the fact that the system has reached its ultimate capacity. Increasing the transmission power does not increase the transmission rate of the system. On the contrary, it will cause more interference to nearby users.

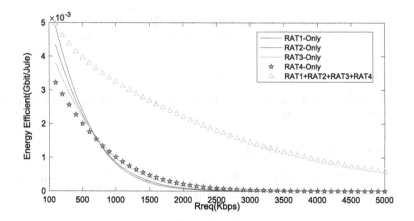

Fig. 2. Energy efficiency changes with the request rate

6.2   Effect of Control Parameter V on Energy Efficiency

Figure 3 shows that we can strike a balance between power and latency. For example, if the network controller selects $0 \; leV \; le20$, the before algorithm is better than splitting. In particular, the proposed algorithm can increase the energy efficienct of our way with the same traffic latency.

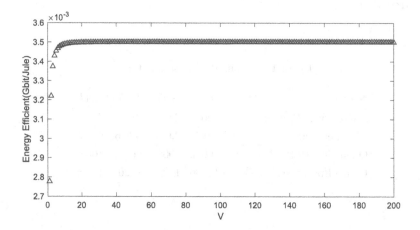

Fig. 3. Energy efficiency changes with the control parameters V

6.3   The Effect of Average Queue Length on Energy Efficiency

Figure 4 displays that the longer the queue, the lower the energy efficienct of the system will be. When the request capacity is a constant, the longer the queue,

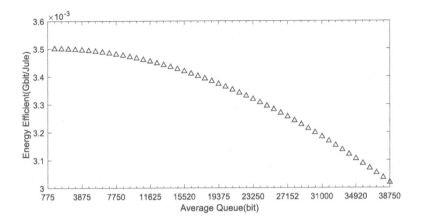

Fig. 4. Energy efficiency changes with the average queue

the longer the time of the packet will leave the send buffer. After the maximum time limit, packet loss and out-of-order will occur. At this time, the receiver will require retransmission, resulting in increasing energy consumption and reducing energy efficiency.

7   Conclusions

In this paper, a concurrent multipath transfer traffic splitting strategy based on energy efficiency maximum is proposed, and Lyapunov optimization method is utilized to obtain the optimal splitting ratio. Through simulation, we know that while guaranteeing the transmission rate requested by the user, it can effectively improve energy efficient of the system, reduce the power consumption of the system, and decrease the transmite delay of the data. The essence of the algorithm in this paper is to make a trade-off between delay and power. In line with the concept of green communication proposed by the fifth generation mobile communication. In the future, we will consider using random geometric methods to partition the interference. It is not necessary to ensure the QoS of the requesting user but also the QoS of the user under the access network that joins concurrent transmission network.

References

1. Cao, Y., et al.: A LDDoS-aware energy-efficient multipathing scheme for mobile cloud computing systems. IEEE Access **5**(99), 21862–21872 (2017)
2. Wang, W., et al.: Beamforming design for energy-constrained full-duplex two-way relaying system. J. Commun. (2018)
3. Ma, X., Sheng, M., Zhang, Y., Xijun, W., Chao, X.: Concurrent transmission for energy efficiency of user equipment in 5G wireless communication networks. Sci. China Inf. Sci. **59**, 1 (2016). https://doi.org/10.1007/s11432-015-5507-3d

4. Gu, Y., Wang, Y., Cui, Q.: A stochastic optimization framework for adaptive spectrum access and power allocation in licensed-assisted access networks. IEEE Access **5**, 16484–16494 (2017)
5. Wang, W., Wang, X., Wang, D.: Energy efficient congestion control for multipath TCP in heterogeneous networks. IEEE Access **6**, 2889–2898 (2018)
6. Peng, Q., et al.: Multipath TCP: analysis, design, and implementation. IEEE/ACM Trans. Netw. **24**(1), 596–609 (2016)
7. Sarwar, G., et al.: eCMT-SCTP: improving performance of multipath SCTP with erasure coding over lossy links, pp. 476–483 (2013)
8. Verma, L.P., Sharma, V.K., Kumar, M.: New delay-based fast retransmission policy for CMT-SCTP. Int. J. Intell. Syst. Appl. **10**, 3 (2018)
9. Xue, K., et al.: DPSAF: forward prediction based dynamic packet scheduling and adjusting with feedback for multipath TCP in lossy heterogeneous networks. IEEE Trans. Veh. Technol. **67**(2), 1521–1534 (2018)
10. Trivedi, P., Singh, A.: Stochastic multi-path routing problem with non-stationary rewards, pp. 1707–1712 (2018)
11. Low, S.H.: A duality model of TCP and queue management algorithms. IEEE/ACM Trans. Netw. **11**(4), 525–36 (2003)
12. Arianpoo, N., Aydin, I., Leung, V.C.M.: Network coding as a performance booster for concurrent multi-path transfer of data in multi-hop wireless networks. IEEE Trans. Mob. Comput. **16**(4), 1047–1058 (2017)
13. Aslam, M.A., Hassan, S.A.: Analysis of linear network coding in cooperative multi-hop networks. Wirel. Pers. Commun. **8**, 1–15 (2017)
14. Liu, J., et al.: Joint congestion control and routing optimization: an efficient second-order distributed approach. IEEE/ACM Trans. Netw. **24**(3), 1404–1420 (2016)

RPMA Low-Power Wide-Area Network Planning Method Basing on Data Mining

Yao Shen, Xiaorong Zhu[✉], and Yue Wang

College of Telecommunication and Information Engineering,
Nanjing University of Posts and Telecommunications, Nanjing 210003, China
xrzhu@njupt.edu.cn

Abstract. A network planning method based on data mining was proposed for Random Phase Multiple Access (RPMA) low-power wide-area network (LPWAN) with large density of base stations and uneven traffic distribution. First, a signal quality prediction model was established by using the boosting regression trees algorithm, which was used to extract the coverage distribution spacial pattern of the network. Then, the weighted K-centroids clustering algorithm was utilized to obtain the optimal base station deployment for the current spacial pattern. Finally, according to the total objective function, the best base station topology was determined. Experimental results with the real data sets show that compared with the traditional network planning method, the proposed method can improve the coverage of low-power wide-area networks.

Keywords: Low power wide area network · Boosting regression trees
Weighted K-centroids · Base station deployment

1 Introduction

With the rapid development of the Internet of things, the number of interconnected devices will be expected to increase to 50 billion, and the traffic volume will increase by more than a thousand times [1]. Traditional short-range wireless technologies and cellular network technologies cannot meet the diversified IoT traffic requirements. Therefore, a new communication pattern, Low Power Wide Area Network (LPWAN) [2]. LPWAN [3] mainly includes NB-IoT, LORA, RPMA and other wireless communication technologies, which can support a large number of devices to access the network. Specially, RPMA can support 60x to 1300x more endpoints for a given network relative to Sigfox and LORA. Moreover, compared with their defect in capacity scalability, PRMA leverages a Time Division Duplex (TDD) approach to provide huge capacity. So, PRMA is a radically new technology with many performance benefits, which is worth studying.

However, for LPWAN such as RPMA, the large density of base station, 2–3 km coverage distance and uneven traffic distribution [4] make the deployment of base stations difficult. Therefore, LPWAN network planning has a great challenge. It should be properly deployed and optimized to improve the network service quality according to its own characteristics. For LPWAN network planning, base station deployment determines the overall performance of the network. However, the determination of the

J. Zheng et al. (Eds.): ADHOCNETS 2018, LNICST 258, pp. 115–125, 2019.
https://doi.org/10.1007/978-3-030-05888-3_11

base station site is a NP-hard problem. It is not scientific to use the traditional location model to analyze the various factors of the site problem, which may lead to the dimension catastrophe of the variables and constraints in the model. In addition, for network planning, when the coverage is considered, the traffic distribution also need to be concerned, where spatio-temporal characteristics need to be addressed and integrated, which makes the problem more complex and designing a reasonable network planning scheme more important.

Now, a lot of researches have been done in network planning. Wang et al. [5] developed an approximation algorithm to address the budgeted base station planning problem in Het Nets, where they aimed to maximize the traffic demand points number with a given budget. Ghazzai et al. [6] proposed an optimal LTE wireless planning method to determine the minimum number and the optimal location of base stations under the constraints of cell coverage and capacity. For network planning, besides the number and location of base stations, energy efficiency is also an important target. So Yang et al. [7] aimed to establish a mathematical model to minimize power consumption for LTE cell planning. Wang et al. [8] employed a cutting-edge territory division to deal with the cell planning problem in Het Nets with the use of load balancing, based on the goal to guarantee users QoS and seamless coverage. The method can reduce the total deployment cost and improve the system performance. The above schemes are mainly for cellular network planning. For LPWAN, most of them survey on its technology, and no reasonable planning scheme has yet been proposed. What's more, the proposed network planning methods were based on a large number of assumptions, which have limitations in application. An effective planning method to quickly plan and deploy a large number of base stations has not fundamentally proposed.

To solve the above problems, big data analytics are combined with network planning in this paper, based on the application of LPWAN in communication system. The paper transforms the base station location problem from the traditional model-driven to data-driven, with massive data as the main analysis line, which overcomes the shortcomings of the traditional network planning model and combines the clustering algorithm to explore a data-driven base station location method so as to improve the level of rationalization of the site selection.

2   System Model

RPMA was design to provide a secure, large coverage footprint with tremendous capacity and low-power connectivity in the global 2.4 GHz band. It is the ideal technology to build a public network to connect many billions of devices for both Brown Field applications, and the even more exciting Green Field applications.

According to the characteristics of RPMA network, a novel network planning method based on data mining is presented in this paper, as shown in Fig. 1. Firstly, considering the coverage objective of network planning, the measured data of RPMA network are collected. Based on the network planning knowledge database, preliminary cleaning and analysis of measured data are required by removing attributes with many repeated and default values to improve the quality of the data, which make them more suitable for specific data mining methods. Through the analysis, we need determine the characteristics that affect the quality of signal coverage and save the analysis results in the knowledge base. Then, with the goal of minimizing the loss function, a signal quality prediction model is trained by inputting the above data into the boosting regression trees model for predicting the network coverage under the current base station deployment. According to the obtained network coverage, by extracting the coverage weight value, we employ the weighted K-centroids clustering algorithm with the location data of base station and test points to achieve the base station deployment that adapts to the current coverage. Finally, we set the total planning objective function to decide whether it is the best base station topology.

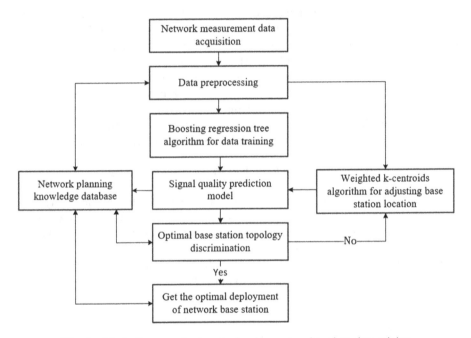

Fig. 1. Block diagram of network planning system based on data mining

3   Signal Quality Prediction Model

As shown in Fig. 1, we focus on the optimization of the coverage blind area and the weak coverage area, by analyzing the weak coverage problem in the wireless network, and adjust the location of base stations according to the network coverage, so that the adjusted base station topology can meet the required coverage effect. Generally, regional weak coverage is mainly caused by insufficient received signal strength, and the specific factors are involved in three aspects: (1) The factors affecting the coverage at base station, such as transmitting power, antenna azimuth, antenna height, antenna gain, etc.; (2) The factors of signal transmission path, such as path loss and shadow fading caused by obstruction; (3)The influence of interference on coverage, such as co-channel interference in the overlapped areas of multiple adjacent base stations, and multipath interference caused by the surface reflections of buildings and mountains to the radio reflection.

All in all, the received signal quality at a certain location in the network is basically related to the three factors, which is the result of combining these factors. Therefore, we consider the mapping relationship between the signal quality and these factors in this paper, that is, to predict the quality of the signal, which is used to assist the final site location of base stations.

3.1 Data Feature Selection

First, we need to carry out preliminary cleaning and analysis of the data by removing the attributes with many repetitions and default values, such as UL Per, Network State and so on. For Deploy Region, latitude and longitude are considered to represent the location difference characteristics of base stations, so it can be eliminated. In addition, combined with the above coverage factors, the irrelevant attributes such as Last Connect Time and Last Connect Address are eliminated. Finally, base station location B_loc (including latitude and longitude), base station height $B\_alt,$ base station power B_power, antenna height A_height, and terminal location P_loc (including latitude and longitude) are selected as input features. The features are integrated into a record:

$$x_k = B\_loc_k, B\_alt_k, B\_power_k, A\_height_k, P\_loc_k \qquad (1)$$

The set of these records serves as the training dataset for the signal quality prediction model. Since RPMA network employs power control, the uplink received signal strength is always near the reception sensitivity, so the terminal downlink received RSSI is used as an indicator for measuring signal quality, that is, the output variable. The process of establishing wireless network data model is to find the mapping function f between them by training existing data sets:

$$y_k = f(x_k) \qquad (2)$$

The value y_k is the predicted signal quality value under given input characteristic variables x_k.

3.2 The Establishment of Signal Prediction Model

In this paper, we use the boosting regression trees algorithm [9] to construct the above function. Boosting Regression Trees (BRT) algorithm completes the learning task together by integrating multiple base learners–decision trees, which is one of ensemble Learning methods. Compared with the single regression algorithms, such as linear regression and logistic regression, BRT algorithm has better generalization performance by integrating multiple decision trees, thereby improving the prediction accuracy of the model. In addition, BRT algorithm can automatically fit the interaction of independent variables and is less prone to overfitting, so the generalization error is lower. The BRT model can be given by the addition model of M decision trees:

$$f_M(x) = \sum_{m=1}^{M} T(x; \gamma_m) \tag{3}$$

Each tree is given by:

$$T(x; \gamma) = \sum_{j=1}^{J} c_j I(x \in R_j) \tag{4}$$

where $\gamma = \{(R_1, c_1), (R_2, c_2), \ldots, (R_J, c_J)\}$ represent the divided areas $R_1, R_2, \ldots, R_J$ of each tree on the input variable set and the constants $c_1, c_2, \ldots, c_J$ on the corresponding area, J is the number of the leaf nodes of the decision tree.

BRT adopts the forward stepwise algorithm to learn each decision tree from the front to the back, that is, learning parameters of each tree by optimizing the following loss function:

$$\hat{\gamma} = \arg \min_{\gamma_m} \sum_{i=1}^{N} L(y_i, f_{m-1}(x_i) + T(x_i; \gamma_m)) \tag{5}$$

In which the loss function is square error, which is the squared sum of the difference between the predicted value and the actual value of the sample:

$$L(y_i, f_{m-1}(x_i) + T(x_i; \gamma_m)) = (y_i - f_{m-1}(x_i) - T(x_i; \gamma_m))^2 \tag{6}$$

Where $e_m = y_i - f_{m-1}(x_i)$ means the residuals of the data fitted by the current model. Therefore, BRT algorithm is used to solve the regression problem, which only needs to fit the residual of each model. The specific algorithm process is shown as follows:

(1) Set $f_0(x) = 0$.
(2) For m = 1,2,...,M:
   a. Calculate the residuals of the current model:

$$e_m = y_i - f_{m-1}(x_i), i = 1, 2, \ldots, M$$

   b. Fit the residuals to learn a regression tree $T(x; \gamma_m)$ and update

$$f_m(x) = f_{m-1}(x) + T(x; \gamma_m)$$

(3) Get the BRT model of the problem:

$$f_M(x) = \sum_{m=1}^{M} T(x; \gamma_m)$$

4   Position Adjustment of Base Station

Typical K-means algorithm partitions the data set $X = \{x_1, x_2 ..., x_n\}$ with n points into K clusters according to the set distance similarity, and the cluster set is expressed by $C = \{c_1, c_2, ..., c_k\}$. Generally, the Euclidean distance is used as a similarity measure between two points, and data points are divided into the nearest clusters.

In typical K-means algorithm, each data point has same importance for locating the location of the cluster center. However, we treat the base station position selection as a weighted problem based on coverage distribution spatial patterns in this paper, which means that each point in the space no longer has an equivalent impact on cluster centers. A weight is introduced to measure influence degree of each point on the base station position, and a weighted K-centroids algorithm is proposed.

The input of this algorithm includes n terminal data point set $P = \{p_1, p_2, ..., p_n\}$ and initial base station positions $B = \{b_1, b_2, ..., b_k\}$. Planning network based on the existing base station site, the current sites and the number of base stations can be used as the initialization parameter of the algorithm, that is, the initialization centers and the number of clusters. In this algorithm, normalized distance is used to determine which cluster the data points belong to, which is called the membership function [10]:

$$f(b_j|p_i) = \frac{\|p_i - b_j\|^2}{\sum\limits_{j=1}^{k} \|p_i - b_j\|^2} \qquad (7)$$

After all data points are assigned, the location of base station is adjusted iteratively in the algorithm, which is mainly considered from distance influence and coverage weight. For distance influence, compared to the terminals close to the base station with smaller distance influence, the terminal signals far from the base station may be worse, which is due to obstructions from buildings and path loss of signal propagation, so forane terminals have a greater distance influence on base station. We employ the above membership function $f(b_j|p_i)$ to measure the distance influence. For coverage weight, the optimization of base station location aims to ensure that the received signal of the terminal within the coverage of the base station can be as good as possible, so we are concerned with the terminal with poor coverage and give it a greater impact weight on the location adjustment of the base station. According to the coverage spatial pattern obtained in the previous stage, a corresponding weight $w(p_i)$ is generated for each data point. With $f(b_j|p_i)$ and $w(p_i)$, the iterative formula for each base station location is given by:

$$b_j = \frac{\sum\limits_{i=1}^{n} f(b_j|p_i) w(p_i) p_i}{\sum\limits_{i=1}^{n} f(b_j|p_i) w(p_i)} \qquad (8)$$

The weighted K-centroids algorithm process is shown as follows:

(1) Use the location and number of existing base stations as the initial cluster center locations and cluster number;
(2) By membership function $f(b_j|p_i)$, each data point p_i is assigned to the cluster where its nearest base station b_j is located;
(3) Adjust each base station location b_j with the membership function $f(b_j|p_i)$ and spatial pattern weight $w(p_i)$;
(4) Repeat steps (2) and (3) until b_j no longer changes.

The network topology obtained by the weighted K-centroids algorithm has been optimized for the current network coverage, but it is not necessarily the final optimal result. It still needs to carry on coverage prediction analysis and optimize base station positions again based on the analysis results. Until the following total objective function is met, an optimal network topology is finally obtained.

The total objective function of the entire planning process:

$$\min \sum_{i \in \{i|y_i \leq \bar{y}\}} (y_i - \bar{y})^2 \tag{9}$$

Where y_i represents the coverage strength RSSI predicted by the BRT algorithm at some point, $\bar{y}$ is a theoretically good signal coverage threshold to meet the coverage standard, and $i \in \{i|y_i \leq \bar{y}\}$ represent test points with signal quality values below the threshold in the area, which means that the signal coverage of the test point is poor. The least square error of the two is used as the objective function for the iteration termination of the entire planning process.

5 Simulation Analysis and Performance Evaluation

The experimental data is derived from the real measured data of 37 RPMA network and drive test data of 131454 test points after data cleaning, including base station basic information data, terminal test point data and corresponding geographic location data. The data is used to verify the feasibility of the proposed method for optimal base station deployment, and the experimental results are visible with python matplotlib tools.

5.1 Result and Analysis of Signal Prediction Model

Before applying the BRT algorithm, three parameters need to be determined to adjust its learning process. The first is the number of base learners. With the increase of its number, the BRT algorithm on training data may be improved. However, the number of base learners exceeds a certain value, which may cause over-fitting. The second is the size of the base learner, which represents the degree of interaction between multiple features captured by the BRT model, and the depth of the tree is used to control the size of the base learner. For the selection of the two parameters, GridSearchCV grid tracking method in sklearn is used in this paper, which can traverse multiple combinations of parameter values that need to be optimized according to the given data set through cross validation until the optimum parameters are obtained. The number of base learners is 530, and the depth of trees is 11 in this paper. Finally, in order to prevent over-fitting on training data, the regularization factor (i.e., learning rate) is introduced to measure the impact of each base learner on the final result. This value is set to a smaller constant below 0.1, which is set to 0.1 in this paper.

Then, 85% of the dataset is selected as the training data set, and 15% is the test data set. The horizontal axis in Fig. 2 represents the number of iterations (i.e., the number of basic learners), the vertical axis represents loss error values, and two lines represent test errors and training errors of each iteration respectively. It is found that the training error and the test error are gradually decrease with the increase of the number of iterations, which indicates that the fitting effect on the data sets increases gradually with the increase of the number of iterations. The test shows that the test error is higher than the training error due to the difference between the test set and the training set, which makes the learning ability of the model on the unknown data set weaker than the original training data set and is a normal phenomenon. In addition, the trend of the two curves also indicates that the parameters obtained by GridSearchCV are appropriate.

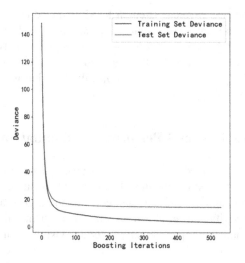

Fig. 2. Relationship between loss error and number of base learners

5.2   Determination of Optimal Base Station Deployment

The left of Fig. 3 shows the collected initial base station locations and test point distributions. The base station location is marked with a blue star point, and the dot marks the test point location. The color depth of the dot represents the RSSI value. The darker the red is, the lower the RSSI value is, and the worse the signal coverage is. It shows that there are still many weak coverage areas in the initial base station deployment. The RSSI unit in the Fig. 3 is dBm.

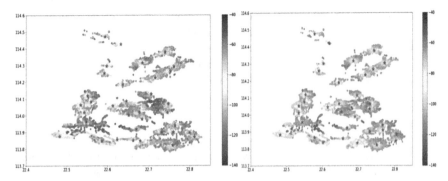

Fig. 3. The left is initial base station locations and change of RSSI value of test points, the right is final base station locations and change of RSSI value of test points (Color figure online)

In this paper, base stations are deployed based on the coverage distribution spatial pattern, and RSSI is used to measure the weight of the coverage strength. Combined with the weighted K-centroids algorithm, the base station location is determined, which is judged by the total objective function. Table 1 shows the total objective function value of each planning iteration, which means that the smaller the value, the better the coverage quality. We can see that the total objective function value gradually decreases with the increase of the number of iterations in the table. That is, the signal coverage gradually improves until the termination of the 10th iteration, and the minimum value of the total objective function is 535.41. The right of Fig. 3 shows the final base station locations and the change of RSSI value of test points, and the dark red region is less than that in the left of Fig. 3, which means that employing the proposed planning method helps improve signal coverage. The right is the corresponding clustering result, the location of base station is marked with a black star point and the location of test point is marked with a dot. Dots with the same color belong to the same base station cluster nearest to them.

Table 1. Total objective function values for each iteration

Iterations	Total objective function values
1	640.93
2	581.79
3	554.43
4	548.89
5	548.66
6	547.08
7	546.87
8	539.41
9	535.54
10	535.41

In order to verify the superiority of the proposed method, we compare the proposed method with the K-means based optimization method [11]. By calculating the total objective function value of each iteration, its iteration result tends to 584.22. Therefore, the method proposed in this paper can better improve the signal coverage rate compared with the K-means based optimization method.

6   Conclusion

In this paper, we have proposed a network planning method based on data mining. First, the overall network is preliminarily analyzed by using the measured data, and the features of coverage quality are selected. Then, the BRT algorithm and K-centroids algorithm are employed to extract the coverage distribution spatial pattern of the network, and the optimal RPMA network base station deployment is obtained. Finally, the feasibility of the proposed method is verified by using the measured data. Compared with conventional K-means based optimization method, this method can improve the coverage quality of LPWAN well, and has a certain reference value for the network planning.

In actual network planning, the base station deployment needs to consider many factors, and we only consider the coverage objective of the network planning in this paper. Therefore, in future work we will introduce capacity objective, and optimize the base station deployment combined with the two objectives, making the network planning more perfect.

Acknowledgements. This work was supported by National Science & Technology Key Project of China (2017ZX03001008), Natural Science Foundation of China (61871237), Postgraduate Research & Practice Innovation Program of Jiangsu Province (KYCX17_0766) and Natural Science Foundation of the Higher Education Institutions of Jiangsu Province (16KJA510005).

References

1. Patel, D., Won, M. Experimental study on low power wide area networks (LPWAN) for mobile internet of things. In: IEEE 85th Vehicular Technology Conference (VTC Spring), Sydney, NSW, pp. 1–5 (2017)
2. Hernandez, D.M, Peralta, G., Manero, L., et al.: Energy and coverage study of LPWAN schemes for industry 4.0. In: 2017 IEEE International Workshop of Electronics, Control, Measurement, Signals and their Application to Mechatronics (ECMSM), Donostia-San Sebastian, pp. 1–6 (2017)
3. Xiong, X., Zheng, K., Xu, R., Xiang, W., Chatzimisios, P.: Low power wide area machine-to-machine networks: key techniques and prototype. Commun. Mag. IEEE **53**(9), 64–71 (2015)
4. Krupka, L., Vojtech, L., Neruda, M.: The issue of LPWAN technology coexistence in IoT environment. In: 2016 17th International Conference on Mechatronics - Mechatronika (ME), Prague, pp. 1–8 (2016)
5. Wang, S., Zhao, W., Wang, C.: Budgeted cell planning for cellular networks with small cells. IEEE Trans. Veh. Technol. **64**(10), 4797–4806 (2015)

6. Ghazzai, H., Yaacoub, E., Alouini, M.S., et al.: Optimized LTE cell planning with varying spatial and temporal user densities. IEEE Trans. Veh. Technol. **65**(3), 1575–1589 (2016)
7. Yang, Z.H., Chen, M., Wen, Y.P., et al.: Cell Planning based on minimized power consumption for lte networks. In: IEEE Wireless Communications and NETWORKING Conference. IEEE (2016)
8. Wang, S., Ran, C.: Rethinking cellular network planning and optimization. IEEE Wirel. Commun. **23**(2), 118–125 (2016)
9. Friedman, J.H.: Greedy function approximation: a gradient boosting machine. Ann. Stat. **29** (5), 1189–1232 (2001)
10. Wen, R., Yan, W., Zhang, A.N.: Weighted clustering of spatial pattern for optimal logistics hub deployment. In: 2016 IEEE International Conference on Big Data (Big Data), Washington, DC, pp. 3792–3797 (2016)
11. Kanungo, T., Mount, D.M., Netanyahu, N.S., et al.: An efficient k-means clustering algorithm: analysis and implementation. IEEE Trans. Pattern Anal. Mach. Intell. **24**(7), 881–892 (2002)

Localization and Tracking

Mobility Assisted Wireless Sensor Network Cooperative Localization via SOCP

Sijia Yu[1(✉)], Xin Su[2], Jie Zeng[2], and Huanxi Cui[3]

[1] University of Electronic Science and Technology of China, Chengdu, China
ysj_17@mail.tsinghua.edu.cn
[2] Beijing National Research Center for Information Science and Technology,
Tsinghua University, Beijing, China
{suxin,zengjie}@tsinghua.edu.cn
[3] Chongqing University of Posts and Telecommunications, Chongqing, China
haoxuan_c@mail.tsinghua.edu.cn

Abstract. Cooperative sensor localization plays an essential role in the Global Positioning System (GPS) limited indoor networks. While most of the earlier work is of static nodes localization, the localization of mobile nodes is still a challenging task for wireless sensor networks. This paper proposes an effective cooperative localization scheme in the mobile wireless sensor network, which exploits distance between nodes as well as their mobility information. We first use multidimensional scaling (MDS) to perform initial location estimation. Then second-order cone programming (SOCP) is applied to obtain the location estimation. To make full use of the mobility of nodes, we further utilize Kalman filter (KF) to reduce the localization error and improve the robustness of the localization system. The proposed mobility assisted localization scheme significantly improves the localization accuracy of mobile nodes.

Keywords: Cooperative localization · Wireless sensor network
Multidimensional scaling · Second order cone programming
Kalman filter

1 Introduction

In many sensor network applications, the availability of accurate information on the location of the node is essential, such as target tracking and detection, cooperative sensing and energy-efficient routing. Cooperative localization is a relatively new concept, trying to overcome the limitations of traditional settings, in addition to the measurement between nodes and anchor nodes, distance measurement among nodes is also considered. Many studies have shown

Supported by the National S&T Major Project (No. 2018ZX03001004), Science and Technology Program of Beijing (No. D171100006317002) and the Ministry of Education and China Mobile Joint Scientific Research Fund (Grant No. MCM20160105).

J. Zheng et al. (Eds.): ADHOCNETS 2018, LNICST 258, pp. 129–138, 2019.
https://doi.org/10.1007/978-3-030-05888-3_12

that accurate inter-node distance measurement can be achieved using techniques such as sound signals or Ultra Wide Band (UWB) technology. This provides a broad application space for cooperative localization.

MDS is a widely used cooperative localization algorithm [2,11]. It can accurately restore the topological relationships among nodes under precise distance measurement between nodes. Authors in [3] proposed a cooperative localization method which not only utilized the initial results of the fingerprint-based algorithm but also used MDS to refine the location estimates for multiple users simultaneously. Another approach is to relax the original non-convex localization problem to obtain a convex optimization problem, which can be efficiently solved using existing algorithms. The two main convex relaxation techniques which utilized widely are SOCP [4,5], and semidefinite programming (SDP) [6,7]. Compared to SDP relaxation, SOCP relaxation is weaker, but its structure is simpler and potential to be solved faster.

At present, most studies about cooperative localization focus on the localization of static nodes. However, in practical applications, the localization of mobile nodes deserves more attention. Recently, authors in [1] studied the problem of maximum likelihood (ML) localization via SDP in the case where mobile sensor nodes utilize their movement information in the localization. In [9], the authors used RSS measurements for distance estimation and formulated the localization problem as an SDP. The inertial measurement unit (IMU) data is used to improve the localization performance further. However, SDP is not suitable for mobile nodes due to its high complexity. Extend Kalman filter (EKF) is widely used in the mobile nodes tracking algorithms is proposed in [8]. Authors in [10] utilized pair-wise range measurements and relative velocity measurements between communicating nodes to obtain the relative positions by EKF. However, EKF is a sub-optimal method compared to KF because it uses a Jacobian matrix to apply KF to nonlinear systems. Although this method expands the application space of KF, the consequences will be severely divergent in a strongly nonlinear scenario. Moreover, EKF has high computational complexity due to the calculation of the Jacobian matrix, which is not appropriate for real-time localization systems.

In this paper, we propose a novel cooperative localization scheme based on node's mobility in the indoor environment, combines the advantages of MDS and SOCP to improve the accuracy and robustness of the mobile localization system. To better take advantage of the node's mobility information, we apply KF to fuse the location estimation of SOCP-based and velocity-based. Simulation results are presented to confirm that mobility information and KF can effectively improve the localization accuracy.

2   System Model

We consider a 2-dimensional mobile wireless sensor network, there are N_s mobile nodes with unknown position and N_a anchor nodes with known position. Each mobile node move independently from their position at time instant t to a new time instant $t+1$, for $t = 1, 2, ..., N$, where N is the total number of observation time instants. In addition, we assume that each mobile node could obtain its velocity which is assumed to be constant between two successive time instants. Let a_k be the position of the k-th anchor node and $x_i^{(t)}$ be the position of the i-th mobile node at time instant t. Let $\mathcal{W}$ be defined as $\mathcal{W} = \{(i, t), 1 \leq i \leq N_s, 2 \leq t \leq N\}$. The velocity between time instants $t - 1$ and t is denoted by $v_i^{(t)}$

$$v_i^{(t)} = (x_i^{(t)} - x_i^{(t-1)})/\Delta T + w_i^{(t)}, \forall (i, t) \in \mathcal{W} \tag{1}$$

where ΔT is the sampling length and $w_i^{(t)}$ is the measurement noise which follows a zero-mean Gaussian distribution $N(0, \sigma_e^2)$. Let us define $\mathcal{A}$ as $\mathcal{A} = \{(i, j, t) | \, \|x_i^{(t)} - x_j^{(t)}\| \leq R\}$, where R is the communication range, $i = 1, 2, ..., N_s$, $j = 1, 2, ..., N_s + N_a$, $t = 1, 2, ..., N$. The distance measurement between the i-th mobile node and the j-th node at time instant t is denoted by $\delta_{ij}^{(t)}$

$$\delta_{ij}^{(t)} = \left\| x_i^{(t)} - x_j^{(t)} \right\| + n_{ij}^{(t)}, \forall (i, j, t) \in \mathcal{A} \tag{2}$$

where $n_{ij}^{(t)}$ is the measurement noise which follows a zero-mean Gaussian distribution $N(0, \sigma_\lambda^2)$.

The localization problem can be described as that given the distance measurement between nodes and the instantaneous velocity vector of each node, estimating the location of all mobile nodes in the network.

3   Cooperative Localization

The proposed algorithm utilizes the velocity and distance measurement to locate multiple mobile nodes simultaneously. Figure 1 illustrates the overall system architecture.

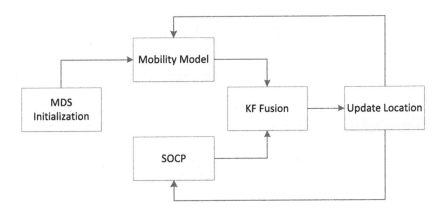

Fig. 1. System architecture.

The localization system uses MDS to perform initialization. Then according to distance and velocity measurement, we derive the localization problem as a non-convex optimization problem and utilize the SOCP relaxation method to estimate the position of nodes. In addition to this, we apply a mobility model based on velocity information and precious estimation to obtain the other location estimation. The KF fusion algorithm is used to enhance the location estimation further.

3.1 MDS-Based Initialization

Firstly, according to the distance between nodes at the initial time, we build the distance matrix D:

$$D = \begin{bmatrix} \delta_{12}^2 & \delta_{12}^2 & \cdots & \delta_{1n}^2 \\ \delta_{21}^2 & \delta_{22}^2 & \cdots & \delta_{2n}^2 \\ \vdots & \vdots & \ddots & \vdots \\ \delta_{n1}^2 & \delta_{n2}^2 & \cdots & \delta_{nn}^2 \end{bmatrix} \tag{3}$$

where δ_{ij} is the distance measurement at time instant 0.

Let us define the true location of the nodes as $X^{(0)} = [x_1^{(0)}, x_2^{(0)}, \ldots, x_n^{(0)}]$, and the corresponding estimated location is $\widehat{X}^{(0)} = [\widehat{x}_1^{(0)}, \widehat{x}_2^{(0)}, \ldots, \widehat{x}_n^{(0)}]$. It can be shown that [11]

$$B \triangleq (X^{(0)})^T X^{(0)} = -\frac{1}{2} JDJ \tag{4}$$

where $J = I - \frac{ee^T}{n}$, I is the $n \times n$ identity and e is the n-dimensional vector of all ones, $n = N_s + N_a$. B is symmetric and positive definite, and we can perform eigenvalue decomposition of B

$$B = Q\Lambda Q^T \tag{5}$$

Then we sort the eigenvalues of matrix B in descending order and select the first two largest eigenvalues to form the matrix Λ', the corresponding eigenvector matrix is Q', the relative coordinates of n nodes are approximated by

$$\overline{X}^{(0)} = Q'\Lambda'^{1/2} \tag{6}$$

Finally utilizes the Procrustes analysis [12] to convert the relative location to absolute location $\widehat{X}^{(0)}$.

3.2 SOCP-Based Localization

Let $\mathcal{D} = \{\delta_{ij}^{(t)} | (i, j, t) \in \mathcal{A}\}$ be the set of all available distance measurement and $\mathcal{V} = \{v_i^{(t)} | (i, t) \in \mathcal{W}\}$ be the set of velocity measurement. Given $\mathcal{D}$, $\mathcal{V}$, and the location of mobile nodes estimated from last time instant $\widehat{X}^{(t-1)}$, the location estimation $\mathcal{X} = \{x_i{}^{(t)}|(i,t) \in \mathcal{W}\}$ at time instant t can be obtained by maximizing the conditional probability distribution function [1]

$$f(\mathcal{D},\mathcal{V},\widehat{X}^{(t-1)}|\mathcal{X}) = f(\mathcal{D}|\mathcal{X})f(\mathcal{V},\widehat{X}^{(t-1)}|\mathcal{X})$$

$$= \prod_{(i,j,t)\in\mathcal{A}} \frac{1}{\sqrt{2\pi\sigma_\lambda{}^2}} \exp -\frac{(\delta_{ij}{}^{(t)} - \|x_i{}^t - x_j{}^{(t)}\|)^2}{2\sigma_\lambda^2} \times$$

$$\prod_{(i,t)\in\mathcal{W}} \frac{1}{\sqrt{2\pi\sigma_e{}^2}} \exp(-\frac{\|v_i{}^{(t)} - (x_i{}^{(t)} - \widehat{x}_i{}^{(t-1)})/\Delta T\|^2}{2\sigma_e{}^2}) \qquad (7)$$

By taking the logarithm to the above equation, the localization problem can be written as

$$\min_{\mathcal{X}} \sum_{(i,j,t)\in\mathcal{A}} \frac{(\delta_{ij}{}^{(t)} - \|x_i{}^{(t)} - x_j{}^{(t)}\|)^2}{\sigma_\lambda{}^2} + \sum_{(i,t)\in\mathcal{W}} \frac{\left\|v_i{}^{(t)} - (x_i{}^{(t)} - \widehat{x}_i{}^{(t-1)})/\Delta T\right\|^2}{\sigma_e{}^2} \qquad (8)$$

(8) is non-convex, to obtain SOCP relaxation of (8), we first define $\mathcal{M} = \{m_{ij}{}^{(t)}|(i,j,t) \in \mathcal{A}\}$, $\mathcal{S} = \{s_i{}^{(t)}|(i,t) \in \mathcal{W}\}$, (8) can be written as the following equivalent form

$$\min_{\mathcal{X},\mathcal{M},\mathcal{S}} \quad \sum_{(i,j,t)\in\mathcal{A}} (m_{ij}{}^{(t)})^2 + \sum_{(i,t)\in\mathcal{W}} (s_i{}^{(t)})^2$$

s.t.
$$\frac{1}{\sigma_\lambda}\left|\delta_{ij}{}^{(t)} - \|x_i{}^{(t)} - x_j{}^{(t)}\|\right| \le m_{ij}{}^{(t)}, (i,j,t) \in \mathcal{A} \qquad (9)$$

$$\frac{1}{\sigma_e}\left\|v_i{}^{(t)} - (x_i{}^{(t)} - \widehat{x}_i{}^{(t-1)})/\Delta T\right\| \le s_i{}^{(t)}, (i,t) \in \mathcal{W}$$

Next we define $\mathrm{u} \triangleq \{m_{ij}{}^{(t)}|(i,j,t) \in A, s_i{}^{(t)}|(i,t) \in \mathcal{W}\}$ and $\mathcal{Q} = \{q_{ij}{}^{(t)}|(i,j,t) \in \mathcal{A}\}$. Then we can obtain the following SOCP problem

$$\min_{\mathcal{X},\mathcal{Q},u,v} \mathrm{v}$$

s.t
$$\|u\|^2 \le v$$
$$\left\|x_i{}^{(t)} - x_j{}^{(t)}\right\| \le q_{ij}{}^{(t)}, (i,j,t) \in \mathcal{A} \qquad (10)$$
$$\frac{1}{\sigma_\lambda}\left|q_{ij}{}^{(t)} - \delta_{ij}{}^{(t)}\right| \le m_{ij}{}^{(t)}, (i,j,t) \in \mathcal{A}$$
$$\frac{1}{\sigma_e}\left\|v_i{}^{(t)} - (x_i{}^{(t)} - \widehat{x}_i{}^{(t-1)})/\Delta T\right\| \le s_i{}^{(t)}, (i,t) \in \mathcal{W}$$

3.3   Fusion Algorithm

Given the position of the mobile node at the last time instant and velocity information, we can easily get the current node's position in each time instant by the following mobility model

$$x_i{}^{(t)} = x_i{}^{(t-1)} + \Delta t \bullet v_i{}^{(t)} \cos\theta_i{}^{(t)}$$
$$y_i{}^{(t)} = y_i{}^{(t-1)} + \Delta t \bullet v_i{}^{(t)} \sin\theta_i{}^{(t)} \qquad (11)$$

The proposed localization system applies KF to fuse the position estimation provided by velocity-based and SOCP-based algorithm. At each time instant t, the state of the nodes is represented by $\widehat{X}^{(t)} = [\widehat{x}_1^{(t)}, \widehat{x}_2^{(t)}, \ldots, \widehat{x}_n^{(t)}]^T$.

The KF estimates a posteriori state $\widehat{X}^{(t|t)}$, given the above algorithm location estimates $z^{(t)}$, and $z^{(t)} = X'$, where X' is the location estimated by SOCP.

According to the dynamical system model and measurement model, the state equation and measurement equation of the localization system are formulated as follows [13]

$$\widehat{X}^{(t)} = F\widehat{X}^{(t-1)} + v^{(t)} + w^{(t-1)} \tag{12}$$

$$z^{(t)} = H\widehat{X}^{(t)} + r^{(t)} \tag{13}$$

where $F = I_{2N}$, $H = I_{2N}$, w and r are the process noise and measurement noise, which covariance matrix are Q and R. The KF equations can be derived as Prediction equations

$$\widehat{X}^{(t|t-1)} = F\widehat{X}^{(t-1|t-1)} + u^{(t)} \tag{14}$$

$$P^{(t|t-1)} = FP^{(t-1|t-1)}F^T + Q^{(t-1)} \tag{15}$$

Update equations

$$K^{(t)} = P^{(t|t-1)}H^T(HP^{(t|t-1)}H^T + R^{(t)})^{-1} \tag{16}$$

$$\widehat{X}^{(t|t)} = \widehat{X}^{(t|t-1)} + K^{(t)}(z^{(t)} - HX^{(t|t-1)}) \tag{17}$$

$$P^{(t|t)} = P^{(t|t-1)} - K^{(t)}HP^{(t|t-1)} \tag{18}$$

4   Simulation Results

We assume that there are ten mobile nodes and five anchor nodes in a $50\,\text{m} \times 50\,\text{m}$ area. The nodes follow the Markov mobility model at each time instant, each node randomly selects a velocity and a direction, where velocity is uniformly distributed between 0 and ν_{max}. Upon reaching the boundary, the node keeps the velocity while moving in the opposite direction. The distance, velocity, and direction errors are 5% respectively. The performance of different algorithms is compared using RMSE and CDF through MATLAB simulations, where all expectations are calculated empirically over 1000 independent runs.

We first studied the positioning performance of static nodes using the MDS algorithm and SOCP relaxation. Figure 2 is the RMSE curves of MDS and SOCP algorithm over ranging error under the static scenario, both of which increase with the increase of ranging error. Combining the CDF of Fig. 3, we can see that the MDS has higher localization accuracy than the SOCP. This is because SOCP relaxes the objective function and only obtains suboptimal location estimation. Moreover, in the static scenario, the objective function only contains the distance information between the nodes, without the help of the velocity vector. The positioning scene diagram in Fig. 4 further validates this result.

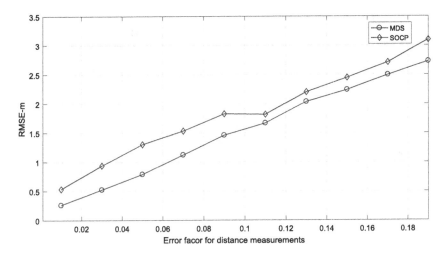

Fig. 2. The RMSE curves of MDS and SOCP against distance measurement error when nodes are static.

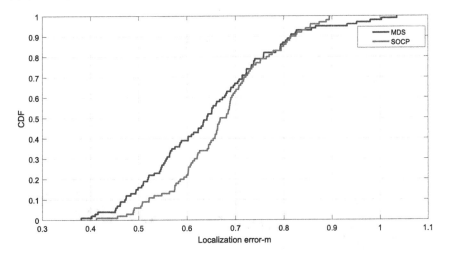

Fig. 3. The CDFs of MDS and SOCP against distance measurement error when nodes are static.

Figures 5 and 6 respectively show the comparison of the RMSE and CDF between the four algorithms when nodes are moving. Figure 5 shows that the MDS-based localization algorithm has the largest localization error compared to the other three algorithms. The RMSE of velocity-based location estimation shows an upward trend with time. Although the localization error of the velocity-based at the beginning is less than that based on the SOCP relaxation algorithm, the performance of the SOCP relaxation algorithm quickly increases over time and exceeds the velocity-based algorithm. This is due to that it relies on the

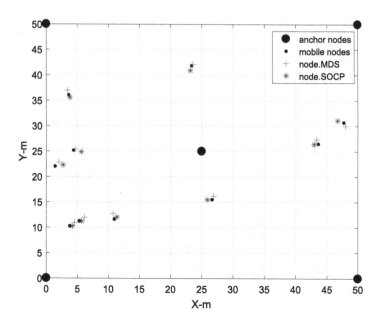

Fig. 4. Location of static nodes estimated by the MDS and SOCP.

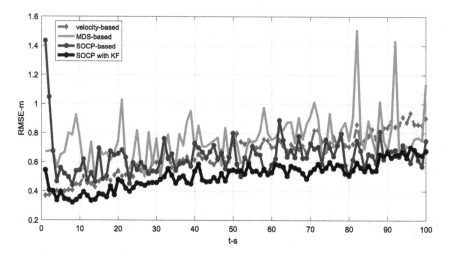

Fig. 5. The RMSE curves of the four algorithms when nodes are moving.

location estimation at the last moment, and the error will accumulate over time. After the SOCP-based relaxation algorithm has incorporated the mobile information, the localization error is significantly lower than that of the MDS. The CDF of Fig. 6 further validates this result. The Kalman filter is applied to fuse the velocity-based location estimation with the location estimation of the SOCP relaxation algorithm, which improves the localization accuracy and robustness

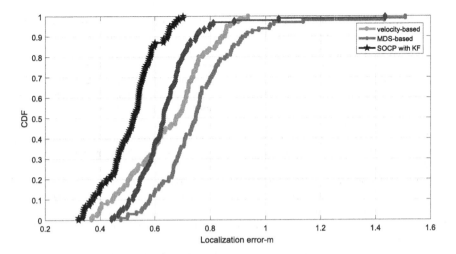

Fig. 6. The CDFs of the four algorithms when nodes are moving.

of the entire localization system. As can be observed in Fig. 6, the localization error after fusion is within 0.8 m, which is better than other algorithms.

5   Conclusion and Future Work

In this paper, we proposed a new cooperative localization scheme of exploiting the distance and mobility information of nodes in the process of localization under mobile wireless network. We utilized the node's mobility to enhance the SOCP-based relaxation localization algorithm and further applied KF to improve the positioning accuracy and robustness of the localization system. The simulation results confirm the effectiveness of the localization scheme. Cooperative localization in heterogeneous networks and NLOS environment will be the focus of our further work.

References

1. Salari, S., Shahbazpanahi, S., Ozdemir, K.: Mobility-aided wireless sensor network localization via semidefinite programming. IEEE Trans. Wireless Commun. **12**(12), 5966–5978 (2013)
2. Shang, Y., Rum, W.: Improved MDS-based localization. In: Joint Conference of the IEEE Computer and Communications Societies (2004)
3. Chen, L., Yang, K., Wang, X.: Robust cooperative Wi-Fi fingerprint-based indoor localization. IEEE Internet Things J. **3**(6), 1406–1417 (2016)
4. Srirangarajan, S., Tewfik, A.H., Luo, Z.Q.: Distributed sensor network localization using SOCP relaxation. IEEE Trans. Wireless Commun. **7**(12), 4886–4895 (2008)
5. Tseng, P.: Second-order cone programming relaxation of sensor network localization. SIAM J. Optim. **18**(1), 156–185 (2017)

6. Biswas, P., Liang, T.C., Toh, K.C., et al.: Semidefinite programming approaches for sensor network localization with noisy distance measurements. IEEE Trans. Autom. Sci. Eng. **3**(4), 360–371 (2006)
7. Vaghefi, R.M., Buehrer, R.M.: Cooperative localization in NLOS environments using semidefinite programming. IEEE Commun. Lett. **19**(8), 1382–1385 (2015)
8. Vaghefi, R.M., Amuru, S.D., Buehrer, R.M.: Improving mobile node tracking performance in NLOS environments using cooperation. In: IEEE International Conference on Communications (2015)
9. Wang, X., Zhou, H., Mao, S., et al.: Mobility improves LMI-based cooperative indoor localization. In: Wireless Communications and Networking Conference (2015)
10. Dong, L.: Cooperative network localization via node velocity estimation. In: IEEE Conference on Wireless Communications & Networking Conference (2009)
11. Borg, I.: Modern Multidimensional Scaling: Theory and Applications (2009)
12. Gower, J.C., Dijksterhuis, G.B.: Procrustes Problems. Oxford University Press, Oxford (2004)
13. Welch, G., Bishop, G.: An introduction to the Kalman filter, vol. 8, no. 7, pp. 127–132 (1995)

A Lightweight Filter-Based Target Tracking Model in Wireless Sensor Network

Chao Li[1], Zhenjiang Zhang[2(✉)], Yun Liu[1], Fei Xiong[1], Jian Li[1], and Bo Shen[1]

[1] Key Laboratory of Communication and Information Systems,
Beijing Municipal Commission of Education,
Department of Electronic and Information Engineering,
Beijing Jiaotong University, Beijing, China
{15111037,liuyun,xiongf,lijian,bshen}@bjtu.edu.cn
[2] School of Software Engineering, Beijing Jiaotong University, Beijing, China
zhangzhenjiang@bjtu.edu.cn

Abstract. Target tracking is an important research in Wireless Sensor Network (WSN), which detects and estimates the event source based on the data of multiple sensors. In this domain, the accuracy of tracking, the choosing of communication nodes and the real-time performance are the main direction of research. In this paper, the local density and distributed filter are investigated. Based on those above, a lightweight filter-based target tracking model is proposed, which use the local density to determine the communication nodes, and use the distributed filter to reduce the interval of sampling. The simulation shows the local density-based communication algorithm is stable and flexible.

Keywords: Local density · Distributed filer · Target tracking
WSN

1 Introduction

Wireless sensor network (WSN) is a typical Ad Hoc network which is highly distributed and self-organized [1, 2], which has many popular applications, such as target tracking, industrial process monitoring and control, air pollution monitoring, and machine health monitoring, and so on.

Target tracking is an important research which detects and estimates the event source based on the data of multiple sensors [3, 4]. Sometimes, kinds of interferences decrease the accuracy of measurements. Therefore, a filter is adopted to weaken the impact of these interferences.

The filter is used to extract a wanted signal from unwanted interferences. When the system dynamics and observation models are linear, the Kalman filter (KF) [5] can be used to calculate the minimum mean squared error (MMSE) estimate. And in most cases, the sensor nodes are always deployed in the harsh environment, without being recharged or replaced [6, 7]. Therefore, energy efficiency in in-network data processing is very important for WSN.

J. Zheng et al. (Eds.): ADHOCNETS 2018, LNICST 258, pp. 139–143, 2019.
https://doi.org/10.1007/978-3-030-05888-3_13

In this paper, a lightweight filter-based target tracking model in WSN is presented, which reduce the computing overhead of sensor nodes. The rest of the paper is organized as follows. In Sect. 2, the related works are introduce. In Sect. 3, the lightweight filter-based target tracking algorithm is introduced. A multi-stable system is structured to verify the proposed algorithm in Sect. 4. And the conclusion of this work in Sect. 5.

2   Related Works

Tracking moving target using WSN technology is a thought-provoking and well-established research area. Most of related researches can be divided into two parts: face-based and filter-based. The face-based target tracking algorithms usually divide the network into regions, cells, grids, clusters, trees, etc., and track the target in a distributed manner. Bhuiyan et al. [8] proposed target tracking algorithm with monitor and backup sensors in WSN. And then they consider target tracking using "face prediction," instead of "target location prediction in faces" presented in their previous work to get the full advantages from this face-based tracking [9].

And in filter-base target tracking algorithms, Both Beard et al. [10] use the Bayesian estimation method to track the target. Moreover, Yang et al. [11] present a sequential fusion estimation method for maneuvering target tracking in asynchronous wireless sensor networks.

Face-based target tracking algorithms utilize several sensor nodes around the target, which make these algorithms more energy-efficient. And filter-based target tracking algorithms have general requirements on node management and node distribution.

In this paper, a lightweight filter-based target tracking model in WSN is presented to reduce the demands on sensor nodes and increase the fault tolerance. In this algorithm, a definition of local density is proposed, which is used to confirm the communication probability of neighbor nods. And a communication probability is structured to confirm the communication nodes.

3   The Lightweight Filter-Based Target Tracking Model

3.1   The Local Density

In WSN, the sensor nodes are deployed in the monitor field randomly, and the distribution is not uniform strictly. Then, the definition of local density is presented naturally, which express the density for each node. In WSN, the local density of node i can be calculated according to the formula as follows:

$$\rho_i = \frac{N_i}{S_i},\tag{1}$$

where S_i is the monitor area of node i, and N_i is the number of sensor nodes in S_i.

In WSN, a target can be monitored by many nodes around it. And in general, not all the nodes which monitor the target transmit the message to the base station. Therefore, the local density can be used to calculate the communication probability for each node.

3.2 Communication Probability of Nodes

In this part, the communication probability for each node should be confirmed. In this probability, two relevant factors are considered. The first one is the local density and another one is the distance between the nodes to target. Then the communication probability is given according to these two factors.

$$P_c(p,d) = \min\left\{ k_1 \frac{n_0}{\pi R^2 \rho} \frac{(R-d)}{R}, k_2 \frac{(R-d)}{R}, 1 \right\}, \tag{2}$$

where R is the detection radius, n_0 is the expectation number of communication nodes, k_2 is given constant and k_1 is an auxiliary constant. For a known WSN, k_2 can be confirmed according to the formula $\sum P_c(\rho,d) = n_0$ when k_1 is given.

3.3 Distributed Filter Algorithm

In most filter-based target tracking algorithms, it is assumed that the target moves in the uniform rectilinear motion between two interfacing time instant with an uncertain noise. Obviously, the estimate is more precise if the time instant is shorter. However, in one time instant, the WSN should calculates the estimate and communicates. And in most cases, sensor node computes the estimate value according to the relevant filter method, which may prolong the minimum time instant.

On the other hand, the filter-based target tracking algorithms usually obtain the estimate according to the state equation and measurement equation. And these two equations can be computed in sensor nodes and base station, respectively. The distributed filter algorithm is shown as follows (Table 1):

Table 1. The distributed filter algorithm (for the kth iteration)

Time (T)	Sensor nodes (SNs)	Base station (BS)
$\text{Max}\{2T_{trans} + T_{cal}, T_{cal'}\}$	Receive the state parameters (T_{trans}) Calculate the $(k+1)^{th}$ estimated value for each node (T_{cal}) Transmit the value to BS (T_{trans})	Calculate the $(k+1)^{th}$ state parameters ($T_{cal'}$)
$\text{Max}\{T_{collect}, 2 T_{trans} + T_{fusion}\}$	Collect the measurement data ($T_{collect}$)	Receive the estimated value (T_{trans}) Fusion all the values (T_{fusion}) Transmit the $(k+1)^{th}$ final estimated value and the $(k+1)^{th}$ state parameters (T_{trans})

Compared with the common filter algorithms, the distributed filter algorithm can save half of filter time at most.

4 Simulation

In this part, 1000 sensor nodes are deployed in the 200×200 area randomly, and MATLAB is used to simulate. Firstly, a target is generated for 100 times randomly, and the distribution of number of communication nodes is simulated and shown in Fig. 1.

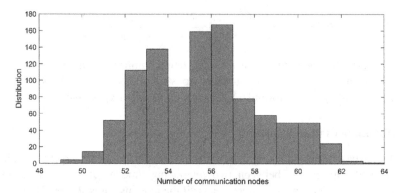

Fig. 1. The distribution of number of communication nodes

In this simulation, the target locates inside the monitor area, which means the minimum distance between the target and the edge of monitor area is longer than the radius of investigation. And

$$n_0 = 0.5\bar{n}, k_1 = k_2 = 3.$$

In this case, Fig. 1 shows that the numbers of communication nodes are focus between 51 and 62. The mean and variance of this distribution are 55.6028 and 6.9465. On the other hand, the expectation of communication nodes $n_0 = 55.5230$. Therefore, the proposed communication probability can satisfy the requirement of WSN.

Then, the parameters k_1 and k_2 are discussed respectively and shown in Fig. 2. In this simulation, $n_0 = 0.6\bar{n} = 63.8748$. As shown in Fig. 2, when $k_2 < 1.3$, the expectation of communication nodes (Ecom) can't arrive at n_0 with $k_1 \in [1, 10]$. Besides, when $k_1 \in [6, 6.3]$, k_2 is stable around n_0.

According two simulations above, the proposed local density-based communication algorithm ensure a stable communication nodes with suitable parameters.

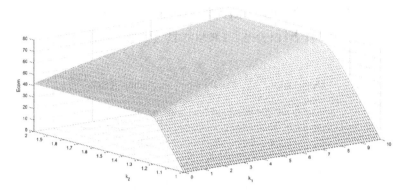

Fig. 2. The expectation of communication nodes with different k_1 and k_2

5 Conclusion

In this paper, a lightweight filter-based target tracking model is presented, which chose stable communication nodes, reduce the interval of sampling and increase the accuracy of estimate. And the simulations discuss how to confirm the parameters and show a well performance in stable on communication.

References

1. Fantacci, R., et al.: A network architecture solution for efficient IOT WSN backhauling: challenges and opportunities. IEEE Wirel. Commun. **21**(4), 113–119 (2014)
2. Xiang, W., Zhou, Y., Wang, N.: An energy-efficient routing algorithm for software-defined wireless sensor network. IEEE Sens. J. **16**(20), 7393–7400 (2016)
3. Mahboubi, H., et al.: An energy-efficient target-tracking strategy for mobile sensor networks. IEEE Trans. Cybern. **47**(2), 511 (2016)
4. Zhou, Y., Wang, N., Xiang, W.: Clustering hierarchy protocol in wireless sensor networks using an improved PSO algorithm. IEEE Access **5**, 2241–2253 (2017)
5. Evensen, G.: The ensemble kalman filter: theoretical formulation and practical implementation. Ocean Dyn. **53**(4), 343–367 (2003)
6. Marques, B., et al.: Energy-efficient node selection in application-driven WSN. Wirel. Netw. **23**(3), 889–918 (2017)
7. Babu, S.S., et al.: Trust evaluation based on node's characteristics and neighbouring nodes' recommendations for WSN. Wirel. Sens. Netw. **06**(8), 157–172 (2014)
8. Bhuiyan, M.Z.A., et al.: Target tracking with monitor and backup sensors in wireless sensor networks, pp. 1–6 (2009)
9. Bhuiyan, M.Z.A., et al.: Local area prediction-based mobile target tracking in wireless sensor networks. IEEE Trans. Comput. **64**(7), 1968–1982 (2015)
10. Beard, M., et al.: Bayesian multi-target tracking with merged measurements using labelled random finite sets. IEEE Trans. Signal Process. **63**(6), 1433–1447 (2015)
11. Yang, X., et al.: Hybrid sequential fusion estimation for asynchronous sensor network-based target tracking. IEEE Trans. Control Syst. Technol. **25**(2), 669–676 (2017)

Radio-Map Search Algorithm Based on Steepest Descent Principle

Deyue Zou[1(✉)], Yuwei Shi[2], and Shuai Han[3]

[1] School of Information and Communication Engineering,
Dalian University of Technology, Linggong str. 2, Dalian 116024, China
zoudeyue@dlut.edu.cn
[2] Academy of Opto-Electronics, Chinese Academy of Sciences,
Dengzhuang South str. 9, Beijing 100089, China
shiyuweilinshi@163.com
[3] Communication Research Center, Harbin Institute of Technology,
Yikuang str. 2, Harbin 150080, China
hanshuai@hit.edu.cn

Abstract. For most of the Ad-Hoc systems, position information is very important. Indoor scenario is a blind area of Global Navigation Satellite System (GNSS) service, which affects the application of Ad-Hoc technology. Fingerprint positioning technology is one of the most popular indoor localization methods. Searching strategy is one of the key techniques of fingerprint positioning. Because the data amount of the radio-map, which is used as the database of the system, is very big. Currently, the main accelerating measure of radio-map searching is clustering. But clustering brings some problems to the system, such as jittering and jamming. This paper proposes a novel radio-map searching strategy. Based on the steepest descent principle, the searching order is changed in the proposed method, compared with traditional clustering-positioning strategy. Thus, the radio-map is used in one piece, which is different from the traditional clustering-matching strategy. Simulations and experiments verified that the positioning accuracy of the proposal is better than that of the traditional method.

Keywords: Database searching · Indoor positioning · Fingerprint localization Steepest descent principle

1 Introduction

Fingerprint localization technology is widely studied in indoor positioning area, because it utilizes the shadowing and reflection of complex indoor scenarios, which blocks the application of traditional positioning technologies, especially the GNSS service. Generally speaking, fingerprint technology is a matching process, between user calibrated sample and a big database, which is named as the radio-map. As the data amount of the radio-map is extremely large, an efficient searching method is definitely important for a fingerprint positioning system. Currently, the most popular searching method is clustering. The radio-map is arranged into several clusters, before positioning process. The user equipment (UE) has to identify which cluster is it in. Thus, the

© ICST Institute for Computer Sciences, Social Informatics and Telecommunications Engineering 2019
Published by Springer Nature Switzerland AG 2019. All Rights Reserved
J. Zheng et al. (Eds.): ADHOCNETS 2018, LNICST 258, pp. 144–153, 2019.
https://doi.org/10.1007/978-3-030-05888-3_14

positioning process is divided into two steps: clustering and matching. Clustering strategy is widely studied. In paper [1] three clustering methods, K-means, affinity propagation and fussy C means, are summarized in order to make balance between the positioning accuracy and the computing complexity. Received signal strength (RSS) based clustering and micro-cell based radio map construction methods were combined in paper [2] to reduce the computational burden of fingerprint positioning. Clustering and principal component transformations in which the number of training data is reduced, compared with traditional system is used in paper [3]. Even in compression perception based fingerprint positioning system, clustering is necessary. [4] Paper [5] presents a support vector machine -C algorithm which enhances the positioning accuracy for clustering. A partitioning machine learning classifier method includes a clustering task and a classification task is proposed in paper [6]. Clustering can be seen as a kind of initial positioning which provides the final positioning results in some applications [7]. In paper [8], K-Melodies and signal feature extraction algorithms are used to reduce the complexity of clustering. As mentioned in paper [9] domain clustering can be used for indoor position estimation, which can enhance the positioning accuracy. Clustering is one of the most effective methods, especially in floor recognition process. [10] Dynamic clustering is also used in unmodified fingerprint systems. [11] To enhance the robustness of clustering algorithm, paper [12] proposed a novel grid estimation method. But clustering-matching scheme also brings some problems. Firstly, when a user is at the seam of two or more clusters, the positioning result may jitters between the neighbor clusters. This is caused by the Ping-Pong problem of identifying, as the cluster heads of nearby clusters are mostly similar. Secondly, for the same reason, when a user is moving from one cluster to another one, the positioning result may be jammed in the former cluster, which causes the positioning delay. Furthermore, different clustering methods have different problems. If the clusters were arranged manually, the distinction of signal feature space would be affected. If they were arranged automatically by clustering algorithms, the spatial distinction would be affected. This paper provides a novel radio-map searching strategy, which utilizes the prior information of the user's track. There is no necessary to divide the radio-map into pieces in the proposal, the searching order follows the steepest descent principle.

The remainder of this paper is arranged as follows. Section 2 introduces some related knowledge of this paper. Section 3 proves the main algorithm of the proposal. The simulation and experiment are illustrated in Sect. 4, followed by the conclusion and acknowledgment part.

2   Related Works

Fingerprint positioning technology is very suitable for indoor applications, because it utilizes the non-line of sight signal feature, which causes traditional positioning method fails. Fingerprint positioning technology has two steps in application: offline process and online process.

In offline process, the database is established, which is called the radio-map. Radio-map is formed by a large number of reference points (RP). Each RP records the mapping relation of the signal feature and its physical location. The RPs are mostly organized uniformly in the service area. And each RP is extracted by a variety of measurement samples.

The database will be used in online process. The user will use the real-time signal feature, to compare with the RPs in the radio-map. The Euclidean distances will be calculated to characterize the similarity between real-time signal feature and the RPs, as the following equation.

$$D_{Ei} = \|\mathbf{r}_{mi} - \mathbf{r}_r\| \tag{1}$$

Where $\mathbf{r}_{mi}$ means the RSS vector of the i-th RP, and $\mathbf{r}_r$ is the RSS vector of real-time signal.

The nearest K RPs in Euclidean distance will be selected to estimate the user's position. The physical locations of the RPs will be averaged as the final positioning result. This method is called the K nearest neighbor (KNN) algorithm, which is widely used in fingerprint positioning.

Clustering process is similar with positioning process. The RPs are arranged in groups, according to their signal features or their spatial distribution. The mean value of RSS vectors of the RPs in each group is calculated as the cluster head. Cluster heads are used as an upper level RPs, KNN algorithm is also used in cluster identifying, but here K equals to 1. After the clusters identify process, only the RPs of the selected cluster would be used in position calculation. Thus the whole positioning process is divided in two levels: clustering and positioning.

3 Steepest Descent Based Radio-Map Search Algorithm

The steepest descent principle based searching strategy in this paper is proposed based on the following two prerequisite:

(1) The track of the user is continuers;
(2) The Euclidean distance has a monotonous relationship with the physical distance, as shown is Fig. 1.

The simulation scenario of this figure is a single room with 4 APs. Assuming the radio-map is tiled on the X–Y side. The TP is at the (50, 50) point, which is shown by the arrow. The figure illustrates the Euclidean distances between the TP and all the RPs, indicated by the Z-axis. It can be seen that further RPs have bigger Euclidean distances.

The proposed algorithm searches the nearby RPs of the prior-known position, such as the latest position or the forecasted position of the user, in circle order. During the searching process, the K nearest RPs in Euclidean distance would be recorded and refreshed until they are fixed still for a certain time. Before that, the searching center would be changed step by step. At the first step, the prior-known position is selected as the center of the circle. And in the following steps, the center of the circle is the RP that has the smallest Euclidean distance with the TP in the last circle. The searched RPs will not be searched any more. The workflow of this algorithm is shown in Fig. 2.

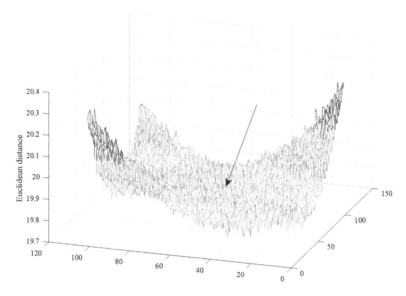

Fig. 1. Monotonous relationship between the Euclidean distance and the physical distance.

Variable N_c in the figure is the searching counter of the algorithm, if this counter reaches a certain threshold L, the searching process stops.

An example of the searching order of this paper is shown in Fig. 3. The radio-map is illustrated by the grids at the bottom of the figure and the latest positioning result of the user, which can be seen as the prior information, is marked by red color and shadows. The searching process is divided in steps, which are shown in different levels and distinguished by different colors. The grids of each level indicate the RPs that covered by this searching step. The color depth of each grid indicates the Euclidean distance between the corresponding RP and the TP. We can clearly find the moving track of the searching center, which are also highlighted in the radio-map by corresponding colors. When the RP selection register keeps unchanged for L steps of searching, as shown by the "Step 8 and so on", the searching process stops.

4 Simulation and Experiment

The effectiveness of the algorithm is verified by simulations. The simulation scenario is established based on cost 231 model. The building structure is shown in Fig. 4. 6 rooms and 1 passage is included, 4 APs are deployed uniformly in the building. Totally 696 RPs are arranged into 7 clusters, according to the structure of the scenario.

Clustering is not necessary in the proposed system, because the scenario is not very big. But in order to compare the performance of the proposal and the traditional clustering-matching strategy, the radio-map is also clustered, as mentioned before. In the simulations, clustered radio-map is only used in traditional system as a compare group. The positioning accuracy simulation is given in Fig. 5.

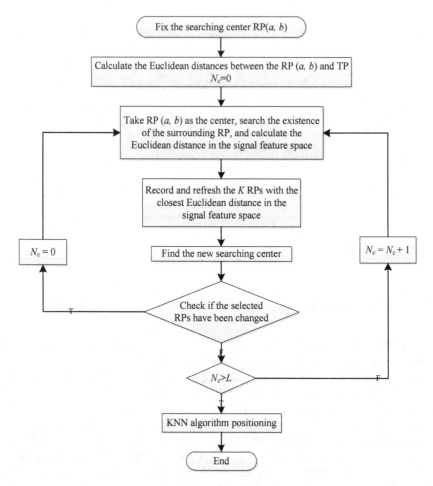

Fig. 2. The workflow of the proposal.

In the searching speed simulation, *RNTF* (RP Number Till Fixed) is used to evaluate the searching speed, which indicates the RP number that need to be covered until the location is fixed. For different searching strategy, the average *RNTF* of the simulation is recorded, as shown in Fig. 6.

It can be seen that when $L = 5$ or $L = 10$, the proposal performs better than the traditional clustering-matching strategy. When L equals to 1, the accuracy is the worst, and the searching speed is nearly the same with traditional algorithm. The increase of L brings no significant accuracy enhancement when $L > 5$, but only brings searching speed decrease. Positioning without clustering is not the most accurate method, and it has to search all the RPs, which makes it the slowest one among all the mentioned methods.

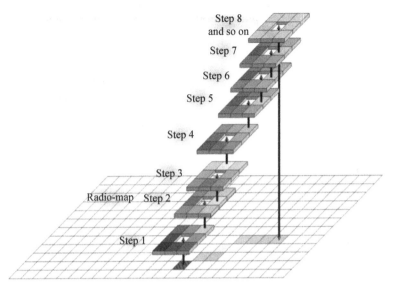

Fig. 3. Searching order of the proposal. (Color figure online)

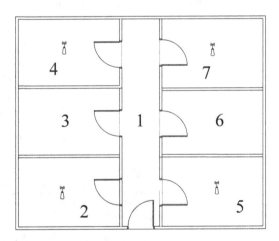

Fig. 4. Simulation scenario.

In order to further verify the system performance, measured data is used in the hardware experiment. The experiment scenario is shown in Fig. 7, and the track of the user is illustrated by the red dots. The experiment results are shown in Fig. 8.

It can be seen that the positioning accuracy of the system is related with the parameter L. An appropriate L value could ensure the system performance and reduces the positioning error. If L is too small, the searching process would be stopped too early before it can find the right RPs. Contrarily, if L is too big, the searching speed would be affected.

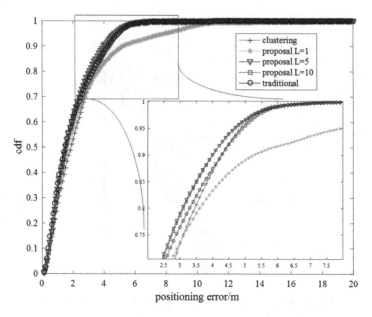

Fig. 5. Positioning accuracy simulations.

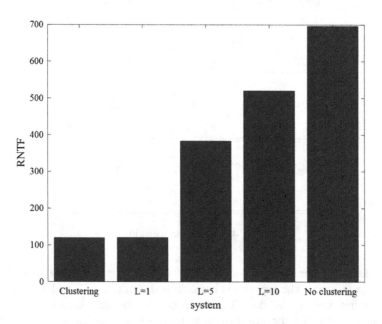

Fig. 6. Search speed comparison.

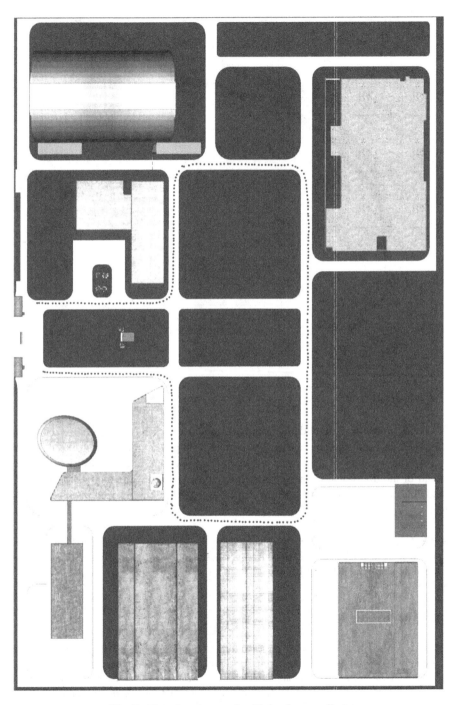

Fig. 7. Experiment scenario. (Color figure online)

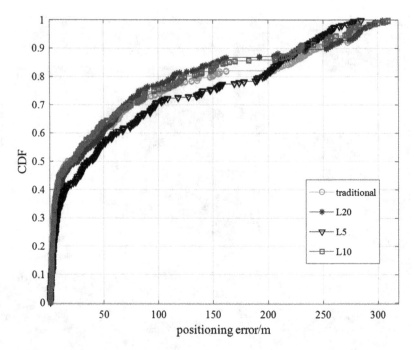

Fig. 8. Experiment results.

5 Conclusion

This paper proposes a novel database searching strategy. This strategy helps the UE to refine the useful information effectively in fingerprint positioning. The proposal utilizes the prior information of the user's track, and searches the radio-map diffusion-liked, instead of the traditional clustering-matching strategy. Simulation shows the proposal could enhance the positioning accuracy and keeps the searching speed in an acceptable level.

Acknowledgment. This research is supported by the Fundamental Research Funds for the Central Universities DUT16RC (3)100, And partly supported by the National Natural Science Foundation of China (NO. 61701072).

References

1. Zou, G., Ma, L., Zhang, Z., Mo, Y.: An indoor positioning algorithm using joint information entropy based on WLAN fingerprint. In: Fifth International Conference on Computing, Communications and Networking Technologies (ICCCNT), Hefei, China (2014)
2. Liu, X., Zhang, S., Zhao, Q., Lin, X.: A real-time algorithm for fingerprint localization based on clustering and spatial diversity. In: International Congress on Ultra-Modern Telecommunications and Control Systems, Moscow, Russa (2010)

3. Li, K., Bigham, J., Tokarchuk, L., Bodanese, E.L.: A probabilistic approach to outdoor localization using clustering and principal component transformations. In: 2013 9th International Wireless Communications and Mobile Computing Conference (IWCMC), Italian, Sardinia (2013)
4. Feng, C., Au, W.S.A., Valaee, S., Tan, Z.: Received-signal-strength-based indoor positioning using compressive sensing. IEEE Trans. Mob. Comput. **11**(12), 1983–1993 (2012)
5. Lee, C.W., Lin, T.N., Fang, S.H., Chou, Y.C.: A novel clustering-based approach of indoor location fingerprinting. In: 2013 IEEE 24th Annual International Symposium on Personal, Indoor, and Mobile Radio Communications (PIMRC), London, England (2013)
6. Premchaisawatt, S., Ruangchaijatupon, N.: Enhancing indoor positioning based on partitioning cascade machine learning models. In: 2014 11th International Conference on Electrical Engineering/Electronics, Computer, Telecommunications and Information Technology (ECTI-CON), Nakhon Ratchasima (2014)
7. Dousse, O., Eberle, J., Mertens, M.: Place learning via direct WiFi fingerprint clustering. In: 2012 IEEE 13th International Conference on Mobile Data Management, Bengaluru, Karnataka (2012)
8. Lin, H., Chen, L.: An optimized fingerprint positioning algorithm for underground garage environment. In: 2016 International Conference on Information Networking (ICOIN), Kota Kinabalu (2016)
9. Zhang, W., Hua, X., Yu, K., Qiu, W., Zhang, S.: Domain clustering based WiFi indoor positioning algorithm. In: 2016 International Conference on Indoor Positioning and Indoor Navigation (IPIN), Alcala de Henares (2016)
10. Zhong, W., Yu, J.: WLAN floor location method based on hierarchical clustering. In: 2015 3rd International Conference on Computer and Computing Science (COMCOMS), Hanoi, Vietnam (2015)
11. Lin, Y.T., Yang, Y.H., Fang, S.H.: A case study of indoor positioning in an unmodified factory environment. In: 2014 International Conference on Indoor Positioning and Indoor Navigation (IPIN), Busan, Korea (2014)
12. Cai, D.: A retail application based on indoor location with grid estimations. In: 2014 International Conference on Computer, Information and Telecommunication Systems (CITS), Jeju, Korea (2014)

Node Scheduling for Localization in Heterogeneous Software-Defined Wireless Sensor Networks

Yaping Zhu[1], Feng Yan[1], Weiwei Xia[1], Fei Shen[2], Song Xing[3], Yi Wu[4], and Lianfeng Shen[1(✉)]

[1] National Mobile Communications Research Laboratory, Southeast University, Nanjing, China
{xyzzyp,feng.yan,wwxia,lfshen}@seu.edu.cn
[2] Shanghai Institute of Microsystem and Information Technology, Chinese Academy of Sciences, Shanghai, China
fei.shen@wico.sh
[3] Department of Information Systems, California State University, Los Angeles, CA 90032, USA
sxing@exchange.calstatela.edu
[4] Key Laboratory of OptoElectronic Science and Technology for Medicine of Ministry of Education, Fujian Provincial Key Laboratory of Photonics Technology, Fujian Normal University, Fuzhou, China
wuyi@fjnu.edu.cn

Abstract. In this paper, a node scheduling scheme for localization in heterogeneous software-defined wireless sensor networks (SD-WSNs) is proposed. An expression to evaluate the connectivity degree of the localized agent is derived, which is used to judge if the agent is connected with an expected number of anchors. The node scheduling scheme is designed on the basis of the software-defined networking (SDN) paradigm, and the state of each anchor is determined by the SDN controller through a flow table via sensor OpenFlow. In the proposed scheme, a timer for each anchor is calculated based on the Cramer-Rao lower bound (CRLB) value and the residual energy. Simulations show that the proposed node scheduling scheme can reduce the number of active nodes while ensuring an expected number of anchors for localization. It can also be shown that the scheme can reduce the energy consumption with only a slight decrease in positioning accuracy.

Keywords: Node scheduling · Localization
Heterogeneous wireless sensor network · Software-defined networking

This work is supported in part by the National Natural Science Foundation of China (No. 61471164, 61601122, 61741102, 61571128), and the scholarship from the China Scholarship Council (No. 201706090053).

J. Zheng et al. (Eds.): ADHOCNETS 2018, LNICST 258, pp. 154–164, 2019.
https://doi.org/10.1007/978-3-030-05888-3_15

1 Introduction

With the development of sensor technology, wireless sensor networks (WSNs) have attracted intensive interest for their variety of promising applications over a decade [1]. Most applications in WSNs are based on the specific locations of sensors, such as environmental monitoring, social networking, asset tracking and indoor navigation [2]. Therefore, sensor positioning in WSNs has been a research topic of particular interest over the past few years.

Considering the resource-constrained characteristic of WSNs, existing researches have made great efforts to reduce energy consumption in the sensor localization algorithms. In [3], a distributed scheduling algorithm based on information evolution is proposed for the cooperative localization. Through neighbor selection and collision control, this scheduling algorithm decreases the complexity and overhead of localization. By decomposing the power allocation problem into infrastructure and cooperation phases, the authors in [4] establish an optimization framework for robust power allocation in cooperative wireless network localization. An effective transmit and receive censoring method is proposed in [5]. This method blocks selected broadcasts and discards less useful incoming information from neighboring nodes, thus, it can reduce the traffic in the localization algorithm.

Recently, an architecture called the software-defined WSN (SD-WSN) has become appealing for application-specific wireless communications [6]. The fundamental idea of software-defined networking (SDN) is introduced into the SD-WSN, which separates the data and control planes. Such a separation makes the SD-WSN programmable and thus the network structure becomes dynamic. The SDN controller in the abstract control plane can centralize the whole network intelligence and dictate the whole network behavior. Therefore, the SDN paradigm can impose a centralized operation for the network management. The physical data plane simply executes flow-based packet forwarding. In order to accommodate to the SD-WSNs, a sensor Open Flow (SOF) is proposed as a southbound interface in [7]. It is worth noting that the SDN technique in SD-WSNs provides a chance to design more flexible node scheduling strategies for the localization algorithms.

In addition, to meet the diverse need of network applications, the heterogeneous WSNs (HWSNs) have become popular recently, in which the nodes possess different software and hardware. The heterogeneity of HWSNs partitions the network tasks, ensuring a more efficient implementation of the overall network function, which can increase the network lifetime, reliability and validity [8]. To adapt to the development of HWSNs, this paper will study the localization algorithms in a more general network that consisting of different kind of nodes. To reduce the energy consumption in HWSN localization, a node scheduling strategy is designed with the support of the SDN technique, in which the state (sleep or active) of anchors at each time slot is determined by the SDN controller. The main contributions in this paper can be summarized as follows.

- An expression to evaluate the connectivity degree of the localized agent is derived in the HWSNs, and is used to judge if the agent is connected with a desired number of anchors.
- To improve the positioning accuracy as well as prolong the network lifetime, a timer for each anchor is calculated based on the Cramer-Rao lower bound (CRLB) value and the residual energy.
- A node scheduling scheme is designed on the basis of the SDN paradigm, and the state of each anchor is determined by the controller through a flow table via SOF.

The remainder of this paper is organized as follows. In Sect. 2, the system model and problem formulation are introduced. The specific node scheduling scheme is elaborated in Sect. 3. In Sect. 4, simulation results and analysis are presented. Finally, Sect. 5 concludes this paper.

2   System Model and Problem Formulation

2.1   System Model

Consider an HWSN with N_b anchors and N_a agents. The anchors in the heterogeneous network can be categorized into K different types. Note that the heterogeneity of anchors is reflected by their communication ranges in the research of localization algorithms. The agents are software-defined that can communicate with any kind of anchor. The positions of anchors are exactly known. The agents are mobile devices with unknown positions and attempt to acquire their locations through the range measurements with anchors. Denote the sets of anchors and agents by $\mathcal{N}_b = \{1, 2, \ldots, N_b\}$ and $\mathcal{N}_a = \{N_b + 1, N_b + 2, \ldots, N_b + N_a\}$, respectively. The position of node i in the network is indicated by the vector $\mathbf{x}_i = (x_i, y_i)^{\mathrm{T}} \in \mathbb{R}^2$ in a two-dimensional (2D) localization system. The distance between nodes i and j is denoted by d_{ij}. Assume that the communication of a type k $(1 \leq k \leq K)$ node follows the binary disc model, in which one can perfectly be connected only within the disc of radius c_k centered at $\mathbf{x}_k$, where c_k is the communication range. The connected region is denoted by disc $\mathcal{A}(\mathbf{x}_k, c_k)$ and the area of communication disc is $\|(\mathbf{x}_k, c_k)\| = \pi c_k^2$.

2.2   Metric Evaluation for Expected Anchor Number

Now, the probability of an agent that is connected with a user-defined number of anchors is derived. By using this probability as a metric, an expected anchor number is ensured during the localization.

The mobile area (MA) of agent a $(a \in \mathcal{N}_a)$ at time slot n is defined as all possible positions of $\mathbf{x}_a^{(n)}$, which is modeled as a disc of radii R_a centered at point $\mathbf{x}_a^{(n-1)}$,

$$\mathbf{x}_a^{(n)} = \mathbf{x}_a^{(n-1)} + R_a \cdot \Theta, \tag{1}$$

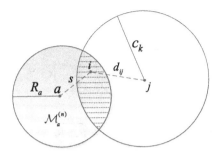

Fig. 1. A point inside the MA of agent a is connected with a type k anchor.

where $\Theta = [\cos\theta, \sin\theta]^{\mathrm{T}}$, and θ is a random variable uniformly distributed in $[0, 2\pi]$. The MA is the set of $\mathbf{x}_a^{(n)}$, which is denoted by $\mathcal{M}_a^{(n)}$ and shown as the gray area in Fig. 1.

Consider a point inside the MA which is at a distance of s from $\mathbf{x}_a^{(n-1)}$. The possible values of s are $0 \le s \le R_a$. Let S denote the variables of s, and the probability density function (PDF) for S is given as $f_S(s) = 2s/R_a^2$. In Fig. 1, a point i in the MA is at a distance of s from agent a, and the anchor j is a type k node having a communication range of c_k. Denote the probability that a node in the MA of agent a can be connected with anchor j by $p_{aj}^{(n)}(s)$. The value of $p_{aj}^{(n)}(s)$ is equal to the ratio of the intersection area (i.e., the shaded area in Fig. 1) to the possible mobile area. To calculate the area of the shaded region, the model is placed into an $x - y$ coordinate plane as shown in Fig. 2. Assume that $c_k > R_a$, the distance between the anchor's position (x_j, y_j) and agent a is d_{aj}. The area is calculated by using the integral of the difference of circle equations enclosing it. Note that, in some cases (Fig. 2b), the area is acquired by subtracting the complementary region from the whole mobile area, and the border value separating these cases is shown in Fig. 2a which is denoted by $d_{aj'}$. Then, the estimate of $p_{aj}^{(n)}(s)$ is given by Eq. (2) for different values of d_{aj} in three cases. For the cases of $c_k \le R_a$, the calculation of $p_{aj}^{(n)}(s)$ follows the similar way. However, in the third case $0 < d_{aj} \le R_a - c_k$, the intersection area corresponding to Fig. 2c becomes πR_a^2 and thus $p_{aj}^{(n)}(s) = \frac{R_a^2}{c_k^2}$.

$$
p_{aj}^{(n)}(s) = \begin{cases}
0, & d_{ij} > c_k + R_a; \\
\dfrac{2\int_0^h (R_a + \sqrt{R_a^2 - y^2} - x_j + \sqrt{c_k^2 - (y-y_j)^2})dy}{\pi R_a^2}, & \sqrt{c_k^2 - R_a^2} < d_{aj} \le c_k + R_a; \\
1 - \dfrac{2\int_0^h (x_j - \sqrt{c_k^2 - (y-y_j)^2} - R_a + \sqrt{R_a^2 - y^2})dy}{\pi R_a^2}, & c_k - R_a < d_{aj} \le \sqrt{c_k^2 - R_a^2}; \\
1, & 0 < d_{aj} \le c_k - R_a.
\end{cases}
$$
$$\tag{2}$$

Take the expected value of $p_{aj}^{(n)}(s)$ as the probability that a point inside the MA of agent a can be connected with anchor j at time slot n, which is written as

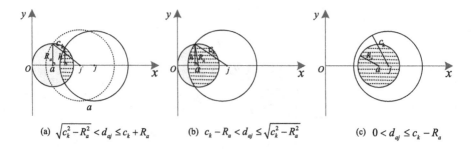

(a) $\sqrt{c_k^2 - R_a^2} < d_{aj} \le c_k + R_a$ (b) $c_k - R_a < d_{aj} \le \sqrt{c_k^2 - R_a^2}$ (c) $0 < d_{aj} \le c_k - R_a$

Fig. 2. The calculation of the intersection area in an $x - y$ coordinate plane.

$$p_{aj}^{(n)} = \mathbb{E}[p_{aj}^{(n)}(s)] = \int_{s=0}^{s=R_a} p_{aj}^{(n)}(s) f_S(s) ds. \tag{3}$$

To ensure an expected number of anchors for each agent during the localization, a probabilistic method is used to set a threshold indicating the degree that an agent is connected with a user-defined number of anchors. Let $B_M^{(n)}(a)$ denote the event that a point in the MA of agent a is connected with M anchors at time slot n, in which the number of type k anchor is m_k, and $\sum_{1 \le k \le K} m_k = M$. Denote all the possible combinations of M anchors with various numbers of each type by $\mathcal{C}^{(n)} = \{\mathcal{C}_1^{(n)}, \mathcal{C}_2^{(n)}, \cdots, \mathcal{C}_Q^{(n)}\}$. The probability of event $B_M^{(n)}(a)$ can be calculated as (omitting the time slot index)

$$P(B_M(a)) = \sum_{1 \le q \le Q} p(\mathcal{C}_q) \prod_{1 \le k \le K, \forall j \in \{k\}} p_{aj}^{m_{qk}}, \tag{4}$$

where $\sum_{1 \le q \le Q} p(\mathcal{C}_q^{(n)}) = 1$, m_{qk} is the number of connected type k anchor in the qth combination. In particular, $p(\mathcal{C}_q)$ can be calculated through the enumeration. To interpret Eq. (4), if $P(B_M^{(n)}(a)) = 0.80$, then, agent a at time slot n has 80% possibility of connecting with M anchors of different types. The following definition provides the degree metric for the level in which the agent is connected with an expected number of anchors.

Definition 1. *The degree metric $\xi_a^{(n)}$ for agent a at time slot n is defined as the integration of $P(B_M^{(n)}(a))$ over the whole MA, i.e., $\xi_a^{(n)} = \int \int_{\mathcal{M}_a^{(n)}} P(B_M^{(n)}(a)) d\mathcal{M}$. This degree describes the overall probability that agent a is connected with M anchors considering all its possible positions at time slot n.*

With this definition, the node scheduling scheme under the premise of satisfying a user-defined degree threshold ξ_{th} is designed. For example, if we set $M = 4$ and $\xi_{th} = 0.85$, it means that the scheme ensures an at least 85% possibility that the localized agent is connected with 4 anchors when scheduling the anchors.

3   SDN-Based Node Scheduling Scheme

To design the node scheduling scheme, the following three aspects are taken into account when selecting the anchors: (1) the benefit that anchor can bring to the localization accuracy; (2) the residual energy of the anchor; (3) the number of anchors for each agent. A timer considering these three factors is set for each anchor. Upon the timer expires, the state of the anchor at every time slot is determined by the SDN controller through a flow table via SOF.

3.1   Timer of Anchor

To select the anchors which are more beneficial to the localization accuracy, the CRLB is used as a measure for the positioning performance. The CRLB is defined as a theoretical lower bound on the variance of the estimator (i.e., position of agent), and can be calculated by taking the inverse of the Fisher information matrix (FIM) [9]. The FIM is defined as

$$\mathbf{F_x} \overset{def}{=} \mathbb{E}_{\mathbf{x}}[\frac{\partial}{\partial \mathbf{x}} \ln f(\hat{\theta}|\mathbf{x}) \cdot (\frac{\partial}{\partial \mathbf{x}} \ln f(\hat{\theta}|\mathbf{x}))^{\mathrm{T}}], \tag{5}$$

in which $f(\hat{\theta}|\mathbf{x})$ is the joint PDF of measurements $\hat{\theta}$ conditioned on $\mathbf{x}$.

For a given network configuration, the CRLB value for the localized agent is unique. Denote the configuration of all anchors and the localized agent a by $\mathcal{T}_a$. When one of the anchors (say anchor j) is taken away from the localization scenario, the CRLB of agent a will increase. Let $\mathcal{T}_a \backslash j$ denote the configuration that anchor j is taken away from the network. A weight factor indicating the quantified value that anchor j contributes to localizing agent a is defined as

$$\omega_{aj} = \frac{1}{\mathrm{tr}\{\mathbf{F}_{\mathcal{T}_a \backslash j}^{-1}\} - \mathrm{tr}\{\mathbf{F}_{\mathcal{T}_a}^{-1}\}}, \tag{6}$$

where, $\mathbf{F}$ is the FIM and $\mathrm{tr}\{\cdot\}$ is the trace of a square matrix.

To prolong the network lifetime, the energy consumption of each node should be kept as balanced as possible, thus, the anchors are selected based on the condition of its remaining energy. Then, considering the anchor's residual energy as well as its contribution to the localization result, the timer of each anchor j is given by

$$t_s(j) = t_0[\alpha \omega_{aj} + \beta(\frac{|e_m - \tau e_j|}{e_m})], \tag{7}$$

where α and β are two coefficients such that $\alpha + \beta = 1$. e_j is the residual energy of anchor j; e_m is the maximum energy at the beginning; τ is a random variable to avoid the same value of residual energy from different anchors; and t_0 is a coefficient to limit the scheduling time.

The timer of each anchor allows anchors for competition to be active. The anchors having smaller weights and more residual energy will have more chances of being scheduled to be active. Once the timeout occurs, the anchor will send a message to the controller to ask for its next state.

3.2 Node Scheduling on the Basis of the SDN Paradigm

A node scheduling scheme is proposed to select a subset of active anchors at each time slot at the same time ensuring an expected number of anchors for localization. The SDN controller in the control plane is responsible for the selection process.

Table 1. Match using CAV in SDN flows (x_coordinate = 13.8, y_coordinate = 15.6)

CAV:	cav_offset	cav_cast	cav_op	cav_value

oxm_type = CAV	cav_offset = 40	cav_cast = int32	cav_op = "="	cav_value = 13.8

oxm_type = CAV	cav_offset = 42	cav_cast = int32	cav_op = "="	cav_value = 15.6

To cater for the special addressing schemes in SD-WSNs, two classes of address in SOF is proposed in [7], i.e., Class-1, compact network-unique addresses and Class-2, concatenated attribute-value pairs (CAV). By exploiting the Open-Flow extensible match (OXM), the flow Matches in these two classes are defined compatible with OpenFlow. In this paper, the flow tables are refined by creating Class-2 flows which defines the Match in the CAV format as illustrated in Table 1. An example of the Match for a flow entry in CAV format using the node's position is shown in Table 1, where the x_coordinate and y_coordinate of a node is assumed to be an int32 stored at offset 40 and 42 of each packet, respectively.

Now, the work mechanism for the SDN-based node scheduling scheme is illustrated for localizing agent a. Before the scheduling round, agent a broadcasts a HELLO message to its neighbors, and anchors which receive this message are set to be active. Each active anchor sends a message with the information of its position, type, initial energy, residual energy and the range measurement with the agent to the controller. The controller stores this information in an information table. Then, the position of agent a is estimated and recorded as the initial position. The timer of each anchor is calculated by the controller and disseminated to the node.

At the beginning of each time slot, the mobile agent a sends a message to activate its neighbors which are within its communication range. The neighbors then send the information to the controller. If the position has been stored before, the controller only updates the residual energy and range measurement; otherwise, a new table containing all the information is constructed. Then, the SDN controller calculates the degree level of agent a as defined in Definition 1. The degree is compared with the predefined degree threshold ξ_{th}. As long as the timer of an anchor expires, it sends a packet to the controller with its new remaining energy. If the agent's current degree is lower than ξ_{th}, this anchor is set to keep active; otherwise, it is scheduled to go to sleep. At the same time, the SDN controller updates the table for this anchor and renews its information. The procedure of the proposed node scheduling scheme is depicted in Algorithm 1.

Algorithm 1. Node Scheduling for Heterogenous SD-WSNs

1: **Initialization:**
2: Time slot n=0;
3: The localized agent sends a HELLO message to its neighboring anchors;
4: Each activated neighboring anchor sends its information (position, type, initial energy, residual energy and the range measurement) via SOF to the SDN controller;
5: The SDN controller constructs an information table for the anchors.
6: **While** $n < N$ (N is the maximum time slot) **do**
7: Once the timer of an anchor expires, it sends a message to the SDN controller;
8: The SDN controller checks whether the address of the anchor is stored in the information table, if stored, updates the information of the anchor; otherwise, constructs a new table for the new anchor;
9: The SDN controller checks whether the current connectivity degree of the agent satisfies the desired requirement, if satisfies, schedules the anchor to sleep; otherwise, sets the anchor to be active;
10: $n = n + 1$.
11: **End while**

---

4 Simulation Results

In this section, the performance of the proposed node scheduling scheme is evaluated through simulation results. Consider a rectangular sensor field of 120 m × 120 m, in which 200 anchors are distributed in a uniform distribution. These anchors are categorized into three types and the communication ranges are $c_1 = 10$ m, $c_2 = 15$ m and $c_3 = 18$ m, respectively. The ratio of these three types nodes is 2:1:1. There are 20 mobile agents moving in the field, with the destination and moving distance at each time slot set between $[0, 2\pi]$ and [1 m, 1.5 m], respectively. Assume that the power consumption at anchors during transmission, reception and sleep modes is 60 mW, 12 mW and 0.03 mW, respectively. The initial energy of each node is assumed to be 30 J.

Figure 3 shows the total remaining energy of nodes in the network. When no scheduling is performed, all the nodes keep active during the tracking process, then the total energy is expended at about the 4/5 stage of the simulation. A great reduction in energy consumption is achieved when the anchors are scheduled to be active or sleep with the proposed node scheduling scheme. According to the scheme, only when the anchor receives the HELLO message from the agent or the command from the SDN controller, will it be active, otherwise it will go to the "sleep" mode. In addition, more energy will be saved when we

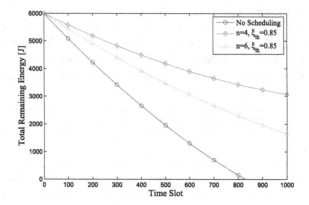

Fig. 3. The total remaining energy in nodes.

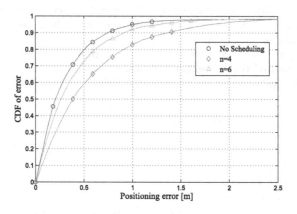

Fig. 4. Comparison of positioning accuracy.

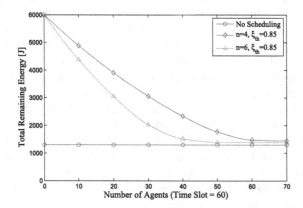

Fig. 5. Total remaining energy for different numbers of agents.

arrange 4 anchors for localizing each agent compared with 6 ones, leading to longer network lifetime.

The cumulative distribution function (CDF) of positioning errors is shown in Fig. 4. When there is no scheduling and all the anchors keep active, average 9 anchors are connected to each agent, which achieves the best performance in terms of localization accuracy among the three cases. The ratio of errors smaller than 0.5 m is reduced to 60% when the required number of anchors is set as 4, while 80% of the errors are controlled in this regime when no scheduling is performed. The distinction between the two schemes with and without scheduling decreases when the number is increased to 6.

Actually, the advantage of the proposed scheme is related to the number of agents. If the number of localized agents in the network is small, only a few anchors are required to be active. However, if the number is large, a high proportion of anchors will be scheduled to be active. In an extreme case, all anchors are activated if there are an awful lot of agents in the network, which is equivalent to the "no scheduling" case. Consider the cases that there are different numbers of agents moving in the network, the comparison of total remaining energy at time slot 600 is shown in Fig. 5. It can be seen that, as the number of agents grows, the remaining energy gets smaller under the proposed scheduling scheme since more anchors are activated. When the number gets large enough, almost all the anchors keep active during the whole localization process, thus, the advantage of the proposed scheduling scheme becomes invalid in terms of network-energy conservation.

5   Conclusion

In this paper, an efficient node scheduling scheme was proposed for the localization in heterogeneous SD-WSNs. The expression to evaluate the connectivity degree of the localized agent has been derived to judge if the agent is connected with an expected number of anchors. The state determination of each anchor has been manipulated by the SDN controller based on the SDN paradigm. Simulation results has shown that the proposed node scheduling scheme ensures an expected number of anchors for the localization. It could also be shown that the scheme prolongs the network lifetime while only slightly decreases the positioning accuracy.

References

1. Borges, L.M., Velez, F.J., Lebres, A.S.: Survey on the characterization and classification of wireless sensor network applications. IEEE Commun. Surv. Tutor. **16**(4), 1860–1890 (2014)
2. Zaidi, S., Assaf, A.E., Affes, S., Kandil, N.: Accurate range-free localization in multihop wireless sensor networks. IEEE Trans. Commun. **64**(9), 3886–3900 (2016)
3. Wang, T., Shen, Y., Mazuelas, S., Win, M.Z.: Distributed scheduling for cooperative localization based on information evolution. In: IEEE International Conference on Communications, Ottawa, Canada (2012)

4. Dai, W., Shen, Y., Win, M.Z.: Distributed power allocation for cooperative wireless network localization. IEEE J. Sel. Areas Commun. **33**(1), 28–40 (2015)
5. Das, K., Wymeersch, H.: Censoring for Bayesian cooperative positioning in dense wireless networks. IEEE J. Sel. Areas Commun. **30**(9), 1835–1842 (2012)
6. Zhu, Y., Xing, S., Zhang, Y., Yan, F., Shen, L.: Localisation algorithm with node selection under power constraint in software-defined sensor networks. IET Commun. **11**(13), 2035–2041 (2017)
7. Luo, T., Tan, H., Quek, T.Q.S.: Sensor OpenFlow: enabling software-defined wireless sensor networks. IEEE Commun. Lett. **16**(11), 1896–1899 (2012)
8. Guidoni, D.L., Mini, R.A.F., Loureiro, A.A.F.: Applying the small world concepts in the design of heterogeneous wireless sensor networks. IEEE Commun. Lett. **16**(7), 935–955 (2012)
9. Dai, W., Shen, Y., Win, M.Z.: Energy efficient cooperative network localization. In: IEEE International Conference on Communications, ICC, Sydney, N.S.W., Australia (2014)

Handover, Scheduling, and Action Recognition

A Speed-Adjusted Vertical Handover Algorithm Based on Fuzzy Logic

Dongdong Yao[1](✉), Xin Su[2], Bei Liu[2], and Jie Zeng[2]

[1] Chongqing University of Posts and Telecommunications, Chongqing, China
yaodongdong@mail.tsinghua.edu.cn
[2] Beijing National Research Center for Information Science and Technology,
Tsinghua University, Beijing, China
suxin@mail.tsinghua.edu.cn

Abstract. The development of wireless communication technology promotes the inevitability of network integration. In order to solve the problems in the process of heterogeneous wireless networks handover, this paper proposes a speed-adjusted vertical handover algorithm based on fuzzy logic. The algorithm periodically acquires motion information of the terminal in the heterogeneous network environment. By using a threshold function based on the simple weighting method and adjusting the threshold value in combination with the speed, the information that is not suitable for handover will be filtered out. Then, the received signal strength (RSS), network available bandwidth, and battery power are normalized and put into a fuzzy logic controller to obtain a comprehensive network performance value (NCPV). Finally, the handover decision is performed according to NCPV. The simulation results show that this algorithm can reduce unnecessary handover with the increase of speed and suppress the generation of ping-pong effect, compared with the traditional algorithm. In addition, this algorithm also considers factors such as network delay, service cost, etc. Those improve the quality of service (QoS) and user satisfaction.

Keywords: Vertical handover · Speed-adjusted · Fuzzy logic

1 Introduction

With the development of wireless mobile communication technology, the future mobile communication network will be a heterogeneous and converged network in which multiple access technologies coexist, cooperate and complement each other. It is clear that various wireless technologies need to be integrated to achieve smooth and seamless handover across technologies to ensure better user experience.

Supported by the National S&T Major Project (No. 2018ZX03001011), Science and Technology Program of Beijing (No. D171100006317002) and the Ministry of Education and China Mobile Joint Scientific Research Fund (Grant No. MCM20160105).

J. Zheng et al. (Eds.): ADHOCNETS 2018, LNICST 258, pp. 167–176, 2019.
https://doi.org/10.1007/978-3-030-05888-3_16

The handover process generally consists of three phases generally, which are divided into network discovery phase, handover decision phase and handover execution phase [1]. Paper [2] proposes an adaptive weight vertical handover algorithm, which can select a suitable network as target handover network according to the type of working application and the adaptive calculating weight vector to user's preference. However, it does not consider the impact of terminal movement on handover. Paper [3] proposes a novel vertical handoff decision algorithm, Self-Adaptive VHO Algorithm which considers the long term movement region and short term movement trend of mobile hosts, achieves a good integrative handoff performance. But this paper does not take into account an important factor: RSS. Paper [4] filtered unsuitable information according to MN's movement trend and received signal strength of WLAN to reduce unnecessary data volume and system overhead. Then put the RSS, network available bandwidth and cost into the fuzzy logic controller, obtain the final comprehensive performance value (VCPN) of the network through normalization, and finally make a decision based on VCPN and dwell time. In article [5], fuzzy logic is applied to the start-up phase of handover, and a multi-objective decision method (MODM) using fuzzy logic is used to select the optimal network in the decision phase, But the impact of speed on the handover performance is still a problem worth considering.

According to the current research situation, this paper designs a algorithm in heterogeneous network environment. The terminal periodically obtains motion information and filters out unsuitable handover information through a preliminary screening of the threshold function based on a simple weighting method, thereby reducing unnecessary system overhead. Then, the RSS, and other factors are normalized and put into a fuzzy logic controller to obtain the NCPV. Finally the terminal perform handover decision based on this value.

The rest of this paper is organized as follows. Section 2 presents related work and a proposed vertical handover decision algorithm is described in Sect. 3. The simulation and analysis is in Sect. 4. Section 5 concludes this paper.

2   System Model

We consider an overlay wireless network composed of WLAN and LTE, as shown in Fig. 1. Suppose that LTE covers the entire service area providing lower data rate and WLAN only covers some portions of the service area providing higher data rate. The vertical handover decision phase is triggered when any of the following events occurs: (a) the MN detects a new wireless link; (b) there is severe signal degradation of the current wireless link; (c) a new service request is made.

3   Proposed Algorithm

In the traditional handover algorithm, due to the large difference between heterogeneous networks, the algorithm cannot improve the user's QoS completely. The speed-adjusted vertical handover algorithm based on fuzzy logic proposed

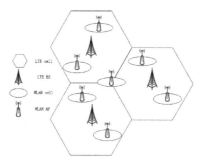

Fig. 1. System model

in this paper can be divided into two phases: initial screening and final decision. The algorithm is shown in Fig. 2.

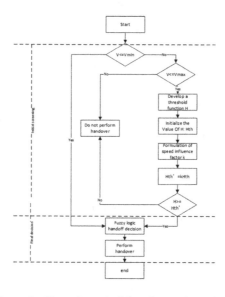

Fig. 2. Flow chart of speed-adjusted vertical handover algorithm based on fuzzy logic

3.1   Initial Screening

The first phase of the algorithm uses the simple weighting method to initially screen the network based on the network delay $delay\_n$, network service fee $cost\_n$, and the distance from the terminal's direction of movement from the BS or AP d_n (n represents the network type) as a multi-attribute parameter. The reason for the initial screening is that if all the parameters are input into the fuzzy logic module, the requirements for the user's mobile device are very high and the processing speed becomes very slow.

Calculation Method of d_n. First of all, we take the distance of the terminal from the Wlan AP as an example in Fig. 3. The center of the circle is the position of the AP. The line connecting the terminal and the AP is the x-axis, and the angle between the x-axis and the extension line of the direction of movement of the terminal is θ. The length of the vertical line extending from the center of the circle to the direction of the terminal is d_n. If the distance from the terminal to the AP is d, then

$$d\_n = d \sin \theta \tag{1}$$

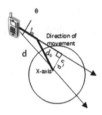

Fig. 3. Schematic diagram of the calculation of d_n

It can be seen from Fig. 3 that the shorter the d_n is, the less appropriate the handover is at this time. The distance d from the AP to the terminal can be calculated by the GPS positioning system of the smart terminal. If the coordinates of the terminal are (x1, y1) and AP coordinates are (x2, y2), then

$$d = \sqrt{(x1 - x2)^2 + (y1 - y2)^2} \tag{2}$$

Assume that the terminal travels a distance of l_0, at this time, the distance from the AP is d_0, which can still be measured by GPS. The value of $cos\theta$ can be given by:

$$cos\theta = \frac{l_0^2 + d^2 - d_0^2}{2dl_0} \tag{3}$$

From this, d_n can be expressed as:

$$d\_n = d \sin \theta = d\sqrt{1 - \frac{(l_0^2 + d^2 - d_0^2)^2}{4d^2 l_0^2}} = \frac{\sqrt{4d^2 l_0^2 - (l_0^2 + d^2 - d_0^2)^2}}{2l_0} \tag{4}$$

Threshold Function and Its Initial Threshold. The selected parameters can effectively prevent some target networks from having better network performance, but the mobile terminal only appears a short time within the coverage area of the network and still perform a handover. It also makes a rough assessment of other network performance, filters out information that is not suitable for handover. This not only reduces the number of unnecessary handovers, but also takes into account the user preference for handover decisions.

Parameter Normalization. Since different network performance parameters need to be compared, and different networks have large differences in performance, the foregoing parameters need to be normalized first. Paper [6] gives the normalized formula of delay,

$$delayi\_n = \begin{cases} 1, \ delay\_n \leq D_{\min} \\ \frac{D_{\max} - delay\_n}{D_{\max} - D_{\min}}, \ D_{\min} \leq delay\_n \leq D_{\max} \\ 0, \ delay\_n \geq D_{\max} \end{cases} \tag{5}$$

Where $delay\_n$ is the connection delay of the target network n, D_{max} and D_{min} are the minimum and maximum delays allowed for user connections, respectively, and $delayi\_n$ is the delay after normalization. The normalized formula of the network service fee $cost\_n$ and the distance d_n of the terminal movement direction from the BS or AP can be expressed as

$$ai = \frac{a_c - a_{\min}}{a_{\max} - a_{\min}} \tag{6}$$

Where ai refers to $costi\_n$ and di_n, and a_{max} and a_{min} refer to their maximum and minimum values, respectively.

Initial Threshold Function and Its Threshold. According to the normalized result of the previous, it is simply weighted to get the expression of the threshold function:

$$H = w_1 * 1/delayi\_n + w_2 * 1/\cos ti\_n + w_3 * 1/di\_n \tag{7}$$

Where w_1, w_2 and w_3 are the weight factors of normalized $delayi\_n$, $costi\_n$ and di_n respectively, and $w_1 + w_2 + w_3 = 1$. In the process of terminal movement, if the new function value of the network is greater than the existing threshold function value, the network can enter the fuzzy logic decision stage, but at the same time it also creates a new problem. In Fig. 3, when the direction of movement of the terminal is constant, that is, d_n remains unchanged, the terminal's moving speed v also affects the staying time of the terminal in the current network coverage. If v is too large and the handover conditions are satisfied at the same time, the handover will also affect the user experience. Therefore, the speed influence factor is needed to balance the influence of the speed on the handover. Since k changes with v, set k to

$$k = \arctan(v/\alpha) + \beta(\beta \in (0, 1]) \tag{8}$$

where α and β are the coefficients of v and adjustable constants, respectively. Derivative of k, we can get

$$k' = \frac{1}{\alpha}(^1/_{1+(\alpha)^2}) \tag{9}$$

When v remains unchanged, the larger α is, the larger the derivative value is, and the steeper the function k is, which means that the function is more sensitive to changes in velocity. But when v is constant, increasing α causes the corresponding k value to decrease. The initial threshold will also be reduced, so proper setting of the initial threshold is crucial. The value of β can be adjusted according to the actual needs of the user. When the other values are constant, the larger the value of β, the larger the value of the initial threshold. When α and β are constant, in the range of vmin<v<=vmax,

$$Hth' = (1+k)Hth \tag{10}$$

It means that as the speed v increases, the value of the threshold function also increases, eliminating unnecessary handovers and suppressing the handover of the terminal when there is a high speed. After repeated experiments, this paper takes $\alpha = 5$, $\beta = 0.5$ and the initial value of Hth is set here as the value of H when $delayi\_n$, $costi\_n$, and di_n take the maximum value.

3.2   Final Decision Based on Fuzzy Logic

After the initial screening by the simple weighting method, other parameters of the network should be put into the fuzzy logic module to enter the final decision phase based on the fuzzy logic. Here, the normalized $RSSi\_n$, the normalized $Bi\_$, and the normalized $batteryi\_n$ are selected as fuzzy inputs, and then the handover decision is made according to the output NCPV.

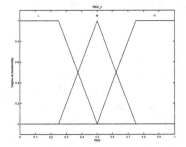
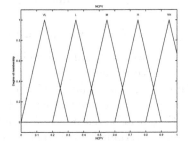

(a) membership functions of RSSi_n   (b) membership functions of NCPV

Fig. 4. Input and output membership functions

First, RSS_n, B_n, and $battery\_n$ should be normalized. The normalization procedure is similar to the previous one, and the normalized formula is shown in formula (6), where ai denotes $RSSi\_n$, Bi_n, and $batteryi\_n$. Then the normalized parameters are fuzzified and then correspond to low (L), medium (M), and high (H) linguistic variables. It is denoted as three fuzzy sets: U(RSSi_n) = U(L, M, H), U(Bi_n) = U(L, M, H) and U(batteryi_n) = (L, M, H). At the same time establish the NCPV language variables and their fuzzy set: U (NCPV) = (VL, L, M, H, VH). The membership functions corresponding to input (take $RSSi\_n$ as an example) and output (NCPV) are shown in Fig. 4 respectively [7].

Some fuzzy rules thus established are shown in the Table 1.

Table 1. Fuzzy rules

RSSi_n	Bi_n	batteryi_n	Output
Low	Low	Low	Very low
Low	Low	Medium	Very low
...	...	...	...
High	High	Medium	Very high
High	High	High	Very high

4   Simulation Analysis

In order to verify the correctness of the above-mentioned algorithm, the LTE and WLAN heterogeneous networks are used as an example to establish a simulation model with MATLAB as shown in Fig. 5. As shown in this figure, the BS of the LTE is located at the origin, its coverage radius is 1500 m, and the carrier frequency is 2000 MHz. The coordinates of the mobile terminal are (40, 0). Wlan1's AP coordinates are (500, 0) and Wlan2's AP coordinates are (980, 360). Wlan's coverage radius is 300 m, carrier frequency is 3400 MHz. The transmission power of LTE and Wlan is 33 dBm and 23 dBm, respectively. Assume that the direction of movement of a terminal at the start of simulation is equal to the angle θ of Wlan1's AP, and its initial value is $\theta = 0.2\pi$ (inside the tangent line). Afterwards, the terminal will move at a constant speed v. At the moment of touching the edge of LTE coverage, another same terminal repeats the above motion with the movement direction of $=(0.2 - 0.02i)\pi$ ($0<i<=10$). Then we change the speed of terminals and repeat the above movement. Since there is no time difference between the previous terminal and the next terminal, it can be regarded as the same terminal. LTE uses the cost231-hata model. The received signal strength is expressed as [8]:

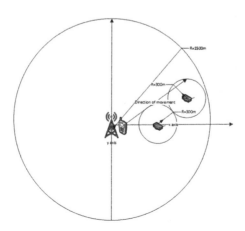

Fig. 5. Simulation model

$$RSS_L = P_{tL} - 127.5 - 35.2\lg d_L \qquad (11)$$

Where P_{tL} is the transmit power of LTE and d_L is the distance of the terminal from the LTE base station BS. The received signal strength of Wlan is expressed as [9]:

$$RSS_W = P_{tW} - 32.5 - 20\lg f_W - 20\lg d_W \qquad (12)$$

Similarly, P_{tW} denotes the transmit power of Wlan in dBm, f_W is the carrier frequency of Wlan in MHz, and d_W is the distance of the terminal from the AP in km. According to the relevant literature, other parameters used in the simulation are shown in the Table 2:

Table 2. Simulation parameters

Parameter	LTE	Wlan1	Wlan2
delay_n	120 ms	80 ms	100 ms
costi_n	0.2	0.05	0.05
B_n	8 Mbps	12 Mbps	10 Mbps
battery_n	6 h *(The maximum power is 24 h)*	6 h	6 h

In the initial screening stage, when vmin<v<=vmax, the weighting factors $w1$, $w2$, $w3$ take 0.6, 0.1, and 0.3, respectively. The simulation results of this algorithm will be compared with RSS-based handover algorithms, handover algorithms based on simple weighting (RSS, network bandwidth, terminal's speed, and battery power) and fuzzy logic-based handover algorithms.

Figure 6 shows comparison of four algorithm handoff times as the speed increases. As can be seen from the figure, compared with other typical handover

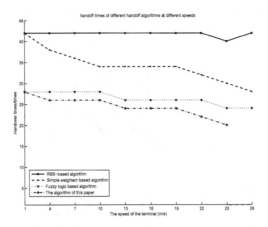

Fig. 6. Comparison of different algorithm handover times

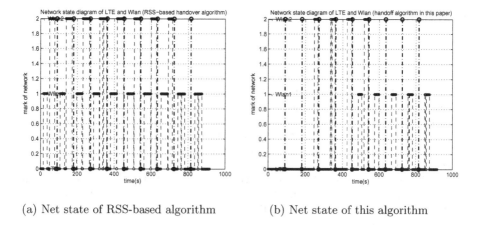

(a) Net state of RSS-based algorithm   (b) Net state of this algorithm

Fig. 7. Network state of two algorithms

algorithms, the number of handovers based on this algorithm is significantly reduced. This algorithm can reduce unnecessary handover with the increase of speed and suppress the generation of ping-pong effect. Especially when the speed is 4–19 m/s, the handoff frequency is stable. As the speed continues to increase, the number of handovers decreases, indicating that the algorithm has an effect on the suppression of higher speed handovers.

Figure 7 shows the network state based on the RSS algorithm and the algorithm in this paper. (2 stands for Wlan2, 1 stands for Wlan1, 0 stands for LTE, and the dash dot line shows the complete movement of the terminal at the same angle). As can be seen from this figure, when the direction of the movement of the terminal and the angle between the APs is large, the algorithm of this paper didn't perform handover, because the larger the angle, the shorter the dwell time of the terminal in the network. In addition, it can better reflect the improvement of the user service quality in the handover decision, because this algorithm also considers the delay, cost and other factors.

5   Conclusion

In this paper, we design a algorithm that based on the speed of the terminal and fuzzy logic decision method. The terminal periodically obtains motion information, and initially filters through a threshold function based on a simple weighting method to filter out information that is not suitable for handover. Then we get the network comprehensive performance value (NCPV) from the fuzzy logic module, and finally perform the handover decision based on this value. Compared with the traditional algorithms, unnecessary handovers are reduced and the complexity of the system is reduced. The user's preference for the network is taken into account, which improves the user service quality and user satisfaction to some extent.

References

1. Chen, W.-T., Liu, J.-C., Huang, H.-K.: An adaptive scheme for vertical handoff in wireless overlay networks. In: Proceedings of Tenth International Conference on Parallel and Distributed Systems 2004, pp. 541–548. IEEE Press, CA (2004). https://doi.org/10.1109/ICPADS.2004.1316136
2. Feng, D., Yajie, M., Fengxing, Z., Shaowu, L.: A multi-attribute vertical handover algorithm based on adaptive weight in heterogeneous wireless network. In: 2014 Ninth International Conference on P2P, Parallel, Grid, Cloud and Internet Computing, pp. 184–188. IEEE Press, Guangdong (2014). https://doi.org/10.1109/3PGCIC.2014.57
3. Liu, M., Li, Z.C., Guo, X.B., Dutkiewicz, E., Wang, M.H.: WLC14-4: SAVA: a novel self-adaptive vertical handoff algorithm for heterogeneous wireless networks. In: IEEE Globecom 2006, pp. 1–5. IEEE Press, San Francisco (2006). https://doi.org/10.1109/GLOCOM.2006.695
4. Tao, Y., Peng, R.: A fuzzy logic vertical handoff algorithm with motion trend decision. In: Proceedings of 2011 6th International Forum on Strategic Technology, pp. 1280–1283. IEEE Press, Harbin (2011). https://doi.org/10.1109/IFOST.2011.6021253
5. Shanmugam, K.: A novel candidate network selection based handover management with fuzzy logic in heterogeneous wireless networks. In: 2017 4th International Conference on Advanced Computing and Communication Systems (ICACCS), pp. 1–6. IEEE Press, Coimbatore (2017). https://doi.org/10.1109/ICACCS.2017.8014702
6. Shen, W., Zeng, Q.A.: Cost-function-based network selection strategy in integrated wireless and mobile networks. IEEE Trans. Veh. Technol. **57**(6), 3778–3788 (2008)
7. Lee, E., Choi, C., Kim, P.: Intelligent handover scheme for drone using fuzzy inference systems. IEEE Access **5**, 13712–13719 (2017)
8. Chen, X., Chen, C., He, J., Guan, X.: Intuitionistic fuzzy handover mechanism for heterogeneous vehicular networks. In: 2017 IEEE/CIC International Conference on Communications in China (ICCC), pp. 1–6. IEEE Press, Qingdao (2017). https://doi.org/10.1109/ICCChina.2017.8330492
9. Zeng, J., Su, X., Gong, J., Rong, L., Wang, J.: 5G virtualized radio access network approach based on NO stack framework. In: IEEE International Conference on Communications 2017, pp. 1–5. IEEE Press, Paris (2017). https://doi.org/10.1109/ICC.2017.7996958

A Self-adaptive Feedback Handoff Algorithm Based Decision Tree for Internet of Vehicles

Wenqing Cui, Weiwei Xia[(⊠)], Zhuorui Lan, Chao Qian, Feng Yan,
and Lianfeng Shen

National Mobile Communications Research Laboratory, Southeast University,
Nanjing 210096, China
{220160838, wwxia, lan_zhuorui, 220160725, feng.yan,
lfshen}@seu.edu.cn

Abstract. In this paper, a self-adaptive feedback handoff (SAFH) algorithm is proposed to address the problem about dynamic handoffs for the Internet of Vehicles (IoVs), aiming at minimizing handoff delay and reducing the ping-pong effect. We first analyze the main attributes and terminal movement trend, and give the respective handoff probability distribution. Based on handoff probability distributions, the structure of multi-attribute decision tree is determined. To update the terminal state, the incremental learning method by feedback mechanism is implemented by adding decision table information at the nodes of the decision tree so as to dynamically catch the splitting attributes of the decision tree. Simulation results show that the proposed SAFH algorithm's time cost is lower than some existing algorithms. Besides, SAFH algorithm also reduces the ping-pong effect and increases the effectiveness of network connections.

Keywords: Internet of Vehicles · Decision tree · Handoff · Feedback decision
Mobile Edge Computing

1 Introduction

With the development of the Internet of Vehicles (IoVs) and wireless access technologies, many vehicles are outfitted with special technologies that tap into the Internet access and provide extra benefits to the drivers. For IoVs, when a mobile vehicle node, which is in a network connection state, moves from one Access Point's (AP's) coverage area to another AP's coverage area, the connection control of the mobile vehicle node is needed to ensure the network connection. From the current serving AP to another AP, this process is named as handoff [1]. The network topology changes faster due to the characteristics of vehicle mobility and high speed, resulting in more inner network handoffs [2]. Realizing rapid handoff in the IoVs can ensure that the users' network connection is stable and the application of IoVs can get better supported[1].

---

[1] This work is supported in part by the National Science Foundation of China (No. 61741102, 61471164, 61601122).

J. Zheng et al. (Eds.): ADHOCNETS 2018, LNICST 258, pp. 177–190, 2019.
https://doi.org/10.1007/978-3-030-05888-3_17

Mobile Edge Computing (MEC) provides an Internet Technology (IT) service environment and cloud-computing capabilities at the edge of the mobile network, within the Radio Access Network (RAN) and in close proximity to mobile subscribers [3]. The aim is to reduce latency, ensure highly efficient network operation and service delivery, and offer an improved user experience. MEC can be used to extend the connected car cloud into the highly distributed mobile base station (BS) environment, and enable data and applications to be housed close to the vehicles. In this paper, we consider an IoVs system that MEC participates in to achieve low latency.

At present, researchers have obtained some research results for the network handoff technology for IoVs [4–9]. The authors in [4] described a location-based handoff scheme of Internet of vehicles. This scheme can accurately predict the points that the vehicle may access and uses a blacklist scheme to eliminate redundant access point in order to reduce the time of scanning access points. In [5], it proposed an urban vehicle handoff scheme based on E-PMIPv6, which can guarantee the continuity of conversation for urban mobile users. It eliminated packet loss to improve handoff performance in each handoff scenario. For the problem of vehicle handoff in mobile micro-cellular networks, the authors in [6] proposed a "mobile extension cell" handoff algorithm. This algorithm focus on outdoor vehicular environments serving end-users with high mobility and it is proved that it is suitable for minimizing packet loss. The authors in [7] reduce handoff delays by predicting vehicle trajectories. To minimizing the handoff cost while satisfying the latency constraints, [7] take a game approach to find the optimal handoff strategies of each type of vehicles. For the problem that existing handoff mechanisms in vehicle networking do not make full use of road information and large handoff delay, the authors in [8] proposed a novel MEC-based handoff mechanism. This mechanism avoided the redundant information exchange between the vehicles and the BS by related deployment operations. The virtual machine migration management solution proposed in [9] first predicted the throughput of the system, and then selected the optimal MEC server for virtual machine migration and handoff. However, the proposed algorithms in the literatures above only presented the utility at the network side, and the terminals' status, which included the service priority and the terminal movement trend, were not under consideration. In this paper, we jointly consider the network parameters and terminals' status to build incremental decision tree by feedback mechanism to realize rapid handoff.

The main contributions of this paper are as follows:

1. We propose a self-adaptive feedback handoff (SAFH) algorithm based decision tree to solve ping-pong effect and delay problem for handoffs in IoVs.
2. This paper jointly consider the network parameters, network load of BS, terminal movement trend and terminals' service requirements to build multi-attribute decision tree.
3. After the vehicle terminal changed its own service state and performed a handoff operation, the vehicle feedbacked decision table information. Incremental learning of the multi-attribute decision tree is implemented so as to dynamically catch the splitting attributes of the decision tree. Consequently, the handoff decision is made according to the rebuilt decision tree.

The rest of this paper is organized as follows: in Sect. 2, the decision tree-based vehicle dynamic handoff algorithm is briefly introduced. Section 3 shows the feedback decision problems based on incremental self-learning algorithm and handoff procedure. And the simulation analysis are given in Sect. 4. In Sect. 5, we summarize the whole work.

2   A Multi-attribute Handoff Decision Based Decision Tree

The system scenario is first described in Sect. 2.1. And parameters of attributes are introduced in Sect. 2.2 because network attributes parameters often affect handoff in IoVs. Then, the decision tree handoff decision method is introduced in Sect. 2.3.

2.1   System Scenario

The system studied in this paper is shown in Fig. 1, it includes vehicle terminals, MEC servers, BSs and cloud center [10]. The vehicle terminals connect to BSs through wireless links. The MEC servers can process and transfer data. It is the edge server which can provide localized cloud services for vehicles. And the handoff decision in this proposed algorithm is performed by the BSs which are assisted by MEC servers. The cloud center connects to MEC severs through the wide area network (WAN). Handoff occurs when the vehicle is traveling between different BSs.

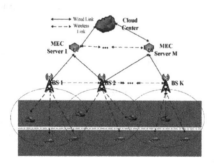

Fig. 1. System scenario

2.2   Multi-attribute Decision

For handoff problem in this paper, we jointly consider the network attribute parameters, terminal movement trend, terminals' service requirements and network load of BS to build decision tree.

A. The Parameters of Network Attribute. The appropriate network attribute parameters are prerequisites for triggering the handoff. Let the target BS network set searched by the vehicle are $S = \{S_k | k = 0, 1, \cdots, K\}$, where K is the total number of target BS, then:

The received signal strength (RSS) reflects the channel quality of the current channel and its expression is:

$$RSS(d) = K_1 - K_2 \lg(d) + \mu(x) \tag{1}$$

Where, K_1 is the transmission power, K_2 is the path loss, K_2 is a constant. d is the distance between the terminal and the BS, $\mu(x)$ is the Gaussian distribution that obeys the parameter $(0, \sigma_1)$, 0 is mean and σ_1 is the variance.

The handoff probability based on the received signal strength network condition attribute parameter is:

$$P_{h1} = P(RSS(d) > \eta) \tag{2}$$

Where, $RSS(d)$ is the target network signal strength, and η is the signal strength threshold required for the terminal to access the network.

B. Terminal Movement Trend. Due to the high-speed movement of the vehicle, the movement tendency, the distance between the terminal and the BS both affect the time for handoffs. The relative movement trend of the vehicle terminal and the BS is shown in Fig. 2. When the vehicle is in position 1, the distance d_1 from the BS 1 is smaller than the distance d_2 from the BS 2. When the vehicle moves to position 2, d_1 is gradually larger than d_2. According to the traditional handoff method, network handoff is required. We use the distance change calculation method to judge the relative motion trend between the vehicle terminal and the BS. It is generally believed that the vehicle's movement trajectory is close to a straight line in a short period of time. The distance between the terminal and the target BS can be calculated from Eq. (1):

$$\Delta D_d = d_2 - d_1 = 10^{\frac{K_1 + \mu(x) - RSS_2}{K_2}} - 10^{\frac{K_1 + \mu(x) - RSS_1}{K_2}} \tag{3}$$

In (3), RSS_1 is the received signal strength between the vehicle mobile terminal and the BS 1, and RSS_2 is the received signal strength between the vehicle mobile terminal and the BS 2. When $\Delta D_d < 0$, it is determined that the terminal is approaching the target BS, which means that the handoff operation needs to be performed; otherwise, it is determined that the terminal is moving away from the target BS.

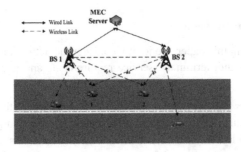

Fig. 2. Relative movement trend between vehicle terminal and BSs

The handoff probability of the terminal motion trend condition attribute is:

$$P_{h2} = P(\Delta D_d < 0) \tag{4}$$

Where, ΔD_d is the distance variation between the terminal and the target BS.

C. Terminal's Services Requirements. Currently, 3GPP defines four basic service types: session services, streaming media services, interactive services, and background services [11]. Among this, the session service has stringent requirements for quality of service (QoS), such as delay and packet loss rate. Therefore, it requires a long network duration. Besides non-conversation services such as streaming media, interactive and background services have a high demand for network transmission rates.

Considering the different services requirements of the vehicle, the network transmission rate is an important index that influences the QoS of the data service and is usually expressed by the link reachable rate as:

$$C_k = Wlb(1 + SNR_k), k = 0, 1, \cdots, K \tag{5}$$

Where, W is the network bandwidth. The handoff probability based on the network transmission rate condition attribute is:

$$P_{h3} = P(C_B > C_A) \tag{6}$$

C_B is the link reachability rate of the target AP's, and C_A is the link reachability rate of the current AP's.

D. Load Balancing of Base Station. The vehicle's movement between the various BSs will make the number of terminals connecting with each BS have obvious dynamic characteristics. It also causes the load of the BS to exhibit a unbalanced characteristic, making part of the BSs overloaded status, which leads to a decrease in system resource utilization, a higher call blocking rate, thereby affecting the user's QoS experience. The load of the BS is defined as the ratio of the occupied network bandwidth to the total bandwidth provided by the BS network, and let L_k be the network load of the BS S_k. Then L_k can be expressed as:

$$L_k = \frac{\sum_{j \in U_k} B_{jk} x_{jk}}{B_{tot,k}} \tag{7}$$

Where, $B_{tot,k}$ denotes the total network bandwidth of BS S_k, U_k denotes all vehicle sets connected to BS S_k, B_{jk} denotes the service bandwidth requested by the terminal j in the set, and $x_{jk} \in \{0, 1\}$ is the access indication amount of the terminal j. If the terminal accesses the network of the BS S_k, then $x_{jk} = 1$; otherwise, $x_{jk} = 0$. The handoff probability based on the network load balancing condition attribute is:

$$P_{h4} = P(L_A > L_B | L_A > \lambda) \tag{8}$$

Where, L_B is the network load of the target BS, L_A is the network load of the current BS, and λ is the threshold value of the heavy load condition.

2.3 Decision Tree Handoff Decision Method Based on Maximum Probability

When there is a session service in the vehicle service, its requirement for network continuity and call drop rate is high, so the MEC server selects the network duration as a priority. When the terminal service is dominated by non-conversation services, the MEC server considers network bandwidth as the first choice. Others, when the terminal's current BS network load is high, the MEC server considers the load balancing among the BS networks as the first choice. Integrating the load situation of the current BS and the target BS, we give priority to switch the vehicle to the BS network with less load. Based on the above analysis, the tree structure of the decision tree is given in Fig. 3.

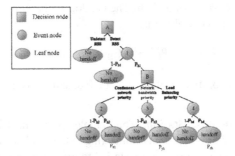

Fig. 3. Structure of multi-attribute decision tree

According to the structure of the decision tree we can get:

$$P_{xhi} = P(h_1)P(h_2|h_1) \tag{9}$$

$$P_{yhi} = P(h_1)P(h_3|h_1) \tag{10}$$

$$P_{zhi} = P(h_1)P(h_4|h_1) \tag{11}$$

The $P(h_1)$, $P(h_2)$, $P(h_3)$ and $P(h_4)$ represent the probability of occurrence of events h_1, h_2, h_3 and h_4 respectively. Therefore, the decision tree-based handoff strategy is a multi-attribute decision based on the maximum probability. That is:

I. When the MEC chooses the network duration priority, If $P_{xh_i} > P_{xh_0}$, we select the ith target BS for network handoff selection; If $P_{xh_i} \leq P_{xh_0}$, the handoff selection is abandoned and the vehicle terminal maintain current network connection.

II. Similarly, when the MEC selects the network bandwidth priority, if $P_{yh_i} > P_{yh_0}$, then we select the ith target BS for network handoff selection, and otherwise the handoff is abandoned.

III. When the MEC selects network load balancing priority, if $P_{zh_i} > P_{zh_0}$, we select the ith target BS for network handoff selection, and otherwise the handoff is abandoned.

Where $P_{xh_i} = \max(P_{xh_1}, \cdots, P_{xh_k})$, $P_{yh_i} = \max(P_{yh_1}, \cdots, P_{yh_k})$, $P_{zh_i} = \max$ $(P_{zh_1}, \cdots, P_{zh_k})$, i represents the ith target BS. And P_{xh_0}, P_{yh_0} and P_{zh_0} are references value of the BS network where the current vehicle terminal is located.

3   Self-adaptive Feedback Handoff Algorithm Based Decision Tree for Internet of Vehicles

During handoff through multi-attribute decision tree, the vehicle movement trend may change. The change of vehicle service status may affect the judgement of the next handoff [12]. Therefore, the self-adaptive incremental learning method based on feedback decision tree is implemented to rebuild the constructed tree.

3.1   Some Definitions About Self-adaptive Incremental Learning

This feedback mechanism implements incremental learning by adding decision table information at the nodes of the decision tree so as to dynamically catch the splitting attributes of the decision tree. Decision table is a special and important knowledge representation system. Decision table is a two-dimensional table, where each row describes an object and each column describes an attribute of the object. Attributes are divided into conditional attributes and decision attributes. According to different conditional attributes, the objects are divided into decision-making categories with different decision attributes. An example of the required decision table is given as follows:

Table 1. Decision table at initial time

	BS network load	Transmission rate	Terminal movement trend	RSS	Decision attribution
1	Medium	High	$\Delta D_d < 0$	High	Y
2	Medium	High	$\Delta D_d < 0$	Low	N
3	Medium	High	$\Delta D_d < 0$	Medium	N
4	Low	High	$\Delta D_d < 0$	High	Y
5	Low	High	$\Delta D_d < 0$	Medium	Y
6	Low	Low	$\Delta D_d < 0$	High	N

Let C indicates condition attributes, $C = \{C_l | l = 1, \cdots, L\}$. In Table 1, C_l are BS network load, Transmission rate, Terminal movement trend and RSS respectively. Let $D = \{Y, N\}$ indicates decision attributes with Y being handoff and N being no handoff. Let E_1 indicates condition class of C_1. In Table 2, $E_4 = \{$High, Medium, Low$\}$. Let T_l denote the number of cases that satisfy the conditional class being E_l when the decision attribute is Y or N, respectively.

This algorithm uses the greatest overall certainty of the condition attribute to the decision table as selection standard of spilt attributes. The definition of the overall certainty and certainty degree of the decision table is given as follows.

Definition 1. *The overall determinacy of the condition attribute C_l for the decision table is defined as:*

$$\mu_c(C_l) = \sum_{i=1}^{n} \max T_{li}/|U| \tag{12}$$

Where, U is the total data sets, $|U|$ is the count of the total data sets. $i = 1, \cdots, n$, n is the number of each condition class E_l.

Definition 2. *The certainty of the condition class E_l for the decision class is defined as:*

$$\vartheta(E_l) = \max T_{li} \bigg/ \sum_{i=1}^{n} T_{li} \tag{13}$$

3.2   The Process of Incremental Learning

The process of the incremental learning is as follows: when a new message is added, the values of μ_c and ϑ are dynamically catched using each decision value stored in each node to determine whether the decision tree needs to be re-adjusted, and the decision tree is re-implemented using the additional information μ_c and ϑ. The great value of μ_c is chosen to be splitting attribute.

At the initial t_1 time, the splitting attribute to start building decision tree is random as the root node is empty. *RSS* is chosen as the root node in this case. Assume that the decision tree generated at the initial t_1 time is shown in Fig. 4, and the root node additional information decision table is shown in Table 2:

Table 2. The root node additional information decision table

	C_1: RSS			C_2: Transmission rate			C_3: Terminal movement trend		C_4: BS network load		
	E_1			E_2			E_3		E_4		
	High	Low	Medium	High	Low	Medium	$\Delta D_d < 0$	$\Delta D_d > 0$	Medium	Low	High
$T_l(D = Y)$ $l = 1, \cdots, 4$	2	0	1	3	0	0	3	0	1	2	0
$T_l(D = N)$ $l = 1, \cdots, 4$	0	1	1	2	0	0	2	0	2	0	0
$\vartheta(E_l)$ $l = 1, \cdots, 4$	1	1	0.5	0.6			0.6		0.67	1	
$\mu_c(C_l)$ $l = 1, \cdots, 4$	0.8			0.6			0.6		0.8		

After the MEC server performed a handoff operation, if the vehicle feeds back its current state as $(E_1 = High, E_2 = Low, E_3 = \Delta D_d < 0, E_4 = High; D = N)$, the $\mu_c(C_l)$ and $\vartheta(E_l)$ are changed respectively, which are shown in Table 3.

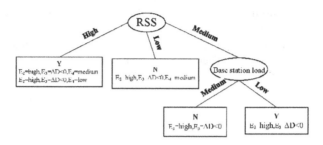

Fig. 4. Decision tree generated at the initial time

Table 3. The root node additional information decision table after feedback

	C_1: RSS			C_2: Transmission rate			C_3: Terminal movement trend		C_4: BS network load		
	E_1			E_2			E_3		E_4		
	High	Low	Medium	High	Low	Medium	$\Delta D_d < 0$	$\Delta D_d > 0$	Medium	Low	High
$T_l(D=Y)$ $l=1,\cdots,4$	2	0	1	3	0	0	3	0	1	2	0
$T_l(D=N)$ $l=1,\cdots,4$	1	1	1	2	1	0	3	0	2	0	1
$\vartheta(E_l)$ $l=1,\cdots,4$	0.67	1	0.5	0.6	1		0.5		0.67	1	1
$\mu_c(C_l)$ $l=1,\cdots,4$	0.67			0.67			0.5		0.83		

Table 4. Medium classification node additional information table

	C_1: RSS			C_2: Transmission rate			C_3: Terminal movement trend	
	E_1			E_2			E_3	
	High	Low	Medium	High	Low	Medium	$\Delta D_d < 0$	$\Delta D_d > 0$
$T_l(D=Y) l=1,\cdots,4$	1	0	0	1	0	0	1	0
$T_l(D=N) l=1,\cdots,4$	0	1	1	2	1	0	2	0
$\vartheta(E_l)$ $l=1,\cdots,4$	1	1	1	0.67	1		0.67	
$\mu_c(C_l)$ $l=1,\cdots,4$	1			0.67			0.67	

From Table 3, μ_c (BS Network Load) $= 0.83$ becomes the maximum value instead of $\mu_c(\text{RSS}) = 0.8$ in Table 2. Therefore, the BS network load is used as the splitting attribute of the root node. According to Eq. (14), $\vartheta(E(medium)) = 0.67$, $\vartheta(E(low)) = 1$, $\vartheta(E(high)) = 1$ respectively. Since $\vartheta(E(low)) > \mu_c$ (BS Network Load), $\vartheta(E(high)) > \mu_c$ (BS Network Load), $\vartheta(E(medium)) < \mu_c$ (BS Network Load), the nodes corresponding to the Low classification and the High classification serve as leaf nodes respectively, and the condition classification Medium continues to split. Therefore, the Medium branch in Fig. 4 is removed and the remainder is denoted as a temporary decision tree T. The instances of Low and High values in T is moved to the leaf nodes corresponding to the new Low and High categories, as shown in Fig. 5. Then, the additional information table is changed rely on the temporary decision tree T, which is shown in Table 4.

In Table 4, according to Eq. (12), $\mu_c(RSS) = 1$ becomes the maximum value to be a splitting attribute of the node. Therefore, the Medium branch in Fig. 5(b) is replaced by RSS node in Fig. 5(a), as shown in Fig. 6. That is the decision tree using SAFH algorithm.

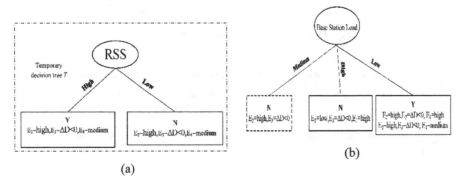

(a)

(b)

Fig. 5. Decision tree generated at intermediate results

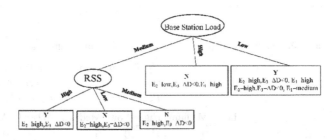

Fig. 6. Decision tree formed after performing a feedback operation

3.3   SAFH Algorithm Based Decision Tree for Internet of Vehicles

In this section, our proposed SAFH algorithm based decision tree is shown in Fig. 7. The two stages of this algorithm are described as follows:

Multi-attribute Handoff Decision Based Decision Tree. The vehicles reports its services requirements to MEC server, MEC server collects network attributes, such as

RSS, transmission rate and BS network load, to calculate handoff probability distribution. Then a multi-attributes decision tree is built to make handoff decision based on maximum handoff according different priorities.

Self-adaptive Feedback Incremental Learning Handoff Method. After the vehicle terminal changed its own service state and performed a handoff operation, the vehicle feedbacked its services requirements and movement trend to MEC server. MEC server update decision table information and incremental learning is used to modify the multi-attribute decision tree. Consequently, the handoff decision is made according to the rebuilt decision tree.

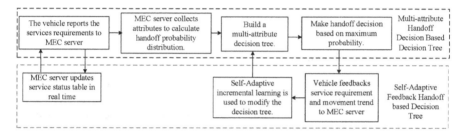

Fig. 7. The flow diagram of SAFH algorithm based decision tree

4 Simulation Results

In this section, we use computer simulations to evaluate the performance of proposed algorithm, and compare the performance of the proposed SAFH algorithm with existing algorithms.

4.1 Simulation Scenario

Based on the system scenario studied in Sect. 2.1, we simulate our proposed SAFH algorithm, comparing with the traditional non-feedback decision tree (NFDT) algorithm [13] and the traditional RSS fuzzy handoff decision algorithm [14]. As shown in Fig. 8, we construct a simulation scenario to evaluate our proposed methods in terms of handoff times and time cost. In the simulation scenario, the signal radius of BS is set to 1000 meters. The signal coverage is circular and the BS is located at the center. In order to facilitate the analysis, the vehicle terminal moves from point A to point E during the simulation. When the vehicle reaches point C, there is session service access. In the simulation experiment, network updating and handover decisions are performed by MEC server every 5 s.

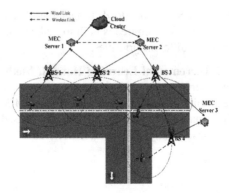

Fig. 8. Simulation Scenario

4.2 Average Handoff Times

When the BS's signal strength changes dramatically in a certain area, the mobile terminal will switch back and forth between the two base stations, which is called the "ping-pong effect" [14]. As shown in Fig. 9, the speed of vehicle is set from 60 km/h to

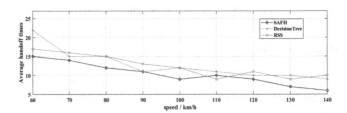

Fig. 9. The average handoff times in terms of vehicle speed

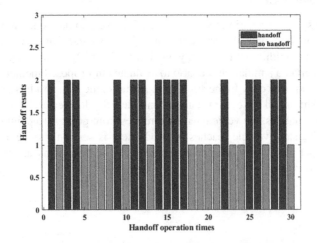

Fig. 10. Handoff case using SAFH algorithm

140 km/h. It shows that the average handoff times decrease as the speed increase. And the average handoff times are lower than NFDT algorithm as well as the traditional RSS fuzzy handoff algorithm. Therefore, the proposed SAFH algorithm can effectively reduce the ping-pong effect, increase the effectiveness of the network connection, and improve the service quality. The Fig. 10 shows a practical handoff case which used the prosed SAFH algorithm, the vehicle terminal experiences 15 handoff operations at a time when its speed is 60 km/h.

4.3   Analysis of Algorithm's Time Cost

We repeated the experiment 10000 times and used the average results to indicate the time cost, because the time cost is a statistical value. From Fig. 11, we can see that the time cost of the proposed SAFH algorithm is generally low. And when the vehicle accessing session service, where travels to the point C, the traditional NFDT algorithm does not have a feedback operation, resulting in a significant increase in time. Besides, the traditional RSS fuzzy handover decision algorithm's time cost is higher than the proposed algorithm. Therefore, the SAFH algorithm proposed in this paper effectively solves the impact on the handoff decisions due to the change of vehicle terminal service status.

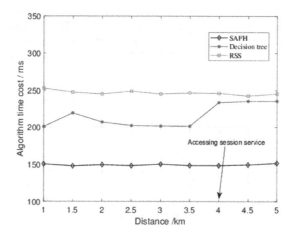

Fig. 11. Preformation time in terms of distance

5   Conclusion

In this paper, we propose a self-adaption feedback handoff (SAFH) algorithm for IoVs based MEC. By vehicle terminal feedback its change of status and movement trends, the MEC server performs pre-trimmed incremental learning on the decision tree to obtain a new type of decision tree. The simulation results show that the SAFH algorithm proposed in this paper is suitable for the handoff decision-making for vehicle terminals with high mobility and frequent business change. The algorithm can effectively reduce the ping-pong effect, increase the effective time of network connection. In addition, our proposed algorithm's time cost is lower comparing with the traditional decision tree handoff algorithm and the RSS-based fuzzy handoff decision algorithm.

References

1. 3GPP: Handover procedures. TS 23.009, v12.0.0 12 (2016)
2. Zuozhao, L., Liu, J.: Application of mobile edge computing in internet of vehicles. Mod. Sci. Technol. Telecommun. **47**(33), 37–41 (2017)
3. Hu, Y.C., Patel, M., Sabella, D., Sprecher, N., Young, V.: Mobile edge computing (MEC): a key technology towards 5G. ETSI. 1.1.1 (2015)
4. Almulla, M., Wang, Y., Boukerche, A.: Design of a fast location-based handoff scheme for IEEE 802.11 vehicular. IEEE Trans. Veh. Technol. **63**(8), 3853–3866 (2014)
5. Bi, Y., Zhou, H., Xu, W.: An Efficient PMIPv6-based handoff scheme for urban vehicular networks. IEEE Trans. Intell. Transp. Syst. **PP**(99), 1–16 (2016)
6. Tselikas, N.D., Kosmatos, E.A.: A handoff algorithm for packet loss optimization in vehicular radio-over-fiber picocellular networks. In: International Conference on Connected Vehicles and Expo, pp. 1074–1079. IEEE Press (2015)
7. Mao, Y., You, C., Zhang, J.: A survey on mobile edge computing: the communication perspective. IEEE Commun. Surv. Tutor. **PP**(99), 1 (2017)
8. Liu, J., Wan, J., Zeng, B.: A scalable and quick-response software defined vehicular network assisted by mobile edge computing. IEEE Commun. Mag. **55**(7), 94–100 (2017)
9. Basudan, S., Lin, X., Sankaranarayanan, K.: A privacy-preserving vehicular crowdsensing based road surface condition monitoring system using fog computing. IEEE Internet Things J. **PP**(99), 1 (2017)
10. Li, L., Li, Y., Hou, R.: A novel mobile edge computing-based architecture for future cellular vehicular networks. In: Wireless Communications and NETWORKING Conference, pp. 1–6. IEEE (2017)
11. 3GPP: Technical specification group services and system aspects. TS 32.102, v9.0.0 9 (2009)
12. Schlimmer, J.C., Fisher, D.H.: A case study of incremental concept induction. In: National Conference on Artificial Intelligence, Los Altos, pp. 496–501 (1986)
13. Bin, M., Wang, D., Cheng, S.: Modeling and analysis for vertical handoff based on the decision tree in a heterogeneous vehicle network. IEEE Access **PP**(99), 1 (2017)
14. He, Q.: A fuzzy logic based vertical handoff decision algorithm between WWAN and WLAN. In: International Conference on Networking and Digital Society, pp. 561–564. IEEE (2010)

Segment-Based Scheduling Algorithm in Cache-Enabled Device-to-Device Wireless Networks

Shaoqin Peng[1(✉)], Bo Chang[1], Liying Li[2], Guodong Zhao[1], Zhi Chen[1], and Qi Wang[1]

[1] National Key Laboratory of Communication, UESTC, Chengdu, China
psq20110607@163.com, changb3212@163.com, gdngzhao@163.com,
chenzhi@uestc.edu.cn, wqforward@163.com
[2] School of Automation Engineering, UESTC, Chengdu, China
liyingli0815@gmail.com

Abstract. In this paper, we study the link scheduling problem in cache-enabled *device-to-device* (D2D) wireless networks considering the *quality-of-service* (QoS) requirement of each scheduled D2D link. We propose a segment-based link scheduling method which consists of two phases, user pairing and link scheduling, to maximize the overall system throughput. We designed a segment factor to control interference among the established D2D links in the link scheduling phase. With the proposed method, interference among different scheduled D2D links can be significantly reduced and the QoS of each link can be guaranteed. Simulation results show that the proposed method outperforms the existing ones in terms of overall system throughput and the number of scheduled D2D links.

Keywords: Scheduling · Cache-enabled · D2D · Wireless networks

1 Introduction

The widely used smart phones and the popularity of tablets have greatly boosted the demand for wireless video services. The videos services will soon occupy most of the wireless data traffic, and lead to a rapid growth in the wireless data traffic [1]. The heavy wireless data traffic has been imposing a significant burden on the current wireless infrastructure. Introducing the caching technique has been a promising solution to solve this problem [2]. Through the caching technique, users can obtain their desired popular files from nearby users via D2D communication links, rather than the *base station* (BS) [3].

Currently, some contributions discuss the link scheduling problem in cache-enabled D2D networks. In [1], the macro-cell is divided into some small clusters

This work was supported in part by the National Natural Science Foundation of China under Grant 61631004 and 61601094.

J. Zheng et al. (Eds.): ADHOCNETS 2018, LNICST 258, pp. 191–201, 2019.
https://doi.org/10.1007/978-3-030-05888-3_18

to reduce intra-cluster interference. However, it ignores the co-channel interference among different clusters. In [4], the authors made some modifications over the conventional *information-theoretic link scheduling* (ITLinQ), called *cached ITLinQ*, where each destination user is connected to the closest source user that caches its requested file. However, the oversimplified user pairing without considering the interference causes performance loss. The *content-centric link scheduling* (CTLinQ) algorithm was proposed in [5] to obtain the maximum number of activated links. In the first phase of CTLinQ, priorities are given to potential D2D links according to their channel gains. This makes the schedule links set settled to a large extent, even though the co-channel interference is considered in the second phase of CTLinQ. However, the latter consideration of interference will degrade the performance of this algorithm in terms of the number of activated links. In [6], the caching and scheduling policies were jointly designed to maximize successful offloading probability. The authors designed a scheduling factor which divided the given duration into some equal-length time slots to control interference among the established D2D links. However, the oversimplified partition limits the performance.

In this paper, we propose a segment-based link scheduling method which consists of two phases for the link scheduling problem in cache-enabled D2D networks. In the first phase, we obtain the set of schedule D2D links according to users' cached file and requested file. In the second phase, we design a segment factor to control interference among the scheduled D2D links. With the proposed method, we can make both the overall system throughput and the number of scheduled D2D links improved. Our results demonstrate the advantages of the proposed method by comparing with the cached ITLinQ method in [4] and the CLTinQ method in [5].

2 System Model and Problem Formulation

2.1 System Model

We consider a cache-enabled D2D wireless network, where a BS with coverage radius R_B is located at the center of a cell. In this paper, we do not consider the mobility of users [7]. We assume that N users distribute uniformly in the coverage of BS. For notational simplicity, we assume that each user has cached a popular file from a file library with M identical size files [8]. Suppose that each user requests one file from the library independently, whose popularity follows Zipf distribution [9]. If we rank M files in terms of popularity in a decreasing order, then the requested probability of the i-th ranked file is given by

$$p_r(i) = \frac{\frac{1}{i^{\gamma_r}}}{\sum\limits_{j=1}^{M} \frac{1}{j^{\gamma_r}}} \quad , \quad i = 1, 2, ..., M, \tag{1}$$

where γ_r is the requested Zipf exponent. Here, the large value of γ_r means that the requests concentrate on the high ranking files.

In the system, a user can obtain its requested file through three ways: self-serve, D2D-Serve or BS-Serve. Here, we mainly discuss the D2D-Serve. We label D2D transmitter (DT) as the user who transmits file, and D2D receiver (DR) as the user who receives file. In our paper, point-to-point link and half-duplex operation modes are assumed [10]. That is, a user can communicate with at most one user, and it cannot transmit or receive files simultaneously. For any DR, only the nearest user who cached its requested file serves as a DT. For any DT, only transmits the file to the nearest user who requests its cached file. In addition, we also assume that all D2D links operate in the same frequency bandwidth, and the cellular links and D2D links operate in orthogonal frequency bandwidth [10].

2.2   Problem Formulation

We define $U = \{u_1, u_2, ..., u_N\}$ as a set of N users, and $V = \{(u_t, u_r)\,|\,u_t \in U, u_r \in U, u_t \neq u_r\}$ as the set of D2D pairs, where (u_t, u_r) is a D2D pair. Here, u_t and u_r represent a DT and a DR respectively. In addition, a D2D pair (u_t, u_r) needs to satisfy the two conditions as follows:

(a) D2D-Serve condition: u_r cannot cache the file requested, it needs to obtain the requested file from other users via D2D link, i.e., $f_c(u_r) \neq f_r(u_r)$, where $f_c(u_r)$ and $f_r(u_r)$ represent the cached file and requested file of u_r, respectively. To obtain the D2D pair (u_t, u_r), u_t needs to cache the requested file of u_r. This means $f_c(u_t) = f_r(u_r)$, where $f_c(u_t)$ represents the cached file of u_t.

(b) D2D range condition: We define d_{u_t, u_r} as the distance between u_t and u_r. In order to establish a D2D communication link, d_{u_t, u_r} should be less than or at least equal to the D2D help distance, i.e., $d_{u_t, u_r} \leq R_{D2D}$, here R_{D2D} is the D2D help distance.

If a D2D pair (u_t, u_r) satisfies the two conditions, it is a potential D2D link. Denote the set of all these potential D2D links as $S = \{(u_t, u_r)\,|\,(u_t, u_r) \in V, (u_t, u_r)$ satisfies conditions (a) (b)$\}$. Then, the set of potential D2D links S is a subset of V.

To indicate the schedule process, we define a binary variable v_{u_t, u_r} as below:

$$v_{u_t, u_r} = \begin{cases} 1, & (u_t, u_r) \in S \text{ and } (u_t, u_r) \text{ is scheduled,} \\ 0, & (u_t, u_r) \in S \text{ but } (u_t, u_r) \text{ is removed} \\ & \text{or } (u_t, u_r) \notin S, \end{cases} \tag{2}$$

where $(u_t, u_r) \in V$. Then, the set of schedule D2D links, which is a candidate set for scheduling, can be expressed as

$$L = \{(u_t, u_r)\,|\,(u_t, u_r) \in V, v_{u_t, u_r} = 1\}. \tag{3}$$

Then L is a subset of set S. Assume that the number of D2D links in the set L is l, i.e., $|L| = l$.

Since we consider the point-to-point link, the following condition needs to be satisfied,

$$\sum_{u_r \in U, u_r \neq u_t} v_{u_r,u_t} + \sum_{u_r \in U, u_r \neq u_t} v_{u_t,u_r} \leq 1, \forall u_t \in U. \tag{4}$$

In addition, the half-duplex operation mode can be expressed as

$$\sum_{u_r \in U, u_r \neq u_t} v_{u_r,u_t} \sum_{u_r \in U, u_r \neq u_t} v_{u_t,u_r} = 0, \forall u_t \in U. \tag{5}$$

After we obtain the set of schedule D2D links L, the *signal-to-interference-plus-noise ratio* (SINR) of $(u_t, u_r) \in L$ can be expressed as

$$SINR_{u_t,u_r} = \frac{P_t d_{u_t,u_r}^{-\alpha}}{\sum_{u_m \in U_T} P_t d_{u_m,u_r}^{-\alpha} + P_n}, \tag{6}$$

where P_t is the transmission power, P_n is the power of noise, α is the path loss exponent, and $\sum_{u_m \in U_T} P_t d_{u_m,u_r}^{-\alpha}$ is the total interference from all the other DTs (constituting the set U_T). In addition, we assume that the transmission power P_t and the power of noise P_n are known to all users [11], thus the DRs of D2D links can obtain their SINR.

To satisfy the users' QoS, the data rate of D2D link $(u_t, u_r) \in L$ has to be greater than or equal to the data rate threshold R_0, i.e.,

$$R_{u_t,u_r} = W \log_2(1 + SINR_{u_t,u_r}) \geq R_0, \tag{7}$$

where W denotes the bandwidth.

This paper aims at maximizing the total system throughput. We define the overall system throughput as S_T, then the problem can be formulated as

$$\begin{aligned}
\max \quad & S_T = \sum_{(u_t,u_r) \in L} W \log_2(1 + SINR_{u_t,u_r}) \\
s.t. \quad & \sum_{u_r \in U, u_r \neq u_t} v_{u_r,u_t} + \sum_{u_r \in U, u_r \neq u_t} v_{u_t,u_r} \leq 1, \forall u_t \in U, \\
& \sum_{u_r \in U, u_r \neq u_t} v_{u_r,u_t} \sum_{u_r \in U, u_r \neq u_t} v_{u_t,u_r} = 0, \forall u_t \in U, \\
& R_{u_t,u_r} \geq R_0, \forall (u_t, u_r) \in L, \\
& v_{u_t,u_r} \in \{0,1\}, \forall (u_t, u_r) \in V.
\end{aligned} \tag{8}$$

Next, we will develop a segment-based link scheduling method to obtain the solution.

3 Segment-Based Scheduling Algorithm

The proposed method consists of two phases: The first phase considers the D2D-serve condition to obtain the schedule D2D links. In the second phase, we design a segment factor to divide a given duration T into two different time slots. We rank the files in library in terms of popularity in a decreasing order. In the meantime, the segment factor also divides the popular files into two segments correspondingly. Thus, the set of schedule D2D links can be divided into two subsets according to the D2D links' transmitting file. The links in two different subsets will be scheduled in different time slots.

3.1   Phase 1: User Pairing

In this phase, we first obtain the set of potential D2D links S. Then, according to (4) and (5), we obtain the set of schedule D2D links. Algorithm 1 shows the details about this user pairing algorithm to obtain the set of schedule D2D links.

Algorithm 1. User Pairing Algorithm.

1: Step 1: The BS collects the users' requested and cached file, i.e., $f_r(u_i)$ and $f_c(u_i)$ $(i = 1, 2, ..., N)$.

2: Step 2: The BS chooses the D2D links which satisfy the conditions (a) and (b), then obtains the set of potential D2D links S.

3: Step 3: For any DR, only the nearest user who cached its requested file can serve as a DT. For any DT, only transmits the file to the nearest user who requests its cached file, the set of schedule D2D links L is obtained finally.

3.2   Phase 2: Link Scheduling

After we obtain the schedule D2D links in the previous step, these links have not been scheduled at this time. Some of them may not meet the requirement on QoS.

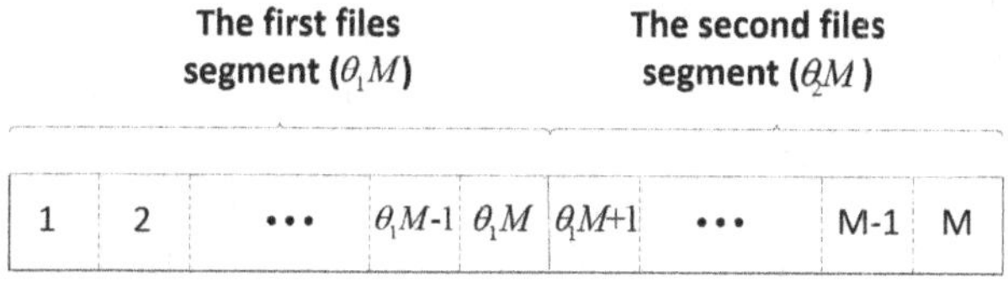

Fig. 1. Illustration of the division of the popular files, where popular files have been ranked in terms of popularity in a decreasing order.

In order to divide the set of schedule D2D links into two subsets, we design a segment factor θ, $\theta \in \{\frac{1}{M}, \frac{2}{M}, ..., 1\}$. This segment factor divides the duration T into two different time slots. The length of the first time slot is $\theta_1 T$, and another is $\theta_2 T$, where $\theta_1 = \theta$, $\theta_2 = 1 - \theta$. After we rank the files in library in terms of popularity in a decreasing order, the segment factor θ also divides the popular files into two segments with length $\theta_1 M$ and $\theta_2 M$ respectively, as shown in Fig. 1. For example, if a file is ranked the top $\theta_1 M$, it will be at the first popular files segment.

Figure 2 illustrates the segment-based link scheduling method, which operates periodically with a given duration T. From the figure, we can observe that k D2D links are scheduled in the first time slot, and another $l - k$ D2D links are scheduled in the second time slot.

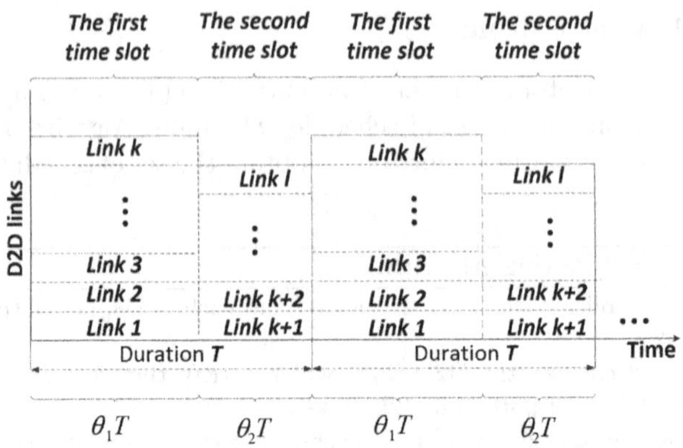

The first time slot	The second time slot	The first time slot	The second time slot

Fig. 2. Illustration of the segment-based link scheduling method for schedule D2D links.

For each established D2D link, there is a file transmitting from the DT to its corresponding DR. Only the D2D link whose transmitting file is in the first files segment can be scheduled in the first time slot, and stays muting in another time slot. While the D2D link whose transmitting file is in the second files segment will be scheduled in the second time slot. That means, the transmitting file of a D2D link decides the time slot that the D2D link will be scheduled. For example, assume that a D2D link $(u_t, u_r) \in L$ transmits the file f_i, $(i = 1, 2, ..., M)$. Then, according to the partition of the popular files, if the file f_i is the top $\theta_1 M$ files, the link (u_t, u_r) will be scheduled in the first time slot, otherwise it will be scheduled in the second time slot.

We assume that the links scheduled in the first time slot belong to the link set L_1, and the others belong to the link set L_2. Both of these sets are subsets of the schedule links set L. The relationships between these sets are given by

$$L = L_1 \cup L_2, \tag{9}$$

and

$$L_1 \cap L_2 = \emptyset. \tag{10}$$

Based on the aforementioned contents, we can rewrite $SINR_{u_t, u_r}$ of $(u_t, u_r) \in L_i$ $(i = 1, 2)$ as

$$SINR_{u_t, u_r} = \frac{P_t d_{u_t, u_r}^{-\alpha}}{\sum_{u_m \in U_{T_i}, i=1,2} P_t d_{u_m, u_r}^{-\alpha} + P_n}, \tag{11}$$

where U_{T_i} is the set of DTs in i-th time slot.

Then, according to [6], the data rate of the D2D link (u_t, u_r) in the i-th time slot is

$$R_{u_t, u_r} = \theta_i W \log_2(1 + SINR_{u_t, u_r}). \tag{12}$$

With the growth of θ, the data rate of the D2D links in the first time slot increases according to (12). Due to the higher ranking files have a higher probability to be requested, the number of links in the first time slot is more than the second time slot. Thus, in order to obtain the maximum system throughput, we have the following expression as

$$\theta_1 > \theta_2. \tag{13}$$

When θ reaches a certain point, the number of D2D links scheduled simultaneously in the first time slot is too large, leading to more interference. This will cause the data rate of the first time slot to decrease, so the optimal θ needs to be obtained.

Based on the schedule D2D links that we obtained in the phase 1, the problem can be expressed as

$$
\begin{aligned}
\max\quad & S_T = \sum_{i=1,2} \sum_{(u_t,u_r)\in L_i} \theta_i W \log_2(1 + SINR_{u_t,u_r}) \\
\text{s.t.}\quad & R_{u_t,u_r} \geq R_0, \forall (u_t, u_r) \in L, \\
& L = L_1 \cup L_2, L_1 \cap L_2 = \emptyset, \\
& \theta_1 = \theta, \theta_2 = 1 - \theta, \theta \in \{\tfrac{1}{M}, \tfrac{2}{M}, ..., 1\}, \\
& \theta_1 > \theta_2.
\end{aligned}
\tag{14}
$$

The overall system throughput consists of the throughput of the two subsets. As mentioned above, the file library has M files, due to (13), we start the search at the $(\frac{M}{2} + 1)$-th file, i.e.,

$$\theta = \frac{\frac{M}{2} + 1}{M}. \tag{15}$$

Although D2D links are scheduled in different time slots, there are still some links may not meet the requirement on QoS. If this happens, they cannot be scheduled finally and have to be removed. However, instead of removing these links together, we remove them one by one. The link that has the minimum data rate will be removed from the set of schedule links successively, until all scheduled D2D links can meet the QoS requirement. Suppose that there are Q_i D2D links in L_i cannot meet the Qos requirement, then the D2D link $(u_t, u_r)_j \in L_i$ which should be removed according to the following expression,

$$j = \arg \min_{1 \leq j \leq Q_i} \{R_{(u_t,u_r)_j}\}, \ (u_t, u_r) \in L_i. \tag{16}$$

In this way, the co-channel interference can be reduced. After removed some links, the links that originally cannot be scheduled may finally meet the QoS requirement.

Algorithm 2 provides the details on how to obtain the optimal θ to maximize the system throughput. Specifically, we start searching at a certain θ, under which we calculate the data rate of scheduled D2D links that meet the QoS requirement. In the meantime, we remove the D2D links which cannot satisfy the requirement one by one based on (16), until all D2D links satisfy the QoS requirement. Then, we obtain the overall system throughput and the number of scheduled D2D links. Next, we conduct the search by repeating the above steps. As a result, we can obtain the optimal θ that maximizes the system throughput.

Algorithm 2. Link Scheduling Algorithm.

1: After user pairing phase: $(u_t, u_r) \in L$
2: **Initialization:** R_0, $S_{Temp} = 0$, $N_{Temp} = 0$
3: **For** $\theta = (\frac{\frac{M}{2}+1}{M}) : \frac{1}{M} : 1$ **do**
4: $\theta_1 = \theta$, obtain the links set L_1
5: **While** $\exists (u_t, u_r) \in L_1, R_{u_t, u_r} < R_0$ **do**
6: calculate $R_{u_t, u_r} = \theta_1 W \log_2(1 + SINR_{u_t, u_r})$
7: remove $(u_t, u_r) \in L_1$ that has the minimum data rate
8: **end while**
9: $\theta_2 = 1 - \theta$, obtain the links set L_2
10: **While** $\exists (u_t, u_r) \in L_2, R_{u_t, u_r} < R_0$ **do**
11: calculate $R_{u_t, u_r} = \theta_2 W \log_2(1 + SINR_{u_t, u_r})$
12: remove $(u_t, u_r) \in L_2$ that has the minimum data rate
13: **end while**
14: calculate the system throughput S_T and the number of scheduled links $N_{Schedule}$
15: **If** $S_T > S_{Temp}$ **then**
16: $S_{Temp} = S_T$
17: $N_{Temp} = N_{Schedule}$
18: **end if**
19: **end for**

---

4   Simulation Results

In the simulation, we assume that each user caches a file according to Zipf distribution with the exponent γ_c. The main simulation parameters are listed in Table 1. For comparison, we provide the simulation results to demonstrate the performance of the cached ITLinQ algorithm in [4] as well as the CTLinQ algorithm in [5].

Table 1. Parameter settings

Parameters	Values
The coverage radius of the BS: R_B	600 m
The D2D help distance: R_{D2D}	100 m
The number of users in the coverage of the BS: N	500
The number of files in the networks: M	1000
The cached Zipf exponent: γ_c	1.2
The requested Zipf exponent: γ_r	0.6
The path loss exponent: α	4
The D2D transmit power: P_t	20 dBm
The noise power density: P_n	-170 dBm\Hz
The bandwidth: W	1 MHz

Figure 3 compares the number of scheduled D2D links versus the data rate threshold. Here, we assume that the number of files is 50, i.e., $M = 50$. From the figure, the number of scheduled D2D links decreases as the data rate threshold increases. This is because if the QoS requirement get stricter, the number of the D2D links which meet the requirement would decrease, then less D2D links can be obtained. We can observe that the performance of the three schemes are better than the CTLinQ and the cached ITLinQ schemes, and the schemes of different segment reach the similar performance. In particular, the complexity of the algorithm will increase as the number of segments grows. Then, it is more efficient to choose the two-segment scheme than the others.

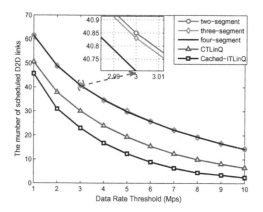

Fig. 3. Performance comparison of different segment schemes in terms of the number of scheduled D2D links, where $R_{D2D} = 100\,\mathrm{m}$, $\gamma_r = 0.6$.

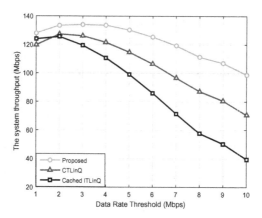

Fig. 4. Performance comparison of different schemes in terms of the overall system throughput, where $R_{D2D} = 100\,\mathrm{m}$, $\gamma_r = 0.6$.

Figure 4 shows the comparison of the overall system throughput between the three methods. From the figure, as the data rate threshold R_0 increases, the system throughput in three methods first increases and then decreases. This is reasonable because as the data rate threshold increasing, there are more D2D links cannot meet the QoS requirement which will be removed in the phase 2. The interference to the existing links will decrease, then the system throughput first increases. As the data rate threshold increasing continually, the number of D2D links which can meet the Qos requirement is decreasing. As the figure shows, while $R_0 \geq 2$, the system throughput starts to drop.

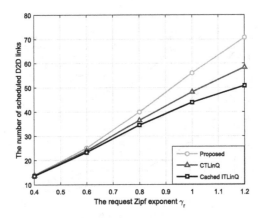

Fig. 5. Performance comparison of different schemes in terms of the number of scheduled D2D links, where $R_{D2D} = 100\,\text{m}$, $R_0 = 1\,\text{Mbps}$.

The impact of the request Zipf exponent is shown in Fig. 5. From the figure, as γ_r increases, the requests are more concentrated on high ranking files, which leads to a higher probability of finding their the requested file in the nearby users' cache. Thus the increasing γ_r raises the number of scheduled D2D links.

5   Conclusions

In this paper, we proposed a segment-based link scheduling method in cache-enabled D2D wireless networks considering the QoS requirement of each D2D link. The first phase obtains the schedule D2D links, and the second phase designs a segment factor to maximize the overall system throughput. Simulation results showed that the performance of the proposed method outperforms the existing cached ITLinQ and CTLinQ methods.

References

1. Golrezaei, N., Mansourifard, P., Molisch, A.F., Dimakis, A.G.: Basestation assisted device-to-device communications for high-throughput wireless video networks. IEEE Trans. Wireless Commun. **13**(7), 3665–3676 (2014)
2. Golrezaei, N., Molisch, A., Dimakis, A., Caire, G.: Femtocaching and device-to-device collaboration: a new architecture for wireless video distribution. IEEE Commun. Mag. **51**(4), 142–149 (2013)
3. Golrezaei, N., Dimakis, A.G., Molisch, A.F.: Wireless device to-device communications with distributed caching. In: Proceedings of Information Theory Proceedings (ISIT), pp. 2781–2785 (2012)
4. Naderializadeh, N., Kao, D.T.H., Avestimehr, A.S.: How to utilize caching to improve spectral efficiency in device-to-device wireless networks. In: Proceedings of Communication, Control, and Computing (Allerton), Monticello, pp. 415–422 (2014)
5. Zhao, G., et al.: CTLinQ: content-centric link scheduling in cache-enabled device-to-device wireless networks. To appear in ICC 2018
6. Chen, B., Yang, C., Xiong, Z.: Optimal caching and scheduling for cache-enabled D2D communications. IEEE Commun. Lett. **21**, 1155–1158 (2017)
7. Akilesh, B., Sathya, V., Ramamurthy, A., Tamma, B.R.: A novel scheduling algorithm to maximize the D2D spatial reuse in LTE networks. In: IEEE International Conference on Advanced Networks and Telecommunications Systems (ANTS), Bangalore, pp. 1–6 (2016)
8. Wang, X., Bao, Y., Liu, X., Niu, Z.: On the design of relay caching in cellular networks for energy efficiency. In: Proceedings of Computer Communications Workshops, pp. 259–264 (2011)
9. Cha, M., Kwak, H., Rodriguez, P., Ahn, Y.Y., Moon, S.: Analyzing the video popularity characteristics of large-scale user generated content systems. IEEE/ACM Trans. Netw. **17**(5), 1357–1370 (2009)
10. Zhang, L., Xiao, M., Wu, G., Li, S.: Efficient scheduling and power allocation for D2D-assisted wireless caching networks. IEEE Trans. Commun. **64**(6), 2438–2452 (2016)
11. Lee, H.S., Lee, J.W.: QoS and channel-aware distributed link scheduling for D2D communication. In: IEEE International Symposium on Modeling and Optimization in Mobile, Ad Hoc, and Wireless Networks, pp. 1–8 (2016)

An Action Recognition Method Based on Wearable Sensors

Fuliang Ma[1], Jing Tan[1], Xiubing Liu[1], Huiqiang Wang[1],
Guangsheng Feng[1(✉)], Bingyang Li[1], Hongwu Lv[1], Junyu Lin[2],
and Mao Tang[3]

[1] College of Computer Science and Technology, Harbin Engineering University,
Harbin 150001, China
fengguangsheng@hrbeu.edu.cn
[2] Institute of Information Engineering, Chinese Academy of Sciences,
Beijing 100093, China
[3] Science and Technology Resource Sharing Service Center of Heilongjiang,
Harbin 150001, China

Abstract. In the field of human action recognition, some existing works are mainly focused on macro actions, e.g., the requirements for action recognition is walking or jumping, while others are concentrated on micro actions, e.g., hand waving or leg raising. However, existing works rarely consider the recognition effect of different sensor wearing schemes with various requirements. In this work, the influences of the wearing scheme on action recognition effect are taken into account, a universal action recognition method to adapt different recognition requirements is developed. First, we present an action layered verification model which includes static action layer, dynamic action layer and joint presentation layer, which is used to provide an optional wearing scheme for each layer and to prevent wrong classification problems. Second, we verify the recognition effect of various wearing schemes under different layers. Finally, an action recognition method based on decision tree is introduced to adapt different requirements. The experiments show that the proposed method achieves a desirable recognition effect in comparison to existing ones.

Keywords: Action recognition · Wearable sensors · Wearing scheme

1 Introduction

Human action recognition is a hot topic in the field of human-computer interaction (HCI) and has received widespread attentions as the techniques of HCI and communication are making continuous improvement [1]. Some existing works are mainly focused on macro action recognition, e.g., the requirements for action recognition is walking or jumping, while others are on micro actions, e.g., hand waving or leg raising [2–5]. Moreover, the earlier technologies to recognize actions by image analysis, captured by the pre-installed cameras [6–9], which is severely affected by the camera accuracy and also incurs privacy concerns. Recently, the wearable sensor-based recognition are coming into interest due to the merits of the sensors, including small size, easy wearing, privacy-protecting, etc. [10–12].

© ICST Institute for Computer Sciences, Social Informatics and Telecommunications Engineering 2019
Published by Springer Nature Switzerland AG 2019. All Rights Reserved
J. Zheng et al. (Eds.): ADHOCNETS 2018, LNICST 258, pp. 202–211, 2019.
https://doi.org/10.1007/978-3-030-05888-3_19

To recognize different kinds of human actions, placing a variety of sensors on different positions is usually employed, e.g., accelerometers on the abdomen for elderly fall detection [13], acceleration and pressure sensors on the sole for recognizing walking, sitting and standing [2], accelerometers in thigh pockets for recognizing athlete's swimming [14], mobile phones with acceleration sensors on leg for recognizing climbing stairs [3], etc. The influences of sensor positions on action recognition are also considered by some researchers. For example, the accelerometer placed on chest has slight advantages on gesture recognition and fall detection [15]. Moreover, the work [16] studies the sensor position calculation for improving the recognition accuracy. In the above studies, the positions and numbers of sensors used to recognize actions are different, which shows that the sensor arrangement is significantly crucial. Although these studies have achieved good results in specific areas, however, the recognition effect of different sensor wearing schemes under different requirements is rarely considered.

In reality, people have different requirements for the action recognition, such as static, dynamic and mixed actions, which is the main problem considered in this work, i.e., designing an action recognition method to adapt different recognition requirements. First, a layered verification model is developed to distinguish different layer actions and verify the recognition effect of the sensor wearing schemes under different layers. Then, we present a universal wearing scheme for actions by comparing the wearing schemes at different layers. Finally, an action recognition method is designed to adapt different requirements.

2 System Model

Figure 1 shows the proposed recognition framework, including data processing, action layered verification model and action recognition model. In the framework, a layered verification model is designed based on the random forest classifier, which can be used to examine various wearing schemes of action recognition on different layers. On this basis, a universal action recognition method after analyzing the sensor for wearing scheme on different layers is developed.

2.1 Data Processing

2.1.1 Data Collection

The Ubisense positioning platform and positioning tags are used for data collection [17]. The platform consists of three components: sensors, positioning tags and positioning platform iLocateTRM, where the positioning tags transmit position information to the sensors via Ultra Wideband (UWB) pulse signal. After receiving the signal, the sensor adopts TDOA and AOA positioning. The algorithm analyzes the tags location and finally transmits it to the iLocate server via wired Ethernet. In an indoor environment, the platform can stably achieve a 3D positioning accuracy of 15 cm.

We place position sensors at 10 positions, including chest (P1), abdomen (P2), left upper arm (P3), left forearm (P4), right upper arm (P5), right forearm (P6), left thigh (P7), left lower leg (P8), right thigh (P9) and right lower leg (P10). Then we build a data set which includes crouch(A1), lying (A2), sitting (A3), standing (A4), walking (A5), tiptoe (stepping on the tip of the toe, (A6), body turn (A7), squat downward (A8), bending arm (A9), raising hand (A10), lifting the leg (A11) and lifting heavy objects (A12). The data set is collected from ten males and ten females. The participants range in height from 1.60 m to 1.78 m, and their weights vary from 50 kg to 85 kg. We continuously collect each action for ten minutes. The Ubisense positioning platform reports the position information of each tags at the frequency of 10 Hz, and the data is saved in the format of <ID, T, X, Y, Z> .

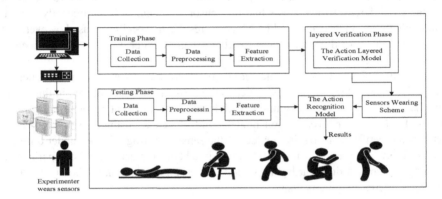

Fig. 1. Action recognition framework.

2.1.2   Data Preprocessing and Feature Extraction

Considering the unavailable noise of raw data, a median filter with a window size of 3 is used. The overlapping time window is a common way to extract features from a time-based data stream. In this paper, we verify the window of 1 to 2 s in consideration of the completeness of actions. Finally the time window size is determined as 1.4 s.

We consider three types of features that include action features, relative features, and statistical features, as shown in Table 1, in which the relative features represent the relationship between any two sensors.

Table 1. Features in detail.

	Features
Motion features	Speed, acceleration, displacement, displacement in the time window, height
Relative features	Relative speed, relative acceleration, relative displacement, relative height
Statistical features	Mean of displacement, standard deviation of displacement, mean of displacement between two sensors, standard deviation of displacement between two sensors

2.2 The Action Layered Verification Model

We design static action layer, dynamic action layer, and joint presentation layer according to the difference in action amplitude and the relationship between limbs. The layers are shown in Table 2.

Table 2. The layers.

ID	Layer	Action	ID	Layer	Action
A1	Static action layer	Crouch	A7	Dynamic action layer	Body turn
A2		Lying	A8		Squat downward
A3		Sitting	A9	Joint presentation layer	Bending arm
A4		Standing	A10		Raising hand
A5	Dynamic action layer	Walking	A11		Lifting the leg
A6		Tiptoe	A12		Lifting heavy objects

The action layered verification model serves the action recognition model. In previous studies, sensor wearing schemes are subjective and empirical. The action layered verification model attempts to explain the effect of the position more objectively. The model provides an optional wearing solution for each layer of action. Then we can adjust the wearing schemes to adapt the requirements (i.e., the requirement for action recognition in the traditional model is to recognize only static actions such as sitting, standing and lying.) of different action recognition.

The data used in this paper is processed during the training phase. First, we use the random forest classifier to layer it in accordance with Table 2. Then the separate classifier is designed for each layer. Under each classifier, we extract a combination of different wearing schemes from the data set to verify a better wearing scheme for each layer. We use four or less sensors to carry out this experiment here, because too many sensors may cause signal interference and waste of resources.

2.3 The Action Recognition Method

The action recognition method includes an action layered model and an action classification model. In the initial stage, the action layered model is used to avoid wrong action classification. Then action classification models are designed for each layer. In action recognition method, the training data set is $D = \{X1, X2, X3, ..., Xn\}$, and feature set is $A = \{A1, A2, A3, .., Av\}$. D belongs to a group of classes $C = \{C1, C2, C3, ..., Cw\}$, and also belongs to a group of classes $L = \{L1, L2, ..., Ls\}$. Here, C is the class of the action, and L is the layer of the action.

The random forest is used as the action layered model, which includes model training and action layering. The processes of model training is as follows: (1) select N samples from the training data set by putting back random samples. (2) Use K features selected randomly to establish a decision tree. (3) Repeat the above two steps m times to generate m decision trees to form a random forest. The processes of action layering is: (1) for the test data, all decision trees are classified one by one. Then we vote to determine the layering result. (2) The layering result L is added as a feature to the raw training data set to form a new training set for action classification. The feature set is represented as $A = \{A_1, A_2, A_3, .., A_v, L\}$.

In action classification model, L is only used to distinguish the layer to which the action belongs. A C4.5 decision tree based classification model is created for each action layer L. The action classification model is constructed as follows: Select the best feature and segmentation point according to the information gain rate, and then split the root node into several sub-nodes according to the best feature and segmentation point. Second, split the sub-node into several sub-segments according to the best feature and segmentation point similarly. The child nodes are recursively split until the recursion end condition is satisfied. There are several cases of recursion end condition: (1) the sample categories in the child nodes are of the same category, (2) the attribute is an empty set, and (3) the feature information gain rate is less than the threshold.

3   Experiment Analysis

In this part, we first analyze and verify each layer of wearing scheme. Then we combine the characteristics of each layer in wearable scheme to verify the action recognition method that applies to all actions. Finally, we validate our scheme on Naive Bayes (NB), Support Vector Machine (SVM) and Artificial Neural network (ANN).

3.1   Action Layered

Table 3 shows that the effects of layered performs very well (99%) and explains the feasibility of the model we proposed. We use the following metrics to show the classification effect: Precision (P), Recall ratio (Recall/R), False Positive Rate (FP Rate), F-Measure. F-Measure is defined as follow.

$$F - Measure = 2 * \frac{P * R}{P + R} \tag{1}$$

Table 3. Layered effects of random forest classifier.

Action layer	Precision	Recall	FP rate	F-measure
Static action layer	0.997	0.996	0.001	0.996
Dynamic action layer	0.990	0.986	0.005	0.988
Joint presentation layer	0.983	0.988	0.009	0.985
Average	0.990	0.990	0.006	0.990

3.2   Layered Verification

3.2.1   Static Action Layer

Static action layer contains four actions A1-A4. We train classifiers for each wearing scheme separately. Figure 2 outlines the results that the positions of wearable sensor have great effect on the recognition quality of the static action layers. It shows that chest and abdomen have the highest recognition rate (96%), arm (P3-P6) performs well (91%) and leg (P7-P10) is the worst (74.8%/67.8%). We examine the feature set and find that the height feature provides useful information, and it performs well when wearable sensors locate in upper body.

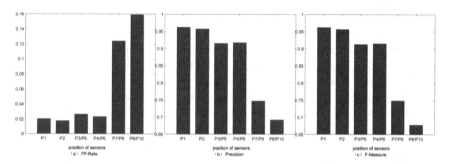

Fig. 2. Static action layers: comparison of performance under different wearing scheme.

3.2.2   Dynamic Action Layers

Dynamic action layers contain four actions A5-A8. We train classifiers for each wearing scheme separately. Figure 3 shows the performance comparison using single sensor under dynamic action layer. The result ($\leq$ 70%) is not satisfactory when we use a single sensor to recognize the action of this layer. Therefore, we combine sensor in the best position P1 with other positions, which has a satisfactory effect (Fig. 4). The chest, arm and thigh have a higher recognition rate ($\geq$ 88.6%), and the standard combination of chest and crus is relatively poor (85.9%). The results show that the increase in the number of sensors and the introduction of relative relationship can improve the recognition performance effectively.

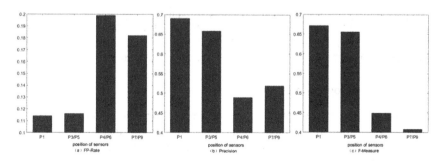

Fig. 3. Dynamic action layer: performance comparison using a single sensor.

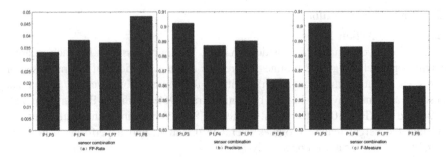

Fig. 4. Dynamic action layer: performance comparison using a combination of two sensors.

3.2.3 Joint Presentation Layers

Joint presentation layer contains four actions A9–A12. We train classifiers for each wearing scheme separately. Using a single sensor cannot represent the complete action of the joint presentation layer, such as raise hand. We directly use the combination of torso, upper extremity and lower extremity position to recognize the action of the joint presentation layer. Because the action includes both upper and lower extremities. Figure 5 shows that combination of three sensors represents the joint presentation layer action well ($\geq 80\%$). Besides, the combination of the left arm (P3, P4) and lower limbs (best 91.7%) is almost higher than that of right arm (P5, P6) and lower limbs. To ensure stability, it is recommended to use the sensor combination on the left body when recognizing the action of the joint presentation layer.

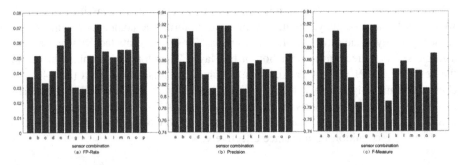

Fig. 5. Joint presentation layers: performance comparison using a combination of three sensors. (Remark: a:{P1, P3, P7}, b:{P1, P3, P8}, c:{P1, P4, P7}, d:{P1, P4, P8}, e:{P1, P3, P9}, f:{P1, P3, P10}, g:{P1.P4, P9}, h:{P1, P4, P10}, i:{P1, P5, P7}, j:{P1, P5, P8}, k:{P1, P5, P9}, l:{P1, P5, P10}, m:{P1, P6, P7}, n:{P1, P6, P8}, o:{P1, P6, P9}, p:{P1, P6, P10}).

3.3 Universal Recognition Method

In the above experiments, we validate the sensor wearing scheme for each layer. We find that there are similarities among each layer's wearing scheme. P1 is an absolutely necessary position in all well-performed wearing schemes. P3, P4, and P7 also perform well in the dynamic action layer and the joint presentation layer. Besides, we find that the combination of {P1, P3, P7} is the best when we choose three sensors in {P1, P3, P4, P7}, and P1 must be chosen. The result is shown in Table 4.

Table 4. The confusion matrix under the specific wearing scheme.

	A1	A2	A3	A4	A5	A6	A7	A8	9A	A10	A11	A12
A1	561	3	4	0	2	0	0	8	0	0	5	0
A2	20	558	0	0	0	0	0	0	0	0	0	0
A3	2	0	550	0	0	0	0	18	0	0	13	0
A4	0	0	0	506	4	27	18	2	27	1	0	10
A5	2	0	1	0	523	10	27	10	0	5	0	5
A6	0	0	0	29	10	455	9	5	27	5	0	25
A7	0	0	0	15	19	16	460	4	21	44	0	12
A8	5	1	12	2	7	3	3	542	0	8	8	6
A9	0	0	0	9	0	23	20	0	472	9	0	40
A10	0	0	0	6	6	5	38	5	5	513	0	15
A11	1	0	15	0	0	0	0	15	0	0	553	0
A12	2	0	0	15	7	31	13	2	102	14	0	399
Precision	0.95	0.99	0.95	0.87	0.91	0.80	0.78	0.89	0.72	0.86	0.96	0.78

The table shows that the static action layer except standing (A4) has well performance under our wearing scheme ($\geq$ 95%). Standing is wrongly classified into {A6, A7, A9, A12}, and these actions are not recognized well ($\leq$ 80%). The reason is that these actions are all based on standing with tiny differences. Besides, we demonstrate that increasing sensors can improve the recognition performance effectively. In Table 5, we analyze the wearing schemes with 4 sensors and give the confusion matrix of the best wearing scheme {P1, P3, P5, P7}.

Table 5. Confusion matrix of the best wearing scheme.

	A1	A2	A3	A4	A5	A6	A7	A8	9A	A10	A11	A12
A1	568	1	1	0	1	0	0	10	0	0	1	0
A2	16	575	0	0	0	0	0	0	0	0	0	0
A3	1	0	574	0	0	0	0	7	0	0	11	0
A4	0	0	0	534	4	18	11	2	2	1	0	8
A5	2	0	1	6	518	11	26	12	0	1	0	5
A6	0	0	0	13	9	513	11	7	22	4	0	26
A7	0	0	0	15	20	7	466	5	4	19	0	23
A8	4	1	7	2	7	6	4	537	1	5	6	5
A9	0	0	0	2	0	8	9	0	522	9	0	52
A10	0	0	0	4	1	9	36	6	6	540	0	9
A11	3	0	5	0	0	0	0	9	0	0	568	0
A12	0	0	0	7	3	26	15	5	62	12	0	474
Precision	0.96	0.99	0.98	0.92	0.92	0.86	0.81	0.90	0.84	0.91	0.97	0.79

3.4   Comparison with Other Classification Methods

In order to show the benefits of our wearing scheme, we compare the performance under the classifiers including DT, ANN, NB and SVM. Figure 6 shows that our wearing scheme outperforms other schemes. Meanwhile in our wearing scheme, the other classifiers perform worse than our DT classifier. Figure 6 shows clearly that DT (90.3%) outperforms other classifiers.

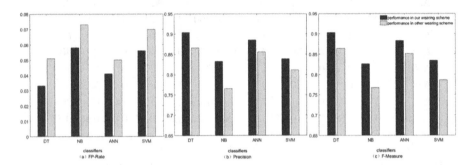

Fig. 6. Comparisons of proposed wearing scheme and classifier.

4   Conclusion and Future Work

In order to adapt different requirements for action recognition, we propose an action layered verification model. It is based on the random forest classifier, which can achieve 99% accuracy of layering. Then we verify wearing schemes of each layer. The experiments show that sensors in chest position provide reliable information in the static action layer, and the recognition rate reaches 96%. It fails to achieve a satisfactory result when we use single sensor to recognize the actions of dynamic action layer. However, using a combination of two sensors located on the chest and arm achieves a recognition rate more than 89%. Besides, three sensors are required at least to recognize the action of the joint presentation layer. Because using a combination of two sensors on the left side of the body and chest, the recognition rate only reaches 86%.

Subsequently, experiments are conducted to identify the overall actions. After a comprehensive analysis of the wearing scheme each layer, we propose an action recognition model based on four sensors. The recognition rate reaches 90.3%. Meanwhile, we verify our wearing scheme on other classifiers. The experiments show that our wearing scheme is also applicable to other classifiers, and the performance of action recognition improves by our wearing scheme.

In the future work, we will find more effective approaches to recognize similar actions and build a complete action recognition system.

Acknowledgement. This work is supported by the Natural Science Foundation of China (No. 615 02118), the Natural Science Foundation of Heilongjiang Province in China (No. F2016009), the Fundamental Research Fund for the Central Universities in China (No. HEUCF180602 and HEUCFM180604) and the National Science and Technology Major Project (No. 2016ZX0 3001023-005).

References

1. Moayedi, F., Azimifar, Z.S., Boostani, R.: Structured sparse representation for human action recognition. Neurocomputing **161**(C), 38–46 (2015)
2. Sazonov, E.S., Fulk, G., Hill, J., Browning, R.: Monitoring of posture allocations and activities by a shoe-based wearable sensor. IEEE Trans. Biomed. Eng. **58**(4), 983–990 (2011)
3. Kwapisz, J.R., Weiss, G.M., Moore, S.A.: Activity recognition using cell phone accelerometers. Acm Sigkdd Explor. Newsl. **12**(2), 74–82 (2016)
4. Liu, Y., Nie, L., Liu, L., Rosenblum, D.S.: From action to activity: sensor-based activity recognition. Neurocomputing **181**, 108–115 (2016)
5. Zhang, M., Sawchuk, A.A.: Human daily activity recognition with sparse representation using wearable sensors. IEEE J Biomed Health Inform **17**(3), 553–560 (2013)
6. Ullah, A., Ahmad, J., Muhammad, K.: Action recognition in video sequences using deep bi-directional LSTM with CNN features. IEEE Access **PP**(99), 1 (2017)
7. Panagiotakis, C., Papoutsakis, K., Argyros, A.: A graph-based approach for detecting common actions in motion capture data and videos. Pattern Recogn. **79**, 1–11 (2018)
8. Alfaro, A., Mery, D., Soto, A.: Action recognition in video using sparse coding and relative features, pp. 2688–2697 (2016)
9. Rautaray, S.S., Agrawal, A.: Vision based hand gesture recognition for human computer interaction: a survey. Artif. Intell. Rev. **43**(1), 1–54 (2015)
10. Saner, H.: Wearable sensors for assisted living in elderly people. Front. ICT **5**, 1 (2018)
11. Bao, Y., Sun, F., Hua, X.: Operation action recognition using wearable devices with inertial sensors. In: IEEE International Conference on Multisensor Fusion and Integration for Intelligent Systems. IEEE (2017)
12. Karungaru, S.: Human action recognition using wearable sensors and neural networks. In: Control Conference, pp. 1–4. IEEE (2015)
13. Zhang, T., Wang, J., Xu, L.: Fall detection by wearable sensor and one-class SVM algorithm. In: Huang, D.S., Li, K., Irwin, G.W. (eds.) Intelligent Computing in Signal Processing and Pattern Recognition. LNCIS, vol. 345, pp. 858–863. Springer, Berlin (2016). https://doi.org/10.1007/978-3-540-37258-5_104
14. Thomas, O., Sunehag, P., Dror, G.: Wearable sensor activity analysis using semi-Markov models with a grammar. Pervasive Mob. Comput. **6**(3), 342–350 (2010)
15. Gjoreski, H., Lustrek, M., Gams, M.: Accelerometer placement for posture recognition and fall detection. In: Seventh International Conference on Intelligent Environments, pp. 47–54. IEEE Computer Society (2011)
16. Mannini, A., Sabatini, A.M., Intille, S.S.: Accelerometry-based recognition of the placement sites of a wearable sensor. Pervasive Mob. Comput. **21**, 62–74 (2015)
17. Stelios, M.A., Nick, A.D., Effie, M.T., Dimitris, K.M., Thomopoulos, S.C.A.: An indoor localization platform for ambient assisted living using UWB. In: International Conference on Advances in Mobile Computing and Multimedia, pp. 178–182 (2008)

Security

Speed Based Attacker Placement for Evaluating Location Privacy in VANET

Ikjot Saini[✉], Sherif Saad, and Arunita Jaekel

School of Computer Science, University of Windsor, Windsor, Canada
{saini11s,shsaad,arunita}@uwindsor.ca

Abstract. The deployment of connected and autonomous vehicles is expected to increase rapidly in the coming decade. For successful operation, it is critical to maintain the security and privacy of the communication messages exchanged among such vehicles. One important aspect of this is to maintain the location privacy of vehicles/users that use unencrypted basic safety messages (BSM) to exchange information with nearby vehicles. The use of temporary identifiers called pseudonyms have been proposed for protecting location privacy. A pseudonym change strategy (PCS) determines the conditions under which pseudonyms should change. The goal is to change pseudonyms in a way that prevents an attacker from linking multiple pseudonyms to the same vehicle. In this paper we explore how an intelligent attacker placement scheme can impact the success rate for linking pseudonyms. We propose a new speed-based attacker placement algorithm that can be used to evaluate different PCS. Simulation results indicate that the proposed scheme is able to increase the rate for successfully linking vehicle pseudonyms.

Keywords: VANET security · Pseudonym change
Attacker placement · Location privacy · Vehicle tracking

1 Introduction

A vehicular ad-hoc network (VANET) [1] consists of a network of vehicles, that exchange relevant information e.g. current vehicle position, vehicle state, traffic conditions, road conditions etc. to improve road safety, reduce traffic congestion and provide a variety of additional services to users. Safety applications require rapid, real-time processing of basic safety messages (BSM) sent by neighboring vehicles. In the USA, BSMs are broadcast using the IEEE 1609 WAVE protocol stack [2], built on the IEEE 802.11p [3] and are unencrypted to reduce processing time. So, anyone in the vehicles transmission range is able to receive BSMs from nearby vehicles and can use the information in successive messages to build a history of previous locations of a vehicle. Such tracking can reveal frequently visited places such as home or office location corresponding to a vehicle and compromises the privacy of the vehicle [4]. The concept of location privacy has

© ICST Institute for Computer Sciences, Social Informatics and Telecommunications Engineering 2019
Published by Springer Nature Switzerland AG 2019. All Rights Reserved
J. Zheng et al. (Eds.): ADHOCNETS 2018, LNICST 258, pp. 215–224, 2019.
https://doi.org/10.1007/978-3-030-05888-3_20

been defined in the literature as a special type of information privacy which concerns the claim of individuals to determine for themselves when, how, and to what extent location information about them is communicated to others [5]. Protecting location privacy is one of the main security challenges in VANETs [6]. To address this issue, a number of researchers have proposed the use of pseudonyms to make vehicle tracking more difficult and improve location privacy [7]. A pseudonym is a temporary identifier issued by a trusted authority. Each vehicle is issued a pool of pseudonyms and corresponding certificates that can be used, when communicating with other vehicles. The temporary certificates associated with pseudonyms also help authenticate messages sent by a vehicle.

Pseudonyms can be effective in hindering vehicle tracking only if they are changed frequently. Otherwise, an attacker may be able to link pseudonyms from the same vehicle based on its history of BSM transmissions. Furthermore, the changing of pseudonyms must be carried out in a way that makes it difficult to link 2 (or more) pseudonyms associated with the same vehicle. There has been a strong research interest in recent years, in the development of effective pseudonym change schemes (PCS) is to prevent such pseudonym linking and a number of different approaches have been proposed in the literature to address this issue [8–10]. These PCS should be evaluated not only with simplistic randomly placed attackers, but also using more sophisticated, traffic-aware attacker placement techniques.

In this paper, we propose a novel speed-based attacker placement strategy that can be used to intelligently select the most advantageous eavesdropping locations for attacking stations, based on traffic patterns and attacker capabilities. We evaluate the performance of the proposed approach and compare it with a uniformly spaced attacker placement for different road types, traffic conditions and attacker capabilities.

The remainder of the paper is organized as follows. In Sect. 2, we discuss the main types of Pseudonym Change Strategies (PCS) in VANET and some existing approaches to vehicle tracking. In Sect. 3 we describe our proposed speed-based attacker placement approach. We present our simulation results in Sect. 4 and conclude in Sect. 5 with some directions for future work.

2   Review

The location information in the vehicular networks is broadcast with a rate of 10 times per second in the safety message. The safety applications rely on this information to prevent potential collisions; however, the information broadcast is in plain text. This allows others to listen the safety messages using the dedicated equipment. The aggregated location and information gives the overall spatiotemporal resource to infer the personal information such as the personal preferences, the workplace or the medical state based on the frequent visits. The pseudonyms are used in place of the vehicle ID as these are temporary identifiers with a limited lifetime. Changing the pseudonyms reduces the ability of the passive attacker to track the vehicle. However, the knowledge of the pseudonym changing scheme and the continuous stream of safety messages with timestamped location updates allow the attacker to successfully correlate the changed pseudonym.

A number of pseudonym changing schemes have been proposed in the last few years. The fixed PCS allows the pseudonym change in a particular area, known as mix zones, or based on fixed time slot, known as periodic PCS. In [9], the concept of mix zone was first introduced and [11] implemented the cryptographic mix zone. The unobserved area is considered as the mix zone where the vehicles change the pseudonym. Also, the mix zone is the region where there are more number of vehicles and more change in the vehicles direction. Such places are intersections, parking lots or gas stations which provide enough confusion for the attacker to detect the pseudonym change. This scheme forces more frequent pseudonym changes which consumes the given set of pseudonyms in less duration. In order to prevent the exhaustion of the pseudonyms, one approach is to reuse the pseudonym for certain time period. As proposed in the most recent standards [12], 20 pseudonyms are valid for a week and the pseudonym change is periodic, i.e., after 5 min the vehicle changes the pseudonym. These schemes have an extent of predictability for the pseudonym change as these are limited to specific location or time.

The dynamic PCS change the pseudonym without predefined location or time period, making it difficult for the attacker to analyze the change of the temporary identifier. Various dynamic pseudonym changing schemes, also known as mix context schemes, are available in the literature. These schemes usually have radio silence when there is a change of pseudonym, otherwise, the change can be directly detected by the attacker. The triggers for changing pseudonyms vary from speed [13] to vehicle density [14]. The trigger-based schemes are excellent because these enable implicit trigger for a change of pseudonym. These are more effective as the attacker is not aware when vehicles are changing pseudonyms and it is not easy to correlate after an implicit trigger. Another advantage is that even if the adversary is monitoring the information, the location and time are not predetermined. Therefore, the prediction of such events is difficult, but is still possible with significant related information such as traffic analysis for the target region. The possible drawback associated with this scheme is that if there is not sufficient number of vehicles, then adversary may trace the target vehicle. Such schemes typically involve group formation for synchronous change to increase the attackers confusion. In [15], a scheme called as synchronous pseudonym change algorithm is proposed, where the status information of the vehicle and the simultaneity of the pseudonym change are considered. The concept of Random Encryption Periods for enhancing the location privacy is introduced in [16]. This PCS uses Public Key Infrastructure along with probabilistic symmetric key distribution. The symmetric key is the group based secret key which is shared among the neighboring vehicles. Weerasinghe [17] introduced the concept of a group based synchronized pseudonym changing protocol. Here the group manager decides the time to change the pseudonym and other group members are informed and after changing the pseudonym, the group is dissolved. Also, the signal strength is changed as the pseudonym is changed.

The speed based changing scheme is one of the dynamic scheme that depends on the speed threshold for the pseudonym change. SLOW was proposed for changing the pseudonym dynamically without predefined location or time. The speed threshold was proposed as 30 Km/h. According to [13], as the vehicle slows down and reaches this threshold, it changes pseudonym while maintaining the radio silence. The radio silence is not desirable for the safety applications, but with respect to the passive attacker, it prevents the continuous information broadcast that reduces the success of the linking attack. The vehicle slows down more in the city either at traffic light intersection or the stop sign causing significant rate of pseudonym change in urban areas. But it is clear that SLOW prevents the disclosure of the pseudonym change, thus, the tracking at the cost of the high number of pseudonyms. VBPC [18] is another velocity-based PCS in which the vehicles are grouped together based on the velocity within a certain transmission range and then the pseudonyms are changed based on the random time period.

3   Proposed Placement Strategy

The performance of a PCS depends on a variety of factors, such as the type of attacker (local or global), the number of attacking stations and the capabilities and communication range of the attacking station. For a local adversary with a limited number of attacking stations, the tracking success depends critically on how the attacking stations are placed. Therefore, it is important to a PCS, with a realistic and effective attacker placement. In our earlier work [19], we have shown that even a simple distance-based placement algorithm is quite effective against a periodic PCS. However, they are less successful when a dynamic PCS is used. In this section, we present a new speed-based attacker placement (SBAP) scheme that can be used for tracking vehicles using a dynamic, context-aware PCS.

3.1   Adversary Model

In our work, we have considered the local passive adversary which has limited capabilities in terms of the equipment. The communication range of the adversary is 300 m. The equipment is also named as attacking or eavesdropping station. The placement of these equipment in the simulation is according to the proposed algorithm, which allows maximum coverage with the given number of equipment. We compared the results of our placement algorithm to the uniformly distributed fixed distance placement. The communication channel is assumed to be reliable. The eavesdropping station is able to clearly listen to all the messages by the vehicles within its range. We model the attacker with limited resources to observe the maximum impact on the privacy protection. The eavesdropping stations provide the information to the central vehicle tracker that records the safety messages and correlate the location, time and pseudonym information from these messages. The vehicle tracker correlates the safety messages of a vehicle by matching pseudonyms based on the multi-target tracking algorithm [20].

3.2 Speed Based Attacker Placement

Speed based PCS relies on the speed of the vehicles. When a vehicles speed falls below a specified threshold, it changes the pseudonym. Such conditions often arise at red light intersections and stop signs. In the remainder of this paper, we refer to an intersection with a traffic light or stop sign as a Traffic/Stop Intersection (TSI). Vehicle speed can also fall below the threshold along sections of roads that experience high traffic congestion. We refer to such areas as high traffic sections (HTS). TSI and HTS are excellent candidate locations for placing attackers. However, it is infeasible wasteful to place attacking stations on all TSI or very closely spaced along a HTS. Therefore, it is necessary to identify potential attacker positions, such that fewer attackers are able to track the most number of vehicles. Successful tracking is more likely to occur when a longer stretch of the road is selected for correlation of the old and new pseudonyms of the vehicle. Therefore, we consider segments that are relatively long (at least 15 km) and have high traffic density.

Algorithm 1. Speed-based attacker placement (SBAP) algorithm

1: Initialize parameters: n=number of available equipment for tracking the vehicles, r_{comm}= Communication range of attacking station
2: Perform traffic analysis to select a set S1 of potential urban road segments for monitoring traffic, where $|S1| = k$ and $s_i \varepsilon S$ is the ith road segment.
3: Repeat steps 4 and 5 until there is no more available attacker equipment
4: For $s_i \varepsilon S1$:
   a: loc_A = the location of the 1st TSI of s_i
   b: Repeat steps i-iv until $loc_A \varepsilon s_i$ == False:
      i. Place attacker at loc_A
      ii. d_{next}=distance from loc_A to the next TSI on s_i after loc_A
      iii. $d_{inter} = \max\{d_{next}, 2.r_{comm}\}$
      iv. $loc_A = loc_A + d_{inter}$
5: For all $HTS_i \varepsilon S2$:
   a: loc_A = the location of the first point in HTS_i that is at a distance of $2.r_{comm}$ from previous attacker on the road.
   b: Repeat steps i-ii until $loc_A \varepsilon HTS_i$ == False:
      i. Place attacker at loc_A
      ii. $loc_A = loc_A + 2.r_{comm}$

An overview of our proposed Speed-based attacker placement is given in Algorithm 1. In step 1, we initialize relevant parameters such as the number of attacking stations (n) to place in the network, the communication range (r_{comm}) of each station. In step 2, we select certain road segments to monitor, based on long term traffic patterns. Two types of road segments are selected:

– A set $S1$ of urban roads segments where attackers will be placed based on TSI locations and
– A set $S2$ of road segments (primarily highways, but may contain some urban roads as well), where attackers will be placed based on traffic congestion.

In step 3, attackers are placed one by one on the selected road segments, based on TSI (step 4) and HTS (step 5), until all positions of interest have been covered or the maximum number of stations (n) have been used. Details of steps 4 and 5 are given below. In step 4, attacking stations are placed based on TSI locations. For each selected road segment s_i on an urban road, the first attacker is placed at the first TSI of the segment. If the distance from the current TSI to the next one is greater than $2.r_{comm}$, then an attacker is placed at the next TSI. Otherwise, next attacker is placed a location $2.r_{comm}$ from the current TSI on the road segment s_i. This placement strategy allows all the TSI along the road segment to be covered using the fewest possible attackers. In step 5, high traffic and/or congested road segments. Attackers are placed at intervals of $2.r_{comm}$ along the entire segment.

4   Results

In our simulations, we considered the area in the city of Windsor, Ontario, Canada. The simulation area contained a 15 Km stretch of Highway (H), as well as Urban(U) areas with the road network consisting of 280 edges (roads) and 120 junctions (intersections) spread in the urban area. We varied the number of available equipment from 10 to 20. This variation is used to investigate the impact of the attacker capabilities in accurately tracking vehicles for longer durations. The vehicular traffic density is varied from low to high. Higher traffic density causes traffic congestion, and this forces speed-based PCS to require more frequent pseudonym changes. To observe the effects of traffic density, we considered three levels of traffic density low (100 vehicles), moderate (200 vehicles) and high (300 vehicles). The average trip time for each vehicle was set to 2 h. We have simulated the highway and urban scenarios with separate synthetic traffics for each scenario which are generated by SUMO [21]. We setup the simulation using OMNET++ [22], SUMO, veins [23]. The trips in the urban scenario are random which means that the vehicles are traveling from different starting points to destination points.

To simulate the attackers and the privacy modules in veins [23], we have used PREXT [24], which provides a unified framework for simulating the PCS used to provide privacy in VANET. PREXT also specifies the attacking modules that listen to BSMs transmitted by the vehicles. We have placed these modules at certain observation points based on preliminary traffic analysis. In our simulations, we have compared the following four attacker placement schemes:

- the proposed SBAP scheme for urban roads (SBAP-U)
- the proposed SBAP scheme for highways (SBAP-H)
- the fixed-interval attacker placement scheme for urban roads (FIAP-U)
- the fixed-interval attacker placement scheme for highways (FIAP-H)

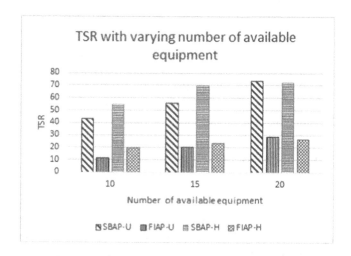

Fig. 1. Comparison of TSR values for different number of attacking stations.

The performance of these approaches is evaluated in terms of the tracking success rate (TSR), which is defined below. We map the location and time information to the respective pseudonyms and predict the vehicles next potential position. When a vehicle comes out of the silent zone, this prediction is used to identify the vehicle by matching the predicted and actual spatiotemporal information. If the matching is done correctly, we count it as a successful tracking event. When the attackers predicted position fails to correctly identify the target vehicle, it is counted as a failed tracking event. We measured the tracking success rate (TSR) as the percent-age of successful tracking events for all vehicles during their trips.

Figure 1 shows how the TSR values vary with the number of available equipment. With more number of equipment, the attacker is clearly able to track more successfully for all placement schemes, as expected. However, the TSR value of FIAP is considerably less than SBAP for both urban roads and highways. This is because for FIAP more pseudonym changes occur out of the range of the eavesdropping stations and hence remain undetected. For example, with 10 equipment in urban scenario, there are many TSIs which are not covered in the range of any attacking station. This significantly reduces the traceability as the vehicles change the pseudonyms while slowing down near TSI. Even as the number of equipment increases, the TSR remains relatively low for FIAP-U, because once a vehicle changes its pseudonym in an uncovered area, this vehicle is classified as a new vehicle by the attacker. With SBAP-U, the traceability

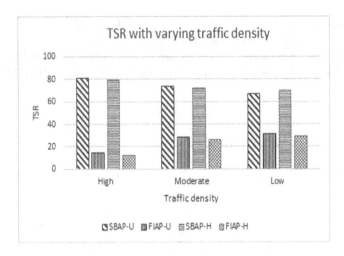

Fig. 2. Comparison of TSR values vs traffic density.

is higher as the stations are placed carefully after analyzing the traffic patterns and the busy intersections, so pseudonym changes are more likely to occur in areas being monitored by attacking equipment. The highways do not have intersections, therefore, only the traffic congestion analysis is helpful in suitable placement based on SBAP. As with urban roads, traceability increases with more number of equipment for both approaches. But, TSR for FIAP-H is consistently lower, since fewer congested areas are covered in the range of attacking stations.

The traffic density is closely related to the pseudonym change in the speed based PCS. In Fig. 2, as the number of vehicles increases, the increased traffic congestion causes the vehicles to slow down, which in turn forces the pseudonym change. If these changes occur in an area monitored by an attacker, more pseudonyms can be linked to each other. This is the case with SBAP (for both urban roads and highways) and therefore traceability increases with traffic density. For FIAP-U and FIAP-H, the rate of pseudonym change also increases with traffic density. However, many of these changes occur in unmonitored areas, so the attacker interprets the new pseudonyms as belonging to new vehicles. Therefore, the overall traceability actually decreases with traffic density. For all road types and ranges of traffic densities, the overall traceability is significantly higher (at least double) for SBAP compared to FIAP.

5   Conclusions

In this paper, we proposed a novel speed-based attacker placement (SBAP) scheme for selecting the locations of attacking stations based on analysis of long term traffic patterns. We have compared our approach to a traffic-unaware fixed interval attacker placement (FIAP) scheme and have shown that the proposed approach consistently outperforms FIAP with an average improvement of 60% in successful vehicle tracking. We conclude that attacker placement has a significant impact on the tracking capability of an attacker, given the same number and capability of attacking stations. The proposed approach can be used to evaluate different PCS and help identify potential vulnerabilities prior to deployment. The SBAP approach presented in this paper is most effective for PCS that use a velocity threshold for triggering pseudonym changes. For our future work, we plan to develop a robust attacker placement technique that be used for other context-aware PCS.

References

1. Harnstein, H., Laberteaux, L.P.: A tutorial survey on vehicular ad hoc networks. IEEE Commun. Mag. **46**(6), 164–171 (2008)
2. IEEE Standard for Wireless Access in Vehicular Environments (WAVE)-Multichannel Operation, IEEE Std 1609.4-2010 (Revision of IEEE Std 1609.4-2006) (2011)
3. Kenney, J.: Dedicated short-range communciations (DSRC) standards in the United States. Proc. IEEE **99**(7), 1162–1182 (2011)
4. Golle, P., Partridge, K.: On the anonymity of home/work location Pairs. In: Tokuda, H., Beigl, M., Friday, A., Brush, A.J.B., Tobe, Y. (eds.) Pervasive 2009. LNCS, vol. 5538, pp. 390–397. Springer, Heidelberg (2009). https://doi.org/10.1007/978-3-642-01516-8_26
5. Duckham, M., Kulik, L.: Location privacy and location-aware computing. In: Drummond, J., et al. (eds.) Dynamic and Mobile GIS: Investigating Change in Space and Time, pp. 34–51. CRC Press, Boca Raton (2006)
6. Emara, K.: Beacon-based vehicle tracking in vehicular ad-hoc networks, Technical report, TECHNISCHE UNIVERSITAT MUNCHEN (2013)
7. Gerlach, M.: Assessing and improving privacy in VANETs. In: Proceedings of 4th Workshop ESCAR, pp. 1–9 (2006)
8. Petit, J., Schaub, F., Feiri, M., Kargl, F.: Pseudonym schemes in vehicular networks: a survey. IEEE Commun. Surv. Tutor. **17**(1), 228–255 (2015)
9. Buttyán, L., Holczer, T., Vajda, I.: On the effectiveness of changing pseudonyms to provide location privacy in VANETs. In: Stajano, F., Meadows, C., Capkun, S., Moore, T. (eds.) ESAS 2007. LNCS, vol. 4572, pp. 129–141. Springer, Heidelberg (2007). https://doi.org/10.1007/978-3-540-73275-4_10
10. Li, M., Sampigethaya, K., Huang, L., Poovendran, R.: Swing and swap: user-centric approaches towards maximizing location privacy. In: Proceedings of the 5th ACM Workshop on Privacy in Electronic Society, pp. 19–28. ACM (2006)
11. Freudiger, J., Raya, M., Felegyhazi, P.P., Papadimitratos, P., Hubaux, J.P.: Mixzones for location privacy in vehicular networks. In: ACM Workshop on Wireless Networking for Intelligent Transportation Systems (WiNITS) (2007)
12. Brecht, B., et al.: Security credential management system for V2X communications. IEEE Trans. Intell. Transp. Syst. **99**, 1–22 (2018)
13. Buttyan, L., Holczer, T., Weimerskirch, A., Whyte, W.: SLOW: a practical pseudonym changing scheme for location privacy in VANETs. In: 2009 IEEE Vehicular Networking Conference VNC, pp. 1–8 (2009)
14. Song, J.H., Wong, V.W., Leung, V.C.: Wireless location privacy protection in vehicular ad-hoc networks. Mob. Netw. Appl. **15**(1), 160171 (2010)

15. Liao, J., Li, J.: Effectively changing pseudonyms for privacy protection in vanets. In: 10th International Symposium on Pervasive Systems, Algorithms, and Networks (ISPAN), pp. 648–652. IEEE (2009)
16. Wasef, A., Shen, X.: Rep: location privacy for vanets using random encryption periods. Mob. Netw. Appl. **15**(1), 172–185 (2010)
17. Weerasinghe, H., Fu, H., Leng, S., Zhu, Y.: Enhancing unlinkability in vehicular ad hoc networks. In: 2011 IEEE International Conference on Intelligence and Security Informatics (ISI), pp. 161–166. IEEE (2011)
18. Ullah, I., Wahid, A., Shah, M.A., Waheed, A.: VBPC: velocity based pseudonym changing strategy to protect location privacy of vehicles in VANET. In: 2017 International Conference on Communication Technologies (ComTech), Rawalpindi, pp. 132–137 (2017)
19. Saini, I., Saad, S., Jaekel, A.: attacker placement for detecting vulnerabilities of pseudonym change strategies in VANET. In: 1st International Workshop on Dependable Wireless Communications (DEWCOM), Chicago, USA (2018)
20. Emara, K., Woerndl, W., Schlichter, J.: Beacon-based vehicle tracking in vehicular ad-hoc networks. Technical report, TECHNISCHE UNIVERSITAT MUNCHEN (2013)
21. Krajzewicz, D., Erdmann, J., Behrisch, M., Bieker, L.: Recent development and applications of SUMO-Simulation of Urban MObility. Int. J. Adv. Syst. Meas. (2012)
22. Andrs, V., Hornig, R.: An overview of the OMNeT++ simulation environment. In: Proceedings of the 1st International Conference on Simulation Tools and Techniques for Communications, Networks and Systems and Workshops, Institute for Computer Sciences, Social- Informatics and Telecommunications Engineering (2008)
23. Sommer, C., German, R., Dressler, F.: Bidirectionally coupled network and road traffic simulation for improved IVC analysis. IEEE Trans. Mob. Comput. **10**(1), 3–15 (2011)
24. Emara, K.: Poster: PREXT: privacy extension for veins VANET simulator. In: Vehicular Networking Conference VNC. IEEE (2016)

HACIT2: A Privacy Preserving, Region Based and Blockchain Application for Dynamic Navigation and Forensics in VANET

Decoster Kevin[(✉)] and Billard David

University of Applied Sciences Western Switzerland in Geneva - HES-SO, Geneva, Switzerland
{kevin.decoster,david.billard}@hesge.ch

Abstract. The current architecture for VANET related services relies on a Client-Server approach and leads to numerous drawbacks. Among them, data privacy concerns and service availability are of prime importance. Indeed, user data collected and stored in servers by providers may be used by third-party services. Particularly for navigation, users submit their GPS position in order to obtain road traffic information and alternative paths. These services treat user privacy for their own purpose (commercial or not) (Beresford and Stajano, 2004) even if GPRD (European Parliament, 2014) is now enforced in Europe. We propose an innovative approach using blockchain technology to avoid the use of third parties services, which enable dynamic navigation rerouting within a fixed geographic zone while ensuring user anonymity. Furthermore, the approach will allow for legal authority to enable forensic analysis of the ledger without unnecessary violation of the user anonymity and privacy.

Keywords: VANET · Raspberry Pi · Android
Navigation · Hyperledger Fabric · Privacy · Blockchain · Forensics

1 Introduction

While many services offer dynamic rerouting navigation based on collaborative data (such as Google maps), none grants the user with a total control of its data. The proof of concept presented in this paper focuses on the collaboration of intelligent cars for determining the best driving route and avoiding traffic jams similarly to what current services do, but without the use of a central Internet service. By forbidding the use of centralized services like Google Maps or Tomtom Go Mobile, the traffic state shared by every users is kept at every peer's side in the form of a shared ledger. This ledger is updated using a consensus algorithm which guarantees that all peers share the same blockchain. Using the cellular network, a user can submit a transaction containing the newly measured road

J. Zheng et al. (Eds.): ADHOCNETS 2018, LNICST 258, pp. 225–236, 2019.
https://doi.org/10.1007/978-3-030-05888-3_21

speed in order to update the ledger. Besides, using the event system of the peers, a user can listen for newly submitted transactions and, if necessary, updates its current navigation instructions by computing the new shortest path given the current road weight states. The proposed project is currently being implemented using the IBM blockchain framework (IBM, 2017) on top of Hyperledger Fabric developed by the Linux Foundation (linux Foundation, 2016), which enable an extensive framework for blockchain technology implementation.

The challenge of this approach is the feasibility of the communication and computing in the mobile device. Indeed, running a blockchain node requires computations and communication capacities which can lead to difficulties in a dynamic mobile network. We will discuss the pros and cons and propose a system using an external device such as a Raspberry Pi to delegate the computing and the storage of the peer client. A consequent part consists in designing an efficient communication protocol between the mobile device and the computing unit.

To handle the geographic graph, OpenStreetMap (OpenStreetMap contributors, 2017) files, GraphHopper Java library (Graphhopper dev, 2017) and OSMAnd Android library (OSMAnd dev, 2017) are respectively used for the map file, the graph handler and the dynamic navigation UI on Android.

Finally, using this innovative approach, the application can enable forensics capabilities. As a matter of fact, legal officers should access navigation path in the immutable ledger without violating user anonymity. For instance, we can foresee that in case of an accident, a user would have an interest to prove its behaviour. This is possible using the data transaction chain.

2   Related Work

The problem of navigation in VANET using only local information has been widely studied this last decade. For instance, the authors of (Wang et al., 2017) propose an anonymous and secure navigation schemes in VANET. While they satisfy all requirements for security and privacy, they still assume the use of third parties as Trusted Authorities (TA) to de-anonymize the car ids. Furthermore, they use direct vehicle communication (through Wifi or radio wave communication) within a dynamic ad-hoc network and as a result, only partial and local information regarding the traffic is shared among moving nodes, as opposed to a system that centralizes all road traffic information such as Google Map.

To the best of our knowledge, although the security in VANET is a well-researched field (Raya and Hubaux, 2007), no paper fully addresses the forensics concern. Indeed, no work already proposes a system enabling dynamic rerouting and forensics for the mobile device using a fully implemented blockchain technology. For instance, (Leiding et al., 2016) uses blockchain in VANET. However, they use it for monetary applications such as an automatic smart contract for insurance or tolling and uses Ethereum to host the smart contracts (see (Wood, 2014)). Without the need for a monetary support (and thus proof of work through mining), our blockchain can achieve consensus without computationally expensive proof-of-work, for instance with Practical Byzantine Fault tolerance (PBFT) algorithm.

3   Hyperledger Fabric

Hyperledger Fabric (HF), developed by the Linux Foundation, proposes a framework for developing permissioned blockchain technology. As opposed to bitcoin network, the access to the blockchain is controlled by an entity called the *Membership Service Provider*, which grant access to users and peers with the cryptographic material (certificate and keys) delivered by a certificate authority (CA).

The blockchain includes a ledger of transactions but also a representation of the world state through a key-value database. Access, queries, modifications and Smart contract are defined using the blockchain rule called Chaincode. This allows efficiently querying and modifying the dataset without having to analyse the whole chained data transactions.

We distinguish 3 different types of nodes:

- *Peers*: a basic node which stores an up-to-date copy of the ledger and chaincode rules. It continuously keeps tracks of information through the gossip protocol running among all peers, see (Shah et al., 2009).
- *Client* (user): Which consists of the end-user who owns an authorized cryptographic material. It runs an SDK which grants him access to the peers API functions. The client connects to a peer to submit transaction proposals.
- *Orderer*: The orderer is a special peer node, whose role is to gather and order validated transactions until a block can be made and broadcasted to all peers. It can either be running on a server (centralized) but can be chosen randomly among peers (peer elected to act as the Leader peer).

To update the ledger, a client creates a transaction and sends it to one or several peers for endorsement (depending on chaincode rules). Once the transaction meets the endorsement policy, it is forwarded back to the client who sends it to the orderer for verification and broadcasting. Upon verification, the orderer broadcasts the transaction to all peers that will check it and update the ledger accordingly. An extensive documentation of the Hyperledger Fabric framework can be found in (linux Foundation, 2016).

4   System Model

Inside our system model, we distinguish the *traffic congestion detector* client, which is the module in charge of detecting a traffic jam situation and submitting speed changes to the shared ledger and the *dynamic navigation rerouting* server, which is the module in charge of detecting a road speed change (from an HF event) on a user's path and recompute the route accordingly.

4.1   The Chaincode

The following listings show how the chaincode fits into our application. In Listing 1.2, we state the different assets accessible in the ledger. Note that all users are only identified with a unique random ID and that a road asset contains an ID *roadId*, a list of submitted speeds *speeds* (and the corresponding list of associated timestamps *timestamps*) and the edge segment default speed *defaultSpeed* initialized from OpenStreetMap predefined tag information. Finally, the transaction *SubmitSpeedChange* which, given a new speed *newSpeed* and new timestamp *newTimestamp* for a road asset whose ID is *assetId*, modifies the *roadAsset* using the function shown in listing 1.1.

Furthermore, in listing 1.1, we observe the transaction *onSubmitSpeedChange* that fires an event *SubmitSpeedChangeNotification* when submitted. Basically, it simply appends the new speed and timestamps to the corresponding stored list within that asset. It ensures that the list size is no longer than N, a predefined constant, defined in function of the number of edges in the geographically bound map. Indeed, greater is N, more storage for the initial state database will be required.

Last but not least, all aforementioned functions are accessible through a REST API on the device storing the peer node, this allows cross-platform and convenient communication in the local network interface between our graph handler and the Hyperledger Fabric peer.

```
function onSubmitSpeedChange(x) {
    push(submitSpeedChange.roadAsset.timestamps, x.newTimestamp, MAX_NUMBER);
    push(submitSpeedChange.roadAsset.speeds, x.newSpeed, MAX_NUMBER);
    return getAssetRegistry('org.hacit.hes.RoadAsset')
        .then(function (assetRegistry) {
            var event = getFactory().newEvent('org.hacit.hes', '
SubmitSpeedChangeNotification');
            event.roadAsset = x.roadAsset;
            emit(event);
            return assetRegistry.update(x.roadAsset);
        });}
```

Listing 1.1. Chaincode

```
event SubmitSpeedChangeNotification { --> RoadAsset roadAsset }
participant User identified by assetId { o String assetId }
asset RoadAsset identified by roadId {
    o String roadId
    o Integer [] timestamps
    o Double defaultSpeed
    o Double [] speeds }
transaction SubmitSpeedChange {
    o Double newSpeed
    o String assetId
    o Integer newTimestamp
    --> RoadAsset roadAsset }
```

Listing 1.2. Ledger Model

4.2   Traffic Congestion Detector Client

Given an accumulated list of the user's GPS coordinates, we find the corresponding edge and extracts its road ID r using a map matching algorithm provided by the GraphHopper library (Newson and Krumm, 2009). Figure 1b shows the process for a user to update its current speed cs measured at timestamps ts to the corresponding road asset r (in the ledger) and thus, the process to create the proper corresponding transaction tx.

The challenge in this step is to decide whether or not the vehicle is in a traffic jam, or simply stopped at the red light for example. Basically, it gathers GPS coordinates until it detects that the road has changed. By computing the average speed in the middle part of this GPS trace, we can apply a threshold to decide if there is congestion.

4.3   Dynamic Navigation Rerouting Server

The other module is the dynamic navigation server, which listens for ledger update (*i.e.* new events submitted by peers). Alongside the main algorithm, we created a speed extractor, that given all submitted speed changes for a given road, extract the current road speed while removing outliers, using unsupervised clustering.

Algorithm. The process describing our dynamic navigation is shown in Fig. 1a and can be summarized as follows:

– An event is fired for a given road id: The HF module connects to our OSM graph handler with a POST request through the *localhost* interface, in order to send the road id and the corresponding list of speeds S and timestamps T (defined in Listing 1.2).
– The Graph Handler feeds the speeds and timestamp list to a speed detector, which will perform Algorithm 1 in order to find the weight from the most recent speed cluster centre while removing outliers.
– If the road modified is within the future road path, and if the change is significant, the user recomputes the navigation path against the up-to-date weighted graph.

Speed Extractor. The HF peer forwards the list of speeds S and timestamps T contained within the road Asset whose is firing the event. The goal of the speed extractor (described in Algorithm 1) is to cluster the 2D dimensional array $X = [T, S]$ and finds the earliest cluster using the *DBScan* algorithm, initially proposed in (Ester et al., 1996), using the Java library (Apache Fondation, 2017). Once the centre cx, cy is found, we forward cy (*i.e.* the speed) to the graph handler.

If there is not enough data or if the clustering fails, we simply use the weighted average Eq. (1) so that speed measurements with earlier timestamps have more weight:

$$\hat{s} = \frac{\sum_{i=1}^{N} w_i s_i}{\sum_{i=1}^{N} w_i} \quad \text{with} \ \ w_i = 1 - \frac{t_i}{\sum_{j=1}^{N} t_j}$$

$$\Rightarrow \hat{s} = \frac{\sum_{i=1}^{N} s_i}{N - 1} - \frac{\sum_{i=1}^{N} t_i s_i}{(N - 1) \cdot \sum_{i=1}^{N} t_i} \tag{1}$$

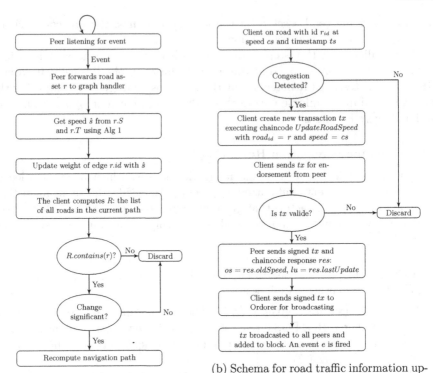

(a) Schema for dynamic navigation rerouting

(b) Schema for road traffic information update to shared ledger

Fig. 1. Procedures

5 Communication System

This section aims to describe how the system communicates between all the modules presented in the previous Sect. 4. Particularly, how and where are executed the HF peer loop, the Graph handler loop and the UI client for dynamic navigation in both the external device (*i.e.* Raspberry Pi) and mobile device (*i.e.* Smartphone).

5.1 Peers on External Device

A Raspberry Pi is a small computer having a dedicated operating system running Linux. The version 3 Model B contains 1 GB RAM, Wifi antenna and an external SD card for storage, see (Upton and Halfacree, 2014). Therefore, it has enough capabilities to run efficiently the HF peer node and the graph handler on such device. It communicates with the mobile device through wifi as shown in Fig. 2a,

---

Algorithm 1. Speed extractor algorithm

Require: X a 2-D array

1: **function** EXTRACT SPEED(X)
2:     $cx \Leftarrow Null$
3:     $cy \Leftarrow -Inf$
4:     **if** $shape(X)[2] > 15$ **then**
5:         $db \Leftarrow dbscan(X, eps : 4.5, min : 5)$
6:         $labels \Leftarrow db.labels\_$
7:         **for** k in $unique(labels)$ **do**
8:             $mask \Leftarrow (labels == k)$
9:             $x \Leftarrow X[mask]$
10:            $[cxx, cyy] \Leftarrow mean(X)$
11:            **if** $cyy < cy$ **then**
12:                $cx \Leftarrow cxx$
13:     **if** cx is $Null$ **then**
14:         $t \Leftarrow X[0, :]$
15:         $v \Leftarrow X[1, :]$
16:         $cx \Leftarrow weightedAverage(t, v)$ ▷ "Equation (1)"
    return cx

---

to exchange new road path to the UI, or new speed estimate alongside GPS coordinate.

Then, we have two servers, the graph handler running on port 4567 and the HF module running on port 8080 and we expose the REST client with the following API:

- The mobile Android app:
  1. *updatePosition*: PUT request to submit current speed and position.
  2. *getPathStatus*: GET request returning *true* if path was modified since last query.
  3. *getPath*: GET request to retrieve the list of navigation instructions. It will immediately update the current navigation instruction to the user interface.
  4. *initializeJourney*: POST request to initialize the graph handler with the destination and starting point.
  5. *updatePath*: PUT request to force the re-computation of the shortest path using Dijkstra algorithm (Dijkstra, 1959), return the newly computed navigation instruction.
- The HF module Client:
  1. *putRoadAsset*: PUT request executed whenever the *HF* module detects a new event (*i.e.* a road speed update) and forward the corresponding road asset to the graph handler.
- The graph handler Client (to HF module server):
  1. *postTransaction*: Executed by the graph handler whenever a traffic jam is detected. It forwards the transaction to the HF module, in addition with the road ID, new speed, and timestamp. After some time, this should fire an event for all listening peers on the network.

We assume that the initial ledger state contains all edges within the imported OSM file. This can be done while creating and instantiating the production chaincode by the administrator before deploying the peer's network.

5.2   Internet Connection and UI Client on Mobile Device

A prerequisite for our system to work, the HF module needs to be connected to the internet. Therefore, we share the connectivity of the Android device with the raspberry pi and thus connect it to the internet through the Android Wifi Access Point. The pre-configured device will automatically try to connect to the router (*i.e.* The android device) and will obtain IP address 192.168.43.155 once the user enables *shared   connectivity*. This IP is then used to perform the REST client calls, expressed in the previous part, between the two devices.

Finally, once initialization is completed and first navigation path instructions are received, the application opens *OSMAnd* dynamic navigation (see Fig. 2b) through Intent and the *OSMAnd* API. While the UI shows the navigation, a background process is continuously checking for new path updates, and if any, sends the updated path instructions to the *OSMAnd* UI. This causes *OSMAnd* to drop the current instructions for the new ones, and thus, updating the UI.

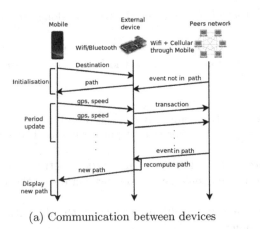

(a) Communication between devices   (b) OSMAnd UI

Fig. 2. The system

5.3   Limitations

The presented blockchain application, running on the mobile device, leads to several complications:

- *The communication burden and latency:*
  The system relies on the cellular network shared by the mobile device to listen to other peers and submit transactions. Therefore, we expect a fair use of the

user's cellular plan. Nowadays, it is common to have unlimited bandwidth usages but most of the data will be synchronized through WIFI before the user drives with the up-to-date system. Moreover, the responsiveness of the system is bounded to the block broadcasting frequency, which can be tuned to meet a trade off between resources usage and more frequent information updates. We are confident that submitting a new block every few minutes is feasible.

– *The storage cost:*
Table 1 shows the different ledger sizes regarding the size of the initial asset for the transactions and road asset initialization. Overall, we expect a ledger of around $842\,MB$ $(317 + 525)$ for one day of utilization for the average Geneva traffic per day (500000 transactions). By having a ledger pruning mechanism inside the chaincode rules, we can guarantee that the data size does not exceed a certain limit. Given the storage size available on our device, we can easily extend these limits to more than dozen of gigabytes.

– *The geographically bounded application:*
In this project, we assumed the use of our system within the boundary of the city of Geneva. Indeed, we realized that most traffic information is only useful within close range for most of the users. From that conclusion, we assumed the use of a chaincode (*i.e.* ledger) per geographically bounded zone (*e.g.* city). In the future, other zones will be used and a system acting as CA to assign dynamically users to the proper chaincode (*i.e.* area) will be studied and implemented.

– *User incentive:*
As every dynamic navigation system, the efficiency of the routing is directly related to the quality and quantity of the data. More user use the system, more precise can the routing be. As for every blockchain application, the principal of decentralization makes the system more complicated to use for the end-user and is often the bottleneck for world-wide acceptance.

5.4 Case Study

Let's imagine a person using our system going to work in a croweded city. At first, he will have to take the station (external device), which was synchronizing/charging at home, with him. The station will automatically connect

Table 1. Ledger size per asset size

Asset	Road		Transactions	
nb	1	68580	1	50000
size (MB)	0.48	317	0.11	525

to the mobile device while the user opens the specific system app. Upon navigation initial instruction, the station will listen for new transaction (*i.e.* road traffic update) and if necessary, forward new instructions to the end-user through the mobile application. In the background, the station will perform all processes to keep the distributed ledger up-to-date and handle user's GPS position (and thus, traffic information). Upon arrival, the user will synchronize the station with the local WIFI and charge it until next departure.

Such scenario will be numerically simulated to assess the performance of the overall system.

6   Forensics

The architecture of the proposed application allows any user to have access to the history of transactions and thus, it enables forensics.

6.1   Ledger Back-Crawling

The architecture allows forensics capabilities for judiciary or insurance claims. With a public shared and immutable ledger provided by the permissioned blockchain, all users can access all submitted transaction and thus, the history of road speed modifications. In another words, by crawling the ledger of chained transactions and given a specific user ID, one can extract the transactions submitted by this user. Thus, given the list of all these submitted transactions, one can extract the road segment ID alongside the corresponding timestamps and speed to create a navigation timeline for this user. The user can then guarantee that he had signed the extracted transactions using his private key.

The efficiency of the forensics system is directly related to the frequency at which the user submits transactions. In another word, if the user does not submit any transaction, there will be no possibility to backtrack his whereabouts. As such, we only provide with this system a tool to help the judiciary or insurance to make the decision, as an extension to the main application.

6.2   A Word on Privacy

Regarding our back-crawling algorithm and the confidentiality of our system in general, we grant access to the application through cryptographic material obtains from our CA. Even though the state database contains only the up-to-date list of road asset, the ledger contains the transactions submitted by any user, hidden behind his *userId*.

Although our approach is not anonymous, it is close to pseudonymous (similar to the bitcoin network, see (Androulaki et al., 2013)). However, one can analyse the ledger and extract meaningful pattern that can lead to the real user's identity.

Fortunately, Hyperledger Fabric will introduce in the version 1.2 a privacy technology known as Zero-Knowledge (ZK) Proof-based implemented has an Identity mixer (Au et al., 2006) and ZK-AT (Zero-Knowledge Asset Transfer). As a result, the identity of the participant issuing the transaction will stay hidden behind the identity mixer and thus, guaranteeing total privacy, similar as what is used in cryptocurrencies such as ZCash.

7   Conclusion

7.1   Summary

This project proposes an innovative variant for a decentralized system of navigation that emancipates the user from using a centralized service. Instead of communicating directly with nearby cars to retrieve only local traffic information, the users submit through cellular network global information about the traffic. This information is stored in assets within a permissioned ledger and can be updated with transactions. A system of event listens for new transactions (and thus, traffic update from other users) which forwards the information to another module handling the locally stored weighted graph. If necessary, the shortest path is recomputed and forwarded to the navigation user interface running on the mobile device making the navigation dynamic.

By using an external device such as a Raspberry Pi to run the blockchain and graph modules, we delegate the computing and storage cost to a unit able to easily handle all processes and make the experience as user-friendly as possible. The user can just plug the device to the car power and share his or her mobile wifi connection.

Furthermore, every user can access the shared ledger and thus, retrieve the list of submitted transactions for forensics purposes. By having a zero-knowledge mechanism implemented in the next version of Hyperledger Fabric, we will be able to guarantee that the identification of the user is not possible and thus, protecting his or her privacy.

7.2   Future Works

Our work so far was to design and implement a system able to dynamically route user using blockchain technology. However, a numerical simulation must be undertaken in order to optimize several parameters such as the size of the array in a road asset (currently equals to 100), the real latency, the storage cost and the ledger pruning time, the bandwidth used or the percent of user using our application in order to make it efficient.

In that manner, we are currently working on a numerical traffic simulation of Geneva, where a percent of the agents (acting as a driver) use our decentralized system. The simulation uses the framework Sumo (Krajzewicz et al., 2012). After these parameters are optimized, we will perform a full-size test assessing the functionalities of our system.

Moreover, an interesting variant would be to use a Road Side Unit (RSU) to store the ledger. In other words, these units would act as a peer for the blockchain network. The cryptographic material identifying a user and the graph would still be stored on the user's mobile side alongside the SDK to create transactions. Once a user comes into range within the RSU, it will send the list of congestion information as transactions and expect the RSU to sign them and send back the list of transactions since the user last connects. However, as of now, the feasibility of such system is not known and must be studied.

References

Androulaki, E., Karame, G.O., Roeschlin, M., Scherer, T., Capkun, S.: Evaluating user privacy in bitcoin. In: Sadeghi, A.-R. (ed.) FC 2013. LNCS, vol. 7859, pp. 34–51. Springer, Heidelberg (2013). https://doi.org/10.1007/978-3-642-39884-1_4

Apache Fondation: Commons Math Java library (2017). http://commons.apache.org/proper/commons-math/userguide/ml.html

Au, M.H., Susilo, W., Mu, Y.: Constant-size dynamic k-TAA. In: De Prisco, R., Yung, M. (eds.) SCN 2006. LNCS, vol. 4116, pp. 111–125. Springer, Heidelberg (2006). https://doi.org/10.1007/11832072_8

Beresford, A.R., Stajano, F.: Mix zones: user privacy in location-aware services. In: Proceedings of the Second IEEE Annual Conference on 2004 Pervasive Computing and Communications Workshops, pp. 127–131. IEEE (2004)

Dijkstra, E.W.: A note on two problems in connexion with graphs. Numer. Math. 1(1), 269–271 (1959)

Ester, M., Kriegel, H.-P., Sander, J., Xu, X., et al.: A density-based algorithm for discovering clusters in large spatial databases with noise. In: KDD, vol. 96, pp. 226–231 (1996)

European Parliament: European Parliament legislative resolution of 12 March 2014 on the General Data Protection Regulation. Technical report (COM(2012) 0011 C7–0025/2012 2012/0011(COD)) (2014)

Graphhopper dev: Graphhopper Java Librairy (2017). https://www.graphhopper.com/

IBM: IBM Blockchain Platform (2017). https://ibm-blockchain.github.io/develop/. Accessed 21 Apr 2018

Krajzewicz, D., Erdmann, J., Behrisch, M., Bieker, L.: Recent development and applications of SUMO - simulation of urban mobility. Int. J. Adv. Syst. Meas. 5(3&4), 128–138 (2012)

Leiding, B., Memarmoshrefi, P., Hogrefe, D.: Self-managed and blockchain-based vehicular ad-hoc networks. In: Proceedings of the 2016 ACM International Joint Conference onPervasive and Ubiquitous Computing, pp. 137–140. ACM (2016)

Linux Foundation, T.: HyperLedger Fabric docs (2016). https://hyperledger-fabric.readthedocs.io/en/release/. Accessed 21 Nov 2017

Newson, P. Krumm, J.: Hidden markov map matching through noise and sparseness. In: Proceedings of the 17th ACM SIGSPATIAL International Conference on Advances in Geographic Information Systems, pp. 336–343. ACM (2009)

OpenStreetMap contributors: Planet dump (2017). https://planet.osm.org. https://www.openstreetmap.org

OSMAnd dev: OSMAND (2017). https://osmand.net/

Raya, M., Hubaux, J.-P.: Securing vehicular ad hoc networks. J. Comput. Secur. 15(1), 39–68 (2007)

Shah, D., et al.: Gossip algorithms. Found. Trends® Networking 3(1), 1–125 (2009)

Upton, E., Halfacree, G.: Raspberry Pi User Guide. Wiley, Hoboken (2014)

Wang, L., Liu, G., Sun, L.: A secure and privacy-preserving navigation scheme using spatial crowdsourcing in fog-based vanets. Sensors 17(4), 668 (2017)

Wood, G.: Ethereum: a secure decentralised generalised transaction ledger. Ethereum Proj. Yellow Pap. 151, 1–32 (2014)

A Lightweight Security and Energy-Efficient Clustering Protocol for Wireless Sensor Networks

Guangsong Yang[1,2] and Xin-Wen Wu[2(✉)]

[1] Jimei University, Xiamen 361021, FJ, China
[2] Griffith University, Gold Coast 4215, QLD, Australia
x.wu@griffith.edu.au

Abstract. Most applications based on wireless sensor networks (WSN) have devices with constraints of limited energy and computational/storage capabilities. The traditional security mechanisms are not desirable to these applications. A lightweight security and energy-efficient clustering protocol was proposed in this paper to solve the security problem in the clustering-based sensor networks. Firstly, a lightweight security algorithm is proposed to meet the security requirements, which reduces the communication overload by using the transmission key index. Secondly, in the process of clustering, the base station (BS) and cluster head (CH) use lightweight authentication procedure to verify the identities hierarchically, to reduce the risk of attacks from malicious nodes posing as BS or CH. Thirdly, the proposed protocol is analyzed in the aspects of security and energy consumption. Simulation results show that the proposed protocol not only enhances the network security but also improves the energy efficiency.

Keywords: Lightweight security · Energy-efficient protocol · Clustering WSN

1 Introduction

Wireless sensor networks based on clustering methods have been proved to improve system throughput, reduce system delay and save energy. Some clustering protocols, such as Low-Energy Adaptive Clustering Hierarchy (LEACH) [1], solve the problem of energy efficiency by selecting cluster heads periodically. However, the dynamic nature of the topology also brings challenges to the existing security schemes.

Like most routing protocols in WSN, LEACH is vulnerable to a variety of security attacks [2], including interference, deception, replay, and so on. However, because it is a cluster-based protocol, it basically relies on CH for data aggregation and routing. If an intruder pretends to be a CH, intrusion and selective forwarding can be carried out to destroy the network. Moreover, the intruder may inject forged sensor data into the networking in some way.

Many of the security schemes used in the classic computer networks are not suitable for WSN. For example, the scheme based on public key distribution is easy to

© ICST Institute for Computer Sciences, Social Informatics and Telecommunications Engineering 2019
Published by Springer Nature Switzerland AG 2019. All Rights Reserved
J. Zheng et al. (Eds.): ADHOCNETS 2018, LNICST 258, pp. 237–246, 2019.
https://doi.org/10.1007/978-3-030-05888-3_22

be cracked by malicious nodes because of the requirement of the global key. The applications these schemes pose a significant security vulnerability.

There were lots of works about the security based on LEACH [2]. LEAP [3] is a local key allocation scheme among neighbor nodes, which is very effective for static networks. But in LEACH, each round may require a new Key distribution, which is inefficient and infeasible.

S-LEACH is the first modified version of LEACH with cryptographic protection against outsider attacks. In S-LEACH [4], each node has two symmetric keys: a pair of keys shared with the BS, and the last key of the key chain held by BS for authentication broadcast. BS authenticates the broadcast of CH through two simple steps. Each CH broadcast advertising message named *adv*, which include ID of CH and MAC (generate by the shared key between BS and CH), BS compiling a legitimate list of CH from these *adv*, and broadcast it to whole network by using μTESLA scheme. Ordinary member nodes can know which *adv* messages they receive from the legitimate nodes, and then select correct CH.

Based on the S-LEACH, other two protocols have been proposed. One is Sec-LEACH [5], another is MS-LEACH [6]. S-LEACH and SecLEACH were proposed by the same authors. S-LEACH is improved by SecLEACH which is based on a random key distribution scheme. In Sec-LEACH, the communication between nodes is protected by a key pre-allocation scheme. The main idea is to generate a large number of keys and their ID when deploying the network, and then randomly assign a group of keys to each node. Each node also is assigned a pair of keys shared with the BS, which are used in nodes and BS. It used random-key pre-distribution and μTESLA for secure hierarchical WSN with dynamic cluster formation. Sec-LEACH applied random key distribution to LEACH, and introduced symmetric key and one way hash chain to provide confidentiality and freshness. Sec-LEACH provides authenticity, integrity, confidentiality and freshness to communications.

MS-LEACH [6] was proposed to enhance the security of S-LEACH by providing data confidentiality to CH authentication using pairwise keys shared between CHs and their cluster members. It does not provide authentication for join request message. There is no key update provisioning for key. It requires multiple unicast communications. This way the energy of a CH can be depleted.

In this paper we proposed a lightweight security scheme for LEACH (which we call LS-LEACH) based on our previous works [9, 10]. The scheme significantly reduces the security overload and provides a higher level of security for distributed and dynamic sensor networks.

The paper is organized as follows, in Sect. 2 the lightweight security protocol for WSN was described. Section 3 proposed a LS-LEACH security protocol based on LEACH. Section 4 presents LS-LEACH performance evaluation. Finally, the concluding remarks and future work are given in Sect. 5.

2 The Lightweight Security Method for WSN

2.1 The Light Weight Security Method

The lightweight security protocol we proposed in [9] based on the work [10] include the process of lightweight encryption, key management and identity authentication, the security is ensured by the procedure of one-key-for-one-file encryption and the security of the key management. Encryption and decryption are executed using a probabilistic encryption procedure or using hashed key.

Firstly, we should prepare a large key store for legitimate users in advance. The key store seed can be stored in the device's hardware security module [8]. When an attacker physically disrupts the device and trying to extract it without successfully authenticating, it will be deleted by the device automatically.

The Structure of proposed lightweight security algorithm is show in Fig. 1. Let S be the sending party and R be the receiving party. Each key $k(\omega)$ is efficiently generated through the key storage seed K and index ω shared by the users and devices (The key is uniquely determined by ω and the seed K in the storage pool). There is no need to transfer keys or maintain them between devices. From the information theory point of view, the key management program is safe, which means that no information about the key is disclosed when the key index is transmitted. Key generation, allocation and usage are specified as follows:

(1) To encrypt x, the sender first needs to pick a random key index ω and seed K in the key store, then generate an encryption key $k(\omega)$ using an efficient algorithm. $k = (k_1, k_2, k_3, \ldots k_n)$ is a key with n bits, $x = (x_1, x_2, x_3, \ldots x_n)$ is information with n bits, the method of Encryption and Decryption are,

$$\text{Encryption} : E_k(x) = (f_k(r), x \oplus h(r))$$
$$\text{Decryption} : D_k(y, z) = h(f_k^{-1}(y)) \oplus z \tag{1}$$

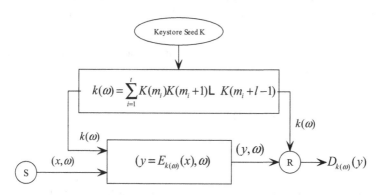

Fig. 1. Structure of proposed lightweight security algorithm

Where, $f_k(x) = (k_1 \oplus x_1, k_2 \oplus x_2, k_3 \oplus x_3, \ldots k_n \oplus x_n)$, $y = E_{k(\omega)}(x), r$ is a random string (independent from the key and plaintext) and h is a random oracle implementation by using a hash function). The seed in key store $K = K(0)K(1)\cdots K(L-1)$ is an L-bit random string, which is used to generate cryptographic keys of length $l(l \ll L)$. Assume $\Omega = (m_1, m_2, m_3, \ldots m_t)$ is a set of cardinality Λ, where t is a positive integer, and $0 \leq (m_1, m_2, m_3, \ldots m_t) \leq L$. Let the elements of Ω act as key indices. For any of $0 \leq \omega = (m_1, m_2, m_3, \ldots m_t)$ in Ω, the Key with length l can be expressed as $k(\omega)$ or $k(m_1, m_2, m_3, \ldots m_t)$, show as

$$k(\omega) = k(m_1, m_2, m_3, \ldots m_t) = \sum_{i=1}^{t} K(m_i)K(m_i+1)\cdots K(m_i+l-1) \qquad (2)$$

Where, $\sum_{i=1}^{t} K(m_i)K(m_i+1)\cdots K(m_i+l-1)$, is bit by bit binary addition.

Here, the sum of the integer m, and j, are related to the module L, so the key store $\Psi = \{k(m_1, m_2, \ldots m_t) : 0 \leq (m_1, m_2, m_3, \ldots m_t) \leq L-1\}$, the number of available keys here is $\Lambda = \binom{L}{t}$

(2) The key index ω with ciphertext (can be placed on the head of the encrypted message packet), are sent to the receiver and encrypted, then $k(\omega)$ are deleted.

(3) The receiver uses ω to regenerate key $k(\omega)$, using the same key index ω and the same key generation process, then used for decryption or authentication verification.

2.2 Identity Authentication Process

When a new legitimate device joins a local network system for the first time, the system administrator configures it through some security method (such as a manual method), so that the device shares it's unique and secret with the HUB or other devices. With this configuration procedure, the new device is also know the identity of other devices. These identities may then be maintained by a hardware security module.

(1) *Identity Authentication*

For any two device D1 and D2, with the unique and secret identity ID_1 and ID_2 respectively. They authenticate each other as follow

Step1. D1 sent the content to D2 as

$$(\omega_1; F_{k(\omega_1)}(ID_1 \| TS)) \qquad (3)$$

Where, ω_1 is a randomly selected key index, TS is a timestamp (used to prevent replay), $F(\cdot)$ is a valid cypher.

Step2. Using the key index ω_1, D2 generates the key $k(\omega_1)$ and decrypts ID_1

$$ID_1||TS = F^{-1}_{k(\omega_1)}(F_{k(\omega_1)}(ID_1||TS)) \tag{4}$$

D2 verifies D1 (obtained from BS or CH) by comparing the decrypted content with the identity of D1;

Step3. Randomly select the key index ω_2 and generate the key $k(\omega_2)$, D2 will send the following content to D1

$$(\omega_2; F_{k(\omega_2)}(ID_2 \oplus ID_1||TS)) \tag{5}$$

Step4. Using the key index ω_2, D1 generates the key $k(\omega_2)$ and decrypts the ID of D2

$$ID_2||TS = ID_1 \oplus F^{-1}_{k(\omega_2)}(F_{k(\omega_2)}(ID_2 \oplus ID_1||TS)) \tag{6}$$

D1 thus obtains the identity of D2.

3   Security Clustering Protocol with Lightweight Method

In this section, a clustering algorithm named LS (Lightweight Security)-LEACH is proposed, which is based on the classical LEACH algorithm combined with our lightweight security method in the process of authentication and clustering.

LEACH protocol employs randomized rotation of the cluster-heads to evenly distribute the energy load among the sensor nodes in the network. The operation of LS-LEACH is similar to LEACH which divided into rounds show as Fig. 2. Each round consists of two phases: a set-up phase and a steady-state phase. During the set-up phase cluster-heads are determined and the clusters are organized. During the steady-state phase data transference to the base station occurs.

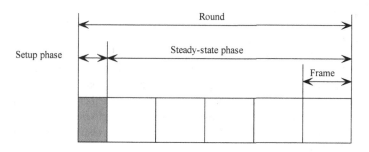

Fig. 2. Timeline of LEACH

The more detailed working process is shown in Table 1.

Table 1. LS-LEACH Protocol.

The algorithm of LS-LEACH Protocol.

Setup phase

Step1. BS $\Rightarrow \Lambda : adv_{BS} (ID_{BS} , \omega_{BS})$

CH $\Rightarrow \Lambda : req_{BS} (ID_{CH}, \omega_{CH}, ID_{BS}, SL)$

BS: Authenticated CH, update *CH_List* and broadcast to the whole network.

A_i : Choose CH according to adv_{CH} and adv_{BS}.

Step2. $A_i \rightarrow$ CH :$join\_req(ID_{A_i} , ID_{CH} , \omega_{A_i})$

Step3. CH $\Rightarrow \Lambda : ID_{CH} , sched(..., \langle ID_{A_i}, t_{A_i} \rangle, ...)$,

Steady-state phase

Step4. $A_i \rightarrow$ CH : $(ID_{A_i} , ID_{CH} , d_{A_i} , \omega_{A_i})$

Step5. CH $\rightarrow$ BS : $ID_{CH} , ID_{BS} , G(..., d_{A_i}, ...)$, ω_{CH}

Symbols defined as below,

A_i ,CH, BS: An ordinary node, a cluster head, and the base station, respectively

Λ : The set of all nodes in the network

$\Rightarrow , \rightarrow$: Broadcast and unicast, transmissions respectively

ID_X : Node X's id

d_X : Sensing report from node X

ID_X , t_{Xi}: Node X's id and its time slot t_X in its cluster's transmission schedule

adv, join_req, sched : String identifiers for message types

G : Data aggregation function

j : Reporting cycle within the current round

SL : Security level, it depend on the length of ω

1. **Setup phase**

   Step 1:
   (1) At the beginning of each round, the BS broadcasts $adv_{BS}(ID_{BS}, \omega_{BS})$ to the whole network. After each sensing node obtains ω_{BS}, it generates $k(\omega_{BS})$ and decrypts ID_{BS} according to Eq. (2), them compared with ID_{BS} in its own memory at initialization phase, to determine whether it is a real BS.
   (2) The self-recommended cluster head sends network access information $req_{BS}(ID_{CH}, \omega_{CH}, ID_{BS}, SL)$ to the BS, and it also can be heard by its neighbor nodes.

(3) BS generate $k(\omega_{CH})$ according to Eq. (2), decrypt out ID_{CH}, and compare with legitimate users in its own database. If an ID_{CH} is satisfied, it means that it is a valid node, then it is listed in the legitimate CH_List of this round, and broadcast $adv_{BS}(ID_{BS}, \omega_{BS}, CH\_List)$ to the whole network.

Step 2: The normal node A_i chooses the closest CH within its coverage based on the RSSI, generates $k(\omega_{CH})$ by ω_{CH}, decrypts ID_{CH} according to Eq. (3). Similarly, it generates $k(\omega_{BS})$ by ω_{BS}, decrypts CH_List. By comparing decrypted ID_{CH} and CH_List, it determine whether the cluster head is a legitimate CH. Then select ω_{A_i} from the k-store, and send the *join_req* request to join the cluster. If a node did not take part in any cluster, he will communicate to BS directly.

Step 3: CH validates the A_i. Then send the TDMA scheduling information to its member nodes.

2. **Steady-phase**

Step 4: A_i send the encrypted monitoring data d_{A_i} to CH by using ω_{A_i}

Step 5: CH aggregate the information from A_i together, and send these data $G(\ldots, d_{A_i}, \ldots)$ and ω_{CH} to the BS. To ensure freshness, ω_{CH} should be updated at each round.

4 Simulation and Evaluation

The security of proposed protocol has been verified in [9, 10]. In this section, we evaluated the energy effectiveness of our scheme through simulation experiments. In the simulation, 100 sensor nodes are randomly distributed in the square region of size 200 m * 200 m and the BS is in the center of this region. The parameters used in the simulation are summarized in Table 2.

Table 2. Simulation parameters.

Parameter	Meaning	Value
n	Size of data packet	4000bit
a	Size of control packet	100bit
E_{DA}	Aggregation energy consumption	5nJ/bit/signal
E_{sedule}	Energy consumption of Schedule	5nJ/bit/signal
E_{init}	Initial energy	10 J
P_r	Receive power	1 mJ /bit
B_t	Threshold of battery	1 J

SecLEACH messages to be 36 bytes long (the default TinyOS message sizes) and LEACH messages to be 30 bytes long. The difference is meant to account for the size difference between the MAC (8bytes [16]) and CRC (2 bytes [12]) – the former present in SecLEACH, but absent in LEACH; and the latter present in LEACH, but absent in SecLEACH.

In our scheme, the additional energy consumption mainly from setup phase. We set the length of $l = k(\omega) = 128(256)$ bits $= 16(32)$ bytes. According the analysis in Sect. 2.1, the length of ω can be selected with different security level.

The average of ten times simulation results is show as Figs. 3 and 4.

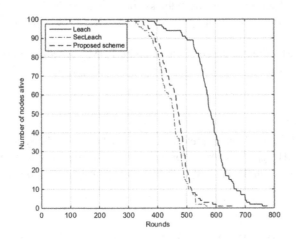

Fig. 3. Dead nodes comparison of different protocol.

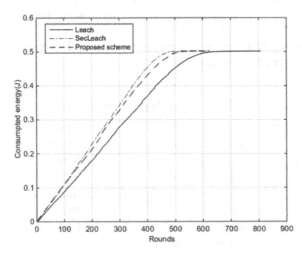

Fig. 4. Energy consumption comparison of different protocol.

Figure 3 shows number of alive nodes using different protocols as rounds varies, We can easily observe that the lifetime of LEACH is longer than that of LS-LEACH and SecLEACH. It is due to some load must be added to ensure safety, nodes cost more energy in certain round leads their death in advance. But LS-LEACH performance is better compared to SecLEACH, because the overload is less than that in SecLEACH.

Figure 4 clearly depicts that LS-LEACH outperforms SecLEACH in terms of energy consumption.

5 Conclusion

In this paper, we proposed a lightweight security leach protocol to enhanced the security and minimize the energy consumption of sensor nodes.

Our contribution in this paper are show as bellow,

(1) We propose a Lightweight Security LEACH (LS-LEACH) protocol, to reduce the overload (both encryption, Decrypt, identity authentication and transmission). Due to the lightweight encryption method, only a few indices need to be sent during node authentication process, so the load is reduced and energy efficiency is improved. Through the node authentication, the multiple ID Sybil attacks and wormhole attacks by malicious node are avoided.

(2) The introduced security mechanism is suitable for distributed scenarios, which enhance the security between nodes authentication, meanwhile avoids energy consumption of distant nodes due to direct transmission.

(3) The level can be controlled by adjust the length of index and key, neighbor nodes can communicate between each other based on the security level.

(4) Due to the network password are update in every round, the freshness is Ensured. Future research work includes how to further to improve the energy efficiency of this protocol by using multi-hop and other method.

Acknowledgement. This research is supported by Science Foundation of Fujian Province (No. 2015J01267), Training Program of FuJian Excellent Talents in University.

References

1. Heinzelman, W.R., Chandrakasan, A., Balakrishnan, H.: Energy-efficient communication protocol for wireless microsensor networks. In: Proceedings of the 33rd Annual Hawaii International Conference System Sciences, pp. 10–15 (2000)
2. Rahayu, T.M., Lee, S.G., Lee, H.J.: Survey on LEACH-based security protocols. In: Advanced Communication Technology (ICACT), pp. 304–309 (2014)
3. Zhu, S., Setia, S., Jajodia, S.: LEAP+: efficient security mechanisms for large-scale distributed sensor networks. ACM Trans. Sens. Netw. (TOSN) 2(4), 500–528 (2006)
4. Ferreira, A.C., Vilaça, M.A., Oliveira, L.B., Habib, E., Wong, H.C., Loureiro, A.A.: On the security of cluster-based communication protocols for wireless sensor networks. In: Lorenz, P., Dini, P. (eds.) ICN 2005. LNCS, vol. 3420, pp. 449–458. Springer, Heidelberg (2005). https://doi.org/10.1007/978-3-540-31956-6_53

5. Oliveira, L.B., Wong, H.C., Bern, M., Dahab, R., Loureiro, A.A.F.: SecLEACH-A random key distribution solution for securing clustered sensor networks. In: Fifth IEEE International Symposium on Network Computing and Applications, NCA 2006, pp. 145–154 (2006)
6. El_Saadawy, M., Shaaban, E.: Enhancing S-LEACH security for wireless sen-sor networks. In: 2012 IEEE International Conference on Electro/Information Technology (EIT), pp. 1–6 (2012)
7. Jolfaei, A., Wu, X.W., Muthukkumarasamy, V.: A secure lightweight texture encryption scheme. In: Huang, F., Sugimoto, A. (eds.) PSIVT 2015. LNCS, vol. 9555, pp. 344–356. Springer, Cham (2016). https://doi.org/10.1007/978-3-319-30285-0_28
8. Paverd, A.J., Martin, A.P.: Hardware security for device authentication in the smart grid. In: Cuellar, J. (ed.) SmartGridSec 2012. LNCS, vol. 7823, pp. 72–84. Springer, Heidelberg (2013). https://doi.org/10.1007/978-3-642-38030-3_5
9. Wu, X.-W., Yang, E.-H., Wang, J.: Lightweight security protocols for the internet of things. In: Proceedings of the 28th Annual IEEE International Symposium on Personal, Indoor and Mobile Radio Communications (IEEE PIMRC 2017), Montreal, Canada, 8–13 October 2017
10. Yang, E.H., Wu, X.-W.: Information-theoretically secure key generation and management. In: Proceedings of 2017 IEEE International Symposium on Information Theory, pp. 1529–1533 (2017)
11. Yick, J., Mukherjee, B., Ghosal, D.: Wireless sensor network survey. Comput. Netw. 52(12), 2292–2330 (2008)

Power Allocation for Physical Layer Security Among Similar Channels

Xiangxue Tai[1], Shuai Han[1(✉)], Xi Chen[2], and Qingli Zhang[1]

[1] Harbin Institute of Technology, Harbin, China
hanshuai@hit.edu.cn
[2] Flatiron Institute, Simons Foundation, New York, NY, USA

Abstract. Physical layer security technologies are used to ensure the secure communication when eavesdroppers use infinite computing capabilities to launch brute force attacks. Traditional physical layer security technologies utilized the difference between legitimate channels and eavesdropping channels. However, in certain scenarios, the legitimate channels are similar to eavesdropping channels so that the communication become insecure. In this paper, we especially studied the physical layer security communication among similar channels. An interference relay model was proposed to ensure the security of communication and at the same time, optimize the power allocation by maximizing the lower bound of the secrecy outage probability. The theoretical secrecy outage probability of the proposed power allocation scheme was derived. Simulation results show that the proposed scheme is superior to a uniform power allocation scheme on channel security performance under the same condition. Furthermore, using simulation, we demonstrated that the derivation of secrecy outage probability for the proposed power allocation scheme is valid.

Keywords: Physical layer security · Similar channels
Power allocation · Interference relay

1 Introduction

Physical layer security is an information theoretical approach to achieving confidentiality at the physical layer [1]. Physical layer security technologies can resist quantum attack and play a key role in secure communications. Currently, there are several studies discussing physical layer security technologies. Precoding/beamforming technologies played a vital role physical layer security. In paper [2], two novel schemes were proposed to enhance the security performance using precoding-aided spatial modulation (PSM): one used the random antenna selection (RAS) technique to generate zero-forcing precoding matrices with randomly

This work is supported by the National Natural Science Foundation of China (No. 91438205 and No. 61471143).

J. Zheng et al. (Eds.): ADHOCNETS 2018, LNICST 258, pp. 247–257, 2019.
https://doi.org/10.1007/978-3-030-05888-3_23

activated transmit antennas; the other was an improved version of RAS-PSM by introducing the time-varying artificial noise into RAS-PSM. Another precoding scheme was proposed for multiple input multiple output (MIMO) system [3] where two cases were analyzed as: (1) all CSI (Channel State Information) with legitimate channels at the transmitter could maximize the signal to noise ratio (SNR) of the receiver and the secret rate: (2) the transmitter used an improved Lloyd algorithm to construct the codebook. This scheme quantified the precoding and finally obtained a low-complexity postcode scheme to offset the SNR loss. Moreover, in recent years artificial noise technologies became more important in physical layer security communication. Artificial noise tech-nologies can jam the eavesdropper so as to improve the security capacity. Nowadays, artificial noise technologies mainly included zero-space noise based on MIMO and noise base station deployment based on random geometric model [4]. Artificial noise technologies were often combined with beamforming [5,6]. By jointly optimizing beamforming and the artificial noise vector of all base stations, they minimized the total transmit power, ensured the QoS (Quality of Service) of authorized users and prevented unauthorized users from intercepting information. Some existing conclusions about single antenna eavesdroppers were extended to multi-antenna eavesdroppers. It has been proved that the traditional zero-space artificial noise scheme is the best choice given any system parameters. Random beamforming technology is also used for physical layer security in some cases since it only used partial CSI but can effectively improve the system security. Exploiting full duplexity to enhance physical layer security has received considerable attention [7]. Besides, physical layer security is studied for the fifth generation communication system (5G), where beamforming based on massive MIMO [8] and secure transmission for millimeter wave systems [9] were both studied.

Physical layer security technologies make the information transmit securely by modelling the difference of channel status information (CSI, you should move this to the place where CSI was mentioned for the first time) between legitimate channels and eavesdropping channels. However, if the distance from legitimate receiver to the eavesdropper is too short compared to the distance between the transmitter to legitimate receiver or eavesdropper, the CSI of the legitimate channel will be very similar to that of the wiretap channel. In such cases, existing physical layer security schemes cannot perform transmission securely any more.

In this paper, to solve the security transmission problem when legal channels are similar to wiretap channels, we proposed a power allocation scheme based on a physical layer security model with interference relays. Key performance measurements of physical layer security include the ergodic secrecy capacity and the secrecy outage probability. We derived the expression of optimal power allocation parameters by maximizing the lower bound of ergodic secrecy capacity. In the meanwhile, the secrecy outage probability was also derived to evaluate the performance of the proposed power allocation scheme.

The rest of this paper is organized as follows. The system model is provided in Sect. 2. In section Sect. 3, power allocation to realize physical layer security communication among similar channels is optimized and a optimal power allocation scheme is proposed. Theoretical analysis is performed in Sect. 4 and the secrecy outage probability based on the proposed optimal power allocation scheme is derived. Simulation results are provided in Sect. 5 to evaluate the secrecy performance of the uniform power allocation scheme and the proposed power allocation scheme. We also verify the accuracy of the secrecy outage probability based on optimal power allocation scheme we derived. Section 6 draws the conclusion of this paper.

Our notations are as follows. In this paper, we use x, $\mathbf{x}$, $\mathbf{X}$ to denote a scalar, a vector and a matrix, respectively. $||\mathbf{x}||^2$ represent 2-norm of vector $\mathbf{x}$. If $\mathbf{X} \in \mathbb{C}^{N \times M}$ denotes that $\mathbf{X}$ is a $N \times M$ dimensional complex matrix. $\mathcal{CN}(0, \sigma^2)$ denotes the circular symmetric complex Gaussian distribution with zero mean and covariance σ^2. $\{x\}^+ = \max(0, x)$. $E(x)$ denotes the mathematical expectation of x.

2 System Model

In order to bring difference to legal channels and wiretap channels, we consider adding interference relays to the system, as shown in Fig. 1. The interference node relays interfering signals, which are orthogonal to the channels from the interference relay node to the legitimate receivers. Then, the interfering signals will only reduce the eavesdropper's signal quality.

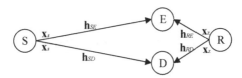

Fig. 1. The physical layer security communication interference relay model for the specific indifference channels

Figure 1 is the proposed physical layer security communication interference relay model for the scenario when channels are not differential enough to ensure secure communication. Source node S represents the transmitter, destination node D represents the legitimate receiver, eavesdropping node E represents the eavesdropping receiver, and relay node R represents the interference relay. The distance from S to D or E is very long so that the distance between D and E can be ignored. Then, S-D channel and S-E channel are very similar. In Fig. 1, we assume that the distance between R and D or R and E is not that long such that the distance between D to E is comparable with it. Then, S-D channel and S-E channel are differential. $\mathbf{h}_{SD}$ denotes the CSI vector from S to D, $\mathbf{h}_{SD} \in \mathbb{C}^{N_s \times 1}$, where N_s is the number antennas of transmitter S. $\mathbf{h}_{SE}$ is the CSI vector from S to E, $\mathbf{h}_{SE} \in \mathbb{C}^{N_s \times 1}$. Especially, $\mathbf{h}_{SE} = \mathbf{h}_{SD}$. $\mathbf{h}_{RD}$ is the CSI vector from R to

D, $\mathbf{h}_{RD} \in \mathbb{C}^{N_r \times 1}$. $\mathbf{h}_{RE}$ is the CSI vector from R to D, $\mathbf{h}_{RE} \in \mathbb{C}^{N_r \times 1}$. $\mathbf{x}_s$ is the useful signal which S transmits to D, $\|\mathbf{x}_s\|^2 = 1$. $\mathbf{x}_z$ is the interference which R transmits to E. $\mathbf{x}_z$ is pseudo random complex Gaussian noise and is orthogonal to $\mathbf{h}_{RD}$, namely $\mathbf{h}_{RD}\mathbf{x}_z = 0$. Besides, $\|\mathbf{x}_z\|^2 = 1$.

Assume that the total power constraint of the system is P which is the sum of the transmitting power of S and R. We introduce a power allocation factor as λ so that the power of S is λP and the power of R is $(1 - \lambda)P$. Assume that the receiving antenna gain of E and D are the same. Then the signals received at D and E can be respectively expressed as:

$$y_d = \sqrt{\lambda P} \mathbf{h}_{SD}^H \mathbf{x}_s + \sqrt{(1-\lambda)P} \mathbf{h}_{RD}^H \mathbf{x}_z + n_d, \tag{1}$$

$$y_e = \sqrt{\lambda P} \mathbf{h}_{SE}^H \mathbf{x}_s + \sqrt{(1-\lambda)P} \mathbf{h}_{RE}^H \mathbf{x}_z + n_e, \tag{2}$$

where y_d is the signal received at the destination node D and y_e is the signal received at the eavesdropping node E. n_d is the complex Gaussian random noise received at the destination node D, $n_d \sim \mathcal{CN}(0, \sigma_d^2)$. n_e is the complex Gaussian random noise received at the eavesdropping node E, $n_e \sim \mathcal{CN}(0, \sigma_e^2)$.

Because $\mathbf{h}_{RD}\mathbf{x}_z = 0$, the signal to noise ratio γ_d at the destination node D can be expressed as

$$\gamma_d = \frac{\lambda P \|\mathbf{h}_{SD}\|^2}{\sigma_d^2}. \tag{3}$$

And the signal to noise ratio γ_e at the eavesdropping node E can be expressed as

$$\gamma_e = \frac{\lambda P \|\mathbf{h}_{SE}\|^2}{(1-\lambda)P \|\mathbf{h}_{RE}\|^2 \cos\theta + \sigma_e^2}, \tag{4}$$

where θ is the angle which obeys uniform distribution between $\mathbf{h}_{RE}$ and $\mathbf{x}_z$, $\theta \in (-\frac{\pi}{2}, \frac{\pi}{2})$.

Then the instantaneous secrecy capacity can be expressed as

$$C_s(\lambda) = [\log_2(1 + \gamma_d) - \log_2(1 + \gamma_e)]^+. \tag{5}$$

Due to $\mathbf{h}_{SE} = \mathbf{h}_{SD}$, $\sigma_d^2 = \sigma_e^2$, $(1-\lambda)P \|\mathbf{h}_{RE}\|^2 \cos\theta > 0$, we can get $\gamma_d > \gamma_e$. Hence, $C_s > 0$. Therefore, the system model can achieve physical layer security communication among indifference channels.

3   A Optimal Power Allocation Scheme to Realize Physical Layer Security Communication Among Similar Channels

3.1   Power Allocation Optimization

The secrecy performance of system is relevant to the secrecy outage probability. The bigger the secrecy outage probability is, the better the secrecy performance is. Hence, it is meaningful to optimize secrecy outage probability.

Assume that the minimum transmission rate that ensures normal system secure operation is R_s, the secrecy outage probability can be expressed as

$$P_{out}(R_s) = Pr[C_s(\lambda) < R_s]. \tag{6}$$

Let $\gamma_{SD} = \dfrac{P\|\mathbf{h}_{SD}\|^2}{\sigma_d^2}$, $\gamma_{RD} = \dfrac{P\|\mathbf{h}_{RD}\|^2}{\sigma_d^2}$, $\gamma_{SE} = \dfrac{P\|\mathbf{h}_{SE}\|^2}{\sigma_e^2}$ and $\gamma_{RE} = \dfrac{P\|\mathbf{h}_{RE}\|^2 \cos\theta}{\sigma_e^2}$, then the Eqs. (3) and (4) can be expressed as

$$\gamma_d = \lambda\gamma_{SD}, \tag{7}$$

$$\gamma_e = \frac{\lambda\gamma_{SE}}{(1-\lambda)\gamma_{RE}+1}. \tag{8}$$

Submitting Eqs. (3), (4) and (5) into Eq. (6) and simplifying, the secrecy outage probability can be rewritten as

$$P_{out}(R_s) = Pr[g(\lambda) < 2^{R_s} - 1]. \tag{9}$$

where

$$g(\lambda) = (1 - 2^{R_s})\lambda\gamma_{SD} + (1 - 2^{R_s})(1-\lambda)\gamma_{RE} + \lambda(1-\lambda)\gamma_{SD}\gamma_{RE}.$$

In [10], $Pr[g(x) \le t] \ge 1 - E(x)/t$. Hence, we can get

$$P_{out}(R_s) \ge 1 - \frac{E[g(\lambda)]}{2^{R_s} - 1}. \tag{10}$$

The lower bound of the secrecy outage probability can be expressed as $1 - \dfrac{E[g(\lambda)]}{2^{R_s} - 1}$. Because it is difficult to maximize the secrecy outage probability, we try to maximize the lower bound of the secrecy outage probability. Then, the optimal power allocation factor λ^* should make the secrecy outage probability maximum, which can be expressed as

$$\lambda^* = \arg\min_{0<\lambda<1}(1 - \frac{E[g(\lambda)]}{2^{R_s} - 1}). \tag{11}$$

The Eq. (11) is equivalent to

$$\lambda^* = \arg\max_{0<\lambda<1} E[g(\lambda)]. \tag{12}$$

Above all, the $E[g(\lambda)]$ can be expressed as

$$\begin{aligned} E[g(\lambda)] = {}&- E[\gamma_{SD}]E[\gamma_{RE}]\lambda^2 + [(1 - 2^{R_s})(E[\gamma_{SD}] - E[\gamma_{RE}]) \\ & + E[\gamma_{SD}]E[\gamma_{RE}]]\lambda + (1 - 2^{R_s})E[\gamma_{RE}]. \end{aligned} \tag{13}$$

According to Eq. (13), $E[g(\lambda)]$ is a quadratic function. The maximum point is its extreme point. Namely, the optimal power allocation factor λ^* is the extreme point of $E[g(\lambda)]$. Hence, the optimal power allocation factor λ^* can be expressed as

$$\lambda^* = \frac{1}{2} + \frac{2^{R_s} - 1}{2P} \left(\frac{1}{E[\|\mathbf{h}_{SD}\|^2]} - \frac{\pi}{E[\|\mathbf{h}_{RE}\|^2]} \right). \tag{14}$$

From Eq. (14), we can see that the optimal power allocation factor λ^* is relevant to $E[\|\mathbf{h}_{SD}\|^2]$, $E[\|\mathbf{h}_{RE}\|^2]$, P and R_s. Hence, when P and R_s is fixed, the optimal power allocation factor λ^* will not change until the statistics channel state information of channel $\mathbf{h}_{SD}$ and $\mathbf{h}_{RE}$ change. Besides, when $P \to \infty$, $\frac{2^{R_s} - 1}{2P} \left(\frac{1}{E[\|\mathbf{h}_{SD}\|^2]} - \frac{\pi}{E[\|\mathbf{h}_{RE}\|^2]} \right) \to 0$, $\lambda^* \to \frac{1}{2}$. Therefore, when the total power constraints P is large enough, this optimal power allocation based on the lower bound of secrecy outage probability has the same secrecy performance on secrecy outage probability as the fixed uniform power allocation scheme of which power allocation factor λ^* is equal to 0.5.

3.2   A Power Allocation Scheme

According to the optimal power allocation factor λ^*, a power allocation scheme is proposed which is summarized in the following procedure.

1: Source node S gets the channel state information from S to D ($E[\|\mathbf{h}_{SD}\|^2]$). Relay node R feeds back the channel state information from R to E ($E[\|\mathbf{h}_{RE}\|^2]$) to the source node E.

2: Source node S calculates the power allocation factor λ^* according to the equation (14).

3: Source node S infroms the λ^* to the Relay node R.

4: Send the useful data safely. The transmitting power of the source node S is λP and the transmitting power of the interference relay is $(1-\lambda)P$. Meanwhile, Source node S checks whether the statistics channel static information has changed.

5: If the statistics channel static information has changed, return to perform step 2. channel static information has changed.

The power allocation factor λ^* is determined at S with the statistics CSI. Then the power allocation factor is fed back to R. The system conduct the transmission in a secure way and check if the statistics CSI has changed at the same time. S will update λ^* if the statistics CSI has changed.

This proposed power allocation scheme has the following characteristics. First, this scheme achieves the physical layer security communication when the distance between a legitimate receiver and a eavesdropping receiver is too short if compared to the distance between a transmitter and a legitimate receiver/eavesdropping receiver. It solves the security issue when legal channels are similar to eavesdropping channels. Second, it can get a better security performance on erodgic secrecy capacity and secrecy outage probability compared to the uniform power allocation scheme (as demonstrated in the next section). Third, compared to the power allocation scheme using instantaneous CSI, this scheme only requires the statistics CSI, which is available in most applications. Finally, this scheme only updates the power allocation factor when the statistics CSI changes. It will save signaling overhead.

4   Performance Theoretical Analysis

Due that the optimal power allocation is based on the lower bound of secrecy outage probability. Hence, it is meaningful to derive the secrecy outage probability under this power allocation scheme.

The expression of secrecy outage probability has been given in Eq. (9). Let

$$\gamma_{SD} = \frac{P\|\mathbf{h}_{SD}\|^2}{\sigma_d^2}, \gamma_{RD} = \frac{P\|\mathbf{h}_{RD}\|^2}{\sigma_d^2}, \gamma_{SE} = \frac{P\|\mathbf{h}_{SE}\|^2}{\sigma_e^2} \text{ and } \gamma_{RE} = \frac{P\|\mathbf{h}_{RE}\|^2 \cos\theta}{\sigma_e^2},$$

the power allocation can be rewritten as

$$P_{out}(R_s) = P_r[ax_1 + bx_2\cos\theta + cx_1x_2\cos\theta < t], \tag{15}$$

where

$$a = \frac{(1 - 2^{R_s})\lambda P}{\sigma_d^2}, \ b = \frac{(1 - 2^{R_s})(1 - \lambda)P}{\sigma_e^2}$$

$$c = \frac{\lambda(1 - \lambda)P^2}{\sigma_d^2\sigma_e^2}, \ t = 2^{R_s} - 1 \tag{16}$$

$$x_1 = \|\mathbf{h}_{SD}\|^2, \quad x_2 = \|\mathbf{h}_{RE}\|^2$$

Obviously, $a < 0$, $b < 0$, $c > 0$, $t > 0$. Besides, they are all const. Hence, the secrecy outage probability can be triple integrals which is

$$P_{out}(R_s) = \iiint_Q p(x_1)p(x_2)p(\theta)dx_1dx_2d\theta, \tag{17}$$

where Q is the restrictions and follows

$$Q: ax_1 + bx_2\cos\theta + cx_1x_2\cos\theta < t, \tag{18}$$

$p(x_1)$, $p(x_2)$ and $p(\theta)$ are respectively the probability density functions of x_1, x_2 and θ. Furthermore, We can get the integration interval more intuitively in Fig. 2.

Due to each element in $\mathbf{h}_{SD}$ and $\mathbf{h}_{RE}$ obeys the complex Gaussian random distribution, $\|\mathbf{h}_{SD}\|^2$ and $\|\mathbf{h}_{RE}\|^2$ follow χ^2 distribution. Assume that θ follows uniform distribution. Then the probability density functions of x_1, x_2 and θ can be expressed as

$$p(x_1) = \begin{cases} \dfrac{1}{2^{N_r}\Gamma(2N_r)\sigma_{SD}^{2N_r}}x_1^{N_r-1}e^{-\frac{x_1}{2\sigma_{SD}^2}}, & x_1 > 0 \\ 0, & x_1 \leq 0 \end{cases} \tag{19}$$

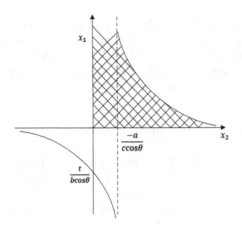

Fig. 2. The integration interval Q

$$p(x_2) = \begin{cases} \dfrac{1}{2^{N_r}\Gamma(N_r)\sigma_{RE}^{2N_r}} x_2^{N_r-1} e^{-\dfrac{x_2}{2\sigma_{RE}^2 N_r}}, & x_2 > 0 \\ 0, & x_2 \le 0 \end{cases} \qquad (20)$$

$$p(\theta) = \begin{cases} \dfrac{1}{\pi}, & \theta \in (-\dfrac{\pi}{2}, \dfrac{\pi}{2}) \\ 0, & otherwise \end{cases} \qquad (21)$$

where $\sigma_{RE}^2 = \dfrac{E[\|\mathbf{h}_{RE}\|^2]}{2N_r}$ and $\sigma_{SD}^2 = \dfrac{E[\|\mathbf{h}_{SD}\|^2]}{2N_r}$.

Then the final expression of the secrecy outage probability is

$$P_{out}(R_s) = \frac{1}{\pi} \int_{-\frac{\pi}{2}}^{\frac{\pi}{2}} (1 - e^{\nabla_1} \sum_{k=0}^{N_r-1} \frac{1}{k!}(-\nabla_1)^k d\theta$$

$$+ \frac{1}{\pi} \int_{-\frac{\pi}{2}}^{\frac{\pi}{2}} \int_{-\frac{a}{c\cos\theta}}^{\infty} p(x_2)[1 - e^{-\nabla_2} \sum_{k=0}^{N_r-1} \frac{1}{k!}\nabla_2^k] dx_2 \, d\theta, \qquad (22)$$

where ∇_1 and ∇_2 are respectively

$$\nabla_1 = \frac{a}{2c\cos\theta\sigma_{RE}^2}, \qquad (23)$$

$$\nabla_2 = \frac{t - bx_2\cos\theta}{2(cx_2\cos\theta + a)\sigma_{SD}^2}. \qquad (24)$$

5 Numerical Results and Analysis

In this section, we conduct simulations and evaluate the erodgic secrecy capacity and the secrecy outage probability of the proposed physical layer security scheme.

The secrecy outage probability of the system using the optimal power allocation scheme ($\lambda = \lambda^*$) has been compared to the fixed uniform power allocation scheme ($\lambda = 0.5$).

5.1   Analysis of Secrecy Outage Probability

Figure 3 shows the erodgic secrecy capacity performance against total transmit power P for the proposed power allocation scheme ($\lambda^* = 0.5$) and the fixed uniform power allocation scheme ($\lambda = 0.5$). We assume that $N_s = N_r = 2, 4, 8$, $N_d = 1$ and $N_e = 1$. All the channels of the system are the Rayleigh fading channels. The noise power at D or E is normalized, as $P = P/\sigma^2$. Hence, the signal-to-noise ratio of the total transmitted power varies from 1 dB to 15 dB. We set the minimum transmission rate $R_s = 1.5$ bit/s/Hz.

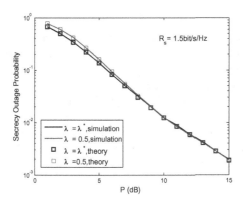

Fig. 3. Secrecy outage probability against total transmit power P for the proposed power allocation scheme and the fixed uniform power allocation scheme

In Fig. 3, it can be seen that the total power constraint P has a positive effect on the secrecy outage probability. When the total power constraint P is fixed, the secrecy outage probability of the system using the optimal power allocation scheme is smaller than the system using the uniform power allocation scheme. And for our power allocation scheme, the secrecy outage probability curve of the simulation results fits the one of Eq. (22) theoretical numerical results, based on which, it can be derived that the theoretical result of secrecy outage probability is correct.

5.2   Analysis of Ergodic Secrecy Capacity

Simulation conditions are the same as those in section A. Here, the minimal data rate R_s to ensure the system communication keeping secret is set to 1.5 bit/s/Hz, which also means if the data rate is smaller than R_s, the system cannot communicate in secure way. The secrecy outage probability against total

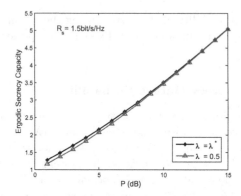

Fig. 4. Erodgic secrecy capacity against total transmit power P for the proposed power allocation scheme and the fixed uniform power allocation scheme

transmit power P for the proposed power allocation scheme ($\lambda^* = 0.5$) and the fixed uniform power allocation scheme ($\lambda = 0.5$) are shown in Fig. 4.

We can see that the greater the total power constraint P, the better the erodgic secrecy capacity performance of the system will be. Moreover, when the total power allocation constraint P is fixed, the optimal power allocation scheme we proposed can ensure a bigger erodgic secrecy capacity than the uniform power allocation scheme. Hence, as for the erodgic secrecy capacity performance, our proposed power allocation scheme is better than the fixed uniform power allocation scheme.

6   Conclusion

In this paper, we solved the challenging problem existing in traditional physical layer security communications, when the difference between legal and eavesdropping channels is not enough to meet the security requirement for information transmission. We specifically studied the power allocation between source node and interference relay node in physical layer security communication with interference relay. We optimized the power allocation through the minimization of lower bound of secrecy outage probability. Further, we developed a power allocation scheme, analyzed its advantages and derived its theoretical secrecy outage probability. Simulation results demonstrated that the proposed power allocation scheme has a better ergodic secrecy capacity and a lower secrecy outage probability than a uniform power allocation scheme.

References

1. Liang, Y., Poor, H.V., Shamai (Shitz), S.: Information theoretic security. Found. Trends Commun. Inf. Theory **5**(4–5), 355–580 (2008)
2. Huang, Y., Zheng, B., Wen, M., et al.: Improving physical layer security via random precoding. In: IEEE GLOBECOM Workshops, pp. 1–6 (2017)
3. Geraci, G., Egan, M., Yuan, J.H., et al.: Secrecy sum-rates for multi-user MIMO regularized channel inversion precoding. IEEE Trans. Commun. **60**(11), 3472–3482 (2012)
4. Wang, H.M., Wang, C., Zheng, T.X., Quek, T.Q.S.: Impact of artificial noise on cellular networks: a stochastic geometry approach. IEEE Trans. Wirel. Commun. **6**(99), 1–5 (2016)
5. Lu, Y., Xiong, K., Fan, P., Zhong, Z.: Optimal coordinated beamforming with artificial noise for secure transmission in multi-cell multi-user networks. In: 2017 IEEE International Conference on Communications (ICC), France, Paris, pp. 1–6 (2017)
6. Mei, W., Chen, Z., Fang, J.: Artificial noise aided energy efficiency optimization in MIMOME system with SWIPT. IEEE Commun. Lett. **21**(8), 1795–1798 (2017)
7. Li, Q., Zhang, Y., Lin, J., et al.: Full-duplex bidirectional secure communications under perfect and distributionally ambiguous eavesdroppers CSI. IEEE Trans. Sig. Process. **65**(17), 4684–4697 (2017)
8. Yaacoub, E., Al-Husseini, M.: Achieving physical layer security with massive MIMO beamforming. In: 2017 11th European Conference on Antennas and Propagation (EUCAP), Paris, France, pp. 1753–1757 (2017)
9. Ying, J., Wang, H.-M., Zheng, T.-X., et al.: Secure transmissions in millimeter wave systems. IEEE Trans. Veh. Technol. **66**(9), 7809–7817 (2017)
10. Abramowitz, M., Stegun, L.A.: Handbook of Mathematical Functions with Formulaes, Graphs, and Mathematical Tables. Dover Publications Inc., New York (1974)

Miscellaneous Topics in Wireless Networks

A Decision Tree Candidate Property Selection Method Based on Improved Manifold Learning Algorithm

Fangfang Guo, Luomeng Chao, and Huiqiang Wang[✉]

Computer Science and Technology, Harbin Engineering University,
Harbin 150001, China
{guofangfang,wanghuiqiang}@hrbeu.edu.cn

Abstract. When the traditional decision tree algorithm is applied to the field of network security analysis, due to the unreasonable property selection method, the overfitting problem may be caused, and the accuracy of the constructed decision tree is low. Therefore, this paper proposes a decision tree selection method based on improved manifold learning algorithm. The manifold learning algorithm maps the high-dimensional feature space to the low-dimensional space, so the algorithm can acquire the essential attributes of the data source. According to this, the problems of low accuracy and overfitting can be solved. Aiming at the traditional manifold learning algorithms are sensitive to noise and the algorithms converges slowly, this paper proposes a Global and Local Mapping manifold learning algorithm, and this method is used to construct a decision tree. The experimental results show that compared with the traditional ID3 decision tree construction algorithm, the improved method reduces 2.16% and 1.626% in false positive rate and false negative rate respectively.

Keywords: Network security · Decision tree · Manifold learning algorithm

1 Introduction

Decision tree is an inductive learning algorithm that is widely used in security analysis, data mining and other fields. Because it is a heuristic algorithm, the unreasonable selection method of the property will directly result in a large deviation of the decision tree results, and it will easily lead to overfitting problem. This is also one of the key issues of the decision tree algorithm [1]. In the field of security analysis, the above problems are particularly evident, which will lead to high false negative rate and false positive rate in network security monitoring systems.

At present, the research on the decision tree mainly focuses on the following two aspects. The first is how to combine other algorithms to improve the accuracy of the algorithm [2]. The second is how to improve the performance of the algorithm by improving the property selection method in the decision tree construction process [3–5]. In the field of network security analysis, data source usually uses log data.

J. Zheng et al. (Eds.): ADHOCNETS 2018, LNICST 258, pp. 261–271, 2019.
https://doi.org/10.1007/978-3-030-05888-3_24

Because the log data has a large number of features, the complexity of the traditional decision tree algorithm is high and training model will take a long time. Therefore, the traditional algorithm cannot meet real-time requirements of the complex network environment security monitoring system represented by the cloud.

Manifold learning is an unsupervised learning algorithm, which is mainly used to reduce the dimension of high-dimensional data. The features extracted after the manifold learning process represent the important and essential features of the dataset [6]. Its characteristics can solve the problem of property selecting of the decision tree, and it can help decision tree algorithm select the proper feature to reduce the probability of overfitting. However, the manifold learning algorithm's convergence speed is slow and sensitive to noise data. Therefore, this paper proposed a Global and Local Mapping manifold learning algorithm (GALM) to improve the performance of the manifold learning.

According to this, this paper proposed a decision tree candidate property selection method based on GALM. The rest of the paper is structured as follows. In the second part of the article, the improved manifold learning method GALM is introduced; The third part introduces how to use GALM algorithm to construct decision tree, and the fourth part analyzes its advantages; In the last part, the effectiveness of the proposed algorithm is verified through experiments.

2   Global and Local Mapping Manifold Learning Algorithm

Manifold learning is an unsupervised learning method, which "manifold" represents the space homeomorphic with Euclid space in the local. Its main idea is the points in the high-dimensional observation space can be regarded as a manifold formed in the observation space by a few independent variables. Therefore, if one method can effectively find the internal main variables, it can reduce the dimension of the data set. Manifold learning can be divided into two categories: one is based on global considerations, such as Isometric Mapping [7] (ISOMAP); the other is based on local considerations, such as LLE [8] and LE [9]. LE is a locally embedded Laplacian-eigenmaps. Compared to LE, LLE algorithm tries to maintain the linear relationship among samples in the neighborhood. However, both types of algorithms have their own advantages and disadvantages. The first type of manifold learning algorithm has a slow convergence rate and it is not suitable for tasks with large data volumes. Although the convergence speed of the second manifold learning algorithm is faster, it is more sensitive to noise data. In order to solve the above problem, this article proposed Global and Local Mapping manifold learning algorithm (GALM).

The main ideas of GALM are as follows: First, local low-dimensional data representations are generated using a highly efficient local embedding method. Then, this method uses the global high-dimensional data to adjust the local low-dimensional data topology. Several definitions are given before describing the algorithm.

Definition 1 Geodesic: The geodesic distance is the shortest distance between two points on the manifold. The geodesic calculation uses Euclidean distance, the definition of Euclidean distance between two points is as follows:

$$G(X_i, X_j) = \sum_{k=1}^{n}(X_{ik} - X_{jk})^2 \tag{1}$$

where X_i and X_j represents the position of the point in space, $X_i = (X_{i1}, X_{i2}, \ldots, X_{in})$, $X_j = (X_{j1}, X_{j2}, \ldots, X_{jn})$.

Definition 2 Harmonic average normalization: Before reducing the data dimension, it is necessary to normalized the average of geodesic. The formula is as follows:

$$\text{dis}(X_i, X_j) = \frac{G(X_i, X_j)}{\sqrt{H(i)H(j)}} \tag{2}$$

where

$$H(i) = \frac{n-1}{\sum_{k=1}^{n}\frac{1}{G(X_i, X_k)}}, \quad k = 1, 2, \ldots, n \tag{3}$$

where $G(X_i, X_j)$ is the geodesic distance between the two points X_i and X_j, and $H(i)$ and $H(j)$ are the harmonic mean values of the two points X_i and X_j.

The main step of the improved manifold learning algorithm proposed in this paper is as follows:

① The k-order neighboring matrices are established by the neighboring rule, the Euclidean distance is used as a measure in this process, If the Euclidean distance between two points is less than ε, then define two points as neighbor, ε represents a threshold;

② For each sample point, it is reconstructed using its neighbors, and the minimum linear reconstruction weight is calculated by formula (4).

$$V_{min} = \left\| X_j - \sum_{j} W_{ij}X_j \right\| \tag{4}$$

where W_{ij} is the linear reconstruction weight and the formula is shown in (5).

$$W_{i,j} = \begin{cases} e^{-\frac{\|x_i - x_j\|^2}{2\delta^2}}, & X_j \in N(i), \\ 0, & \text{else.} \end{cases} \tag{5}$$

where $N(i)$ represents the neighboring point of the point X_i. δ is a tuning parameter, it makes W_{ij} meet condition (6).

$$\sum_j W_{ij} = 1 \tag{6}$$

③ Low-dimensional embedding $\varnothing(y_i)$ of the input sample is calculated by formula (7), y_i represents the mapped node position;

$$\varnothing(y_i) = \left\| y_i - \sum_j W_{ij} y_i \right\|^2 \tag{7}$$

④ In order to make the low-dimensional embedded geodesic lines close to the real geodesic lines, this method use global information to adjust the position of the sample after mapping. The movement of each node satisfies that $1/\theta$ of $dis(x_i, x_j)$ is the distance between the low-dimensional embedded node x_i and x_j (as shown in Fig. 1), where θ depends on the feature scaling, $x_j \in N(i)$. $1/\theta$ of $dis(x_i, x_j)$ is the distance between the low-dimensional embedded node x_i and x_j, where θ depends on the dimension scaling, $x_j \in N(i)$. D_i^{source} is the source node and $P_{i,j}$ represents neighbor node of D_i^{source}. $P_{i,j}^{new}$ is the position after mapped, which is obtained by formula (8). In order to make $P_{i,j}$ select the mapped low-dimension $\varphi(x_i)$, the top k neighboring nodes with the smallest distance loss are selected by formula (9), where π_{ij} represents the weight of each neighboring point.

$$P_{i,j}^{new} = P_{i,j} - \frac{\left(P_{i,j} - D_i^{source}\right)}{\left\| P_{i,j} - D_i^{source} \right\|} \times \frac{dis}{\theta} \tag{8}$$

$$min\theta(Y) = \sum_{i=1}^{n} \left| \varphi\left(y_i - \sum_{j=1}^{k} \pi_{i,j} \varphi\left(y_{i,j}\right) \right) \right|^2 \tag{9}$$

⑤ Reconstruct W through new neighbor node and calculate M according to formula (10), where the first d features of M represent the mapped low-dimensional space coordinates, d represents the scaled spatial dimension.

$$M = (I - W)^T (I - W) \tag{10}$$

The GALM algorithm is shown in Algorithm 1.

Algorithm 1: GALM

Input: Training set: $X = \{x_1, x_2, \ldots, x_n\}, x_i \in R^D$
Output: Reduced dimension dataset: $Y = \{y_1, y_2, \ldots, y_n\}, y_i \in R^d$
begin
Step1. For each $(x_i) \in X$
         Generate y_i randomly
    End For
Step2. For each $(x_i) \in X$
       If $x_j \in X$ and $G(x_i, x_j) < \varepsilon$ **then**
         $N(i) \leftarrow N(i) + x_j$
         Compute W_{ij} using formula (6)
    End
    End For
Step3. Get low-dimensional embedding $\emptyset(y_i)$ using formula (7)
Step4. Calculate $P_{i,j}^{new}$ where $i \in \{1, 2, \ldots, n\}$
Step5. Reconstruct W and get M using formula (10)
return Top d features in M
end

Since the geodesic distance estimated in the high-dimensional space is always larger than the geodesic distance of the low-dimensional embedding manifold, a parameter is required to dynamically adjust the distance between each embedded node and the neighboring node. Since the original data has been reconciled and averaged prior to embed, the low-dimensional embedding manifold is calculated using the distance after the reconciliation. Therefore, the embedding manifold effectively avoid the "point aggregation" problem.

3 Decision Tree Construction Method Based on GALM

The first step in the construction of the decision tree is to use the GALM algorithm to reduce the dimension. It requires that the manifold after the reduction can be spread evenly, thereby reflecting the nature of the feature.

After selecting one feature, the improved method will remove it, and it iteratively select the feature to test. However, this method is also limited, when an evenly distributed manifold cannot be found which can mapping high-dimensional data, traditional entropy calculations need to be performed on the remaining features. The decision tree construction process is shown in Algorithm 2.

Algorithm 2: Construct decision tree method

Input: Training set: $X = \{x_1, x_2, ..., x_n\}$, $x_i \in R^D$, Feature set: $F = \{f_i, i = 1, 2, ..., n\}$

Output: Decision tree model

begin

Step1. While Low-dimensional manifold $F = \{f_i, i = 1, 2, ..., d\}$ not clear **do**

    Run GALM on $F = \{f_i, i = 1, 2, ..., n\}$

Step2. ClassMap <key, value>←0; // randomly initialize

Step3. While F not Null **do**

    Compute attributesSet( ) on F

    For each attributes ∈ attributesSet( ) **do**

      String key←attributes.get(row, columnIndex, destination);

      if(key ∈ ClassMap)

        classmap ← (key, value + 1);

      else

        classmap ← (key, 1);

    End For

    $F \leftarrow F - \{key\}$;

  return classMap(<key, value>);

end

---

4 Complementarity Analysis of Manifold Learning Algorithm and Decision Tree Algorithm

Decision tree is an inductive algorithm, which has the advantages of strong anti-noise ability, high efficiency, etc. However, traditional decision tree generation methods often lead to overfitting. As a data dimension reduction method, the manifold learning method can help the decision tree to select important features, thereby reducing the possibility of overfitting. The comparison between the two algorithm is shown in Table 1.

Table 1. Comparison of Decision Tree and Manifold Learning

Disadvantages of decision tree	Advantages of manifold learning
① When the number of features is large, the unreasonable feature selection rules will lead to deviations in the results of the decision tree model	① Manifold learning algorithms can map high dimensions to lower dimensions, revealing the essential characteristics of the data
② Because it relies on axis-parallel segmentation, it can be difficult to model some relationships	② Manifold learning algorithm improves the efficiency of data analysis by reducing dimensions and reducing some insignificant features
③ When the sample set changes, the decision tree constructed by the algorithm will also change due to changes in the sample set	③ Manifold learning algorithm can select stable and critical feature through dimension reduction measures

5   Simulation Experiment and Performance Analysis

5.1   Experimental Design and Experimental Parameters

(1)   Experimental environment

In order to analyze the performance and effectiveness of algorithm proposed in this paper, we use the Toolbox toolkit and the classic Swiss roll data source to perform experiments on the MATLAB simulation platform.

As shown in Fig. 1, using the existing equipment in the laboratory, cloud monitoring data fusion analysis system based on the log data is set up. The object of analysis is multi-source log data, the specific information of the collected data will be described in detail later. In the experiment, four infrastructures were configured in the Hadoop cluster environment. One of them is set as Master node and the others are Slave nodes.

(2)   Data source

The multi-source log collection is provided by Hadoop's Flume, an acquisition component. After collection, the log data are aggregated to the log receiving server for storage. The log used for security analysis are divided into IDS log, firewall log, and DNS log. The Kali Linux penetration test is used to perform corresponding security event attacks on the target host. The attacks used in this paper include SYN Flood, ICMP Flood, TCP Flood, DNS Flood, and ARP Spoofing. This paper will use the Swiss roll data source to make usability analysis of the GALM algorithm, and to do comprehensive verification in the final analysis stage.

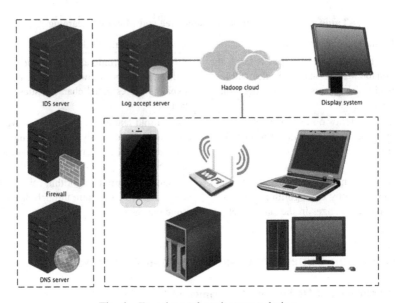

Fig. 1. Experimental environment design

The evaluation of experimental results is divided into two aspects: efficiency and accuracy. In terms of efficiency, the proposed method is compared with LLE, LE, and ISOMAP algorithms, and the improved decision tree algorithm is compared with the ID3 decision tree algorithm. In the aspect of accuracy, the improved decision tree algorithm and ID3 decision tree algorithm are compared in terms of false negative rate and false positive rate.

5.2   Experimental Results and Algorithm Performance Analysis

(1)   GALM algorithm performance analysis

The selected Swiss roll data source is processed by GALM algorithm, traditional LEE algorithm, LE and ISOMAP algorithm respectively. Through the analysis of the processing results, the effectiveness of the low-dimensional manifold formed by dimension reduction through GALM algorithm is verified, then the computational efficiency of GALM is verified.

Figure 2 shows a 3-dimensional manifold image generated by a Swiss roll data source with a quantity of 2000, noise of 0.05. This experiment use GALM algorithm to reduce dimensionality of manifolds to form 2-dimensional manifold respectively. Figure 3 shows the embedded manifold Formed by GALM.

Figure 4 shows a comparison of the running time of GALM, LLE, LE and ISOMAP. It can be seen that at the beginning, the GALM runtime is close to the LLE and LE. As the amount of data increases, the running time of the GALM algorithm will gradually approach the ISOMAP.

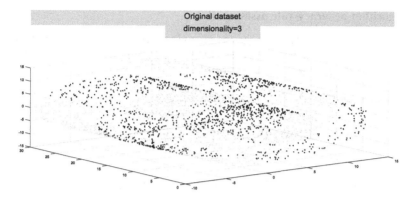

Fig. 2. Swiss roll data Source: 3-dimensional manifold formed by 2000 nodes

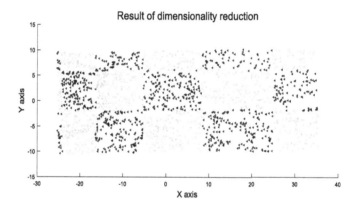

Fig. 3. 2-Dimensional Embedded Manifold Formed by GALM

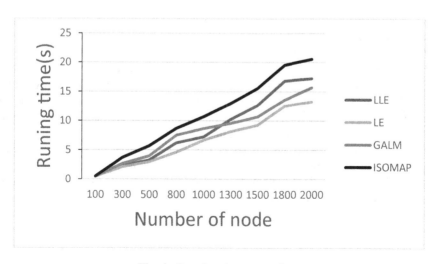

Fig. 4. Running time comparison

(2) **Algorithm accuracy rate assessment**

The log source obtained from the log receiving server is 2.1 GB. The method of constructing the decision tree based on GALM algorithm presented in this paper is compared with the ID3 decision tree construction algorithm.

Figure 5 compares the misjudgment rates of the two algorithms. The experimental results show that compared with the ID3 algorithm, the method proposed in this paper reduces the misjudgment rate by 0.323%, 0.365%, 1.079%, 0.597% and 1.128% respectively for ARP, DNS, UDPS and SYN. Especially for SYN Flood and UDP Flood, it can be seen that the decision tree construction method based on manifold learning shows a good detection effect in terms of false positive rate, so the accuracy of the improved decision tree detection algorithm has been improved overall.

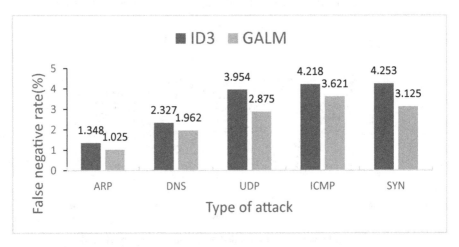

Fig. 5. Comparison chart of False negative rate

6 Conclusion

The manifold learning method has a obvious dimensionality reduction effect on non-linear data, and it can get the nature of the data. This feature can be combined with the classic decision tree algorithm to reduce the overfitting problem. Based on the above ideas, this paper proposes a GALM algorithm, it can select the nature of the data to build a decision tree. The experimental results show that the decision tree constructed using the algorithm proposed in this paper has been improved in accuracy and efficiency of model. The next step will focus on how to combine multi-manifold learning with other security analysis algorithms to effectively solve security monitoring issues in the field of network security situational awareness.

References

1. Kim, S.Y., Upneja, A.: Predicting restaurant financial distress using decision tree and AdaBoosted decision tree models. Econ. Model. **36**(1), 354–362 (2014)
2. Pai, P.F., Changliao, L.H., Lin, K.P.: Analyzing basketball games by a support vector machines with decision tree model. Neural Comput. Appl. **232**, 1–9 (2016)
3. Azad, M., Moshkov, M.: Multi-stage optimization of decision and inhibitory trees for decision tables with many-valued decisions. Eur. J. Oper. Res. **263**, 910–921 (2017)
4. Ai, X., Wu, J., Cui, Z.: Broaden the minority class space for decision tree induction using antigen-derived detectors. Knowl.-Based Syst. **137**, 196–205 (2017)
5. Cicalese, F., Laber, E., Saettler, A.: Decision trees for function evaluation: simultaneous optimization of worst and expected cost. Algorithmica **79**, 1–34 (2013)
6. Zhang, Q., Zhang, Q., Zhang, L.: Ensemble manifold regularized sparse low-rank approximation for multiview feature embedding. Pattern Recogn. **48**(10), 3102–3112 (2015)
7. Tenenbaum, J.B., De Silva, V., Langford, J.C.: A global geometric framework for nonlinear dimensionality reduction. Science **290**(5500), 2319–2323 (2000)
8. Roweis, S.T., Saul, L.K.: Nonlinear dimensionality reduction by locally linear embedding. Science **290**(5500), 2323–2326 (2000)
9. Belkin, M., Niyogi, P.: Laplacian eigenmaps for dimensionality reduction and data representation. Neural Comput. **15**(6), 1373–1396 (2003)

Repairable Fountain Codes with Unequal Repairing Locality in D2D Storage System

Yue Li, Shushi Gu$^{(\boxtimes)}$, Ye Wang, Juan Li, and Qinyu Zhang

Communication Engineering Research Center, Harbin Institute of Technology,
Shenzhen, Guangdong, China
{liyue,lijuan2016}@stu.hit.edu.cn, {gushushi,wangye83,zqy}@hit.edu.cn

Abstract. In this paper, we propose a novel repairable fountain codes (RFC) used in D2D data storage systems for failure data recovery. This RFC has the priority of unequal repairing locality (URL), which can provide unequal data protection for different nodes' bandwidth and power in different areas. The lower locality of URL-RFC can reduce the repair bandwidth in D2D storage system, and tradeoff different nodes' capabilities of transmitting. We firstly give the heterogeneous D2D storage network model, and analysis the communication cost for data download and node repair. Then, the construction method of URL-RFC is given based on generated matrix. Simulation results show that, URL-RFC significant outperforms conventional distributed codes on communication cost in heterogeneous D2D storage system.

Keywords: D2D data storage system · Repairable fountain codes
Unequal repairing locality · Repair and download bandwidth

1 Introduction

The rapid growth of mobile data traffic has caused tremendous pressure on distributed storage systems (DSS) and cellular base stations (BSs). A rising technique called device-to-device (D2D) distributed storage, is proposed to relieve the pressure of BS, which also takes advantage of the increasingly powerful storage capacity of mobile devices [1,2]. Presently, the redundancy has been brought into DSS, such as replication scheme, MDS codes and regenerating code, which have derived some crucial research achievements in the application DSS in D2D networks [3–5]. The focus of these research is on how to reduce the repair cost and download cost of the system.

Repairable fountain code (RFC) is a new family of fountain codes that can be applied to DSS, that is a rateless and systematic code and has low locality [6]. Therefore, this new family of RFC has great application potential in

© ICST Institute for Computer Sciences, Social Informatics and Telecommunications Engineering 2019
Published by Springer Nature Switzerland AG 2019. All Rights Reserved
J. Zheng et al. (Eds.): ADHOCNETS 2018, LNICST 258, pp. 272–281, 2019.
https://doi.org/10.1007/978-3-030-05888-3_25

the D2D distributed storage system with large network heterogeneity (nodes' bandwidth, communication distance, or device reception or transmitting signal power). However, the problem of further reducing the communication cost for the heterogeneous network of D2D distributed storage is still difficult to solve. The research of fountain code in the field of unequal error protection (UEP) in broadcast transmission has been extensive [7,8], and the local reconstruction code have also been studied preliminarily in terms of unequal failure protection [9] in file storage system.

This paper proposes a novel RFC for D2D distributed storage systems, which is mainly used for the repair of failure data. Our new RFC has different priorities for repairing locality (URL) and can provide different data protection for nodes with different bandwidth and power in different areas. The lower locality of URL-RFC can reduce the repair bandwidth cost in D2D storage systems and tradeoff transmission capacity of different nodes. We first give a heterogeneous D2D storage network model and analyze the data download and repair communication cost. Then, based on the generator matrix, the URL-RFC construction method is given. Simulation results show that, in heterogeneous D2D storage systems, the communication cost of URL-RFC is better than that of traditional distributed systems.

The structure of this paper: Sect. 2 gives the system model of heterogeneous D2D distributed storage. In Sect. 3, the constructions method of RFC and the URL-RFC are introduced. In Sect. 4, we analyze the communication cost of the URL-RFC scheme. In Sect. 5, simulation results show that URL-RFC can reduce communication cost. Finally, the Sect. 6 is the summary of the main research in this paper.

2   System Model

We consider the D2D distributed storage system shown in Fig. 1. A base station (BS) can cover two areas at the same time. The mobile devices in the red area have a stronger D2D communication capability than the mobile devices in the green area, because the antenna size and power amplifier capability of the devices in the two areas are different. The yellow cell phone represents the node that requested the file (requester), the blue cell phone represents the new storage node (empty), and the red and green cell phones represent nodes that store the data (helper).

The Working Process of the System is as Follows:
As the nodes enter and exit (Poisson process) the coverage area of the BS randomly, the number of storage nodes in the system may be insufficient, that is, the file data may be lost. The requester will request to download all data with a certain probability, so the lost node (data) must be repaired. When the D2D communication capability is insufficient or does not have the enough number of nodes to repair data, it is necessary to rely on the BS for data download and repair. Due to the differences in device capabilities between heterogeneous areas, there will be differences in the energy costs of downloading data and repairing data between the two areas.

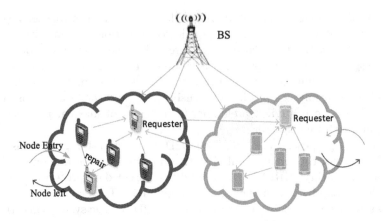

Fig. 1. Heterogeneous D2D distributed storage system model. (Color figure online)

The research work in this article is based on the following basic assumptions:

1. Assume that the data storage space of each node is infinite, and we consider that there is a single file, of size M bits, stored at the BS.
2. We denote by ρ_{BS} the cost of transmitting one bit from the BS, ρ_r the cost of transmitting one bit between nodes in the red area and ρ_g the cost of transmitting one bit between nodes in the green area. We assume that $\rho_r > \rho_g$. The cost for one bit inter-area transmission is set to be the same, which is $\rho_{rg} = \rho_{gr}$.
3. According to pass loss of wireless signals, i.e. lager distance is required, more power is consumed. Therefore, the distance between the nodes of one area is smaller than the distance between the nodes of different areas, and the both are less than the distance from BS to nodes, i.e. $\rho_{BS} > \rho_{rg} = \rho_{gr} \geq \rho_r > \rho_g$.
4. The expected numbers of nodes in red and green areas are N_r and N_g, respectively. The incoming rates of nodes in the two areas are $N_r\lambda$ and $N_g\lambda$, respectively. The instantaneous number of nodes can be described by the $M/M/\infty$ Markov model. The probabilities that the number of nodes in the two areas are i satisfy Eqs. (1) and (2), respectively [10].

$$\pi_r(i) = \frac{N_r{}^i}{i!}e^{-N_r} \tag{1}$$

$$\pi_g(i) = \frac{N_g{}^i}{i!}e^{-N_g} \tag{2}$$

Data Storage: The file is divided into k packets, and k is composed of two parts, k_r and k_g. Then, the two parts are encoded by RFCs with parameters $(n_r, k_r, d(k_r))$ and $(n_g, k_g, d(k_g))$, respectively. Moreover, n is the number of encoding symbols, k is the number of input symbols and d is the repair locality. Finally, the encoded data generated by the two parts of packets are respectively stored in the nodes of red area and green area. For simplicity, we assume

$n_r \ll N_r$, $n_g \ll N_g$, that is, the number of storage nodes is much less than the number of expected nodes, then $\sum_{i=0}^{n_r-1} \pi_r(i) \ll 1$, $\sum_{i=0}^{n_g-1} \pi_g(i) \ll 1$. Therefore, the probability that the number of nodes in the red area is less than n_r can be negligible, while the probability that the number of nodes in the green area is less than n_g can also be negligible.

We consider a uniform allocation in our system model. Hence, each storage node stores α bits, then α is

$$\alpha = \frac{M}{k_r + k_g}. \tag{3}$$

File Download: Assume that the rate of each node requesting a file is ω, and the interval between the requests for the file in the red area and in the green area is $\frac{1}{N_r\omega}$, $\frac{1}{N_g\omega}$, respectively. When the number of storage nodes in the system is greater than or equal to $(1+\varepsilon)(k_r + k_g)$, the file download can be performed through D2D links, i.e. the download requires slightly more data than M bits. Otherwise, the entire file must be downloaded from the BS.

Data Repair: Assume that the departure rate of a node is λ. When the storage node leaves the system, the data stored in the node will also be lost. In order to reduce the power cost of repairing data, we consider to use the nodes in the same area to repair the lost data as much as possible. When the number of storage nodes in the same area is insufficient, the nodes in different areas can be used for repair. If the number of helper nodes is still insufficient, then we can use the BS to repair the data.

We consider the ideal conditions: When a storage node leaves, data repair is performed immediately and there is no repair delay. Because the probability that the number of nodes in the red area is smaller than n_r and the probability that the number of nodes in the green area is smaller than n_g are negligible. So, the storage nodes that can connect to when repairing in both of the two areas are sufficient, that is, the participation of nodes in another area and BS are not needed. In this case, the files can always be stored in the D2D distributed storage system and there is no need to download file from the BS. Therefore, the bandwidth costs of repairing one node's data in the red area and the green area are described as formula (4) and (5), respectively, where $\beta = \alpha$.

$$\gamma_r = d(k_r)\beta \tag{4}$$

$$\gamma_g = d(k_g)\beta \tag{5}$$

3   RFC and URL-RFC

3.1   Construction of RFC

Repairable Fountain Code (RFC) inherit the rateless property of classical fountain codes, so we do not need to pre-determine the number of coded symbols.

Unlike classical fountain codes, the RFC is a systematic code and its parity symbols also have logarithmic sparseness [6].

The repair fountain code divides the source file into k input symbols. The input symbols are encoded by a $k \times n$ generator matrix, resulting in n encoded symbols containing copies of k input symbols and n-k parities symbol. Each parity symbol is generated by a linear combination of $d(k) = clogk$ input symbols selected uniformly at random. The coefficient ω of the linear combination is selected from the finite field F_q, and c is a constant. Therefore, the generator matrix can be represented as $\mathbf{G} = [\mathbf{I_k}|\mathbf{P}]$, as shown in Fig. 2. The identity part of $\mathbf{G}$ corresponds to the systematic symbols, and the matrix $\mathbf{P}$ corresponds to the parity symbols.

$$\mathbf{G[I_k \mid P]} = \begin{bmatrix} 1 & \cdots & \cdots & 0 & \omega_{1,k+1} & \cdots & \omega_{1,n} \\ \vdots & \ddots & & \vdots & \vdots & & \vdots \\ \vdots & & \ddots & \vdots & \vdots & & \vdots \\ 0 & \cdots & \cdots & 1 & \omega_{k,k+1} & \cdots & \omega_{k,n} \end{bmatrix}$$

k input symbol columns   n-k parity symbol columns

Fig. 2. Generator matrix of RFC.

A parity symbol along with the systematic symbols covered by it form a local group. Any symbol in the local group can be reconstructed by the linear combination of other symbols in the local group, and the local goup size is $d(k) + 1$. The RFC trades its low locality with its MDS property, but it still possesses near-MDS property. When downloading the entire file, a very small decoding overhead $\varepsilon > 0$ is required, so that any subset of $k' = (1 + \varepsilon)k$ symbols can reconstruction the file. The maximum likelihood decoding method can be used for decoding, which is equivalent to solving the solutions of k' linear equations.

3.2   Unequal Repairing Locality Based on RFC

In D2D distributed storage systems, the repair cost is an important component of communication cost. If we do not consider the difference in the D2D communication capabilities of the nodes, the repair cost of the nodes in the red area of the Sect. 2 will be particularly large. Therefore, based on the RFC, this paper proposes an unequal repair locality code based on RFC (URL-RFC). This URL-RFC can reduce the repair cost of red area and reduce the overall communication cost. The specific plan is designed as follows:

The k input symbols are divided into k_r and k_g groups in a certain proportion. Let $u_1 \sim u_{k_r}$ represent the first set of input symbols, and $u'_1 \sim u'_{k_g}$ represent the second set of input symbols. Two sets of encoded symbols are generated by the two sets of input symbols and stored in the nodes of the red area and the green area, respectively, as shown in Fig. 3. The first set of n_r encoded symbols contains systematic symbols $v_1 \sim v_{k_r}$ and parity symbols with degree $d(k_r)$. The second set of n_g encoded symbols are similar to the first set. Based on the fourth assumption in Sect. 2, it is not necessary to generate the global parity symbols. The generator matrix $\mathbf{G}[\mathbf{I_k}|\mathbf{P_r}|\mathbf{P_g}]$ in Fig. 4 is composed of three parts, namely a identity matrix corresponding to systematic symbols, $\mathbf{P_r}$ corresponding to the first set of parity symbols, and $\mathbf{P_g}$ corresponding to the second set of parity symbols. The encoding process can be expressed as

$$v = u\mathbf{G}[\mathbf{I_k}|\mathbf{P_r}|\mathbf{P_g}]. \tag{6}$$

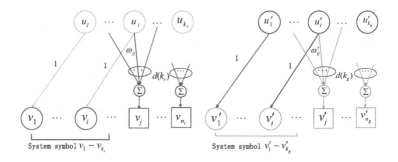

Fig. 3. URL-RFC encoding process. (Color figure online)

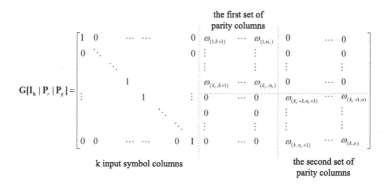

Fig. 4. URL-RFC generation matrix.

When decoding, the new generator matrix $\mathbf{G_S}$ is composed of the columns of the symbols in the available helper nodes, it is a sub-matrix of $\mathbf{G}[\mathbf{I_k}|\mathbf{P_r}|\mathbf{P_g}]$.

If $\mathbf{G_S}$ is full rank, then we can use $u = v\mathbf{G_S}^{-1}$ to decode the input symbol. The condition for $\mathbf{G_S}$ full rank is that the number of helper nodes both in the red area and the green area are equal to or greater than $(1 + \varepsilon)k_r$ and $(1 + \varepsilon)k_g$ respectively. The encoded symbol v_j can be written as

$$v_j = u\mathbf{G}(j) = \sum \omega_{ij} u_i, \tag{7}$$

where $\mathbf{G}(j)$ represents the jth column of the generator matrix $\mathbf{G}[\mathbf{I_k}|\mathbf{P_r}|\mathbf{P_g}]$. When repairing an encoded symbol, we can connect the other symbols in the local group to reconstruct the encoded symbol by formula (7).

4   Repair and Download Cost

In this section we derive the analytical expressions for repair cost (C_{r-URL}), download cost (C_{d-URL}), total communication cost (C_{URL}) of URL-RFC and the repair cost (C_{r-ERL}), download cost (C_{d-ERL}), total communication cost (C_{ERL}) of Equal Repair Locality(ERL-RFC). Consider the system model in Sect. 2, which has the following parameters: N_r, N_g, n_r, n_g, k_r, k_g, M, λ, ω, ε, c, ρ_r, ρ_g, ρ_{rg}, ρ_{gr}, α, γ_r, γ_g. We let $n = n_r + n_g$, $k = k_r + k_g$ and $N = N_r + N_g$. Without loss of generality, let the file size $M = 1$. The cost is defined in cost units per bit and time unit.

Average Download Cost: For ERL, the number of coded symbols in the red and green regions is randomly assigned in proportion to N_r and N_g.

The average download cost of URL-RFC is:

$$C_{d-URL} = \frac{N_r \omega(1+\varepsilon)\alpha(\rho_r k_r + \rho_{gr} k_g) + N_g \omega(1+\varepsilon)\alpha(\rho_{rg} k_r + \rho_g k_g)}{N\omega k\alpha}$$
$$= \frac{(1+\varepsilon)[N_r(\rho_r k_r + \rho_{gr} k_g) + N_g(\rho_{rg} k_r + \rho_g k_g)]}{Nk}. \tag{8}$$

The average download cost of ERL-RFC is:

$$C_{d-ERL} = \frac{N_r \omega(1+\varepsilon)k\alpha(\rho_r \frac{N_r}{N} + \rho_{gr} \frac{N_r}{N}) + N_g \omega(1+\varepsilon)k\alpha(\rho_{rg} \frac{N_r}{N} + \rho_g \frac{N_r}{N})}{N\omega k\alpha}$$
$$= \frac{(1+\varepsilon)[N_r(\rho_r N_r + \rho_{gr} N_g) + N_g(\rho_{rg} N_r + \rho_g N_g)]}{N^2}. \tag{9}$$

Proof: The total request rate of the red area and the green area is $N_r\omega$, $N_g\omega$ respectively. The amount of data to be transmitted using the D2D download file is $(1 + \varepsilon)k\alpha$ bits. For URL, the transmitted data has $(1 + \varepsilon)k_r$ bits from the storage node in the red area and $(1 + \varepsilon)k_g$ bit data from the storage node in the green area. For ERL, the transmitted data has $\frac{N_r}{N}k$ bits from the storage node in the red area and $\frac{N_g}{N}k$ bit data from the storage node in the green area. Normalize the total download data $N\omega k\alpha$, we get the formula (8) and (9).

Average Repair Cost: Assuming only one lost data is repaired at a time, the average repair cost of URL-RFC is:

$$C_{r-URL} = \frac{n_r \lambda \gamma_r \rho_r + n_g \lambda \gamma_g \rho_g}{n\lambda\alpha} = \frac{k_r c \log(k_r)\rho_r + k_g c \log(k_g)\rho_g}{k}. \tag{10}$$

Proof: The number of storage nodes leaving the red and green areas in unit time is $n_r \lambda$, $n_g \lambda$ respectively, and the bandwidth cost of repairing a lost data is $\gamma_r \rho_r$, $\gamma_g \rho_g$ respectively. Normalize the total repair data $n \lambda \alpha$ to get the formula (10).

The average repair cost for ERL-RFC is:

$$C_{r-ERL} = \frac{n_r \lambda \gamma(\frac{n_r-1}{n-1}\rho_r + \frac{n_g}{n-1}\rho_{gr}) + n_g \lambda \gamma(\frac{n_g}{n-1}\rho_{rg} + \frac{n_g-1}{n-1}\rho_g)}{n\lambda\alpha}$$
$$= \frac{d(k)[\rho_r N_r(N_r k - RN) + 2\rho_{gr}N_r N_g k + \rho_g N_g(N_g k - RN)]}{N^2(k-R)}. \tag{11}$$

where, $\gamma = d(k)\beta = d(k)\alpha = c\log(k) \cdot \frac{M}{k}$, $R = \frac{k}{n}$.

Proof: The amounts of data to be transmitted using D2D repair both in the two area is γ bits. When the storage node in the red area leaves the system, it needs $\frac{n_r-1}{n-1}$ parts of data from the red area with a cost of ρ_r and $\frac{n_g}{n-1}$ parts of data from the green area, with a cost of ρ_{gr}. When the storage node in the green area leaves the system, it is similar to the red. Normalizetotal repair data $n\lambda\alpha$ to get the formula (11).

Total Average Cost: The total average cost is defined as the sum of the average download cost and the average repair cost.

The total cost of URL-RFC is:

$$C_{URL} = C_{d-URL} + C_{r-URL}, \tag{12}$$

$$C_{ERL} = C_{d-ERL} + C_{r-ERL}. \tag{13}$$

5   Simulation and Results

This section compares the total cost of URL-RFC and ERL-RFC under different conditions. In the simulation, the common parameter values are given as follows. Code rate is $R = \frac{1}{2}$, and input symbols number is $k = 100$. The constant $c = 4$ in the encoding symbol degree of RFC, and the decoding overhead $\varepsilon = 0.1$.

In Fig. 5, we select three different communication power cost ratios $\rho_{gr} : \rho_r : \rho_g$, which are 3:2:1, 5:3:1 and 10:5:1. We can see that, the communication cost of URL-RFC is less than ERL-RFC at three different ratios. As the ratio increases, the gain difference of the URL-RFC compared to the ERL-RFC also increases.

In Fig. 6, we change the ratio of the number of input symbols allocated in the two areas under the total input symbols fixed, and consider the influence of the number of nodes in the two areas on the communication cost. When the number of encoded symbols in the green area increases and the coded symbols in the red area decrease correspondingly, it can be seen that the overall communication cost is continuously decreasing. This is because k_g increases the k_r reduction, which reduces the locality of the encoded symbols in the red area, so that the repair cost of the red area nodes is reduced. Since we calculate the average cost of transmitting unit bits, the change in the number of nodes in the two areas

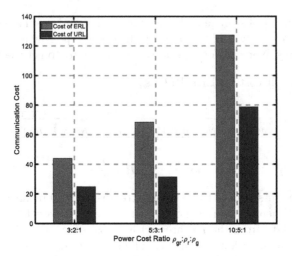

Fig. 5. Comparison of communication cost between URL-RFC and ERL-RFC under different power cost.

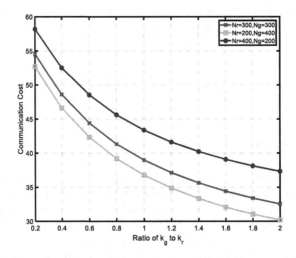

Fig. 6. Comparison of communication cost of URL-RFC under different ratio of $k_g : k_r$. (Color figure online)

has little effect on the result. However, it can be seen that when the number of nodes in the red area is large, the communication cost is larger than the other two cases.

In summary, URL-RFC can reduce the overall communication cost of the heterogeneous D2D distributed storage network. When using URL-RFC, in order to reduce the communication cost of the network, we should allocate input symbols as many as possible to the green area if the number of nodes in the green area is sufficient.

6 Conclusions

In this paper, we introduce an unequal repairing locality code based on repairable fountain codes (URL-RFC) used in heterogeneous D2D data storage systems. It can provide unequal data protection for different nodes transmission capacity in different areas. The lower locality of URL-RFC can reduce the repair cost in D2D storage system, and tradeoff different node capabilities of transmitting. We firstly give the heterogeneous D2D storage network model, and analysis the communication cost for data download and repair. Then, the construction method of URL-RFC is given based on generated matrix. Simulation results show that, URL-RFC significant outperforms conventional distributed codes of communication cost in heterogeneous D2D storage system. And we show that assigning symbols to green areas as much as possible will have lower communication cost.

Acknowledgments. This work was supported in part by the National Natural Sciences Foundation of China under Grant 61701136, Grant 61501140 and Grant 61525103, and China Postdoctoral Science Foundation Grant 2018M630357, and Shenzhen Basic Research Program under Grant JCY2017081114233370 and Grant ZDSYS20170728090330586.

References

1. Wang, L., Wu, H., Han, Z.: Wireless distributed storage in socially enabled D2D communications. IEEE Access **4**, 1971–1984 (2017)
2. Pääkkönen, J., Hollanti, C., Tirkkonen, O.: Device-to-device data storage for mobile cellular systems, pp. 671–676 (2013)
3. Pääkkönen, J., Hollanti, C., Tirkkonen, O.: Device-to-device data storage with regenerating codes. In: Jonsson, M., Vinel, A., Bellalta, B., Tirkkonen, O. (eds.) MACOM 2015. LNCS, vol. 9305, pp. 57–69. Springer, Cham (2015). https://doi.org/10.1007/978-3-319-23440-3_5
4. Pedersen, J., Amat, A.G.I., Andriyanova, I., Brännström, F.: Distributed storage in mobile wireless networks with device-to-device communication. IEEE Trans. Commun. **64**(11), 4862–4878 (2016)
5. Pedersen, J., Amat, A.G.I., Andriyanova, I., Brännström, F.: Optimizing MDS coded caching in wireless networks with device-to-device communication (2018)
6. Asteris, M., Dimakis, A.G.: Repairable fountain codes. IEEE J. Sel. Areas Commun. **32**(5), 1037–1047 (2014)
7. Luo, Z., Song, L., Zheng, S., Ling, N.: Raptor codes based unequal protection for compressed video according to packet priority. IEEE Trans. Multimedia **15**(8), 2208–2213 (2013)
8. Chen, Z., Xu, M., Yin, L., Lu, L.: Unequal error protected jpeg 2000 broadcast scheme with progressive fountain codes, pp. 1–5 (2012)
9. Hu, Y., et al.: Unequal failure protection coding technique for distributed cloud storage systems. IEEE Trans. Cloud Comput. **PP**(99), 1 (2017)
10. Miller, S., Childers, D.: Probability and Random Processes, 2nd edn (2012)

Channel Impulse Response Analysis of the Indoor Propagation Based on Auto-Regressive Modeling

Jinpeng Liang[1]([✉]), Wenjun Lu[2], Yang Liu[1,2], Qiong Wu[1,3],
Baolong Li[1,3], and Zhengquan Li[1]

[1] Key Laboratory of Advanced Process Control for Light Industry,
Jiangnan University, Wuxi 214122, China
lzq722@sina.com
[2] Jiangsu Key Laboratory of Wireless Communications,
Nanjing University of Posts and Telecommunications, Nanjing 210003, China
[3] National Mobile Communications Research Laboratory, Southeast University,
Nanjing 210096, China

Abstract. A novel statistical channel impulse response model at 2.6 GHz is proposed for the indoor stairs and corridor environment. The model is based on the frequency domain auto-regressive (AR) process. The samples of the complex frequency response can be described as the output of the AR transfer function driven by a Gaussian white-noise process. In this model, the number of poles of the AR transfer function is determined by the significant paths of radio propagation. The paths depend on the reflectors of different propagation environment. The accuracy of the AR modeling has been verified by utilizing the root-mean-square error and root-mean-square delay spread as metrics. The model is also compared with the conventional tapped delay line model. The proposed model can be useful for the development and design of future communication.

Keywords: Channel impulse response · Stairs and corridor
Auto-regressive process · Radio propagation

1 Introduction

The stairs and corridor are not only an entrance/exit in our daily lives, but also an integral part of communication integration in future intelligent buildings. Furthermore, these areas can be utilized for deploying emergency communications and monitoring systems. Therefore, it is necessary to design a communication system that satisfies the requirements of data transmission in terms of quantity, quality and speed. Also, understanding the comprehensive and complex characteristics of channel in the stairs and corridors is very important for the communication system design [1–4].

The propagation characteristics of stairs and corridors are researched in [5–7] by using image-based ray tracing methods. In fact, the wireless propagation channel can be modeled by channel impulse responses (CIRs), which can be described as a time-varying linear filter. The CIR is an important characteristic of the channel. It can be

© ICST Institute for Computer Sciences, Social Informatics and Telecommunications Engineering 2019
Published by Springer Nature Switzerland AG 2019. All Rights Reserved
J. Zheng et al. (Eds.): ADHOCNETS 2018, LNICST 258, pp. 282–291, 2019.
https://doi.org/10.1007/978-3-030-05888-3_26

used to predict and compare the performance of different communication systems, and provide many important channel parameters, such as root-mean-square (RMS) delay spread and coherent bandwidth. In general, researchers tend to describe the CIRs as a tapped delay line (TDL) in time domain [8, 9]. Some researchers successfully applied the concept of clusters to the multipath arrival of channels [10, 11], and suggested that the formation of clusters is related to the spatial structure of buildings. However, in order to accurately describe the original channel of measured environment, a large number of delay taps and complex parameters are needed. For ray tracing methods, the deterministic modeling method requires a very accurate input database, which includes many details and parameters of the measured site.

In this paper, we put forward a novel frequency domain autoregressive statistical model at 2.6 GHz. The selected band is intended to mimic the band 41 in the time division duplexing-long term evolution (TDD-LTE) system. This model is based on three different indoor conditions: the line-of-sight (LOS) stairs environment, the non-line-of-sight (NLOS) stairs environment and the corridor environment. In the autoregressive (AR) modeling process, it is found that the distribution of poles is related to the structure and reflectors of the indoor environment. At the same time, we will also use the traditional TDL model to verify the accuracy and superiority of the proposed model.

In Sect. 2, the measurement environment and the frequency domain measurement system are described. Section 3 proposes a frequency domain autoregressive model for the indoor stairs and corridor environment. In Sect. 4, the results of AR modeling are compared with the TDL model, and the relationships between the poles of AR transfer function and reflectors of measurement environments are analyzed. The conclusions of the study are summarized in Sect. 5.

2 Measurement Environment and Settings

The selected stairs in our measurement campaign is located in a typical office building. The structure of the stairs measurement is shown in Fig. 1(a). We select two consecutive stairs for measurement in the building. There are 14 and 9 stair steps in the down direction and up direction, respectively. The size of each stair step is 120×28 15 cm, as shown in Fig. 1(a). What calls for special attention is that there is a crossbeam made of concrete over the second stair step in the up direction. The height of transmitting (Tx) antenna is 1.9 m. Further, the height of receiving (Rx) antenna under LOS circumstance (Rx1–Rx14) is 1 m, while the NLOS measurement is operated on the eighth and ninth stair steps in the up direction (Rx21 and Rx22) and the height of receiving antenna is 1.9 m. As shown in the Fig. 1(b), the position of corridor is at the exit of the stairs. The transmitter is fixed on the corridor while the receiver is moved along the corridor with the interval of 2 m at each receiving point (indicated as Rx31–Rx35) among the measurement campaign. The ceiling made of plaster is 3.2 m above the floor and the floor is made of marble. Both of the measurements for the transmitting and receiving antennas in the corridor are 1.5 m. What's more, there is no movement during all the measurements to make sure the channel can be considered to be time-invariant.

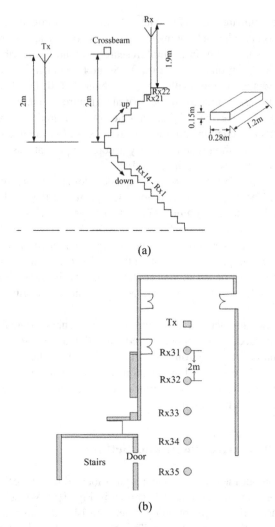

Fig. 1. The experimental environment. (a) The structure of the measured stairs environment. (b) The geometry of the measured corridor environment.

Figure 2 displays a rough diagram of the measurement system. The core equipment of the entire system is an Agilent 8720ET vector network analyzer (VNA). The detailed information of the frequency domain measurement system can be referred to in [12]. For convenience, the experiments were divided into two groups: stairs measurement and corridor experiment. The stairs measurement is conducted at 2.5–2.69 GHz with 201 frequency domain sweep points, while the corridor experiment has 801 sweep points in 2.35–2.85 GHz band.

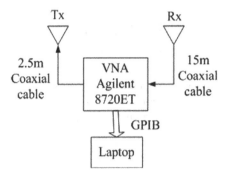

Fig. 2. The diagram of the measurement system.

3   Frequency Domain Autoregressive Modeling

The frequency response of stairs channel at frequency $H(f_n)$ measured in Sect. 2 can be considered as a random process, which is described by an AR process. The frequency domain AR model of order P is given by the following:

$$H(f_n) + \sum_{k=1}^{P} a_k H(f_{n-k}) = W(f_n), \ n = 1, 2, \ldots, N \tag{1}$$

where $H(f_n)$ is the sample of the complex frequency response at frequency f_n, $n = 1$, $2\ldots, N$, N represents the number of sweep points of the measurement system. The symbol a_k, $k = 1, 2\ldots, P$ signifies the complex coefficients of AR model. $W(f_n)$ is a zero-mean complex Gaussian white-noise process.

In general, the frequency response can be regarded as the output of a linear filter with transfer function $G(z)$ driven by the excitation signal $W(f_n)$. The AR transfer function can be obtained from the z-transformation of Eq. (1).

$$G(z) = \frac{1}{1 + \sum\limits_{k=1}^{P} a_k z^{-k}} = \frac{1}{\prod\limits_{k=1}^{P} (1 - p_k z^{-1})} \tag{2}$$

The AR model can be seen as an all-poles model with parameters p_k in Eq. (2). To characterize the complex model, the P parameters and the variance of excitation signal need to be identified. Many algorithms can be used to achieve the coefficients a_k, for instance, the Levinson algorithm, Burg algorithm, and so on. The coefficients are the result of the Yule-Walker equations in this paper:

$$\sum_{k=1}^{P} a_k R(k - l) = -R(l), \ l = 1, 2, \ldots, P \tag{3}$$

where $R(k)$ is the frequency autocorrelation function defined as follows:

$$R(k) = \begin{cases} \frac{1}{N} \sum\limits_{n=1}^{N-k} H(f_{n+k})H^*(f_n), & k \geq 0 \\ R^*(-k), & k < 0 \end{cases} \tag{4}$$

The autocorrelation function is vital in this process. The average received power can be calculated by using the function in Eq. (4). The variance of the zero-mean white noise can be calculated through the minimum mean square error criteria (MSE).

$$\sigma_v^2 = R(0) + \sum_{k=1}^{P} a_k R(k) \tag{5}$$

In the paper, there are many methods to determine the order of AR model. Specifically, the Akaike information criterion (AIC) and Final Prediction Error (FPE) methods are currently the most widely used methods. The AICs [13] of different frequency responses are calculated by:

$$AIC = 2L - 2\ln(K) \tag{6}$$

where L represents the number of estimated parameters, and K is the maximum likelihood function in this model. The minimum AIC is selected as the order of AR model.

4   Statistical Result and Analysis

The results of power delay profile (PDP) of stair step 1 (Rx1) from AR modeling, the conventional TDL model [8], and the measured data are shown in Fig. 3. The goodness-of-fit of AR modeling and the TDL model are verified by the root-mean-square error (RMSE) evaluation criterion between simulated value and measured data. The algorithm of RMSE is provided as follows:

$$\text{RMSE} = \sqrt{\frac{\sum\limits_{i=1}^{n} \left(X_{simu,i} - X_{meas,i}\right)^2}{\sum\limits_{i=1}^{n} X_{meas,i}^2}} \tag{7}$$

The RMSE of PDP of AR modeling and the TDL model for stair step 1 is 0.037 and 0.108. The graph of the cumulative distribution functions (CDFs) of the RMS delay spread for measured data, AR modeling, and TDL model is shown in Fig. 4. The number of delay taps of TDL model is set to be the same as the order of AR model for the LOS stairs measurement. Both the RMSE and the RMS delay spread prove that AR modeling is in better agreement with the measured data than the TDL model. In addition, the frequency selectivity can be observed from the simulated channel, which is a characteristic that the TDL model does not have. High delay resolution is responsible for the AR model being better than the TDL model.

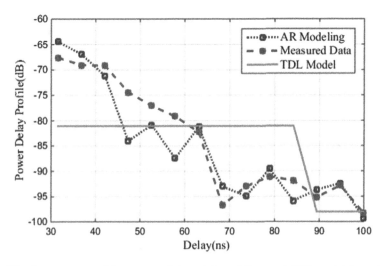

Fig. 3. The time response of the measured data, AR modeling, and TDL model for stair step 1 (Rx1) in the first 100 ns.

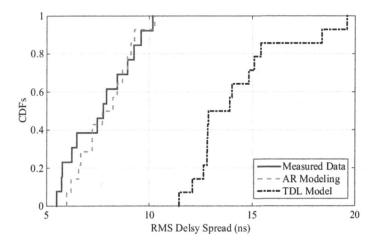

Fig. 4. The distributions of the RMS delay spread for measured data, AR modeling, and TDL modeling in the LOS stairs environment.

The scatter plot of the poles of the fourth quadrant from the transfer function in the stairs measurement is shown in Fig. 5. In this paper, the delay of the significant paths in the time domain is related to the angle of p_k and the arrival time can be calculated by Eq. (8):

$$\tau = \frac{-\arg(p_k)}{2\pi f_s} \tag{8}$$

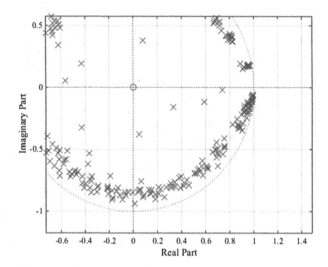

Fig. 5. The scatter plot of poles of AR transfer function in the fourth quadrant for the LOS stairs measurement.

where f_s is the frequency resolution. In the stairs measurement, the resolution in the frequency response is 0.95 MHz. Then the observation window of maximum delay is 1052.6 ns. However, too much redundant information (e.g., the noise and weak signals) is included in the channel impulse response. It is found that the obvious multipath components are unable to be observed when the delay surpasses a certain value. In the LOS stairs measurement, the specific value is determined to be 100 ns in order to reduce the complexity of data. At the same time, we only analyze the distribution of poles in the fourth quadrant of the unit circle. For the 14 stairs steps in the case of LOS, most of stairs have 3 poles in the first 100 ns and there are 5 steps with 4 poles. Pole 4 can be ignored because it is relatively small. Based on the above analysis, there are three, one, and two poles, respectively, for the stairs of LOS, the stairs of NLOS, and the corridor.

Figure 6 shows a graph of the delay of the first three poles in the first 100 ns for the LOS stairs environment. For the analysis reported in [14], the poles close the unit circle can be seen as the significant clusters in multipath propagation. The delay of the first pole is proportional to the distance of the direct path. The time required for the signal to reach the receiving antenna is almost the same as the time for the rays to propagate in free space. However, errors due to the measurement system may have an effect on this result.

Electromagnetic wave propagation in the indoor stairs environment is a fairly complex problem, but the mechanism of signal propagation is of interest for some researchers [7, 15]. In the LOS stairs measurement, the reflectors that cause the paths of signal propagation change are the wall on the left side (on the right of the Rx is the stair handrail), the stairs oblique beam above the Rx, the steps of stairs, and the wall behind the Rx. The delay of the second pole is between 21.74 ns and 42.57 ns, and it increases with the distance of the receiving antenna. The trend caused by the last 4 steps (11, 12,

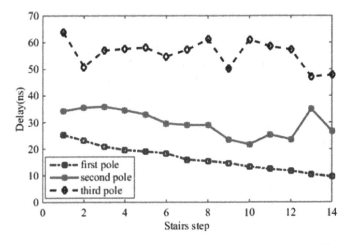

Fig. 6. The graph of the delay of the first three poles in the first 100 ns.

13, and 14) is because of the rays from both of the walls on the left and right sides. Thus, this indicates that the rays reflected from the wall on the left side mainly contribute to the received power. Those rays are unable to directly reach the receiver after one reflection from the steps because of the geometry of measurement environment, unless they are reflected multiple times. However, the final signal to the receiver will be weak and the delay will increase. For pole 3, longer delays (50–60 ns) and smaller modules relative to the first two poles indicate the signals experience at least two or three reflections. The result of the LOS stairs measurement is in disagreement with the observations of other researchers [14, 16]. A two-pole model is applied to describe the indoor radio channel in their research work. The difference can be explained as that even after multiple reflections, the attenuated signal can still reach the receiving antenna because of the special structure of the stairs environment, and it contributes to the received power.

For the NLOS stairs (Rx21, Rx22) measurement, it is reasonable that there exists only one pole within the first 100 ns because there is no direct path. The most obvious path is reflected from the floor in front of the steps to the receiver. In the corridor measurement, there exists two obvious paths: a direct ray similar to the propagation in free space and rays reflected from surrounding walls, ceiling, and floor (wave-guide effect). Accordingly, two significant poles can be seen in the first 200 ns, which is in agreement with the conclusion from [5, 6].

5 Conclusion

The CIR of indoor stairs and corridor at 2.6 GHz is described as a novel frequency domain auto-regressive model, which has higher accuracy than the traditional TDL model and lower complexity compared to ray-tracing methods. The RMSE evaluation criterion and the CDFs of the RMS delay spread are utilized to verify the results. The measured channel frequency response can be interpreted by the location of P poles of transfer function. The locations and magnitude of the poles are related to the reflectors of measurement environment and the mechanism of signal propagation. The number of poles representing the significant paths (clusters) depends on different measurement environments (the LOS stairs, the NLOS stairs and the corridor). The first pole in the LOS case can determine the formation of the first cluster caused by the direct ray. The determination of the second and third cluster depends on single reflected and double reflected (or higher order reflected) rays. These studies are expected to be applied in the development and design of the indoor communication system for stairs and corridor.

Acknowledgments. This work was supported by the National Natural Science Foundation of China under Grant No. 61701197 and 61571108, the Open Foundation of Key Laboratory of Wireless Communication, Nanjing University of Posts and Telecommunication, Jiangsu Province, under Grant No. 2017WICOM01, the Open Research Fund of National Mobile Communications Research Laboratory, Southeast University, under Grant No. 2018D15, the Open Foundation of State Key Laboratory of Networking and Switching Technology, the Fundamental Research Funds for the Central Universities under Grant No. JUSRP11742 and JUSRP11738, the Postgraduate Research & Practice Innovation Program of Jiangsu Provence under Grant No. SJCX18_0646.

References

1. Huang, Y.M.: Signal processing for MIMO-NOMA: present and future challenges. IEEE Wirel. Commun. Mag. **25**(2), 32–38 (2018)
2. Zhu, J.Y., Wang, J.H., Huang, Y.M., He, S.W., You, X.H., Yang, L.X.: On optimal power allocation for downlink non-orthogonal multiple access systems. IEEE J. Sel. Areas Commun. **35**(12), 2744–2757 (2017)
3. Xiao, M., Mumtaz, S., Huang, Y.M.: Millimeter wave communications for future mobile networks. IEEE J. Sel. Areas Commun. **35**(9), 1909–1935 (2017)
4. Xiang, W., Zheng, K., Shen, X.: 5G Mobile Communications. Springer, Cham (2017). https://doi.org/10.1007/978-3-319-34208-5
5. Geng, S., Vainikainen, P.: Millimeter-wave propagation in indoor corridors. IEEE Antennas Wirel. Propag. Lett. **8**, 1242–1245 (2009)
6. Rao, T.R., Murugesan, D., Ramesh, S., Labay, V.A.: Radio channel characteristics in an indoor corridor environment at 60 GHz for wireless networks. In: 5th International Conference on Advanced Networks and Telecommunication Systems, pp. 1–5. IEEE, Bangalore (2011)
7. Lim, S.Y., Yun, Z., Baker, J.M., Celik, N., Youn, H.S., Iskander, M.F.: Propagation modeling and measurement for a multifloor stairwell. IEEE Antennas Wirel. Propag. Lett. **8**, 583–586 (2009)
8. Zhao, X., Kivinen, J., Vainnikainen, P.: Tapped delay line channel models at 5.3 GHz in indoor environments. In: 52nd Vehicular Technology Conference, pp. 1–5. IEEE, Boston (2000)
9. Yu, Y., Liu, Y., Lu, W.J., Jin, S., Zhu, H.B.: Modeling and simulation of channel power delay profile under indoor stair environment. IET Commun. **11**(1), 119–126 (2017)
10. Suzuki, H.: A statistical model for urban radio propagation. IEEE Trans. Commun. **25**(7), 673–680 (1977)

11. Saleh, A.A.M., Valenzuela, R.: A statistical model for indoor multipath propagation. IEEE J. Sel. Areas Commun. **5**(2), 128–137 (1987)
12. Liu, Y., Yu, Y., Lu, W.J., Zhu, H.B.: Antenna-height-dependent path loss model and shadowing characteristics under indoor stair environment at 2.6 GHz. IEEJ Trans. Electr. Electron. Eng. **10**(5), 498–502 (2015)
13. Emanuel, P., Kunio, T., Genshiro, K.: Selected Papers of Hirotugu Akaike. Springer, New York (1998). https://doi.org/10.1007/978-1-4612-1694-0
14. Morrison, G., Fattouche, M., Zaghloul, H.: Statistical analysis and autoregressive modeling of the indoor radio propagation channel. In: 1st International Conference on Universal Personal Communications, pp. 97–101. IEEE, Dallas (1992)
15. Yang, C.F., Wu, B.C.: A ray-tracing/PMM hybrid approach for determining wave propagation through periodic structures. IEEE Trans. Veh. Technol. **50**(3), 791–795 (2001)
16. Howard, S.J., Pahlavan, K.: Autoregressive modeling of wide-band indoor radio propagation. IEEE Trans. Commun. **40**(9), 1540–1552 (1992)

Predicting Freezing of WebRTC Videos in WiFi Networks

Suying Yan[1], Yuchun Guo[1(✉)], Yishuai Chen[1], and Feng Xie[2]

[1] Beijing Jiaotong University, Beijing, China
[2] ZTE Inc., Shenzhen, China
{13120210,ychguo,yschen}@bjtu.edu.cn, xie.feng@zte.com.cn

Abstract. WebRTC is an open source project which enables real-time communication within web browsers. It facilitates web-based multimedia applications, e.g. video conferencing and receives great interest from the academia. Nevertheless understanding of quality of experience (QoE) for the WebRTC video applications in wireless environment is still desired. For the QoE metric, we focus on the widely accepted video freezing event. We propose to identify a freezing event by comparing the interval of receiving time between two successive video frames, named *F-Gap*, with a threshold. To enable automatically tracking of video freezing, we modify the original WebRtc protocol to punch receiving timestamp on the frame overhead. Furthermore, we evaluate the correlation between video freezing and quality of service (QoS) in WiFi network based on experiments in typical indoor environment. We build a machine learning model to infer whether QoE is unacceptable or not in the next time window based on current QoS metrics. Experiments verify that the model has good accuracy and the QoE state is mainly relevant to quality metrics of *Round-Trip Time*, *Link Quality* and *RSSI*. This model is helpful to highlight the providers in system design and improve user experience via avoiding bad QoE in advance.

Keywords: WiFi · WebRTC · QoS · Freezing · Machine learning

1 Introduction

Wireless video real-time communication (RTC) is becoming a killer application on mobile devices, such as Apple Facetime, Google Hangout, and Microsoft Skype, etc. Evaluation results of these applications are reported in [1]. Recently, the open source project WebRTC which enables RTC within webpages, has received great interest from both academic and industry. Most popular web browsers support WebRTC without the needs of installing extra software or plugin.

Supported by National Science Foundation of China under grant No. 61572071, 61271199 and 61301082.

© ICST Institute for Computer Sciences, Social Informatics and Telecommunications Engineering 2019
Published by Springer Nature Switzerland AG 2019. All Rights Reserved
J. Zheng et al. (Eds.): ADHOCNETS 2018, LNICST 258, pp. 292–301, 2019.
https://doi.org/10.1007/978-3-030-05888-3_27

WebRTC also attracts academic interest, such as implementation schemes of WebRTC [2], the congestion control mechanism for WebRTC [3], and video conferencing system design [4,5] based on WebRTC for general realtime communication or specialized purpose like tele-health. However, understandings of QoE for WebRTC video or RTC video is still limited [6] due to tediousness of the traditional methods of measuring user experience (e.g., MOS) corresponding to video quality (e.g., Peak Signal-to-Noise Ratio). Nowadays with the previllance of online service, it is widely accepted to characterize QoE with objective quality metrics, e.g., buffering rate or bitrate [7], which are easily to obtained in a large scale. Authors of [8] analyzed performance of WebRTC video in terms of throughput, jitter, and packet loss under different LTE scenarios. Authors of [9] focused on the comparison of smartphone configurations (e.g., CPU) on quality ratings under WiFi network. A recent study reported that the freezing event is an indicator of QoE that users care most [10]. Thus, in this paper, we focus on the occurence possibility of freezing event as a metric of WebRTC video QoE.

To predict WebRTC video freezing in WiFi networks, we need to answer the following three questions:

(1) *How to identify and track WebRTC video freezing?* Answer to this question is the first step for the prediction. We find that the time interval between two successively received frames, named *F-Gap*, can serve as a proper metric to identify a freezing event. However, it is non-trivial to obtain the value of F-Gap as WebRtc provides sending timestamps instead of receiving ones, but the sending time cannot be used due to the delay variance. Authors of [11] proposed to camera video playing screen with a stopwatch setting aside as timestamps and recover the timing text of each frame from the camera records with OCR (optical character recognition) tool afterwards. Thanks to the openness of WebRTC, we modify the original WebRtc protocol to insert receiving timestamps at each frame to enable the metric *F-Gap* to be obtained directly and the video freezing event to be identified in realtime.

(2) *How to build comprehensive measurements to evaluate the correlation of video QoE state with wireless quality?* To make this evaluation effective, we systematically design and conduct extensive measurement experiments in a typical indoor WiFi environment. During the experiments, we collect the values of F-Gap and two types of network QoS metrics: (a) wireless signal/link quality metrics, including Signal Quality, received signal strength indicator (RSSI), etc.; (b) network data transfer quality metrics, including packet loss rate and Round Trip Time. QoE state can be further inferred based on setting a proper threshold for the F-Gap.

(3) *How to predict QoE state of whether WebRTC's video freezing is unacceptable from wireless network's QoS metrics?* Based on the observation that wireless network quality correlates with the QoE state of whether the freezing ratio is unacceptable, we propose a practical model predicating video freezing event in the next time window based on the quality in current time window. This model can be used for the system to adjust service strategy in real time during a video call or for the user to avoid to access to the service if a freezing is predicted.

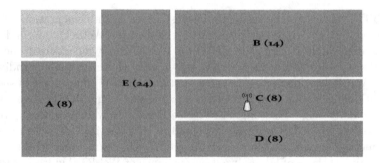

Fig. 1. Indoor measurement environment

In a word, our freezing evaluation method, measurement observation, and prediction model provide valuable insights for improving performance of wireless WebRTC-based video communication system. The remain of this paper is organized as follows. Section 2 describes our experimental methodology. Section 3 introduces our measurement results and the correlation analysis of the wireless network quality metrics and the proposed QoE metric in terms of video freezing state. Section 4 presents the freezing prediction model. Section 5 concludes this paper.

2 Measurement Methodology and Metrics

2.1 Testbed and Experiment Datasets

In this paper, we focus on the typical two-party WebRTC video chat widely used by users in WiFi environment. We set up a testbed consisting of laptops and a 802.11n wireless LAN AP. We modify the official open-source reference protocol of WebRTC to enable monitoring of video freezing events and network quality. We design another program to collect wireless quality. To ensure that the transmitted video contents are consistent and repeatable, we choose a high-definition (HD) video sequence *Big Buck Bunny*, widely used in video-related research, as the video sourceas. We inject this video sequence into WebRTC clients with a virtual video camera tool[1].

As most RTC communication takes place indoors with WiFi access, we consider the typical office usage environment and multi-room home environment as shown in Fig. 1. The AP is placed in room C. The white thick lines are the walls between rooms, and the gray blocks are our experiment spaces. Room A to D are typical office rooms with desks, chairs, computers, and other office supplies. Besides, each room is covered by several other WiFi APs which work in channels that different from our AP. We conducted independent experiments at each seat in these rooms within the AP's signal coverage range. We also divided the space of corridor (i.e., area E) into 62 blocks with of similar size and conducted 10

---

[1] e2eSoft. http://www.e2esoft.cn/vcam/.

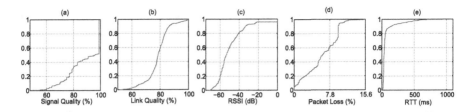

Fig. 2. Distribution of measured wireless network quality metrics.

experiments in each block. Totally we have 620 groups of basic experimental data.

Moreover, we invited 10 volunteers to conduct extra experiments with the following changes compared to the above basic experiments: (1) Use another AP of different type; (2) Play another video sequence with plentiful facial expression change; (3) Each student conducted 20 groups of experiments in random positions and accessed to the video sequence with his/her own laptop. Finally, we choose 50 groups of data with freezing events among these 200 groups of experiments as the extra dataset to verify our model.

2.2 Wireless Network Quality Metrics

To characterize the wireless network quality, we use the following metrics.

- Wireless signal/link quality metrics: We use all wireless physical layer metrics reported by Microsoft Windows 7 OS through its API, including *received signal strength indicator* (RSSI), *Signal Quality* (SQ), and *Link Quality* (LQ).
- UDP transportation quality metrics. As video transportation in WebRTC uses RTP over UDP, we measure *Packet Loss Rate* (Loss) and RTT.

The *cumulative distribution function* (CDF) for each wireless network quality metric is shown in Fig. 2. Our measurement covers a wide range of wireless network conditions. For instance, Fig. 2(c) shows the RSSI ranges from −70 dB to 0 dB, which is the general working range of WiFi network. Likewise, each of other metrics covers working range respectively as shown. Such a result verifies the effectiveness and generality of our measurement methodology.

2.3 QoE Metrics in Terms of Video Freezing

It is widely accepted that users of video services mainly care about the percepted fluency and clarity of video. Video's Structural SIMilarity (SSIM) index of a received frame with the transmitted frame is newly accepted metric of video clarity. However it is impossible to measure SSIM at a receiver client in a real-time scenario. On the other hand, video fluency in terms of freezing ratio is feasible to be measured with our modification of the WebRtc protocol by adding a timestamp of receiving time at the receiver side.

To identify a video freezing event, we first propose a metric *F-Gap*. We define *F-Gap* to be the *time interval or gap between two consecutively received video frames*. Then we compare it with the visual quality metrics. We find that the *F-Gap* is a good video freezing indicator. For a WebRTC video with frame rate of 30 frames/second, the regular interval of two successive frames is 33 ms. When the F-Gap is longer than 33 ms, there are some frames delayed or lost. Due to the limited visual sensitivity of human, short pause between two consecutive frames cannot be sensed by human. Therefore, the detection of freezing event is equivalent to find when the F-GAP is larger than a threshold. Specifically, to determine this threshold value, we ask volunteers to label freezing events they felt, and find that F-Gap of 1 s can be felt visually by human. Thus, We say it is "Freezing" when F-Gap >1 s, otherwise, we say it is "No Freezing".

We find that the F-Gap is correlated to video's Structural SIMilarity (SSIM) index.the freezing time approaches 20% of a session, SSIM would degrade about 0.172. This is because when the network condition is worsen, the video sender will decrease its video encoding rate to ensure the communication smooth. Besides, we change the threshold for F-Gap to 0.5 s, 2 s, 3 s, ..., 10 s, and find that such correlation between F-Gap and SSIM remains the same. This reveals that the F-Gap metric reflects the visual quality partially. Hence it is proper to choose the F-Gap to as the metric to identifying freezing.

Furthermore, the duration of freezing events in a time window above a fraction, say 10% or 30%, of the window is often considered unacceptable QoE. For the prediction of QoE, it is not feasible to make an realtime estimation of the exact time when a freezing occurs. Instead, we will show that it is feasible to make an prediction about whether the QoE is unacceptable or not in the next time window of some length, say 10 s.

3 Correlation Between Wireless Network QoS and Video Freezing

3.1 Statistical Perspective

In this section, we intend to find proper perspective to evaluate the relationship between WebRTC's user freezing and wireless network's quality metrics. Figure 3 plots the temporal variance of the five QoS metrics for an experiment conducted at a position in room B for 5 min. For clearness, we show parts of the result from 210 s to 260 s. The Freezing and No Freezing events are marked with blue '*' and black 'o', respectively. As shown in Fig. 3, the occurrence of Freezing event seems correlated with wireless network QoS. For instance, the Freezing seems correlated with wireless network QoS degradations, e.g. low RSSI and link quality (LQ). However, such a perspective on a single experiment cannot support drawing significant observation.

We then evaluate the correlation of wireless network quality metrics with video freezing statistically in all experiments. To obtain a macroscopic analysis of all experiments, we define a session (or a time window) of a video is of *unacceptable* QoE if the ratio of freezing time is greater than 30% of the whole session (or window).

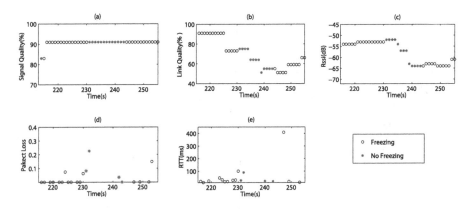

Fig. 3. Variances of wireless network QoS metrics in one experiment.

3.2 Feature Importance: Relative Information Gain

We then calculate the relative information gain [10] of the mean and variance of the five wireless network QoS metrics to F-Gap unacceptable indicator of all experiments, respectively. More specifically, Y denotes the random variable of QoE state (unacceptable, acceptable), X denotes the random variable of a QoS metric. For each random variable X for a QoS metric, we calculate the relative information gain (RIG) of Y against X as

$$RIG(Y|X) = \frac{H(Y) - H(Y|X)}{H(Y)},$$

where $H(Y)$ is the entropy of random variable Y and $H(Y|X)$ is the conditional entropy of Y given random variable X. The relative information gain quantifies how much uncertainty of knowing the F-Gap is unacceptable or not is reduced by wireless network QoS metrics. The higher the information gain, the more correlated the QoS metric is to the QoE state. Table 1 shows the result.

As shown in Table 1, the relative information gain of QoE state against the variance of RTT, the mean of RTT and variance of link quality are 0.136, 0.087 and 0.082 respectively. Thus, we conclude that *the video freezing relates to the wireless network quality metrics, in particular the variance of RTT*. Such a result suggests that the current WebRTC's video freezing problem is mainly due to the volatility of RTT. This finding is reasonable. Although WebRTC congestion control algorithm adjusts the video streaming rate for fluency partially based on variance of network latency, it cannot remedy excessive churns. However, none single QoS metric is strong enough to predicet QoE state so that we will choose to use these metrics integratedly to predict QoE state.

Table 1. RIG of network QoS metrics vs. QoE state.

Feature	RIG
$RTT_{-Variance}$	0.136
RTT_{-Mean}	0.087
Link Quality$_{-Variance}$	0.082
$RSSI_{-Mean}$	0.040
Link Quality$_{-Mean}$	0.035
Signal Quality$_{-Variance}$	0.031
$RSSI_{-Variance}$	0.026
Signal Quality$_{-Mean}$	0.017
Packet Loss$_{-Mean}$	0.012
Packet Loss$_{-Variance}$	0.009

Table 2. Feature importance of QoE models.

Feature	Importance
$RTT_{-Variance}$	0.23
RTT_{-Mean}	0.22
$RSSI_{-Mean}$	0.15
Link Quality$_{-Mean}$	0.13
Link Quality$_{-Variance}$	0.07
Signal Quality$_{-Mean}$	0.07
$RSSI_{-Variance}$	0.05
Packet Loss$_{-Variance}$	0.04
Packet Loss$_{-Mean}$	0.03
Signal Quality$_{-Variance}$	0.01

4   WebRTC Video Freezing Prediction Model

4.1   Model

We intend to build a machine learning model to predict the video freezing of a user's WebRTC video communication session from the wireless network quality metrics. An intuitive idea is to map the QoS metrics into the QoE state in same time window via training a classifier. However, such mapping is not effective in practice as it leave no time for making a scheduling decision accordingly and further deploying it. Hence, to make the prediction feasible and helpful in the network scheduling in practice, we intend to design a model to predict the QoE state in the future with present QoS condition considering the self-correlation of each metric to itself.

We propose a *video freezing prediction model* as follows. We use the measured wireless network QoS metrics in a current time window (say window A) to predict the video F-Gap *unacceptable* event in the next time window (say window B), as shown in Fig. 4. In Window A the wireless network quality metrics is collected historically for predicting the QoE in the next window, i.e. the Window B. As WebRTC use a 10-s video jitter buffer at the receiver side, we use 10 s as the size of window B. We can investigate the size of window A to obtain best prediction performance in our model training. The training and prediction can be done online. During a user's video communication process, we can keep collecting wireless network quality metrics, predicting freezing extent in the next time window, which can be used to in WebRTC's rate control algorithm to improve video playback continuity. Moreover, a WebRTC video call is started up at the magnitude of seconds for establishing connection. Therefore we can use the short window in the maganitude of seconds to estimate the QoE state for users and even make a space for making scheduling decision. This will be verified with the experiment results shown in Fig. 5.

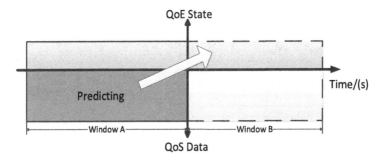

Fig. 4. Prediction window mechanism.

4.2 Performance

We use the wireless network quality features listed in Table 2 to train our video freezing model. For each window, we calculate the mean and variance of each metric, and then use them as the features. Thus, we totally have 10 features. Besides, we mix the basic dataset and the extra-dataset into an integrated dataset, 80% data are randomly selected as the training set and the remaining are used as testing set.

We use *Decision Trees (DTs), Random Forests (RandF), Support Vector Machines (SVM)* and *Extra-Trees classifier (ExtraT)* to train our models and compare their performance. We evaluate the effectiveness of classification methods in terms of the following indexs: *Precision, Recall* and F_1 *score* [12]. Among them, we use F_1 score as the main metric, as it is a comprehensive index which includes precision and recall. Moreover, the prediction accuracy of QoE bad is more important to avoid users' frustration of wrong prediction. Thus, we mainly compare the algorithms' F_1 score of QoE bad prediction results, and our results show the Random Forests method has the highest F_1 score for QoE bad prediction. After extensive experiments, we find that F_1 score returned by SVM is always below 0.3 and the performance of Extra-Trees and Decision Tree fluctuates widely with the size of sliding window A. Based on comparison, Random Forests method performs well and stably. Such a result is reasonable as Random Forests is ensembles of a number of decision trees and is the most successful general-purpose algorithm [13]. Thus, we finally select Random Forests model.

Figure 5 plots the performance of the Random Forests model against the size of sliding window. As shown in Fig. 5, as the size of sliding window A increases from 5 s to 120 s, the F_1 score of the prediction model gradually increases, meaning the model performs better when using more historical data. When the window size is of 5 s, the precision, recall and F_1 score are 87.3%, 60.8% and 7.21 respectively. When the widow size is larger than 17 s, the precision, recall and F_1 score keep relatively stable and larger than 90%, 80% and 0.8, which means the model is of high accuracy. For instance, when the window size is 20 s, the precision, recall and F_1 score of the model are 99.6%, 74.4%, and 0.84, respectively.

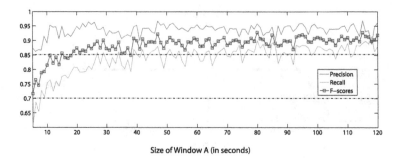

Fig. 5. Performance of QoE prediction model versus the size of Window A.

Thus, in practice, we suggest that the size of sliding window can be selected in the range from 20 to 30 s.

We list the features' importance of the Random Forests model in Table 2. As shown in Table 2, the RTT mean and variance are of top importance. Link quality and RSSI are also important metrics which represent quality on network level and physical level respectively.

5   Conclusions

In this paper, we studied the problem of accurate prediction of user video QoE of WebRTC in WiFi networks. First, we proposed a new, simple, and efficient QoE metric which is based on the time interval between two successive video frames. Second, we conducted 620 basic experiments and some extra experiments in an indoor WiFi environment and showed the strong correlation of WebRTC user QoE with wireless network QoS metrics. Finally, we built a machine learning models to predict a user's WebRTC video communication QoE state based on the current wireless network measurement results. The model can be used by a system to adjust its servicing strategy in real-time during a video call. Experimental result demonstrated that the model is accurate, with F_1 scores above 0.7 with 5 s of measurements and .84 with 20 s of measurements. Moreover, our analysis results and models clearly show that the current WebRTC implementation's QoE problem is mainly due to volatility of RTT. Our QoE evaluation method, analysis results, and prediction models provide valuable insights for wireless WebRTC video communication system design.

For more parameter settings, such as values of several thresholds, and the model targetted for multi-party meeting senario, we plan to make more investigation in the future work.

References

1. Sun, W., Qin, X.: End-to-end delay analysis of wechat video call service in live DC-HSPA+ network. In: Proceedings of International Conference on 6th Wireless Communications and Signal Processing (WCSP), Heifei, China, pp. 1–5. IEEE (2014)
2. Taheri, S., et al.: WebRTCbench: a benchmark for performance assessment of webRTC implementations. In: Proceedings of 13th Embedded Systems For Real-time Multimedia (ESTIMedia), Amsterdam, Netherlands, pp. 1–7. IEEE (2015)
3. De Cicco, L., Carlucci, G., Mascolo, S.: Experimental investigation of the Google congestion control for real-time flows. In: 1st Proceedings of the ACM SIGCOMM Workshop on Future Human-Centric Multimedia Networking, Hong Kong, China, pp. 21–26. ACM (2013)
4. Rodríguez, P., Cerviño, J., Trajkovska, I., Salvachúa, J.: Advanced videoconfer-encing based on WebRTC. In: Proceedings of 9th IADIS International Conferences Web Based Communities and Social Media and Collaborative Technologies, Lisbon, Portugal, pp. 180–184. IADIS (2012)
5. Jang-Jaccard, J., Nepal, S., Celler, B., Yan, B.: WebRTC-based video conferencing service for telehealth. Computing **98**(1–2), 169–193 (2016)
6. Balachandran, A., Sekar, V., Akella, A., Seshan, S., Stoica, I., Zhang, H.: Developing a predictive model of quality of experience for internet video. ACM SIGCOMM Comput. Commun. Rev. **43**(4), 339–350 (2013)
7. Balachandran, A., Sekar, V., Akella, A., Seshan, S., Stoica, I., Zhang, H.: A quest for an internet video quality-of-experience metric. In: 11th Proceedings of the ACM Workshop on Hot Topics in Networks, Seattle, WA, USA, pp. 97–102. ACM (2012)
8. Carullo, G., Tambasco, M., Di Mauro, M., Longo, M.: A performance evaluation of WebRTC over LTE. In: 12th Annual Conference on Wireless On-demand Network Systems and Services (WONS), Cortina d'Ampezzo, Italy, pp. 1–6. IEEE (2016)
9. Vucic, D., Skorin-Kapov, L.: The impact of mobile device factors on QoE for multi-party video conferencing via WebRTC. In: Proceedings of 13th International Conference on Telecommunications (ConTEL), Graz, Australia, pp. 1–8. IEEE (2015)
10. Dobrian, F., et al.: Understanding the impact of video quality on user engagement. ACM **41**(4), 362–373 (2011)
11. Yu, C., Xu, Y., Liu, B., Liu, Y.: Can you see me now? A measurement study of mobile video calls. In: Proceedings IEEE 33rd INFOCOM, Toronto, Canada, pp. 1456–1464. IEEE (2014)
12. Joumblatt, D., Chandrashekar, J., Kveton, B., Taft, N., Teixeira, R.: Predicting user dissatisfaction with internet application performance at end-hosts. In: 32nd Proceedings IEEE INFOCOM, Turin, Italy, pp. 235–239. IEEE (2013)
13. STRATACONF Homepage. http://strataconf.com/strata2012/public/schedule/detail/22658. Accessed 4 Feb 2012

Author Index

Printed in the United States
By Bookmasters